ZHUKOV
AT THE ODER

The Stackpole Military History Series

THE AMERICAN CIVIL WAR

Cavalry Raids of the Civil War
Ghost, Thunderbolt, and
 Wizard
Pickett's Charge
Witness to Gettysburg

WORLD WAR I

Doughboy War

WORLD WAR II

After D-Day
Armor Battles of the
 Waffen-SS, 1943–45
Armoured Guardsmen
Army of the West
Australian Commandos
The B-24 in China
Backwater War
The Battle of Sicily
Battle of the Bulge, Vol. 1
Battle of the Bulge, Vol. 2
Beyond the Beachhead
Beyond Stalingrad
The Brandenburger
 Commandos
The Brigade
Bringing the Thunder
The Canadian Army and the
 Normandy Campaign
Coast Watching in
 World War II
Colossal Cracks
A Dangerous Assignment
D-Day Deception
D-Day to Berlin
Destination Normandy
Dive Bomber!
A Drop Too Many
Eagles of the Third Reich
Eastern Front Combat
Exit Rommel
Fist from the Sky
Flying American Combat
 Aircraft of World War II
Forging the Thunderbolt
Fortress France
The German Defeat in the
 East, 1944–45
German Order of Battle, Vol. 1
German Order of Battle, Vol. 2
German Order of Battle, Vol. 3
The Germans in Normandy

Germany's Panzer Arm in
 World War II
GI Ingenuity
Goodwood
The Great Ships
Grenadiers
Hitler's Nemesis
Infantry Aces
Iron Arm
Iron Knights
Kampfgruppe Peiper at the
 Battle of the Bulge
The Key to the Bulge
Kursk
Luftwaffe Aces
Luftwaffe Fighter Ace
Massacre at Tobruk
Mechanized Juggernaut or
 Military Anachronism?
Messerschmitts over Sicily
Michael Wittmann, Vol. 1
Michael Wittmann, Vol. 2
Mountain Warriors
The Nazi Rocketeers
No Holding Back
On the Canal
Operation Mercury
Packs On!
Panzer Aces
Panzer Aces II
Panzer Commanders of the
 Western Front
Panzer Gunner
The Panzer Legions
Panzers in Normandy
Panzers in Winter
The Path to Blitzkrieg
Penalty Strike
Red Road from Stalingrad
Red Star under the Baltic
Retreat to the Reich
Rommel's Desert Commanders
Rommel's Desert War
Rommel's Lieutenants
The Savage Sky
The Siegfried Line
A Soldier in the Cockpit
Soviet Blitzkrieg
Stalin's Keys to Victory
Surviving Bataan and Beyond
T-34 in Action
Tank Tactics
Tigers in the Mud
Triumphant Fox

The 12th SS, Vol. 1
The 12th SS, Vol. 2
Twilight of the Gods
The War against Rommel's
 Supply Lines
War in the Aegean
Wolfpack Warriors
Zhukov at the Oder

THE COLD WAR / VIETNAM

Cyclops in the Jungle
Expendable Warriors
Flying American Combat
 Aircraft: The Cold War
Here There Are Tigers
Land with No Sun
Phantom Reflections
Street without Joy
Through the Valley

WARS OF THE MIDDLE EAST

Never-Ending Conflict

GENERAL MILITARY HISTORY

Carriers in Combat
Cavalry from Hoof to Track
Desert Battles
Guerrilla Warfare
Ranger Dawn
Sieges

ZHUKOV AT THE ODER

The Decisive Battle for Berlin

Tony Le Tissier

STACKPOLE
BOOKS

Published in paperback in 2009 by
STACKPOLE BOOKS
5067 Ritter Road
Mechanicsburg, PA 17055
www.stackpolebooks.com

ZHUKOV AT THE ODER: THE DECISIVE BATTLE FOR BERLIN, by Tony Le
Tissier, was originally published in hard cover by Praeger, an imprint of Greenwood Publishing Group, Inc., Westport, CT. Copyright © 1996 by Tony Le Tissier.
Paperback edition by arrangement with Greenwood Publishing Group, Inc. All
rights reserved.

Cover design by Tracy Patterson

Printed in the United States of America

10 9 8 7 6 5 4 3 2 1

ISBN 978-0-8117-3609-1 (Stackpole paperback)

The Library of Congress has cataloged the hardcover edition as follows:

Le Tissier, Tony.
    Zhukov at the Oder : the decisive battle for Berlin / Tony Le Tissier.
      p. cm.
    Includes bibliographical references and index.
    ISBN 0-275-95230-4 (alk. paper)
    1. Berlin, Battle of, 1945. 2. World War, 1939–1945—Campaigns—Eastern. 3.
  Zhukov, Georgii Konstantinovich, 1896–1974. 4. Marshals—Soviet Union—
Biography. I.
    Title.
    D757.9.B4T57 1996
    940.54'2131—dc20   95-10099

Dedicated
to those that fought in these battles,
those defending their country and people,
those avenging the rape of theirs,
victims alike
of time and place.

Contents

Maps   xi
Preface   xiii
Acknowledgments   xv

PART I DEPUTY SUPREME COMMANDER

1. The Man   3

2. The Soviets   13

3. The Germans   19

PART II THE BRIDGEHEADS

4. The Vistula-Oder Operation   29

5. The Struggle for the Bridgeheads I   43

    A New Situation   43
    The Kienitz Bridgehead   47
    The Göritz Bridgehead   55
    The Southern Flank   58

6. The Struggle for the Bridgeheads II   63

    The German Command   63
    The Oderbruch   65
    The Reitwein Spur   67
    The Southern Flank   75

The Cost of Attrition   76
The German Deployment   78

7. The Küstrin Corridor and Fortress   79

The Fortress Besieged   79
Closing the Corridor   84
The German Counteroffensive   90
The Fortress Falls   95

8. The East Pomeranian Operation   99

PART III LAUNCHING "OPERATION BERLIN"

9. Planning and Logistics   107

10. Defense in Depth   117

A New Defense Philosophy   117
Manpower   122
Organization and Strengths   124
Deployment   125
Reserves   133
Morale   133

11. Orders and Reconnaissance   137

Zhukov's Conference   137
Zhukov's Directives   138
The Artillery   140
The Armor   143
The Infantry   144
The Air Arm   144
The Air Defense   146
Morale   146
Reconnaissance in Force   148

PART IV THE BIG BATTLE

12. First Day of Battle   157

Let Battle Commence!   157
The Northern Flank   161
The 47th Army   164

The 3rd Shock Army   166
The 5th Shock Army   168
The 8th Guards Army   174
The 69th Army   182
The Frankfurt Fortress   183
The Southern Flank   184
The German Summary   187
The Soviet Summary   188

13. Second Day of Battle   191

The Northern Flank   191
The 47th Army   192
The 3rd Shock Army   194
The 5th Shock Army   197
The 8th Guards Army   199
The 69th Army   204
The Southern Flank   205
The German Summary   206
The Soviet Summary   207

14. Third Day of Battle   209

Reinforcements for the 9th Army   209
The Door Swings Open at Wriezen   210
The Advance on Müncheberg   214
The German Bulwark   221
The Southern Flank   222
The German Summary   224
The Soviet Summary   224

15. Fourth Day of Battle   227

The Northern Breach   227
The Breach at Müncheberg   232
The Isolated Bastion   235
The Southern Flank   235
Defeat and Victory   237

PART V BEYOND THE BREAKTHROUGH

16. The Fate of the German 9th Army   241

17. Stalin Rules   251

Abbreviations and Symbols   261

Appendices   263

I   Organization of a Red Army
         Rifle Division in 1945   265
II   Organization of Red Army
         Tank and Mechanized Formations 1945   266
III   Combatant Strength of the 1st Byelorussian
         Front for "Operation Berlin"   267
IV   Establishment of a German Infantry
         Division in 1945   270
V   Organization of a Volks Artillery
         Corps   272
VI   Combatant Strength of the 9th Army
         on 15 April 1945   273
VII   Armored Strength of the 9th Army
         on 13 April 1945   274
VIII   Allocation of Artillery Resources in
         Support of the 8th Guards Army on
         16 April 1945   277

Notes   279
Bibliography   303
Index   309
Armed Forces Index   321

Photographic essay follows page 180.

Maps

The author has provided his own maps to illustrate the action described in the text. For those who would like to have a general overview at hand, the author recommends the ADAC 1:150,000 map "Deutschland Blatt 21 Von Potsdam bis zur Oder, von Berlin bis Cottbus." More detailed 1:100,000 black and white maps of the area from the prewar "Karte des Deutschen Reiches," as used by the German General Staff, are also available in the series HK 100 DR/Gr, Nos. 245 (Freienwalde), 270 (Wriezen), 271 (Küstrin), 295 (Fürstenwalde), 296 (Frankfurt), 319 (Beeskow) and 320 (Fürstenberg).

These can be ordered by post from:

Landesvermessungsamt Brandenburg
Kartenversand
Robert-Havemann-Strasse 1
15236 Frankfurt/Oder
Germany

1 The Race to the Oder	30
2 The Küstrin Factor	34
3 The Initial Bridgeheads	36
4 The Kienitz-Genschmar Sector	48
5 The Karlsbiese-Kienitz Sector	50
6 The Raegener Division in Action 3-5 Feb 45	56
7 The 33rd Army's Bridgehead	59
8 The Soviet Attack of 2 Mar 45	66
9 The Reitwein Spur	68
10 The Frankfurt Bridgehead	76
11 The Küstrin Battlefield	80

12 Closing the Corridor 22-23 Mar 45 85
13 The German Counteroffensive 27-28 Mar 45 91
14 The East Pomeranian Operation 100
15 Zhukov's Deception Plan 113
16 The "Kurmark" Corner 130
17 Zhukov's Plan of 12 Apr 45 139
18 The Northern Battlefield 16-17 Apr 45 162
19 The 47th Army's and 3rd Shock Army's
   Sectors - 16 Apr 45 165
20 5th Shock Army's Sector – 16 Apr 45 170
21 8th Guards Army's Sector – 16 Apr 45 175
22 The Southern Battlefield 185
23 The 47th Army's and 3rd Shock Army's
   Sectors – 17 Apr 45 193
24 5th Shock Army's Sector – 17 Apr 45 198
25 The Seelow Sector and the "Stein-Stellung"
   – 17 Apr 45 200
26 The Way past Wriezen 212
27 The Advance on Müncheberg 215
28 The Northern Breach 228
29 The Müncheberg Breach 231

Preface

This book is a consequence of the collapse of Communism, the Soviet Union and the German Democratic Republic, all of which have opened up avenues of knowledge hitherto denied the public in the interests of political correctness.

Unraveling what occurred in the decisive fighting in the Oderbruch and for the Seelow Heights during the early part of 1945 has proved a fascinating and rewarding task, in which the accounts of Soviet commanders, produced a good twenty years after the event and subject to the current party line, have been of only limited use, whereas German survivors' accounts have proved very illuminating.

Conducting battlefield tours of the area for American, British and German groups convinced me of the need to write up this little-known element of relatively recent history, and I have been delighted with the generous response to my appeals for information from survivors and researchers alike. Sadly, and inevitably, some of my correspondents have died during the preparation of this work, which I hope will serve as a memorial to them and their contemporaries. Of course, in trying to understand what they went through, one cannot apply the freedoms of conscience and of choice of action that we enjoy today, for theirs was a world of rigid conformity and draconian discipline.

Acknowledgments

I would like to thank most warmly all those who have so generously assisted me with source material and encouragement in compiling this book:

Adolf Ayasse, Dr. Fritz-Rudolf Averdieck, Erwin Bartmann, Willi Böse, Col. Steve Bowman U.S. Army, Heinz Breitscheidel, Frau Heidemarie Daher, Dr. Anton Detter, Oberst a.D. Theodor von Dufving, Dr. Erich Fellmann, Jürgen Fiehne, Hermann Freter, Ernst-Christian Gädtke, Prof. Dr. (Med.) Wolfgang Gebhardt, Oberst a.D. Horst Grabow, Erich Hachtel, Gerhard Hahn, Dorothée Freifrau and Ludwig Freiherr von Hammerstein-Equord, Major Winfried Heinemann, Dekan a.D. Hartmut Heinrici, Oberst a.D. Harry Hermann, GenLt. a.D. Hans-Joachim von Hopffgarten, Alfons Jenewein, Friedrich Kaiser, Kurt Keller II, Frau Marianne Klein, Dr. Hans-Werner Klement, Fritz Knüppel, Fritz Kohlase, Werner Kortenhaus, Erwin Kowalke, Prof. Dr. Werenr Kroemer, Erwin Kruse, Günter Labes, Dr. Richard Lakowski, Oberst a.D. Dibbert Lang, GenMaj. a.D. Rudi Lindner, Major Vladimir V. Lukin, the "Mook wi" Old Comrades Association of the 20th Panzergrenadier Division in Hamburg, Captain Thomas Pike U.S. Army, Heinz Rall, Artur Römer, Oberstlt. a.D. Wolfgang Ruff, Friedhelm Schöneck, Joachim Schneider, Richard Schulte, Julius M. Schultz, Hans-Ulrich Seebohm, Christian Seeger, Lt. Col. Jevgeni Simanovich, GenMaj. a.D. Hans Spiegel, Helmut Stahl, Oberst a.D. Dr. Karl Stich, Hans Sturm, Karl-Hermann Tams, Dr. Hans J. Teller, Hermann Thrams, Gerd Wagner, Oberstlt. a.D. Helmut Weber, Ottmar Weis, Lennart Westberg, Horst Wewetzer, Horst Wilke, Oberst a.D. E. Wittor, Col. Tim Wray U.S. Army, Oberst a.D. Horst Zobel.

I would also like to thank Progress Publishers, Moscow, for permission to quote from Soviet literary sources, Chronos-Film GmbH for the use of photographs taken from original Soviet film footage in their archives, and also the Seelow Museum for some of their photographs.

CONVENTIONS

The word "detachment" as used for a subdivision of armored and artillery regiments by the Germans (*Abteilung*) and Soviets, is translated as "battalion" for convenience.

"Frankfurt-an-der-Oder", although not hyphenated in German, has been hyphenated here to conform to English usage, while the double "s", as in "Booßen", is given as "Boossen".

Postwar variations of place-names used in the text are quoted in parentheses in the Index.

GDR alterations of names such as "Neu Lewin" into "Neulewin" have been ignored, but should be expected on current maps of the area.

Timings in Soviet accounts are presumed to be Moscow Time and have therefore been converted to German Summer Time.

Waffen-SS ranks are given as normal army equivalents, such as "SS-Major" and so on.

The pattern of narration is generally north to south, east to west.

PART I

Deputy Supreme Commander

CHAPTER 1

The Man

The artillery bombardment that launched "Operation Berlin" was the mightiest that had ever been recorded. It started with an ear-shattering crack as tens of thousands of guns, mortars and rockets of all calibers opened fire simultaneously. Every available weapon, whether specifically targeted or not, participated in the terrifying opening salvo of this twenty-five-minute bombardment.

The volume of fire was so great that the earth trembled from the impact for miles around. In Berlin, some forty miles away, telephones jumped off their cradles and pictures fell off the walls.

The orchestrator of this extraordinary event with its cast of over three-quarters of a million players was Marshal of the Soviet Union Georgi Kontantinovich Zhukov, Deputy Supreme Commander of the Soviet Armed Forces, already twice Hero of the Soviet Union and undoubtedly the most outstanding military figure to emerge on the Soviet side during the Second World War, or the Great Patriotic War of 1941-1945 as it was described in the Soviet Union.

Who then was this man Zhukov?

Unfortunately the conventions of the Stalinist era allow us little indication of his true personality. Even today he is presented rather like a cutout picture of a hero, lacking any third or human dimension. It seems that he was married twice and had three daughters, but the intensity and devotion with which he tackled his career could not have left much time for family life. Not even his own *Reminiscences and Reflections* give us much of a clue as to his real character and personality.

Zhukov was born into a poverty-stricken peasant family on 19 November 1896 in the village of Strelkova in the province of Kaluga. His father worked as a cobbler, while his mother worked in the fields or as a carter, all for pitifully small sums. He had a sister two years older than himself and then a younger brother who died within a year of being born. He attended the local village school for three years, as was the custom, leaving at the age of ten with top marks and a yearning for further educaion. Shortly before his twelfth birthday he was apprenticed to his furrier uncle in Moscow on a four-and-half-year term. His uncle had clawed his way to being a successful businessman the hard way and ruthlessly exploited his staff, nephew included, for an eleven-hour working day. Nevertheless, Zhukov had acquired a zest for reading at his village school and after about a year he started attending night school. By the end of 1912 Zhukov had completed his apprenticeship and was a fully qualified furrier, continuing to work for his uncle.

Then came the First World War and in August 1915 Zhukov was conscripted into the cavalry. On completion of basic training with its lessons in brutal discipline, he was selected for NCO training and eventually sent to the front with a detachment of the 10th Dragoons. His subsequent war experience gained him two St. George's Crosses, one for capturing a German officer and another for a reconnaissance mission in which he was concussed by an exploding mine.

Zhukov then witnessed the collapse and disintegration of the Tsarist forces under revolutionary pressure before enlisting in the 4th Regiment of the 1st Moscow Cavalry Division of the Red Army in August 1918. This was a time when the newly founded Soviet government was under threat both from anti-Communist factions and troops sent into the country by the governments of Germany, France, the United Kingdom, the United States and Japan. Zhukov took an active part in the Civil War that ensued, and his service in the elite cavalry formations under commanders such as Timoshenko, Budyenny and Voroshilov, who were later to form part of Stalin's inner circle, was to stand him in good stead. In September 1919 he was wounded by a hand grenade, whose splinters entered his left side and thigh. While in the hospital he contracted typhus and took a while to recover, but was then sent on a commanders' course as a trainee sergeant major before returning to active service. As the war continued he gradually rose in rank through troop to squadron commander. On one day in 1921 he had two horses killed under him in action and was awarded the Order of the Red Banner for his deeds.

Then in May 1923, the Civil War being over, he was appointed commander of the 39th Buzuluk Cavalry Regiment at the age of only twenty-six and began an intensive course of self-education in military science while at the same time engaging in the intensive training of his regiment for modern warfare, adding a private three to four hours of study on top of a twelve-hour working day. The following year he was sent to the Higher Cavalry School in Leningrad on what became a one-year course with three other students that were also to become Marshals of the Soviet Union: Bagramyan, Rokossovsky and Yeremenko. He returned in 1925 to the 7th Samara Cavalry Division, where he was given command of the new 39th Melekess-Pugachevsk Cavalry Regiment. In May Zhukov was promoted to commander of the 2nd Cavalry Brigade in the same division.

In late 1929 Zhukov was sent to a refresher course for higher-level commanders in Moscow at the highly interesting time of the exchange of military expertise under the secret clauses of the revised Russo-German Rapallo Pact of 1926. (However, he did not attend any of the staff courses held in Germany as has sometimes been alleged.) A year later he was appointed Assistant Cavalry Inspector of the Red Army under the famous Marshal Budyenny, in which capacity he worked on cavalry combat training in close cooperation with the Combat Training Division. Much attention was paid to developing modern equipment and in particular to the evolution of a new kind of tank soldier and battlefield cooperation between mechanized, armored, cavalry and infantry units.

In 1932 he was given command of the 4th Cavalry Division in Byelorussia. By 1935 this division had achieved such an all-round high standard of proficiency that Zhukov personally and the division were both awarded the Order of Lenin. In 1936 the division was renamed the 4th Don Cossack Division, and a year later Zhukov briefly assumed command of the 3rd Cavalry Corps before taking over the 6th Cossack Cavalry Corps. While continuing his military studies, he again concentrated on the combat use of cavalry within a mechanized army, seeing clearly that the future lay with armored and mechanized formations. The horrific purge of army commanders in 1936 and 1937 left him untouched, presumably protected by the "cavalry club" of Stalin's close chums, but thereafter he is said to have kept a bag packed in case of sudden arrest. Then at the end of 1938 Zhukov was given the post of Deputy Commander of the 1st Byelorussian Military District, controlling the training of the cavalry units and tank brigades within the district, which in wartime would have given him command of a force of four to five cavalry divisions and three to four independent tank brigades.

At the beginning of June 1939 he was summoned to Moscow by the Commissar for Defense. There he was briefed on the Japanese army's incursion into Mongolia, where the Red Army's 57th Special Corps was deployed in support of the Mongolian army, before being flown out to report back on the situation. As a result of his subsequent reports, Zhukov was ordered to replace the corps commander, and the Soviet forces in Mongolia were heavily reinforced as the 1st Army Group. With these forces he conducted his first modern battle, inflicted a humiliating defeat on the Japanese at the end of August at the battle of Kharkin Kol, in which the Japanese sustained 50,000 casualties, including 18,000 killed, against Zhukov's 9,000 casualties, and were driven back across the frontier. This victory gained him his first award of the gold medal of Hero of the Soviet Union.[1]

One of the army commanders not to come out too well of the situation as Zhukov had found it was Ivan Stepanovich Koniev, a recent convert from the role of political commissar in the Red Army. Zhukov's success only exacerbated Koniev's jealous annoyance, providing the seed for the bitter rivalry that was to ensue between them, carefully nurtured by Stalin for his own ends. As Boris Nicolaevsky wrote in his book *Power and the Soviet Elite*, Stalin, with his great talent for exploiting human weaknesses, had

> quickly sized up Koniev and cleverly used his feelings towards Zhukov. If we trace the history of Stalin's treatment of the two soldiers, the chronology of their promotions and awards, we shall see that as early as the end of 1941 Stalin was grooming Koniev, the politician, as a rival whom he could play off against the real soldier, Zhukov. This was typical of Stalin's foresight and bears all the marks of his style. He confers honours on Zhukov only when he has no choice, but on Koniev he bestowed them even when there was no particular reason for doing so. This was necessary in order to maintain the balance between the 'indispensable organiser of victory' and the even more indispensable political counterweight to him.[2]

Zhukov's work in Mongolia fortunately kept him out of the Red Army's debacle in the 1939-1940 Winter War against Finland, and in May 1940 Zhukov was ordered back to Moscow, where he met Stalin for the first time. He was then given command of the Kiev Special Military District, the largest in the Soviet Union, as a full general under the Red Army's new rank structure. Clearly both men made a good impression on each other at this first meeting. Stalin came to trust him and to respect his military ability, and their relationship became relatively close, bearing in mind Stalin's inherent distrust of others. Zhukov was to accept Stalin's authority without question, whether he thought him right or wrong, in the same spirit in which he demanded total obedience from his own subordinates.

Then on 1 February 1941 Zhukov was appointed Chief of the General Staff. The Red Army was in urgent need of reform and particularly weak in the quality of its commanders, as the war with Finland had shown. He wanted a well-disciplined, efficient army, properly organized and equipped with the minimum political interference in the command structure, but time was too short. On 22 June the Germans invaded the Soviet Union in a surprise attack that swept aside the Red Army with ease and made enormous inroads into the country.

One of the measures taken by the Soviets to counter this emergency was to set up the Stavka of the Supreme Command. This was in effect a small discussion and briefing group which was to enable Stalin to make uncluttered decisions about the conduct of the war, and was a separate entity from both the State Defense Committee covering all aspects of the country's commitment to war and the General Staff of the High Command.

The Stavka consisted of only seven members, including Stalin, his old chum Marshal Budyenny, his foreign adviser Molotov, and Zhukov as Chief of the General Staff. A system then evolved whereby members or delegates of the Stavka would be dispatched to trouble spots to report, advise and supervise as necessary, a role that Zhukov was destined to fulfill at least fifteen times in the Great Patriotic War, as this conflict came to be called.

Under this system, in due course operational plans drawn up by the individual fronts (or army groups) had first to be cleared by the General Staff for approval by the Stavka, whose operational reserves could then be allocated to ensure the success of specific tasks. One result of this was that no plan could be attributed to any individual commander.

However, the Stavka system enabled Stalin to play the role of supreme commander with increasing confidence, and Zhukov, despite his outstanding achievements, was to experience a gradual loss of influence with Stalin as the war progressed.

At the end of June 1941 Zhukov was sent to Kiev and Tarnopol to check on the Southwestern Front only to be abruptly relieved of his post as Chief of the General Staff after advising the abandonment of Kiev to an enraged Stalin. Instead, while retaining membership on the Stavka and the title of Deputy Commissar for Defense, he was appointed Commander of the Reserve Front, which was forming east of Smolensk. Almost immediately he became involved in the battle for Jelnya, winning the first Soviet victory of the war.

Shortly afterward he was sent to organize the defense of Leningrad, taking over command of that Front and the Baltic Fleet from the totally incompetent Voroshilov. Within a month he had established a secure defensive system and restored the shattered morale. The Germans were checked in front of Leningrad, which they now proposed starving out while they switched their attention toward Moscow. On 6 October Zhukov was recalled to resume command of the Reserve Front before Moscow, now under direct threat, and four days later the Reserve and Western Fronts were combined under his command as the new Western Front. The previous commander, Koniev, had just lost half a million men in the Vyazma/Bryansk pocket[3], but Zhukov asked for him to be kept on as his deputy, a post filled only for a week. This was the first occasion these two actually served together and it could not have been a happy combination. There followed the winter battle for Moscow, which was to last until April 1942 and bring a decisive victory over the German invaders.

The precariousness of Zhukov's position vis-à-vis Stalin as the fledgling supremo were clearly seen in early 1942 when the latter, exuberant over the success of Soviet arms before Moscow, called for a concerted counteroffensive on all fronts. Zhukov argued that there were insufficient resources for such a venture and recommended a concentration of effort on his own front, where he could guarantee a measure of success, while standing firm on the others. Stalin refused to accept this argument and pressed ahead with his plan. Zhukov dutifully struck out at Army Group "Mitte", into whose rear area he made deep penetrations by the skillful use of cavalry and paratroops, but meanwhile Stalin was milking Zhukov's front to reinforce others, with the result that the operation failed to achieve its aim of destroying the German army group.

Stalin remained convinced that the Germans would try for Moscow once more with their summer offensive, whereas all indications were that they were planning something in the south, and again in March he pressed for a general counteroffensive. It was only when the Germans thrust out toward Stalingrad and the Caucasus that Stalin realized that his miscalculations in the military field had led to this major disaster. Zhukov was recalled to Moscow on 26 August, appointed Deputy Supreme Commander and sent off to Stalingrad to clear the mess. Before leaving he obtained Stalin's consent to the restoration of unitary command, clipping the powers of the commissars that had been introduced in the panic of the invasion the previous year, thus greatly simplifying the command function. Within three months of Zhukov's arrival the Soviets were able to launch massive attacks on the flanks of the German salient, closing the ring on the German 6th Army, which was eventually forced to capitulate on 2 February 1943 after one of the most humiliating defeats in German history. On 19 January, the day the German blockade of Leningrad was broken, Zhukov was promoted Marshal of the Soviet Union, but by this time he was investigating a failure by Koniev to eliminate a German salient as Stalin had ordered. Zhukov's promotion coincided with the reintroduction of shoulder boards denoting rank in the Soviet Armed Forces and also the recognition of a separate officer status. A month later he received the first Order of Suvorov (First Class) to be awarded for his triumph at Stalingrad.

Zhukov's next major task was the planning, preparation and conduct of the battle of Kursk, where it was correctly anticipated that in opening their summer offensive the Germans would attempt to reduce the Soviet salient astride that city from their own salients to the north and south. In this role he was instrumental in persuading the Stavka to amass massive reserves for the battle.

The German attack on 4 July was immediately met by a devastating artillery barrage and by such a dense net of antitank defenses that during the first week of the action the Soviets claimed to have destroyed nearly 3,000 German tanks and killed 70,000 German troops. Soviet losses were even higher but they could afford them better than the Germans. By 27 August the German salients had been eliminated and the Soviets were poised to cross the barrier of the Dnieper and liberate the Ukraine.

Stalin was now pressing for the liberation of Soviet territory and Zhukov was given the task of supervising the Voronezh and Steppe Fronts, the latter under Koniev. These were shortly to be renamed the 1st and 2nd Ukrainian Fronts respectively. Bridgeheads were established across the Dnieper and Kiev taken as the Soviet armies drove west. However, when the commander of the 1st Ukrainian Front was wounded in action, Zhukov was obliged to take over, dropping his responsibility for the supervision of the 2nd Ukrainian Front, thus for the first time becoming a fellow front commander to Koniev in March 1944. Zhukov's front launched an attack that advanced them 350 kilometers in five weeks, bringing him the first Order of Victory to be awarded.

Zhukov was then briefly recalled to Moscow to work on the plans for a summer offensive for the retaking of Byelorussia, code-named "Operation Bagration," leaving the 1st Ukrainian Front temporarily in Koniev's hands. At the end of May Zhukov was detailed to supervise the 1st and 2nd Byelorussian Fronts and, in the second phase of the operation, the 1st Ukrainian Front as well. The offensive was launched on 23 and 24 June, and by the middle of August the Soviet troops had closed up to the Vistula opposite Warsaw and established bridgeheads on the west bank further south. This success gained Zhukov his second award of the golden star of a Hero of the Soviet Union.

Zhukov's next task was to supervise the 3rd Ukrainian Front's assault on Bulgaria, which turned out to be a walkover as the Bulgarians met them with open arms, overthrowing their fascist government as they did so.

Zhukov returned to the supervision of the 1st and 2nd Byelorussian Fronts at the end of September 1944, but the following month he was summoned back to Moscow once more. Stalin told Zhukov that the western front had been so shortened by their advance, and with it the number of individual fronts so reduced, that from now on they would all be controlled directly from the Stavka. Zhukov would have command of the 1st Byelorussian Front aimed at Berlin and would retain his title of Deputy Supreme Commander, meaningless though they both knew it to be. Marshal Rokossovsky would move over from the 1st to the 2nd Byelorussian Front, while Marshal Koniev would retain the 1st Ukrainian Front.

Zhukov must have been greatly disappointed in this decision, for he already had experience of supervising the three fronts concerned in "Operation Bagration," and he had fully expected Stalin to focus his attention on the forthcoming operations in Hungary, where much of the remaining German resources were being concentrated in defense of the only remaining oil fields available to them. But it was not to be; he was to revert to being a Front commander. In effect it was a serious and humiliating demotion for him, placing him on a par with his deadly rival and previous subordinate, Koniev.

As early as July of that year Stalin had been talking as if he assumed the war with Germany were already won, and was discussing the possible political and military results. Now he was planning on these lines, with the political factors far outweighing the military ones. The implications for Zhukov emerge within the span of this book, which describes how all his leadership qualities were put to the test in the final stages of the war.

Again Zhukov wanted to see the Red Army well disciplined, proficient and well led by professionally minded officers. Although he had been a member of the Communist Party since 1919, he remained openly hostile to the inclusion of political commissars in the command structure of the Red Army, a daring position to take in the political climate of the day. His rival Koniev stemmed from that source, but his friend Konstantin Konstantinovich Rokossovsky, who had been one of the victims of Stalin's purge, imprisoned and tortured, sentenced to death and then released and rehabilitated to use his skills of command in the Great Patriotic War with the sentence still hanging over him, served as a constant reminder of the precariousness of all their positions.

Of Zhukov as a planner, Marshal A.M. Vasilevsky, who served with him as a member of the Stavka in a similar role, wrote:

> In the constellation of Soviet generals who so conclusively defeated the armies of Nazi Germany, he was the most brilliant of all.
>
> At all stages of the war, in strategic, tactical and organisational matters, Zhukov was always clear-headed and sharp, bold in his decisions, skilled in finding his bearings, in anticipating developments and picking the right instant for a decisive stroke. Making the most fateful of decisions, he was astoundingly cool and level-headed. He was a man of extraordinary courage and self-possession. I have never seen him flustered or depressed not even at critical moments. On the contrary, at moments like that he was only more forceful, more resolute, and more concentrated.[4]

In fact Zhukov had two senior political commissars on the staff of the 1st Byelorussian Front, Lieutenant General K.F. Telegin as his "Member of the War Council" and Lieutenant-General S.F. Galadzev as his Head of the Political Department, both of whom carried more weight than his other heads of arms and services.[5]

In his early days of command Zhukov had had a reputation for firmness and fairness in his dealings with his men, not asking of them more than he could do himself, although his own standards in fitness, horsemanship and general competence were high. As he grew older and more senior in rank he had become increasingly intolerant of incompetence in officers and other commanders. It is said that his bodyguard doubled as a mobile court-martial and execution squad. He was known to have a fierce temper and to ride roughshod over his subordinates, who both feared and respected him, but his popular image with the troops was as the bringer of victory and they knew that he too had gone through the ranks the hard way.

Nevertheless, he had a reputation for utter determination and ruthlessness in achieving his objectives, regardless of the cost in human lives, and for demanding instant and absolute obedience to orders. In an army of millions the keys to success lay in strategy, logistics and determination, and Zhukov was master of all three. He lay great stress on personal reconnaissance and concise briefings. Having ensured good planning and adequate resources for the attack, he left the execution to the subordinates, ensuring that they gained their objectives, irrespective of the cost.

Here we see the contrast with his Western counterparts, whose experiences in the First World War had made them and their home countries opposed to any wastage of human life. But in Stalin's Soviet Union with its millions of deaths through imposed starvation, deportation and indiscriminate massacre, human life was of little account. Military reports quoted enemy losses but did not bother with their own. Of the over 20 million deaths of Soviet citizens originally attributed to the Great Patriotic War, Russian historians now attribute less than 10 million to deaths on the battlefield or in German captivity.[6]

CHAPTER 2

The Soviets

At the beginning of 1945 the Soviets had some 6,000,000 troops on their western front facing some 2,100,000 Germans and their allies. Rather than deploy them evenly across the front, the Soviets maintained a system of reserves under the Stavka that enabled them to concentrate an even greater superiority in numbers in men and equipment at their points of main effort when required.

The Red Army in the field was sustained by the Soviet Union's own massive industrial effort and lend-lease items provided by the Western Allies. For instance, at this stage of the war about two-thirds of all Soviet military vehicles were of American origin, many of the troops wore boots and uniforms of either British or American manufacture, and the frontline troops existed almost entirely on American-supplied concentrated foodstuffs. Their devastated heartland was quite incapable of sustaining such vast numbers of men in the field unaided, and these vehicles provided their armies with the necessary mobility to defeat the Axis forces ranged against them. The Germans thus tended to regard the arrival of an Allied convoy in Russia as the herald of the next offensive.[1]

Despite all the difficulties involved, Soviet industry in 1944 alone was able to produce a staggering 29,000 tanks and self-propelled assault guns (SPGs), 122,500 guns and mortars, 40,300 aircraft and 184 million shells, mines and bombs.[2]

The Soviet lines of communication were based on their railway system, linking their fronts with the war industries, ports and sundry centers of production. The distances involved were enormous, with nearly 2,000 miles separating the war industries grouped in the Ural Mountains from the Vistula, and half the lease-lend supplies coming all the way across Siberia from the Pacific ports. The Russian gauge being wider than the European, the railway tracks had to be adapted and repaired as they advanced across Poland into Germany. This was usually done by ripping up the four pins holding a rail to each sleeper and relaying with only two pins, a system that was speedy of execution but led to a weaker track. Railheads were then set up as close to the front as circumstances allowed, from where local distribution was effected by horse and motor transport.[3]

Breakdowns of the composition of the various types of Red Army infantry, armored formations and mechanized formations are given in the Appendices of this book. However, it should be noted that establishments were frequently well under strength and that even at full strength a Red Army division was only half the size of its German equivalent.

The quality of the troops in the various arms was reflected by the system of allocation of recruits, which was by order of intelligence rating to the air arm, artillery, engineers, armor and finally infantry. However, manpower was beginning to run short, so released prisoners of war and slave laborers were promptly armed and incorporated into the infantry formations, a measure which did nothing to increase their quality.

Formations within or combining these arms were again divided into various categories. Of these the elite were those with the "Guards" appellation, which was awarded to regiments and superior formations that had distinguished themselves in battle, such as Chuikov's 64th Army, which had been renamed the 8th Guards Army after the battle of Stalingrad. This title brought increased rations but also demanded the maintenance of the highest standards in discipline, training and combat. Guards regiments and formations could be found throughout the first echelon formations, but when grouped into Guards armies they normally carried more firepower than the others, and their establishments tended to be larger.[4]

The cavalry formations remained an elite from the Civil War, all bearing Guards titles, and incorporated a mechanized element as developed in the interwar years. This arm was by no means obsolete, for with the vast, wild expanses involved in the Great Patriotic War, the cavalry provided a vital extension to the scope of the mobile and foot elements of other arms. Small mounted detachments also served in the traditional role as scouts and messengers in the infantry units.

The air force remained subordinate to the army, and was divided into Strategic, Tactical and Transport Commands. The Strategic Command of long-range bombers was the least used and least effective, but the Tactical Command had a wide range of combat aircraft, and was used extensively as another form of artillery support in the front line. In concept the air force was primarily another battlefield arm, an extension of the artillery, with little strategic value.[5]

The Il-2 Shturmovik fighter-bomber was the most popular aircraft for the ground-attack role. Late in 1944 air liaison units were attached to the headquarters of armies, corps and leading brigades to provide radio links for the improvement of air-ground liaison. Even if the liaison units' radios failed it was still technically possible to communicate through the tanks' own radios.[6] Curiously, the Po-2, an open two-seater biplane, was also extensively used for artillery spotting and reconnaissance purposes, but particularly for night bombing in First World War style, with the observer dropping light bombs or clusters of grenades by hand. The Germans called them "sewing machines" after the sound of the engine, but they were effective enough in harassing the frontline areas at night, and were often flown by all-female crews.

The primary role of the engineers was to be found in bridging the various water obstacles encountered. The main resources were held at front level, but allowance had to be made for far-penetrating mobile units to have adequate bridging resources. For instance, a tank army would require three to four girder bridges, two of them with a capacity of sixty tons, apart from its supporting arms' requirements.[7]

The artillery was regarded by the Soviets as the king of the battlefield and came to be used in concentrations of extraordinary density when Stavka reserves were allocated in support of specific operations. The backbone of the artillery was provided by the 76mm and 122mm towed guns, but there were also independent artillery regiments of extra powerful artillery pieces like the 152mm mounted on an open tracked carriage. Another artillery weapon was the 120mm heavy mortar.

A particularly strong element of the artillery was formed by armored self-propelled guns (SPGs) known as the SU-76, SU-85, SU-100 and the JSU-122 and JSU-152, carrying guns of those calibers, mounted on tank chassis and, except for the SU-76, all fully enclosed and organized into independent regiments according to type. However, the open-topped SU-76 was the most common. Originally a tank destroyer, the 76.2mm gun with sixty rounds that it carried in an open superstructure on a T-70 tank chassis was no longer suitable for that role, so it was now deployed in direct infantry support as a light assault gun, and organized into battalions of three batteries, each of four guns. The SU-122, mounted on a KV tank chassis, was organized in medium SPG regiments of sixteen guns and used in support of infantry divisions. Then came the heavy assault guns in the form of the SU-152 on a KV tank chassis, and the ISU-122 and ISU-152 on a "Stalin" tank chassis, all of the calibers indicated being organized into Guards heavy SPG brigades consisting of twelve batteries with sixty-five guns in all.[8]

A devastating addition to this armory was the Katyusha multiple-rocket launcher mounted on open truck-beds and known to the Germans as "Stalin-organs". Various versions were produced, the original mounting thirty-six rockets of 82mm with a range of 6,000 meters, followed by a heavier edition of sixteen rockets of 132mm and a range of 9,250 meters. The largest rockets were 310mm. This weapon was issued to specially formed Guards units of NKVD troops.[9]

The Soviets also had a comprehensive antiaircraft artillery organisation for the protection of their troops and installations.

The Soviet armor was very good indeed. By concentrating production on just a few simplified designs, the Russians had produced some of the most outstanding fighting vehicles of the war, roughly finished though they might appear. The new sixty-ton JS-2 (Stalin) tank carried a powerful 122mm gun and twenty-eight shells with separate cartridges for it, a formidable fighting machine. But the main component of the Soviet armoured force was the robust thirty-six-ton T-34/85 with an 85mm gun and carrying seventy-six rounds. There was also the light T-70 tank with its 45mm, which was used mainly for the protection of tactical headquarters in battle. However, radios were scarce and generally limited to commanders' vehicles, so that communication between tanks in action was often difficult. The Guards armored units were usually equipped with the latest "Stalin" and T-34/85 tanks, but the 2nd Guards Tank Army was particularly well supplied with American equipment, including the M4 "Sherman" tanks, several thousand of which had been provided under lend-lease, this presumably being the 76mm gun version, and a few British "Valentines." However, Soviet production figures for 1944 amounted to a record 29,000 tanks and self-propelled assault guns (SPGs), of which 2,000 were JS-2s, 11,000 T-34/85s, and over 3,000 SPGs with guns of 100mm, 122mm and 152mm caliber.

For tank destroyers the Soviets had the SU-85 and SU-100, carrying forty-eight and thirty-four rounds respectively, mounted on a T-34 chassis, the SU-85 being organized into battalions of twenty-one guns, and the SU-100 into Guards SPG brigades of sixty-five guns each.[10]

In support of this armor there was a most effective system of vehicular recovery and repair through damaged vehicle assembly points, whose workshops were able to put back into service a good half of all such vehicles recovered.[11]

At the bottom of the scale, the infantry were divided between Guards, Shock and normal infantry armies, these sometimes being organized as combined-arms armies, that is, each consisting of three infantry and one armored corps. The Shock armies had stronger artillery resources than the normal infantry armies, as they were designed to breach enemy fortifications at the beginning of an offensive.[12]

The remaining infantry armies were generally of a much lower caliber. Although well equipped with light arms, their artillery and all their transport was horse-drawn. Having the lowest priorities for clothing and rations, their uniforms were often in rags and they were expected to virtually live off the land. Consequently, on the move they presented an extraordinary spectacle, reminiscent of previous Asiatic invasions, with livestock being driven alongside ungainly caravans of commandeered wagons piled high with loot. Their training was minimal and their discipline poor, authority often being exercised by their officers at pistol point.[13]

Human life was of little value in Soviet considerations, and least of all in the penal units, of which each front had up to three battalions and each army from five to ten companies. Men of field officer rank and upward were sent to the penal battalions and men of junior officer rank downward to the penal companies, all as "penal privates," where they could regain their rank and decorations either by distinguished conduct, posthumously after being killed in action, or after fully recovering from wounds as fit to return to duty. These units were used for the most difficult and dangerous tasks, such as swamping enemy positions by sheer weight of numbers, or for advancing first over minefields to clear the way for others. Not only did they cater for the disciplinary cases, but they were also a convenient means of purging real or potential opponents of the regime from the ranks.[14]

The 1st Byelorussian Front had a chemical warfare battalion equipped with poison gas with them in the field, but this was not used. Other chemical warfare battalions at army level specialized in laying smoke screens to cover various operations.

Discipline in the Red Army varied greatly from unit to unit, but throughout bouts of heavy drinking would lead to serious breakdowns in discipline and acts of violence. Generally the Soviet soldier had a good and close relationship with his officers, which was not so readily extended to his commissars, for whom he had a natural distrust, despite his gullibility. His basic characteristics were those of the Russian peasant, and the qualities of patriotism, obstinacy, tenacity, endurance and cunning stood him in good stead as a soldier. He tended to be unpredictable in his moods and could easily become apathetic, morose or unruly in his behavior. Although slow-witted and cautious in his approach, he was by no means lacking in courage.[15]

Each Soviet army had from one to three NKVD (Ministry of the Interior) regiments attached, depending upon the situation. These units were not intended for use as fighting troops, but for providing a rear screen to the parent formation, preventing desertion, and for controlling the civilian population in the rear areas.[16]

The part played by women in the Soviet armed forces should not be underestimated. They were to be found extensively in the Rear Services in all sorts of roles, but were also to be found in the combatant units as signalers and down to company level as medical orderlies as well as political workers, and some even formed tank, infantry and engineer units or specialized as snipers. Some drove the amphibious vehicles used in assault river crossings, and there were all-female squadrons flying the Po-2 biplane night bomber previously mentioned.[17]

Also fighting under Soviet command were the recently raised 1st Polish Army, soon to be joined by the 2nd, the 1st Polish Composite Air Corps with 390 combat aircraft, and various other Polish units, including a tank brigade and a cavalry brigade. These had originally been founded from prisoners taken when Poland was overrun in 1939 and then subjected to lengthy political indoctrination. Their numbers had later been augmented by partisans and recruits called to the colors by the so-called Lublin Government after the "liberation" of their country.[18]

The Red Army depended upon its officer corps for the maintenance of discipline rather than on the NCO backbone found in most other national armies. Morale was the responsibility of commissars and political workers under the Political Department. The higher command structure coordinated by the Stavka under Stalin has already been described. Once the operational plans had been agreed at these levels, the front commanders had some freedom of interpretation of the general principles. Lesser-formation commanders were grouped into military councils with their chiefs of staff and political advisers, the latter being known simply as Member of the Military Council, and were allowed some initiative in the execution of their orders; but none was allowed at unit level, where immediate and unquestioning fulfillment was demanded upon pain of death.[19]

The Russian style of fighting basically still involved using troops on a massive scale, flooding the battlefield with men in successive waves, advancing almost shoulder to shoulder, attacking time after time with complete disregard for casualties until the objective was gained. In the latter part of the war they were also able to use tanks in the same manner and to prepare the way with earth-shattering bombardments from massed artillery and rocket launchers. Facing up to such attacks required strong nerves from skilled soldiers.

CHAPTER 3

The Germans

In contrast to the tight system of centralized control exercised by the Soviets, the German command structure was an uneasy mess. Adolf Hitler, the Führer of the Third Reich and Supreme Commander of the German Armed Forces, exercised his authority from remote command posts in which he had become more and more removed from the reality of the world in which his subjects lived, suffered, fought and died unheeded. On 16 January 1945 he moved into his new command bunker beneath the Old Chancellery in the Wilhelmstrasse.[1]

During the years of Nazi rule Hitler had established himself as an absolute dictator, who expressed his will to the nation by means of Führer-Orders and Führer-Decrees, while the rest of the Nazi leaders indulged in a behind-the-scenes struggle for power among themselves. His physical and mental health had suffered considerably from the strains of office, lack of exercise and possibly the attentions of his private physician, Professor Morrell, whose prescriptions have subsequently aroused some criticism. The assassination attempt of 20 July 1944 had done nothing to alleviate this condition, and since then a baleful mistrust of the General Staff, and also of Göring and his Luftwaffe, had been grafted on his megalomania and ferocious despotism.[2]

He firmly believed that his presence alone was sufficient to galvanize all energies in the right direction, and that all orders to retreat, however justifiable, inevitably led to disaster. He also believed that the situation was bound to change in his favor, this belief being based partly on the expected appearance of some new secret weapons (for which there were no longer any production facilities), partly on the conviction that the Allies would fall out when the Anglo-American armies met up with the Soviets, and partly on an absolute faith in his own star.[3]

His entourage did everything to encourage him in these beliefs, and nothing to bring about a sense of reality to the Führerbunker during this final stage of the war. Were the consequences not so drastic, the events in the bunker would have all the elements of a farce. In an oppressive atmosphere of noisy air-conditioning

19

and sweating concrete walls, with no distinction between night and day, Hitler's courtiers kept up their internecine struggle with malicious gossip, slandering those absent and disguising the truth from each other. Despite Hitler's obvious deterioration, his presence overwhelmed reason and sane judgment in all of them, and his military staff were as obsequious as the rest.[4]

The General Staff, once a strong contender in the power struggle, had been utterly broken by the purge following the unsuccessful assassination attempt of 20 July 1944, and its representatives in his entourage were now mere sycophants. Only Colonel General Heinz Guderian, who had been appointed Chief of Staff of the Oberkommando des Heeres (OKH Army GHQ) following the coup, had the nerve to stand up to him, but this led to endless rows and eventually Guderian's dismissal. Permanently with Hitler in the Führerbunker was Field Marshal Wilhelm Keitel, nominal Chief of the Oberkommando der Wehrmacht (OKW Armed Forces GHQ) with his headquarters in Berlin-Dahlem, but in practice acting as Hitler's personal Chief of Staff and issuing orders in the Führer's name. The OKW Chief of Staff, Colonel General Alfred Jodl and Guderian were obliged to spend most of their time shuttling back and forth between the Führerbunker conferences and their own secret wartime headquarters in the vast bunkers known as Maybach I and II respectively, some twenty miles south of the city at Zossen-Wunsdorf.[5]

In December 1941 Hitler had supplemented his role as Supreme Commander of the Armed Forces by taking over as Commander in Chief of the Army with the following announcement:

> Anyone can do the little job of directing operations in war. The task of the Commander in Chief is to educate the Army to be National Socialist. I do not know any Army General who can do this the way I want it done. I have therefore decided to take over command of the Army.

He then further complicated the command structure by directing the Eastern Front operations exclusively through the OKH, whose responsibilities in other theaters were then given to the OKW, thus obliging the two headquarters to compete against each other over resources for their respective spheres of responsibility.[6]

His attitude to the General Staff, of whose work he insisted on approving every detail, comes out clearly in this outburst to Guderian on one occasion:

> There's no need for you to try and teach me. I've been commanding the German Army in the field for five years and during that time I've had more practical experience than any gentlemen of the General Staff could ever hope to have. I've studied Clausewitz and Moltke and read all the Schlieffen papers. I'm more in the picture than you are![7]

One has to read Colonel General Heinz Guderian's book to realize how intolerable Hitler's conduct as a commander was toward the General Staff and what pressure persons like himself was placed under as a result of this. For instance, in January 1945 as the Soviets lauched their Vistula-Oder Operation and the fall of Warsaw was imminent, the heads of Guderian's Operations Department, a colonel and two lieutenant colonels, were arrested and interrogated by the Gestapo over the pertinent signals and their reactions to them. Although Guderian took full responsibility and suggested he be interrogated rather than lose that vital element of his staff, it was only after lengthy, time- and energy-wasting interrogations that he could ill afford, that the two lieutenant colonels were released, but the colonel was shunted around from one concentration camp to another until captured by the Americans. The essence of the problem lay in Hitler's Führer system of unquestioning obedience to orders clashing with the General Staff's system of mutual trust and exchange of ideas, against a background of Hitler's class consciousness and genuine distrust of the General Staff following the failed putsch.[8]

Hitler's last headquarters in the Führerbunker suffered the serious defect of not being equipped with the normal communications facilities of the Führer headquarters he had set up and occupied elsewhere in Europe during the course of the war. This was in part due to scale, for accommodation was extremely cramped in the Führerbunker itself, although more space could have been made available in the bomb-proof shelters beneath the New Chancellery building. However, the only communications facilities installed in the Führerbunker were a one-man switchboard, one radio transmitter and a radio telephone, which was depended, as previously mentioned, upon an aerial suspended from a balloon over the Führerbunker.[9]

The head of the Luftwaffe, the once flamboyant Reichs Marshal Hermann Göring, had been rightly blamed for its many shortcomings and was now a discredited figure, but he still occasionally attended conferences in order to display his loyalty to the Führer.[10]

Joseph Goebbels, like the other party leaders, combined several titles and responsibilities acquired in the scramble for power. Although most commonly known for his role as Minister of Public Enlightenment and Propaganda, he remained the original Gauleiter of Berlin, and was now also Reichs Defense Commissar for Wehrkreis III (Berlin-Brandenburg). To counter depression and defeatism his Ministry issued an endless stream of propaganda, which continued to hold out hope until the very end, while simultaneously threatening traitors and defeatists with the most dire penalties.

One of Goebbels's responsibilities as Gauleiter was the raising of the Berlin quota of Volkssturm units as part of the overall concept for defense. The Volkssturm had originally been raised the previous autumn as a form of home guard, intended purely for local defense and fortification construction, from men of sixteen years upward capable of bearing arms in an emergency but otherwise not physically fit for active service. The majority came from the upper age bracket and included many First World War veterans. They were organized into companies and battalions in their home districts, but with no set establishments, so that the Berlin battalions varied in strength from 600 to 1,500. Unit commanders were appointed by the party, some being veterans with military experience and a strong sense of duty, others mere political warriors. The only common issue was an armband, uniforms being either varied (even captured British battle dress being used) or nonexistent. Training was conducted on weekends and in the evenings when there was no construction work to do, and some three-day courses were offered at SA camps, but no Volkssturm troops were trained up to the combat role that came to be expected of them as the enemy engulfed their homeland. The Wehrmacht had no responsibility for this party-sponsored organization in the Home Guard role, which was meant to be armed, equipped and maintained entirely from local resources, but was obliged to take over those units later committed to the Eastern Front.[11]

However, in his capacity as a Reichs Defense Commissar, Goebbels took an active interest in events on the Eastern Front, making frequent visits of inspection and liaising directly with the field commanders.

Hitler's system of leadership was reflected in the state and composition of the German Armed Forces. One particularly confusing aspect was the use of corps and army headquarters taken out of reserve to command new formations to which they automatically gave their titles, irrespective of their composition or function. Thus the Vth SS Mountain Corps commanded only one Waffen-SS formation and no mountain troops, and the XIth SS Panzer Corps consisted primarily of ordinary infantry units.[12]

The basic framework of the German ground forces was still that of the army, most commonly known by the overall title of the Wehrmacht. However, after the abortive coup of 20 July 1944, the army had been seriously weakened by the great purge of officers that followed and by the Nazi leaders' distrust of the survivors. Political officers (NS-Führungsoffiziere) had been appointed to all units and formation headquarters for the purpose of promoting the Nazi spirit and to spy on possible dissidents. Reichsführer-SS and Chef-der-Deutschen-Polizei (State SS and Police Chief) Heinrich Himmler, who was also Minister of the Interior, had been given command of the Reserve or Home Army, an appointment of considerable influence in the army hierarchy, covering as it did all recruitment, training, development and allocation of equipment. Since then all new recruits had been assigned to the newly constituted Volkswehr (People's Army) of Volks Grenadier (Infantry) and Volks Artillery units, which were intended to form the nucleus of a more politically reliable postwar army. The latter were also given priority of equipment over the army, which thus suffered deficiencies of the same important equipment that the Volkswehr then wasted through lack of combat experience.

Under the operational command of the Wehrmacht, although technically an entirely separate organisation, were Himmler's own troops of the Waffen-SS, consisting of Panzer (Armored), Panzergrenadier (Motorized Infantry), cavalry and mountain formations, as well as foreign volunteer elements such as the "Nordland," "Wallonien," "Nederland" and "Charlemagne" Divisions, but as a result of hard usage most of these formations were now drastically reduced in strength. They had priority of equipment over the army and, as part of Himmler's extensive empire, they even had their own sources of supply from SS slave-labor factories. The Waffen-SS, however, like many Nazi Party organizations, was not all that they appeared to be on the surface. Their revolutionary training methods, based upon special storm-trooper tactics developed late in the First World War, had been initiated by Felix Steiner, later to become an SS general, and they were renowned for the irresistible ferocity of their attacks and indifference to casualties. As the war progressed they expanded considerably, but also suffered tremendous losses in their spearheading of attacks. Unable to compete with the conscription laws directed at the Wehrmacht, they had been obliged to recruit elsewhere and had become so diluted with foreign volunteers and non-ethnic Germans, and so indifferent to the higher command while maintaining an arrogant spirit of elitism, that they were now curiously like the French Foreign Legion in outlook, a closed community with their own rules and loyalties. By 1945 the faith of the SS generals in Hitler was wavering, and they no longer believed in final victory. Handicapped by second-rate reinforcements and wrestling with a crisis of conscience over foreign volunteers, the Waffen-SS had become a prey to ideological doubts and now followed leaders whose loyalty to the state was suspect.[13]

Under Himmler's aegis as Minister of the Interior, *Marsch* (field) battalions were raised from police, fire brigade, customs and border guard resources, equipped with smallarms and sent into the the field to serve under their own officers.

Apart from the air support provided by Colonel General Ritter von Greim's 6th Air Fleet over this combat zone, the Luftwaffe contributed three categories of troops to the land battle.[14]

First there were the parachute units. Although many of their personnel had never received parachute training, being early selections from nonflying branches of the service, they had been trained and indoctrinated in the elitist traditions of the parachutists, and these units had long been employed as shock infantry with the army. However, at this stage replacements for casualties from further selections, including aircraftless aircrew, were being incorporated into these units without the benefit of the normal training and indoctrination.

Second, the flak, or antiaircraft artillery, corps of the service, which provided 90 percent of all German antiaircraft defense, was represented in all army formations down to divisional level, usually under their own command and control structure. In addition to providing antiaircraft cover for headquarters installations, supply dumps and communications centers, flak batteries were also frequently successfully used as mobile artillery against strong points or in the antitank role, for which the 88mm gun was famous. Unlike their counterparts in most armies, the flak corps had started life as an elite body and remained so in the field, individual batteries often fighting heroically until finally overrun or destroyed.

Lastly there were the Luftwaffe field divisions, which had first been formed in 1942 and eventually attained a strength of 200,000 men, or one-tenth of the entire service. They had originally been formed from men skimmed from the training organizations, flak and other ground service units, but had been lightly armed and committed as infantry, only to suffer enormous losses in consequence. By April 1945 the original units had virtually ceased to exist, but in these last desperate days more units were raised in the same manner and committed to battle. This measure was greatly facilitated by the Luftwaffe system of having all their ground staff organized into companies and battalions on their bases, but of course these units lacked all but the men's own personal weapons for this new role, had no combat experience and could be expected to be of only limited value when committed as infantry.

However, the continuing strength of the Wehrmacht lay in its tactical skills, its command system in the field, and its ability to reorganize quickly at all levels. Time and time again the Germans were able to trounce their opponents by means of their superior skills, despite a vast imbalance of numbers. One weak point, however, lay in their antitank defense doctrine, which we will come to later.

German field headquarters were kept small and well forward so as to maintain close contact with subordinate commanders, who in turn used experienced officers as their liaison links with those headquarters. The staff officers were highly trained and able to make quick decisions, for their philosophy was that the unexpected could always happen and one must be able to react decisively. Consequently there was a high degree of personal contact and mutual confidence in the command structure. The system of *Auftragstaktik* left the initiative of how a given objective was to be achieved to the subordinate commander, thus achieving maximum flexibility of response to any given situation.[15]

The establishment of a German infantry division of this period is given in Appendix IV. Of note is the growing use of and dependence upon the cheaply manufactured, handheld antitank weapons known as the *Panzerschreck* and *Panzerfaust*. Effective at short range, these weapons were widely available, and captured stocks were often a welcome addition to the Soviet armory. Because of the prevalence of this type of weapon, the German armor was often protected with a metal skirting around the hull and turrets so as to induce detonation before the missiles could penetrate. Another measure taken against close-quarter fighting was the painting with *Zimmerit*, an antimagnetic paste, as an antidote to the application of magnetic devices.

The Germans had a variety of tanks, SPGs and tankhunters (*Jagdpanzer*) available, although the desperate situation reached by 1945 meant that units were being raised and equipped with anything that was available. The Panzer IV had seen service throughout the war in various production series and was now equipped with a 75mm 48-caliber gun to enable it to stand up to the Soviet T-34/85. The later German tanks all owed inspiration to the T-34, which had proved itself so superior in design when first encountered in 1941. The first of these was the 45-ton Panzer V "Panther" with a 75mm 70-caliber gun and carrying seventy-nine rounds. Then came the 55-ton Panzer VI "Tiger I" with an 88mm 56-caliber gun and ninety-two rounds, followed by the 70-ton Panzer VI "Tiger II", or "Königstiger", with an 88mm 71-caliber gun carrying eighty rounds. The latter was designed to dominate the battlefield, as it could when properly handled, being able to take on any number of T-34s without itself sustaining damage. It was in fact the most powerful tank produced in the Second World War, but its sheer size, weight and mechanical unreliability counted against it.

As a simpler form of construction, the turretless versions of these tanks were used as tankhunters or destroyers. There was the Jagdpanzer IV/70 mounting a 75mm 70-caliber gun, the "Panzerjäger Panther" *Jagdpanzer* mounting a 88mm 70-caliber gun, and the Jagdpanzer VI "Jagdtiger", actually derived from the "Königstiger" and mounting a 128mm 55-caliber gun, with an all-up weight of seventy tons. There were still some of the earlier models around, such as the *Jagdpanzer* "Ferdinand" or "Elefant," which the Soviets were to encounter near Müncheberg and in Berlin.[16]

A lighter series of tankhunters were to be found in the "Hetzer" and "Marder" range mounted on the well-proven and reliable LT-38 Czech tank chassis. The Jagdpanzer 38(t) "Hetzer" mounted a 75mm 48-caliber gun in an all-enclosed body, whereas the "Marder III" had a 75mm 46-caliber gun mounted behind a gun shield with open top and rear.

In addition to these armored vehicles, the Germans had experimented with a variety of SPGs, of which the most common was the Sturmgeschütz III on the old Panzer III chassis and mounting a 105mm howitzer. There were also two armored flak vehicles, the Flakpanzer IV "Möbelwagen" mounting a single 37mm gun and the Flakpanzer IV "Wirbelwind" with a quadruple 20mm gun mounting, both types being devastating when used against infantry.

However, Allied bombing was seriously affecting the German war industry. Production had been greatly reduced and the railway communications seriously disrupted. Most serious of all was the lack of motor fuel of all kinds, whose production centers had become a priority target in the Allied bombing offensive. Of all strategic targets this certainly proved the most effective, but its value was not fully appreciated until fairly late in the war, and not actually implemented until 1945. Fuel had already been in critically short supply for some months and was having a telling effect on operations everywhere.

Another, perhaps little-known, but equally serious aspect was the effect of the lack of zinc and copper for the production of brass cartridges for small arms ammunition. A metal substitute dipped in lacquer to prevent rusting had been introduced, but this resulted in the rounds jamming as soon as the weapon became heated. Consequently machinegun barrels had to be changed and cleared at the end of each burst, and the riflemen were obliged to kick or hammer the bolts of their weapons open with a bayonet or entrenching tool between rounds, thus reducing their rate of fire to that of an early musketeer.[17]

PART II

The Bridgeheads

CHAPTER 4

The Vistula-Oder Operation

The summer offensive of 1944 had brought the Soviets across Byelorussia and central Poland up to the line of the Vistula, where three large bridgeheads had been secured on the west bank. The next major offensive was planned for mid-January 1945, and Zhukov was heavily involved in the general planning for this during late October and early November 1944 before taking over command of the 1st Byelorussian Front on 16 November.

One aspect that arose was the disposition and strength of the Soviet forces to be used in the clearance of East Prussia and the Courland Peninsula, which would be on the northern flank of the Berlin group of fronts, that is, the 1st Byelorussian and the 1st Ukrainian. Both Zhukov and General Antonov of the General Staff suggested the reinforcement of the 2nd Byelorussian Front by one more field army, but Stalin did not agree. This turned out to be a serious error of judgment, for the task of clearing East Prussia of the mass of German troops concentrated there proved to be a far slower process than the "Berlin" fronts' advance to the west, resulting in a dangerous gap opening between the 1st and 2nd Byelorussian Fronts.

The Red Army was now operating outside its sovereign territory and therefore no longer had the benefit of intelligence and support from its partisan units, which had been so helpful until then. Camouflage and deception, jointly known as *Maskirovka*, were of increasing importance to disguise and protect Soviet operations and formed an essential part of the operational planning.

Another aspect was the behavior of the Soviet troops now that they were outside their homeland. An East Prussian village recaptured after Soviet occupation was found to have had all its inhabitants massacred, a subject that Goebbels was able to exploit to the full in ensuring a stiff resistance by the German troops in the defense of their homeland. In Poland behavior was little better and the Political Department had a hard job putting it across that the troops were to act as liberators and not as conquerors. Certainly behavior toward the

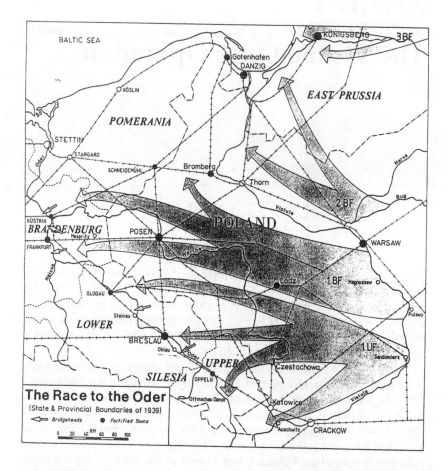

The Race to the Oder
(State & Provincial Boundaries of 1939)

⟸ *Bridgeheads*   ● *Fortified Towns*

0   20   40 KM 60   80   100

German population could not be effectively restrained until the fighting was completely over, for the lust for revenge after all the atrocities perpetrated by the Nazi regime against the Soviet people had hitherto been fostered by the Department and was now too great to be suppressed overnight as a result of a change in official policy.

For the 1st Byelorussian Front the Warsaw-Lodź Operation plan, as it was first called, involved breaking out of its two bridgeheads, eliminating the German forces in the area between Warsaw and Radom, and then pushing forward via Lodź to Posen to form a line extending north to Bromberg and south toward Breslau, which the 1st Ukrainian Front should by then have reached in its clearance of Upper Silesia. Nothing detailed was planned beyond that stage, for the outcome of the type of breakthrough battle envisaged could not be gauged with any accuracy.

Zhukov planned the launching of his operation in order of a reconnaissance in force followed by a thirty-minute barrage. If that appeared to have stunned the Germans sufficiently, the main attack would follow immediately. This would be conducted by the infantry supported by tanks, SPGs and aircraft. Once a breach had been opened in the main defenses the armor would be let through to push ahead as fast as possible, splitting the surviving German groupings and beating them back to their alternative defense lines.

Koniev began his offensive with the 1st Ukrainian Front on 12 January, followed by Rokossovsky with the 2nd Byelorussian Front on the 13th, and finally Zhukov with the 1st Byelorussian Front on the 14th. By the time Zhukov attacked, the 9th Army opposing him was fully alert, but to little avail. By the end of the 15th the German defensive system had been destroyed and Zhukov's 1st and 2nd Guards Tank Armies were through and advancing up to 100 kilometers beyond their start lines. To the south Koniev's forces were enjoying similar success with a rapid advance.

Hitler reacted to the collapse of the front on the Vistula by sacking the Army Group "A" and 9th Army commanders, and replacing them with Colonel General Ferdinand Schörner and General Theodor Busse, but Army Group "A" was renamed Army Group "Mitte" and the 9th Army went to Army Group "Weichsel" (Vistula). The latter was taken over on 25 January by Heinrich Himmler, who immediately set off in his luxurious personal train to Deutsch-Krone in Pomerania with neither the necessary direct communications link to the Wehrmacht command network nor maps, apart from one which the newly appointed operations officer happened to bring along with him four days later. No sooner had he issued his first orders than the Soviet advance forced him to withdraw westward again. The ineptness of this appointment continued with his chief of staff, SS-Brigadier Lammerding, who appeared on the 27th, but proved to have no staff experience.[1]

The Soviet advance was favored by frozen ground, little snow, and iced-up waterways that could take the weight of the infantry and light artillery pieces, so that built-up areas could more easily be bypassed. The move was so swift that the Soviets were constantly catching the Germans unprepared, their defenses unmanned. Consequently, on 17 January, the day the two "Berlin" fronts drew abreast and Warsaw fell, Stalin ordered Zhukov to reach the Bromberg-Posen line by 2 or 4 February.

The advance continued with increasing speed. Posen was reached on the 22nd and Bromberg taken the next day, a full week ahead of schedule. However, the important communications center of Posen, where seven railway lines and six major roads met, was not to be taken that easily. It was a genuine nineteenth-century fortress city with an inner citadel and a ring of massive forts manned by a garrison of some 12,000 troops of various kinds. The city could not be allowed to hold up the advance, so the leading troops pressed on and Colonel General Chuikov of the 8th Guards Army was detailed to supervise the reduction of the fortress with four of his divisions and two from the slower-moving 69th Army that appeared later. The siege was to last until 23 February, an important delaying factor on the part of the Germans.

In his capacity as army group commander, Himmler ordered SS-General Friedrich-Wilhelm Krüger of the Vth SS Mountain Corps based in the Meseritz area to try and block the Soviet advance on Berlin. Headquarters Vth SS Mountain Corps then had the 433rd and 463rd Reserve Infantry Divisions under command, deployed along the north-south line of the Odra River and the prewar frontier defences against Poland known as the Tirschtiegel Riegel (defensive belt). Massive though these partly-completed Maginot-like defenses were, they had long been stripped of their guns for the Atlantic Wall, and so failed to present the expected obstacle to the Soviet advance. Volksturm and other scratch units were sent to reinforce the corps. Then on 26 January, the "Grossdeutsch-land" Replacement and Training Brigade based in the Guben-Cottbus area, and about to be renamed the "Kurmark" Panzergrenadier Division on 1 February, was ordered to dispatch a battle group immediately to the Vth SS Mountain Corps via Frankfurt-on-the-Oder and follow with its remaining units as soon as possible. The brigade's armored reconnaissance battalion had already set out by rail on 22 January to the relief of the Posen garrison but was stopped short of its destination and eventually had to fight its way back, reaching the Oder near Grünberg at the end of the month after many adventures.[2]

On 26 January, the day his troops crossed the 1939 German border, Zhukov submitted a plan, approved by the Stavka the following day, which stipulated that the 1st Byelorussian Front's forces were to reach the line Berlinchen/ Landsberg/Brätz by 30 January, and went on to say:

> By the same day the tank armies shall gain control of the following areas:
> The 2nd Guards Tank Army Berlinchen, Landsberg, Friedeberg: the 1st Guards Tank Army Meseritz, Schwiebus, Tirschtiegel.
>
> Upon reaching this line, the formations, particularly the artillery and the logistical establishments shall halt, supplies be replenished and the combat vehicles put in order. Upon full deployment of the 3rd Shock and 1st Polish Armies, the Front's entire forces shall continue the advance on the morning of the 2nd February, 1945, with the immediate mission of crossing the Oder in their drive, and shall subsequently strike out at a rapid pace toward Berlin, directing their main effort at enveloping Berlin from the northeast, the north and north-west.[3]

Zhukov went on to issue orders on 27 January that included:

> There is evidence that the enemy is hastily bringing up his forces to take up defensive positions on the approaches to the Oder. If we manage to establish ourselves on the western bank of the Oder, the capture of Berlin will be guaranteed.

> To carry out this task each army will detail one reinforced rifle
> corps ... and they shall be immediately moved forward to reinforce the
> tank armies fighting to secure and retain the position on the west bank of
> the Oder.[4]

Zhukov continued his planning and the next day further details emerged.
The 5th Shock Army was to thrust toward Bernau, northeast of Berlin, the 8th
Guards Army toward Buckow, Alt Landsberg and Weissensee, and the 69th
Army toward Frankfurt-an-der-Oder, Boossen and Herzfelde, all three armies
operating between the water boundaries formed by the Finow Canal in the north
and the Spree River in the south.

On the basis of his instructions of the 27th, the front's armies widened the
arc of their advance toward the Oder, sending strong vanguards ahead of each
army, corps and division. The threat of rising temperatures forced them to
quicken their pace even further in the hope that the ice would still be holding
when they reached the Oder and thus simplify their crossing. A medal that had
been struck the year before for commanders gaining bridgeheads no doubt acted
as an added incentive.

The armored vanguards of each corps consisted of a reinforced brigade
operating thirty to forty kilometers ahead of the main body, while the infantry
armies formed similar vanguards from their own integral armor and motorized
infantry units to operate up to sixty kilometers ahead of the main body. These
were flexible distances, of course. As the fighting was done almost exclusively
by the vanguards, the main body followed in column of route and only deployed
when larger enemy forces were encountered, thus enabling the infantry armies to
maintain virtually the same pace as the armored ones.

However, in this approach across a wide arc the front was uncomfortably
split by both the Warthe estuary (Warthebruch) and further back by the gap in
the lines of communication caused by the Posen Fortress. The Soviet vanguards
were therefore fortunate that they did not come up against any properly organized resistance.

Both the 2nd Guards Tank Army, less one corps already detached to cover
the front's exposed northern flank, and the 5th Shock Army passed through
Landsberg north of the Warthebruch on the 30th, heading for Kienitz on the
Oder, which they reached on 31 January.

The 1st Guards Tank Army and those elements of the 8th Guards and 69th
Armies not involved in the siege of Posen fanned out south of the Warthebruch,
with the 33rd Army even further south on the front's left flank. The 44th Guards
Tank Brigade, vanguard of the 11th Guards Tank Corps (1st Guards Tank
Army), broke through the "Tirschtiegel Riegel" astride Meseritz, pushing
forward along the axis Tauerzig-Polenzig-Göritz, to reach the Oder on 2
February. The main body was unable to take advantage of its vanguard's success

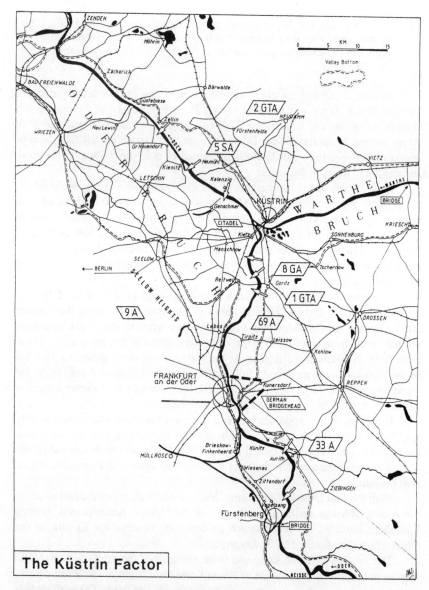

The Küstrin Factor

and had to fight its way through the old German border defenses, which took the whole of the two days of 30 and 31 January to do.[5]

The first units of the 1st Byelorussian Front to force the Oder, crossing the ice at 0600 hours on 31 January, were from General Nikolai Erastovich Berzarin's 5th Shock Army, the 2nd and 3rd Battalions of the 1006th Rifle Regiment (266th Rifle Division, 26th Guards Rifle Corps). They were able to cross the ice and take the village of Kienitz completely by surprise, together with the manor of the same name and several individual farms in the area, all within an hour, establishing a bridgehead four kilometers wide and two deep. The weight-carrying capacity of the ice prevented the moving over of vehicles and heavy artillery. Only fifteen 76mm guns of the 507th Antitank Artillery Regiment and the sixteen 120mm mortars of the 2nd Battalion of the 489th Mortar Regiment could be transferred across to reinforce the bridgehead.[6]

All of the other guns, the tanks and the SPGs had to remain on the east bank. Thus only half of the vanguard could be deployed in the bridgehead. However, improvement of the ice-crossing points enabled the ice to carry more weight and eventually 184 guns and mortars were transferred across.[7]

During the course of this first day more units of the 26th Guards Rifle Corps reached the Oder, as did the 219th Tank Brigade (1st Mechanized Corps, 2nd Guards Tank Army). The 283rd and 286th Guards Rifle Regiments of the 94th Guards Rifle Division immediately reinforced the defense of the bridgehead and enabled an expansion to a width of six kilometers and a depth of two and a half, encompassing the village of Gross Neuendorf in the north to just short of the hamlet of Sophienthal in the south, thereby considerably improving the circumstances for the defense, who could now concentrate more strength and equipment to counter enemy attacks. Furthermore, it was possible to distance the crossing points from the direct line of enemy fire.[8]

However, Zhukov's often-quoted description of this event is surprisingly inaccurate:

> At the moment the detachment burst into the town of Kienitz, German soldiers were blissfully walking the streets, and officers were sitting in a restaurant. Trains on the Kienitz-Berlin line were running on schedule, and communications were operating normally.[9]

This is imaginative nonsense, for Kienitz is actually just a small village then standing on a narrow-gauge railway linking the villages of the Oderbruch with the flanking towns of Wriezen and Fürstenwalde. A German documentary film made on this subject several years later found the same baker and his assistant that had been virtually the only persons awake in the village when the Soviets crossed on the frozen ice in the early hours of the morning, following the tracks of farmers that had been gathering firewood on the eastern side. A train carrying six antiaircraft guns and some sleeping Reichsarbeitsdienst (RAD) troops was captured intact at the village station with thirteen officers and sixty-three youngsters. Only a few lightly clad individuals fled across the fields to get away to warn the incredulous officials in the nearest town of Wriezen. The Soviets also liberated fifty-seven Soviet prisoners of war employed on the land at Amt Kienitz. The Wehrmacht bulletin for 31 January erroneously reported that tanks and about 2,000 infantry had formed a bridgehead at Kienitz.[10]

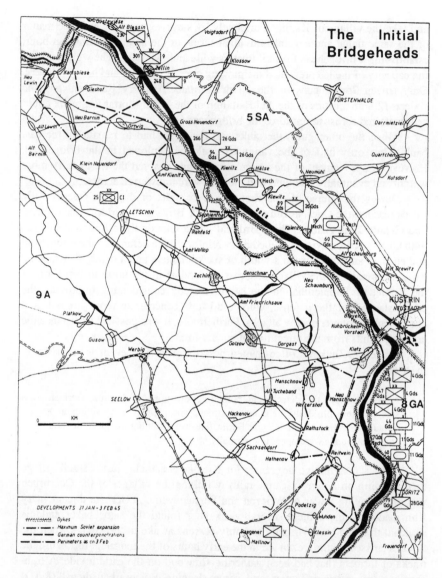

The Initial Bridgeheads

Colonel General S.I. Bogdanov's 2nd Guards Tank Army also assisted with this Kienitz bridgehead, sending across a motorized rifle battalion of the 219th Tank Brigade on 31 January to reinforce the defense. But the tanks could not cross, so they probed to the south until they met fierce resistance on the outskirts of Küstrin. Six of these tanks burst right into the marketplace of Küstrin-Neustadt, where four of their number were destroyed before the rest could withdraw to the northeastern edge of the town.[11]

The first Soviet troops to arrive on the Oder south of the Warthebruch divide were from Colonel General Vassily Ivanovich Chuikov's 8th Guards Army's 4th Guards Rifle Corps's vanguard, who appeared just to the south of Küstrin on 1 February, having followed the main road through Schwerin and Kriescht. At Sonnenburg they were shocked to find a Gestapo prison whose over 700 inmates had just been indiscriminately executed in the prison yard ahead of the Soviet advance, only four having survived the massacre by chance.[12]

Further south another of Colonel General M.I. Katukov's 1st Guards Tank Army's vanguards, the 20th Guards Mechanized Brigade (8th Guards Mechanized Corps), followed the route Meseritz-Zielenzig-Drossen to also arrive at Göritz, while the 1st Guards Tank Brigade of the same corps followed the highway from Schwiebus and Reppen toward Frankfurt-an-der-Oder. Here it ran into the main body of the "Kurmark" Panzergrenadier Division east of Reppen on the 27th and forced the Germans back to Kunersdorf, but then ran out of fuel only five kilometers short of the Oder on the site of the battlefield where an earlier Russian army had assisted the Austrians to defeat Frederick the Great in 1759. The new "Kurmark" stemmed from from veterans of the "Grossdeutschland" Panzergrenadier Division and Katukov described the fighting at Kunersdorf as the fiercest encountered in the whole of the Vistula-Oder Operation. The German troops later withdrew about a kilometer, forming a bridgehead around Dammvorstadt, the east bank suburb of Frankfurt-an-der-Oder, that was to hold until the defenders were withdrawn on the night of 21-22 April and the road bridge blown.[13]

Even further south, the 33rd Army appeared on the banks of the Oder at Aurith, having come via Ziebingen, and crossed the river to establish a bridgehead at Vogelsang just north of Fürstenberg. The German inhabitants were immediately evacuated from the area the Soviets had seized. Ad Hoc units were thrown into desperate counterattacks against this bridgehead but failed to dislodge the Soviets. One company of young Wehrmacht recruits had only 13 left alive out of 135 after their first week in action.[14]

The essential was to establish bridgeheads on the west bank of the Oder before the Germans could occupy and defend that natural obstacle. For all the Soviet units involved it entailed a final desperate effort and considerable courage to effect, for the ice had reached a critical stage in which it could break up at any moment and nowhere was strong enough to take any heavy equipment.[15]

Appreciating the vulnerability of his troops in this situation to air attack, Chuikov obtained the release of the 16th Antiaircraft Artillery Division from the Front's resources, but this formation ran out of fuel on the way and did not arrive until the morning of the 3rd.

Chuikov describes the scene:

At 1000 hours on the 2nd February I visited the observation post of General Glazunov commanding the 4th Guards Rifle Corps. The OP had been set up in the ruins of a fort outside the village of Säpzig, south of Küstrin. The corps had already deployed along a dike between Küstrin and Göritz, poised to cross the Oder. A wide river it was, lined with dykes. Our troops were concentrated on the eastern bank. The ice on the river was so brittle that even the infantrymen, let alone the heavy equipment and tanks, could move across it only at great peril. We had no organic crossing facilities, and yet the troops, under cover of artillery fire, began to make their way to the far bank, carrying poles, planks and bundles of brushwood. On their way they laid planking and improvised footbridges. Here and there they managed to get antitank guns to the opposite bank by putting them on improvised skis and pushing them over the ice.

Unfortunately, German aircraft soon put an end to the crossing. Flying in nines and sevens, Focke-Wulf fighters swooped over the crossing points, bombing and strafing our troops. How badly we needed General Seredin's antiaircraft gunners! But they were still on their way. Neither were there any Soviet fighters in sight: they [were in the course of being transferred] to airfields closer to the Oder and were also short of fuel. In the meantime, the German pilots had a field day, flying so low at times it seemed that their propellers would touch the heads of our men. The antitank gunners and machine-gunners joined battle against the planes. It is hard to say how many holes they made in them, but I did see two Focke-Wulfs come down in flames. A captured German pilot said that the Luftwaffe had been ordered at all costs to prevent the Russians from crossing the Oder.

And this they did. We were compelled to discontinue the crossing until nightfall. But when we resumed it the conditions were even more difficult, since on top of being brittle the ice had now been holed by bombs in many places.

Although only small units made it to the opposite bank during daylight hours, they still managed to secure minor bridgeheads there.[16]

In accordance with Chuikov's instructions, during the course of 2 February, elements of the 35th and 47th Guards Rifle Divisions (4th Guards Rifle Corps) managed to establish a small bridgehead near Neu Manschnow, meeting no resistance. Their scouts in one of their customary advance probes captured two German staff officers on the Küstrin-Seelow highway, who confirmed that the German General Staff had been unaware of the latest developments in this area. (In fact General Busse's headquarters had been located at Golzow as late as 30 January.) Surprise had been complete. Another small bridgehead was established southeast of Reitwein by the 79th Guards Rifle Division (28th Guards Rifle Corps), whose scouts pushed forward as far as Reitwein village by 1600 hours, driving a Reichsarbeitsdienst battalion they encountered back to the confines of the manor farm on the far side. (These 200 youths, only partly armed with rifles, were there to help the local authorities shepherd the refugees passing through from Göritz, and had not been expected to perform as infantry.)[17]

Then at 1500 hours the 20th Guards Mechanized Brigade (8th Guards Mechanized Corps, 1st Guards Tank Army) reached the Oder near Göritz. They were joined later that evening by the 40th Guards Tank Brigade (11th Guards Tank Corps, 1st Guards Tank Army), whose commander, Colonel A.K. Babadshanian, immediately started organizing a crossing, assisted by the arrival of the 20th Pontoon Battalion at 1900 hours.[18] The 273rd Battalion of his 27th Guards Motorized Rifle Brigade, using boats they found, joined part of the 57th Guards Rifle Division northeast of Reitwein, and seven tanks were ferried across to both of the bridgeheads near Göritz before orders were received next day for the redeployment of the tank armies necessitating their return to the east bank.[19]

The redesignated Vistula-Oder Operation had been an outstanding military success, but the extent of the success brought its own problems with it. Rokossovsky's 2nd Byelorussian Front had been unable to keep pace on the northern flank for lack of sufficient forces, the very point that Zhukov and Antonov had raised with Stalin the previous autumn, and now Zhukov was having to redeploy a considerable part of his forces to meet the threat of gathering German reinforcements in the Stargard area to his north. The reference to the 3rd Shock and 1st Polish Armies in his orders of 26 January involved their moving forward into the first echelon to join the 61st Army for that purpose. On the 31st he sent an urgent signal to Stalin asking for Rokossovsky's 70th Army to be ordered forward to help fill this gap, but to no avail; he did not even get a reply. For the moment there seemed to be a slippage of understanding between front and Stavka on what was actually being achieved on the ground. It may be that at this stage the Stavka were too preoccupied with preparations for the Yalta Conference, which was to last from 4 to 11 February, to keep pace with events on the ground.[20]

Another major problem was that the speed of advance had caused the vanguards to outstrip their lines of supply. In many cases vehicles had to be temporarily abandoned for lack of fuel. The supply columns were having to cover enormous distances to reach them from the Vistula, where the railway bridges were being hastily rebuilt, and on return journeys every second truck having to be towed back in order to save fuel. Even captured alcohol stocks were being used to supplement vehicle fuel. Ammunition of all kinds was running dangerously low, and Chuikov's 8th Guards Army was obliged to use captured German guns and ammunition to make up for these deficiencies. Battle casualties were not being replaced and many formations were well under strength and exhausted by the time they reached the Oder. With the thaw the Red Air Force's grass airfields were becoming unusable, so that they could provide little support against the Luftwaffe, which was mainly operating from properly constructed airfields. The sudden thaw also brought floodwaters and made the movement of heavy equipment extremely difficult.[21]

There had also been a serious breakdown of discipline as the Soviet troops crossed the German frontier and started exacting their revenge, looting, raping, killing and pillaging as they went.[22]

But Zhukov still had his eyes firmly fixed on the main goal, and on 4 February he issued the following "orientation", as he called it:

Attention of Military Councils of all armies, commanders of fighting services and the chiefs of rearguard forces.

Below are tentative calculations for the immediate future and a brief situation estimate:

1.   The enemy confronting the 1st Byelorussian Front has as yet no sufficiently large concentrations for mounting a counterattack.

Nor has the enemy any stable line of defence, but is now defending in a number of directions and is also trying to organise a mobile defence in several sectors. According to preliminary information, the enemy has removed four armoured and five or six infantry divisions from his western theatre and is transferring them to his eastern theatre. At the same time the enemy is continuing to move troops out of the Baltic area and East Prussia.

In all probability, within the next six or seven days the enemy will deploy his arriving forces along the line Schwedt-Stargard-Neustettin so as to cover Pomerania and deny us Stettin and access to the Pomeranian Bay.

The forces being transferred from the west will evidently be deployed in the Berlin area to cover the approaches to the city.

2.   The task of the Front's forces in the next six days is to consolidate their gains by vigorous action; bring forward everything that needs doing so; replenish supplies, bringing them up to a double supply of fuel and two sets of ammunition, and to take Berlin on 15 or 16 February with a sweeping assault.

In order to consolidate the gains, i.e. between 4 and 8 February, it is necessary:

a.   for the 5th Shock, 8th Guards, 69th and 33rd Armies to seize bridgeheads on the west bank of the Oder. Consequently, it is preferable that the 8th Guards and 69th Armies share a common bridgehead between Küstrin and Frankfurt.

It would also be good if the bridgeheads of the 5th and 8th Armies could possibly be merged;

b.   for the 1st Polish Army, the 47th and 61st Armies, the 2nd Guards Tank Army and the 2nd Guards Cavalry Corps to throw the enemy back beyond the line Ratzeburg-Falkenburg-Stargard-Altdamm-Oder River, and then to leave a covering force to await the arrival of the 2nd Byelorussian Front and redeploy along the Oder for a breakthrough;

c.   to complete the liquidation of the Posen-Schneidemühl enemy grouping by 7 to 8 February;

d.   to note that the means of reinforcement for the breakthrough will be no more than what the Front currently holds;

e.   for armoured and self-propelled artillery units to put back in service equipment now in running order and medium repair states by 10 February;

f.   for the Air Force to complete its deployment and to have at least six refuelling supplies at its airfields.

g.   for the Front, army and immediate rear units to be in full
readiness for the decisive phase of the operation by 9 or 10 February.[23]

His specific orders to the 5th Shock Army read:

Attention of the Military Council, Corps Commanders and Division
Commanders of the 5th Shock Army:
The 5th Shock Army has been assigned an especially important
mission, that of holding the bridgehead on the west bank of the Oder and
expanding it at least up to 20 km in frontage and 10 to 20 km in depth.
I ask that you all understand your historic role in carrying out your
mission and, after explaining this to your men, to demand that they display
the utmost fortitude and courage.
Unfortunately, we cannot yet help you with aircraft, because all the
airfields have been turned into bogs and the planes cannot take off. Enemy
planes are flying from Berlin aerodromes with concrete runways. I
recommend:
1.   to dig in deep;
2.   to organise massive anti-aircraft fire;
3.   to move to night combat operations, launching each attack with a
limited objective; to repulse enemy attacks during the day. In another
two or three days the enemy will be wiped out.
I wish you and your troops historic success which you not only can, but
must ensure.[24]

Ahead of the Soviets came a wave of German refugees under the horrific
conditions of that winter, some by rail, some in open railway wagons, others by
any means of transport available, many trekking in their farm wagons pulled by
horses or oxen. The villages on their route were crammed with refugees who
were moved on as soon as they had rested to make room for those following.
Many of the older ones and the younger children died from exposure. Even
heavier were the casualties among the columns of emaciated prisoners of war
and concentration camp inmates being evacuated along with them.[25]

CHAPTER 5

The Struggle for the Bridgeheads I

A New Situation

The area of operations in which these bridgeheads were established lay in the flat valley bottom of the Oderbruch, forming a "T" with the similar terrain of the Warthebruch, and was bounded on the eastern side by the marshy banked Oder River, which was from 200 to 300 meters wide, 2.5 to 4.5 meters deep, and had a current of from 0.6 to 1.3 meters per second.[1]

At the end of January and the beginning of February 1945 the Oder was covered with about forty centimeters of ice, which was, however, breaking up from the onset of a thaw, causing the river to broaden up to 380 meters wide and to flood the banks right up to the dikes on either side. These dikes are usually doubled with roads or tracks running along the top and a full-depth gap in between.[2]

There were at this time one passenger and nine vehicular ferries located on the river in the bridgehead area, but none were operational due to the ice. Apart from the rail and road bridges at Frankfurt, the only others were those at Küstrin, where three crossed the Warthe to the citadel on the isthmus between the rivers, two going on to the island in the bend of the Oder opposite, which in turn was connected by two further bridges taking the road and rail connections on to Berlin. This island, known simply as the Oder-Insel, had also been fortified as part of the fortress's defenses, as had part of Küstrin-Neustadt on the east bank of the Warthe, and formed a formidable obstacle in the Soviet path.

From the river the Oderbruch extends westward for distances between ten to fifteen kilometers before butting up against the eroded escarpment of the Seelow Heights, which form the eastern edge of the Lebuser Plateau and run northward from Frankfurt-an-der-Oder to Bad Freienwalde. A small spur extends in a northeasterly direction toward the village of Reitwein, which lies below its tip and gives it its name. This escarpment averages from forty to sixty meters above the Oderbruch, dominating the valley below.

The terrain within the Oderbruch consisted of what seems to be absolutely flat and open landscape generally nine to ten meters above sea level but dipping in the northwest to as low as four meters. Apart from the wooded Reitwein Spur there were only a few small strips of woodland and rows of trees in the valley bottom, mostly running alongside the watercourses, the trees being far fewer in number then they are today. Originally fenland, the terrain is crisscrossed with numerous canals, small rivers, streams and water channels, as well as traces of former courses of the main river, forming natural impediments to the conduct of military operations.

Because of the high water table, thaw conditions and heavy rain, the ground was very boggy, making the digging of trenches and positions extremely diffi-cult, and hampering the movement of men and equipment to the extent that vehicles could not be deployed off the roads and tracks.

On the whole the natural conditions favored the defense. The many ditches and water obstacles, as well as the long-lasting muddiness of the terrain, hindered movement and consequently the execution of attacks on the bridge-heads as much as the development of the latter.

In the flat terrain of the Oderbruch it was essential to seize what cover from view there was and turn it rapidly into cover from fire. Again the advantage was with the defense, for an attacker would be exposed from maximum range onward and lack any ground cover until he dug in. However, early morning mist in the moist conditions that obtained throughout the fighting in the Oderbruch was a factor encountered almost daily.

The character of the villages in the Oderbruch varied considerably in layout, some having their houses concentrated, usually around a manor farm, and some having them scattered, but every building was of value to the defense, for which their strong foundations of ice age rocks made them eminently suitable.[3] Consequently villages and individual buildings such as farms, barns and cottages were all liable to be turned into strong points. The first priority for the Soviet troops was to establish an antitank defense, which was done with those guns that had been brought across into the bridgeheads, and the second to set up an adequate antiaircraft defense, as the bridgeheads and crossing points came under ceaseless air attack.

Although the Soviet advance elements had headed for those places where ferries were already located, the ice prevented their use, and there was no bridging equipment with the forward echelons. Except in the case of the 1st Guards Tank Army, which ferried across a few tanks and SPGs on 2 February, only to have them and the bridging pontoons recalled the same day, no heavy equipment could be got across, and therefore the bridgeheads could only be expanded up to about four kilometers in depth, that is, within feasible protective artillery range from the east bank.

It was now time for the Germans to react. However, at this stage of the war, operations were seriously hindered by Hitler's Führer-Order of 19 January 1945, which started:

I order as follows:
1.   Commanders in Chief, Commanding Generals and Divisional Commanders are personally responsible to me for reporting in good time:
   a.   Every decision to carry out an operational movement.
   b.   Every attack planned in divisional strength and upward which does not conform with the general directives laid down by the High Command.
   c.   Every offensive action in quiet sectors of the front, over and above normal shock troop activities, which is calculated to draw the enemy's attention to that sector.
   d.   Every plan for disengaging or withdrawing forces.
   e.   Every plan for surrendering a position, a local strong point or a fortress.
They must ensure that I have time to intervene in this decision if I think fit, and that my counterorders can reach the frontline in time.[4]

The consequence in the Oderbruch was that attacks of divisional size upward were almost invariably launched on orders issued by the Führer Headquarters, which the intermediary headquarters could only relay in helpless resignation, as these orders tended to ignore basic factors that made such attacks often forlorn hopes in which heavy losses were sustained pointlessly, as Major von Lösecke, commanding the 90th Panzergrenadier Regiment, was later to write:

During the night attacks of 24 and 27 March, first the 3rd Battalion and then the 2nd Battalion of the 90th Panzergrenadier Regiment sustained very high losses of officers, NCOs and men. The loss of many brave soldiers was lamentable, but especially painful was the loss of irreplaceable leaders. Each failure further shattered the confidence of the troops. The responsibility for this was not to be found at Division or Corps, but rather at the highest level, where at their map tables they often no longer felt any responsibility toward the fighting soldiers. If one complained about this, the only answer that came was: "Führer's orders!"[5]

On 2 February, Army Group "Weichsel" was ordered to

bring the advance of the enemy either side of the Warthe toward Berlin to a halt on the Oder, and to establish a continuous front along the Oder line as far as Schwedt with all available forces, and to attack those enemy that have crossed the Oder and throw them back.[6]

The previously planned and already partly constructed "Nibelungen-Stellung" defensive position along the whole length of the west bank of the river was thus to form the new front line, incorporating the fortress bridgeheads of Küstrin and Frankfurt.[7]

When these operations began the 9th Army had had very few troops at its disposal, apart from those in the two fortresses mentioned. Those troops then available had consisted mainly of recently raised and Volkssturm units whose command and control was rendered extremely difficult from lack of trained staff to run corps and divisional headquarters as well as lack of communications equipment at all levels.[8]

For instance, in the sector between the Küstrin-Berlin highway and Frankfurt-an-der-Oder, then the responsibility of the Vth SS Mountain Corps, the only German troops available were a miscellany of units under Major General Adolf Raegener, who had been relieved as commandant of Küstrin by Himmler's nominee that very morning after only a week in that post and given command of the so-called "Raegener" Division. When he arrived at Reitwein at noon, having heard rumors of Soviet troops having been seen near Göritz, Soviet tanks were already firing across the river. He decided to set up his command post in the village of Podelzig on the Reitwein Spur, where he conscripted his own headquarters staff from elderly local landowners hastily pressed back into their reservist uniforms. He had no field communications equipment or support services of any kind, relying on the civilian telephone service to connect him with higher command. In all his division consisted of:

1 Volkssturm battalion (the 7th/108th Franken),
1 RAD battalion at Lebus.
1 Volkssturm battalion from Potsdam at Klessin.
1 field replacement battalion, SA "Feldherrnhalle" Regiment at Wuhden.
1 Ad Hoc battalion at Podelzig.
1 RAD battalion at Reitwein.
3rd Battalion, SS Artillery Training Regiment, near Mallnow.[9]

Nevertheless, the bringing forward of units to assist with the recovery of the Oder sector was carried out very quickly, and the number of tanks and SPGs in the 9th Army also rapidly increased, rising from 289 on 12 February to 390 on 28 February.[10] However, the lack of fuel seriously restricted their use.

The Oberkommando der Luftwaffe (OKL) assisted with the allocation of four detachments each of three heavy antiaircraft batteries for the "Kurmark" Panzergrenadier, 303rd "Döberitz" and 309th "Berlin" Infantry Divisions. Also, to make up for the deficiency of artillery units, antiaircraft defenses were withdrawn from various cities and sent to the Oder front, so that by 28 February some 300 heavy, and 96 medium and light batteries had arrived. These were organized as the 23rd Flak Division, consisting of five motorized flak regiments with a total of 82 batteries, and employed in a dual ground/flak capacity.[11]

The 6th Air Fleet, responsible for this area, was also heavily reinforced and from a strength of 364 aircraft on 6 January, despite combat losses, was increased to 1,838 by 3 February.[12] The main task set the Luftwaffe was the destruction of the crossing points. In an order issued on 6 March by the General Officer Commanding 6th Air Fleet, Colonel General Robert Ritter von Greim, it was stated:

> The bridges thrown over the Oder and Neisse are a critical prerequisite for every major offensive against Berlin and the heart of the Reich. Thus immediate destruction by all means available to every part of the Armed Forces is of decisive significance to this battle and possibly to the war.[13]

Thanks to its bases on permanent airfields in the Berlin area, the 6th Air Fleet was able to increase its sorties from the normal 550 to 600 per day to 1,000 sometimes 2,000, inflicting heavy casualties among the Soviet troops, while Soviet aircraft were bogged down on their temporary airfields by the weather conditions and also lacked aviation fuel due to the poor supply situation.[14]

For use against the Soviet crossing points, the Luftwaffe turned to a flying bomb device that had only been used once before (and that with moderate success) against the "Mulberry" harbors off the Normandy beaches. This was the "Mistel," which consisted of a bomber (Ju 88) packed with explosives and a fighter (Focke-Wulf Fw 190A or Messerschmitt Bf 109) fastened on top. The idea was that the fighter pilot used all three engines to take off, aimed the bomber at the target, then released it to fly on guided by its automatic pilot. The first attack was made on the bridges near Göritz on 8 March by four machines. One had to discharge its load early when it became unmanageable, two hit their targets and the third scored a near miss, destroying several Soviet antiaircraft gun emplacements in the process. Despite its massive destructive power this weapon also proved highly inaccurate in practice, for the pilot had to brave intense antiaircraft fire to approach his target, and in the end only about ten such devices in all appear to have been engaged here.[15]

Apart from aircraft and artillery attacks, frogmen, floating mines and other devices were also used against the Soviet bridges but to little avail, for their wooden construction enabled rapid repair.

The Kienitz Bridgehead

As previously mentioned, when the Soviets first crossed the Oder in the early hours of 31 January, no German troops in formations of any size were prepared to meet them on the west bank. At 1300 hours that day, Major Weikl, commanding a North Caucasian infantry battalion in Küstrin, was ordered to take the 345th Ad Hoc Battalion from the city, connect with the 203rd Ad Hoc

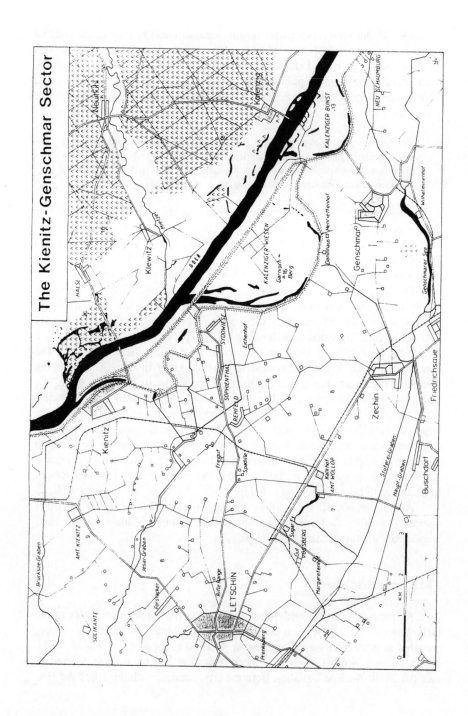

The Kienitz-Genschmar Sector

Battalion from Berlin and form them into a combat group, and then report to Colonel Schimpff, who was establishing his command post in Letschin. The roads west of Küstrin were choked with refugees, so it was 1600 hours before Major Weikl came across Captain Bohl's 203rd Battalion in Zechin. Only assembled that day in Spandau, this battalion had been brought out by Berlin city busses to Zechin. Both battalions then deployed under cover of darkness, with the 203rd taking up a defensive position along the line Sophienthal-Sydowswiese and the 345th covering the west bank of the Oder between there and Küstrin.

At 0100 hours orders came from Colonel Schimpff for the 203rd to attack at 0400 hours up both sides of the Letschin-Amt Kienitz road and to push on to Kienitz itself. For this they would have the support of some driver-training tanks from the NSKK (National Socialist Motorized Corps) school at Wriezen. The German attack happened to coincide with a Soviet attack from Kienitz, resulting in the German battalion, none of whose members knew each other, and armed only with rifles, being driven back to their start point in Sophienthal. Within the next six days the battalion lost half its manpower, either killed and wounded, but the survivors continued to hold out until relieved on 17 February, when they were reallocated to other units.[16]

Despite thick cloud, the famous Luftwaffe Colonel Hans-Ulrich Rudel's tank-busting squadron of Stukas, flying out of Neuendorf-im-Sande, immediately north of Fürstenwalde, attacked the Soviet positions in Kienitz that first day with bombs, cannon and machinegun fire to such effect that the Soviets hastened to bring forward antiaircraft guns and get them across to the west bank.[17]

Fortunately for the Germans, the 25th Panzergrenadier and 21st Panzer Divisions had already been extracted from the fighting against the Americans and French in Alsace in preparation for switching to the Eastern Front, and the 25th Panzergrenadiers were actually on their way to Küstrin by rail with the intention of blocking the Soviet advance before it reached the Oder. Orders for the 21st Panzer Division in the southern Pfalz to entrain for the same destination were issued at 1835 hours on 31 January. These latter orders, however, would take twenty-seven trains and another four to six days to fulfill.[18]

Orders too were given for the formation near the town of that name of the "Müncheberg" Panzer Division from the remnants of experienced units, under the command of the highly decorated Major General Werner Mummert. Considerable priority was given to the equipping and manning of this new division, and later to the replacement of its casualties in vehicles and manpower, but, unlike the deployment of the other divisions, the "Müncheberg" was kept intact in reserve on the main approach route to Berlin until the beginning of March before being committed to action.[19]

The 25th Panzergrenadier Division started arriving on the 31st, its headquarters alighting at Küstrin-Neustadt only to find that the station, congested with refugees, itself was under attack from Soviet armor. As Colonel Professor Erwin Boehm's history of the division relates:

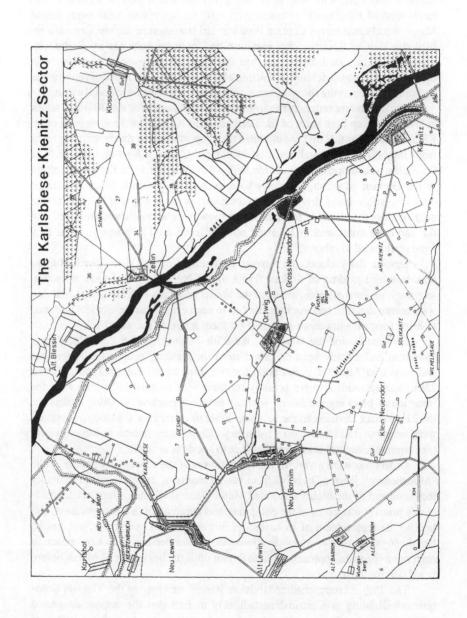

The Karlsbiese-Kienitz Sector

Thus upon the arrival of the train carrying the 1st Battalion of the 25th Artillery Regiment, the first in action was an antitank section, which under Sergeant Sommer shot up three Soviet tanks with Panzerfausts before unloading could begin. There was general chaos in the station area. The guns had to be off-loaded from the wagons by hand. They then went straight into action. Once the German resistance had stiffened, the Russians withdrew to the northeastern edge of the town. That evening the elements of the division that had detrained in Küstrin withdrew in accordance with orders to the west bank of the Oder.[20]

The tanks destroyed in this incident were in fact a British-made Valentine Mark III and two American-made Shermans of the 2nd Guards Tank Army.[21]

The headquarters of the 25th Panzergrenadier Division then withdrew to Gusow, committing the divisional units into action piecemeal on the west bank as they arrived.

Two batteries of the divisional artillery regiment and the 2nd Battalion of the 119th Panzergrenadier Regiment off-loaded with considerable difficulty in Golzow, for panicking supply troops had set light to the tall army store depots standing immediately next to the track, attracting Soviet artillery fire. The railway personnel fled and the train driver had to be caught and forced to take the wagons through the flames one at a time to be unloaded by the troops at the single ramp available. The battalion commander had to order the immediate occupation and defense of the village, leaving only a few men to finish the unloading at the station. Soon afterward orders arrived for them to move to Letschin without delay.[22]

Meanwhile the 1st (APC) Battalion of the latter regiment off-loaded in Werbig, where they were stuck for lack of fuel until the following evening.[23]

At 0400 hours on 1 February Kienitz came under fire from the 6th Battery of the 211th Flak Regiment, now deployed as field artillery, whose guns were manned by sixteen- and seventeen-year-old schoolboys from Berlin-Tegel. The first pause in this artillery fire was the agreed signal for the German attack.[24]

According to Soviet sources, one regimental-sized combat team supported by tanks attacked west and north of Ortwig, while a larger group, also supported by tanks, attacked from Letschin toward Amt Kienitz, but this first attack was beaten back. According to German sources, the 6th Company of the 2nd Battalion, 119th Panzergrenadier Regiment, advanced on Gross Neuendorf from Letschin that day and threw the Soviets back into the village, only to be checked at the village cemetery. Some German aircraft then attacked Kienitz, but this time were met by the fire of antiaircraft guns and two were shot down. More air attacks occurred, and as soon as the aircraft withdrew, the soldiers of the 25th Panzergrenadier Division resumed their attack.

While this fighting was going on, the 9th Rifle Corps arrived at the Oder on the 5th Shock Army's right flank and forced it with the 248th Rifle Division opposite Zellin and the 230th Rifle Division opposite Alt Blessin. The Soviet bridgehead was thus temporarily extended to a width of seven kilometers and a depth of four.[25]

That evening the 1st (APC) Battalion of the 119th Panzergrenadier Regiment and part of their divisional 5th Panzer Battalion, which had just arrived that day, set off from Werbig for Ortwig, arriving early the following morning after local Volkssturm and RAD units had just repelled a Soviet night attack on that village.[26]

At dawn on 2 February aircraft of two Luftwaffe divisions resumed the attack on the Kienitz bridgehead and Soviet units on the east bank of the Oder. Aerial reconnaissance reported that the ice on the Oder was continuing to break up; it was also raining and the day temperature rose as high as 8° Centigrade.[27]

At 0730 hours the 1st (APC) Battalion of the 119th Panzergrenadiers and the 5th Panzer Battalion, together with eight Hetzers of an Army tank-hunting unit, attacked along either side of the Ortwig-Gross Neuendorf road across open ground with air support. Despite encountering heavy antitank gun fire coming from the scattered farm buildings along their way, they managed to force the 895th Rifle Regiment (248th Rifle Division) out of its field positions and broke into Gross Neuendorf at considerable cost in casualties on both sides, taking several prisoners. The latter part of the attack was made in conjunction with one by the now complete 2nd Battalion from the southwest, and together the German troops with seven tanks reached as far as the village church before being checked and obliged to go on the defensive as house-to-house fighting broke out.[28]

For the Soviets this was a near disaster, for their troops were forced back to the line of the Oder dike and the outer edge of Gross Neuendorf, some even being withdrawn to the east bank. Zhukov describes how the 1,500 or so troops holding the Kienitz bridgehead suffered heavy casualties and their guns were knocked out one by one. The last 45mm antitank gun was dragged into a barn for cover by Senior Sergeant Belsky and two soldiers as eight German tanks rolled toward them. With their last thirteen shells five of the German tanks were destoyed at a range of 500 meters and the rest withdrew. For this action Belsky received the award of the Red Banner. In all the 902nd Rifle Regiment claim to have destroyed fifteen German tanks that day, but it took the opportune arrival of the 301st Rifle Division and some fierce fighting over the next two days to secure the Soviet position, which had been seriously dented and fragmented by the German attack.[29]

During that morning of 2 February the bulk of the 1st Mechanized Corps (2nd Guards Tank Army) arrived, and a further small bridgehead was effected near Genschmar in the Kalenziger Bunst by a rifle battalion of the 19th Motorized Rifle Brigade. The newly arrived 1st Battalion of the 35th Panzergrenadier Regiment immediately attacked, driving the Soviets back to the dikes, but were unable to go beyond and clear the bridgehead completely. The Soviets then mounted several counterattacks toward Genschmar in which they lost four tanks.

The 303rd "Döberitz" and 309th "Berlin" Infantry Divisions, under Lieutenant General Dr. Rudolf Hübner and Major General Heinrich Voigtsberger respectively, were deployed straight into the line south of the 25th Panzergrenadiers as they arrived that day, albeit piecemeal as the trainloads dictated, thereby helping to redress the balance.

However, that day the Soviets also crossed the Oder opposite Güstebiese, rapidly establishing another bridgehead some ten kilometers deep that posed a new and potent threat to the 25th Panzergrenadier Division's northern flank.

On 3 February, a day of heavy rain, the bulk of the remaining units of the 25th Panzergrenadier Division arrived in the Oderbruch and all these newly arrived formations were placed under the command of the newly created Headquarters CIst Corps under General Wilhelm Berlin that had been formed from Colonel Schimpff's staff.

The 1st (APC) Battalion of the 119th Panzergrenadiers repelled four Soviet attacks on Gross Neuendorf that morning before being relieved by the 2nd Battalion, and then withdrew to Ortwig to cover the threat from the new Güstebiese bridgehead. The latter proved so serious that the 2nd Battalion was also withdrawn to form a new defensive line north of Letschin, while the 3rd Battalion of the 35th Panzergrenadiers were thrown into an attack northward from Ortwig as they arrived. The easing of pressure resulting from this redeployment gave the Soviets the opportunity to combine their Güstebiese-Kienitz bridgeheads, and the 301st Rifle Division was brought forward to reinforce the position. By the end of 3 February the 5th Shock Army held a continuous bridgehead along the west bank of the Oder from opposite Güstebiese to opposite Kalenzig.[30]

On 4 February the 25th Panzergrenadier Division assembled an armored combat team, consisting of the 5th Panzer Battalion, the 1st (APC) Battalion of the 119th Panzergrenadier Regiment and the 25th Tank-Hunting Battalion, to make an attack on Gieshof from Neu Barnim at 1815 hours. This night attack caught the 1054th Rifle Regiment by surprise, causing the troops to flee and leave behind a supply column for the Germans to capture. The armored combat team was then relieved in Gieshof during the night by the newly arrived 3rd Battalion of the 119th Panzergrenadiers.

Meanwhile the 3rd Battalion of the 35th Panzergrenadier Regiment had been cut off in a farm northeast of Ortwig by Soviet troops using some forty antitank guns, but managed to hold out until nightfall with the assistance of the divisional artillery and then escaped under cover of a heavy snowfall. Further south the 2nd Battalion of the 119th carried out another abortive attack on Gross Neuendorf, and the 1st Battalion of the 35th was involved in some bitter to-and-fro fighting between Genschmar and the dikes.[31]

Soviet scouts, presumably from the 8th Guards Army, were seen as far forward as the Golzow-Alt Tucheband road.[32]

During the period of 4 to 6 February, elements of the 21st Panzer Division unloaded on the open railway tracks between Langsow and Golzow as they arrived and began assembling in the area Golzow-Gorgast-Manschnow. Once fully assembled, this division, which had just been refurbished with up-to-date equipment, consisted of:

> 22nd Panzer Regiment (18 Pz IVs and 29 Pz V Panthers)
> 200th Tank-Hunting Battalion (15 Jagdpz IVs)
> 125th Panzergrenadier Regiment (2 battalions)
> 192nd Panzergrenadier Regiment (2 battalions)
> 21st Armored Reconnaissance Battalion
> 155th Armored Artillery Regiment (3 battalions)

The Panzergrenadier battalions were at about 90 percent of their manpower establishment and the artillery battalions at between 79 and 93 percent.[33].

At 1600 hours on 5 February the 25th Panzergrenadier Division's armored combat group supported the 303rd "Döberitz" Infantry Division in an attack driving northward from Neu Barnim. The armor took their objective, the hamlet of Kerstenbruch, but the infantry attack was mistimed and failed to coordinate with them. Nevertheless, by the end of the day the northern part of the bridgehead had been effectively reduced to a depth of about three kilometers along the line Karlsbiese/Gieshof/Ortwig, and the armored combat group was able to return to the central position at Ortwig.

The 5th Shock Army desperately tried to get some tanks across the river to reinforce the bridgehead. Several fell through the ice but four T-34s managed to cross, enabling the Soviets to extend their bridgehead at Genschmar up to a line running through the center of the village.[34]

On the afternoon of 6 February the 21st Panzer Division was ordered by the CIst Corps to prepare for an attack toward Kietz from Manschnow with a combat group formed from those of its units that had arrived, and then to push northward to clear a front along the Oder as far as Genschmar, where the 25th Panzergrenadier Division's 35th Panzergrenadier Regiment was already heavily engaged. At the same time the 21st Panzer Division was expected to clear the Soviet troops out of Kietz and to escort a supply convoy through to the Küstrin Fortress. Forming up for the attack proved difficult, as the Küstrin-Seelow highway (Route 1) was blocked by a stream of refugees fleeing to the west, and while this was going on the Soviets attacked northward, reaching the line of the Küstrin-Seelow railway and taking Gorgast.[35]

Meanwhile the Soviets were continuing to try and expand and unite their bridgeheads. In the north an attack on Letschin on 7 February was repulsed by the 2nd Battalion of the 119th Panzergrenadier Regiment. At Gross Neuendorf a German attempt with armored support to relieve a platoon of the 1st Battalion that had been trapped at the railway station proved unsuccessful and the platoon was eliminated.[36]

In the center, the 21st Panzer Division, under Colonel Hans von Luck, launched its attack at 0330 hours in rain and poor visibility, but was checked by the fierce resistance put up by the Soviet troops now occupying Gorgast, although two farmsteads northeast of the village were taken, six heavy antitank guns captured or destroyed and one Soviet tank destroyed.[37]

The Göritz Bridgehead

Further south, with the arrival of the 16th Anti-aircraft Artillery Division, the 8th Guards Army was able to resume its crossing operation in daylight on the 3rd. The loss of three aircraft in the first attack of the day obliged the Luftwaffe to change tactics from attacks in mass to individual sorties. Consequently, the balance of the infantry divisions of the 4th Guards Rifle Corps and the 79th Guards Rifle Division (28th Guards Rifle Corps) were able to cross the river with minimal loss, taking their artillery observers with them, although the guns had to remain on the east bank for the time being, as no bridging or ferrying facilities had come forward with the 8th Guards Army's vanguard.[38]

That day saw a rapid and virtually unopposed expansion and connection of these three small bridgeheads. The 35th Guards Rifle Division went on to occupy the southern part of Kietz and some terrain to the west of the village, while the 47th Guards Rifle Division occupied Neu Manschnow about noon and moved on to block the Küstrin-Seelow highway in Manschnow itself.

During the preceding night the only German unit in this part of the valley, an RAD battalion stationed in the village of Reitwein to assist the flow of refugees, was routed in a surprise attack by the 220th Guards Regiment's 6th Company. The latter went on to take Height 81.5 on the wooded tip of the Reitwein Spur the next day, thus obtaining a commanding elevation of some seventy meters over the whole valley bottom. The bulk of the 57th and 79th Guards Rifle Divisions went on to occupy Reitwein village and swept on as far as Hathenow, bypassing the Reitwein manor home farm where the company-sized remnant of the RAD battalion was now ensconced. However, these Soviet forces lacked substance, remaining exceedingly vulnerable without the close support of either armor, artillery or aircraft. One of General Raegener's staff, retired Lieutenant Colonel von Wittich, the squire of Reitwein, took an infantry platoon from Podelzig to reinforce the RAD troops in defense of his property.[39]

The Soviet occupation of Reitwein attracted considerable harassment on 4 February from Stuka dive-bombers and from the German artillery, a battery of which was now located in Sachsendorf, where the roads were still congested with refugees, prisoners of war and concentration camp inmates on the move.[40]

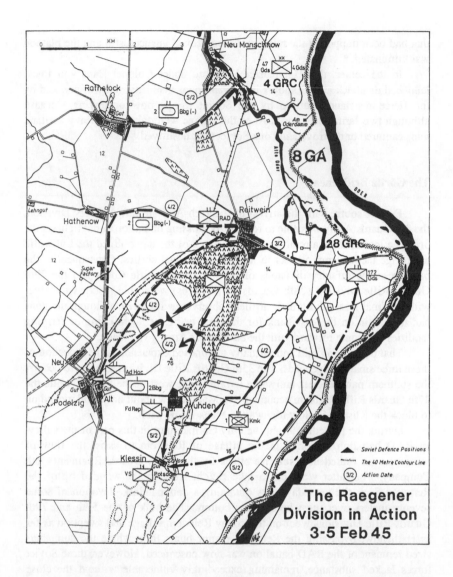

The Raegener Division in Action 3-5 Feb 45

That day SS-General Friedrich-Wilhelm Krüger, then commanding the Vth SS Mountain Corps, responded to Major General Raegener's pleas for assistance over the civilian telephone net, which offered the only means of communication available, with the loan of the "Kurmark" Panzergrenadier Division's designate Ia (operations officer), Major Hans-Joachim von Hopffgarten. That same afternoon the RAD battalion was forced out of Reitwein back onto the Reitwein Spur barely 400 meters from the divisional headquarters, which was informed at 1615 hours that the Soviets were now occupying the tip of the spur with an infantry battalion. The headquarters were then obliged to move to a new location outside Libbenichen.

Meanwhile Major von Hopffgarten managed to obtain the loan of the 1st Battalion, "Kurmark" Panzergrenadier Regiment, and the 2nd Battalion, "Brandenburg" Panzer Regiment, for a counterattack to be carried out at 1700 hours, the plan for which included using the "Raegener"'s "Feldherrnhalle" and Ad Hoc Battalions to clear the top of the Reitwein Spur, while the Panzergrenadier battalion on the right and the Panzer battalion on the left swept the valley bottom on either side and pushed the Soviets back over the Oder.[41]

However, poor visibility, light snow and unfamiliar ground hampered all aspects of this operation. The lack of field communications within the "Raegener" made it impossible to coordinate the night action on the wooded ridge, where the Soviets reacted vigorously, rapidly reinforcing their positions as soon as they came under attack. On the left the Ad Hoc Battalion advanced to within 500 meters of the woods capping the tip of the spur before being forced to dig in, while on the right the "Feldherrnhalle" ran into a Soviet attack only 500 meters from Wuhden and had to do the same. In the bitter fighting in what was again unfamiliar ground to both sides, Guardsman Sergei Mostovoy of the previously mentioned 6th Company, 220th Guards Rifle Regiment, an immensely strong machinegunner, is said to have displayed exemplary courage, continuing to attack with his machinegun's mounting and a shovel once he had run out of ammunition and grenades, and even capturing a German prisoner by tucking him under his arm! Both he and his Company Commander, Guards Senior Lieutenant Afansi Savelyev, were given the award of "Hero of the Soviet Union" for their exploits that night.[42]

The 1st Battalion of the "Kurmark" Panzergrenadier Regiment advanced along the valley bottom between the river and the eastern side of the Reitwein Spur, encountering no Soviet troops until they came to within about 400 meters of the crossing point opposite Göritz, when they encountered an infantry battalion backed by the artillery resources on the east bank that gave them an extremely hostile reception. The Soviet battalion then apparently counterattacked southward along the riverbank, hooking round to penetrate the hamlet of Klessin on the eastern flank of the spur, which was held by the Potsdam Volkssturm Battalion at the time. With its lines of communications thus threatened, the Panzergrenadier battalion was ordered back into divisional reserve at Wuhden, from where it approached Klessin from the north at daybreak on the 5th and engaged and destroyed the Soviet troops of about battalion strength found there.[43]

Meanwhile the bulk of the Panther tanks of the 2nd Battalion, "Brandenburg" Panzer Regiment, had cleared the Soviets out of Hathenow on the far side of the spur and pushed forward as far as Reitwein, where they ran into strong Soviet antitank defenses and were obliged to withdraw again. One Panther company had remained in support of the Ad Hoc battalion to prevent a Soviet breakthrough to Podelzig.[44]

The significance of the Reitwein Spur now came to the fore with both sides struggling to gain mastery as the importance of this elevation was realized. Having gained a foothold, it was vital for the Soviets to hang on and equally vital for the Germans to get them off. The hamlets of Klessin and Wuhden and the ancient fishing town of Lebus overlooking the river valley on the eastern side, together with the villages of Podelzig and Mallnow on the northern side, became key objectives in the vicious struggle to follow.

German reinforcements in the form of the 1st "KS Potsdam" Grenadier Regiment began moving into Sachsendorf on 3 February as the inhabitants of this part of the Oderbruch were evacuated.[45]

On 5 February, the 2nd Battalion of the "Brandenburg" Panzer Regiment launched an attack from Rathstock toward Neu Manschnow with its Panthers but was checked on the line of the Alte Oder, which was already strongly defended. The tanks then took up a blocking position astride Herzershof and Rathstock.[46]

The situation was particularly serious on the southern flank, where the "KS Dresden" Grenadier Regiment, which had only arrived the previous night, found itself defending Podelzig against a Soviet attack launched down the Reitwein Spur. This regiment's immediate counterattack enabled the German troops to dig in on a new line of defense a kilometer from the village, but the overall situation in this area resulted in the 1st (APC) Battalion of the 119th Panzergrenadier Regiment (25th Panzergrenadier Division) being sent to the aid of the "Kurmark," under whose command it remained until the 24th of the month.[47]

From the outset, the failure of the 9th Army to clear the Soviets out of their Oderbruch bridgeheads, despite the narrowness and apparent precariousness of the perimeters, was to prove a decisive factor in the forthcoming battle for Berlin.

The Southern Flank

Franfurt-an-der-Oder had been officially declared a *Festung*, with all that this entailed, on 26 January. General Busse was a native of the city and was to take a personal interest in its defense.

Further south the ventures of the 69th and 33rd Armies presented a different picture. The German bridgehead on the east bank opposite Frankfurt eventually withdrew some distance from its original salient where the "Kurmark" Panzergrenadier Division had stalled the Soviet advance near Kunersdorf, but remained surprisingly large, and the encroachments of the 33rd Army on the west bank between Brieskow and Fürstenberg, although impressive in extent, proved to be of little tactical value. In retrospect, it seems that the principal

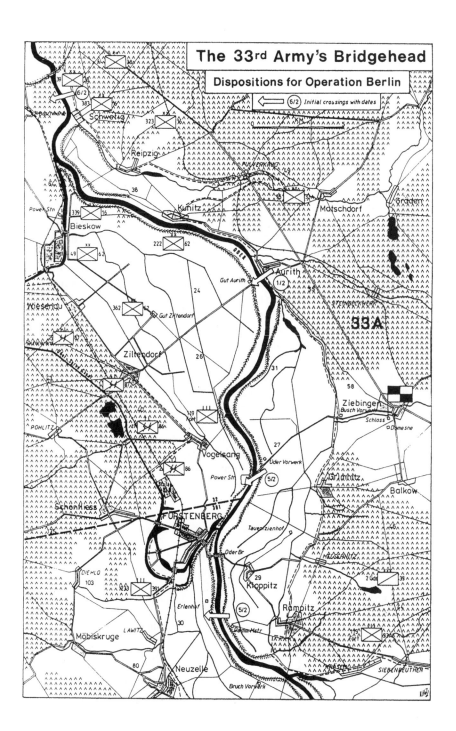

The 33rd Army's Bridgehead

Dispositions for Operation Berlin

6/2 Initial crossings with dates

purpose of the Soviet forces deployed on this southern flank was simply to tie down German resources.

Immediately south of Frankfurt, scouts of the 69th Army reached the Oder and crossed into the Eichwald (Oak Wood) below the railway bridge on 4-5 February, but further troops, apparently from the 77th Guards Rifle Division (25th Rifle Corps), did not arrive to establish a holding until the night of the 8th-9th. The dense wood of the Eichwald lies like a broad letter "J" on a rectangle of flat river meadowland that is boxed in on its northern and western sides by high railway embankments and by the river on its other two sides. The wood connects with the railway embankments at its extremities, the tip of the hook being astride the site of the Buschmühle restaurant, a popular excursion point in prewar days. However, it was not a healthy site for a bridgehead. The meadowland was subject to inundation, so that the Soviet troops had to build their positions and accommodation on piles under cover of the dense trees, or burrow into the sides of the railway embankments. As things developed, the Germans held on to the northern and western embankments down as far as the Buschmühle position and then on to the high ground above the Frankfurt-Brieskow railway line, except for a small incursion across the line near the brick works immediately south of the Buschmühle position. These positions were then stabilized by minefields laid by either side. The open meadowland and the approaches across the river from the east were completely dominated by the arc of German positions before Güldendorf and Lossow a good forty to fifty meters above the valley bed, so that the Soviets could only supply their bridgehead under cover of darkness and were unable to construct any bridges in the area. Troops of the 33rd Army eventually relieved those of the 69th Army in this bridgehead on about 14 January.[48]

As previously related in Chapter 4, the 33rd Army had taken the village of Vogelsang by surprise from its Aurith bridgehead on 2 February. Ernst-Christian Gädtke, a gunner with the "Schill" Combat Team, described the scene in the Vogelsang area when his unit arrived on 7 February.

> The Russians were occupying (certainly uncomfortably) the Oder marshes. A gentle high water had facilitated their crossing but, unfortunately, the winter had become mild and dry, so that one could not hope for a proper inundation.
>
> The Russians had pushed forward a little further between Vogelsang and Fürstenberg, blocking the 112 road between the northern outskirts of Fürstenberg and the southern part of the little village of Vogelsang. Fighting was going on within and around Vogelsang, the front line running through the middle of the place.
>
> In the rest of this area there were some quarries in which the Russians had also established themselves.
>
> The 112 north of Vogelsang was in our hands, and here our front line ran along the edge of the woods east of the road.
>
> The Russians still had no heavy weapons on this side of the Oder, although a bridge was under construction just north of Fürstenberg. On the

east bank, both on and behind the dike, there were light and medium artillery in position, and also some tanks and SPGs dug into the reverse slope. The lack of artillery on this bank was made up by a constantly increasing number of mortars. Behind the far dike there were several batteries of rocket launchers, the highly rated "Stalin-organs".

Conditions on our side were wretched. A few hastily assembled infantry units lay on the edge of the woods and in Volgelsang, mainly territorial reservists and Ad Hoc units, hardly a battle-worthy company to be found among them. Apart from a few insignificant, old, short-barreled 75mm infantry guns, there were no artillery, flak or antitank guns.

From time to time a battery would drive up, fire a few salvos and then drive off again. Somewhere further back were several 200mm howitzers that roared in the direction of the Oder every few days, trying to hit the bridge being built.

The Luftwaffe appeared once or twice, a flight of Ju 87s, and once two or three Me 109s.

Our four worn-out, borrowed, short-barreled SPGs, obsolete for at least the last four years, gave no convincing impression of strength; and in fact would not last much longer.

Apart from us, there was a battery of 105mm SPGs, and a few days later a tank-hunting battalion equipped with SPG IVs (long-barreled 75mm guns) was to turn up, but even then, we did not make much of an impression.[49]

That was Gädtke's impression, but Horst Wilke, a signals NCO with the 32nd SS Volunteer Grenadier Division, whose "bush-telegraph" was indubitably far more effective than the official communications system, reports that on 4 February the artillery available in this sector amounted to a battery of 150mm guns, a Luftwaffe flak battalion with double-barreled 88mm guns, a Reichs-arbeitsdienst battery of 88mm guns, several flak batteries of 37mm and 88mm guns, and one of 120mm guns, as well as the 1st Battery of the 360th Mortar Regiment near Diehlo. The main problem was obtaining the ammunition, although in fact there was plenty of flak ammunition readily available from Berlin if one could find the trucks with fuel to move it.[50]

The important Oder Bridge just south of Fürstenberg was blown on the afternoon of 4 February, one of the German sappers being killed in the process.[51]

The 33rd Army effected a crossing just south of this bridge on 5 February and established a small bridgehead around the Erlenhof farmstead.[52]

CHAPTER 6

The Struggle for the Bridgeheads II

The German Command

The desperate state of the German forces at this juncture is clearly demonstrated by the sending of Volkssturm battalions straight into the line to help plug the gaps. One officer reported that he had been appointed commander of the 7/108th Franconian Volkssturm Battalion in Frankfurt on 10 February. The men had come straight off the train from their hometowns of Rothenburg-ob-der-Tauber, Ansbach, Weissenburg and Dinkelsbühl, having been assembled and equipped in such haste that some had not even had the chance to say farewell to their families. They had been issued desert boots that let in water and brown uniforms and greatcoats that made them stand out against the snow and drew the fire of their own troops taking them for Soviets. Their only weapons were rifles, apart from some grenades, for which no fuses were available. Totally untrained for its role, although about 40 percent of its members had First World War experience, this unit was expected to hold the line between the Mühlental ravine just south of Lebus and the Burgwall, the northernmost point of the Frankfurt Fortress area, and not only to hold the line but face up to repeated Soviet attacks.[1]

When one such Volkssturm battalion, equipped only with Italian rifles, later lost its positions in a Soviet attack, General Busse ordered the court-martial and execution of its sixty-year-old commander. Colonel Langkeit, commanding the "Kurmark", refused to comply with this order, instead giving the man a reprimand, but General Busse then ordered his trial by court-martial at Army Headquarters. Fortunately, in the chaos of the Soviet offensive this case never came to court.[2]

On 11 February, General Busse issued the following instructions to his 9th Army for the destruction of the bridgeheads:

XIth SS Panzer Corps is to destroy the bridgehead Lebus-Kietz in the following stages:
    1.   Occupation of the Reitwein Spur and the heights between Lebus and Küstrin.
    2.   Clearance of the road Münchebc.g-Küstrin including the area between the Alte Oder and the Oder near Küstrin.
    3.   Advance of the front line to the Oderdamm [dike] from the northern edge of Küstrin to left corps boundary.
    4.   Destruction of the enemy forces in the Oderbruch forward of the Lebus-Reitwein heights and advance of the front line up to the west bank of the Oder.
CIst Corps is to:
    1.   Clear the Loose [meadows] and advance up to the Oder.
    2.   Destroy the enemy between [Neu] Lewin and the Loose, inclusive to the former front line on the west bank of the Oder.
    3.   Destroy the Kienitz bridgehead.
    4.   Restore a stable Oder Front from the right corps boundary to Kienitz.[3]

However, by the second half of February the attacks mounted by the 9th Army, even when conducted in considerable strength, no longer posed a significant threat to either of these bridgeheads, the Red Army now being firmly ensconced.

Fritz Kohlase, then in the 303rd Infantry Division's reserve pool of NCOs, wrote of this:

The fighting was both difficult and costly, not least because the bottom of the Oderbruch had become heavy going with the thaw. We heard about it when the supply troops returned at night from attending to the troops in the front line, often bringing back the dead with them. The German counterattacks produced little success. Neu Lewin and Neu Barnim were retaken, but the Soviet troops expanded their lines in other places. When the Russians were able to bring over tanks to the west bank of the Oder and build underwater bridges across the Oder, which persistent attacks by the German side failed to destroy, it was obvious that we would no longer be able to eliminate their bridgehead. However, the order for the introduction of smaller German counterattacks was not given until 9 March.[4]

By 23 February the drastic measures introduced on Himmler's instructions as army group commander to maintain discipline behind the lines were to be seen in the figures of soldiers hanging from improvised gallows along the roadside between Seelow and Alt Tucheband. Colonel Willy Langkeit, commanding the "Kurmark" Panzergrenadier Division, refused point-blank to comply with such orders in his divisional area.[5]

The situation on the Oder front was now of such concern that on Saturday, 3 March, Hitler made a surprise visit to the 9th Army, only his second such visit to a frontline unit during the war. He met General Busse at the headquarters of the CIst Corps at Schloss Harnekop for a briefing and then went on to visit the headquarters of the 309th and 606th Infantry Divisions. Word of his visit proved a considerable morale boost among the troops there, but his driver reported him unusually withdrawn on the return journey.[6]

The Oderbruch

On 8 February the 21st Panzer Division stubbornly resumed its attacks only to meet with equally stubborn resistance. A thrust on the hamlet of Herzershof immediately to the south of Manschnow failed, and an attack from the regained southern part of Gorgast toward the northern part of Manschnow stalled 500 meters short of the main crossroads, where the old fort, now occupied by the Soviets, dominated the approaches from its slight elevation.[7] Another probe eastward from Gorgast gained little ground. However, that evening part of the 22nd Panzer Regiment broke through to Alt Bleyen, reestablishing contact with the beleaguered Küstrin garrison, and enabling a supply convoy to get through. In this attack, which was greatly assisted by the reappearance of Colonel Rudel's tank-busting Stukas, the division claimed to have caused the Soviets the loss of four antitank guns, four heavy machineguns and ninety-five dead.[8]

On the 9th the 21st Panzer Division broadened its hold to a two-kilometer-wide corridor to the Küstrin garrison astride the line of the Gorgast-Alt Bleyen road in some bitter fighting, in which it claimed to have cost the Soviets thirty-seven guns of various kinds, fifteen heavy machineguns, twenty vehicles and 200 dead. However, Hitler had ordered the immediate transfer of this division to the 4th Panzer Army to the south, so at 2000 hours the 303rd "Döberitz" Infantry Division began relieving the 25th Panzergrenadiers in the line to enable the latter to take over responsibility for the Küstrin corridor the next day. The 25th Panzergrenadiers were allocated the three Ad Hoc battalions already in position in the corridor. Supporting attacks by the Stukas ended with Colonel Rudel himself being shot down and obliged to make an emergency landing immediately behind the German front line only 900 meters northwest of Lebus station, where he was removed unconscious from his burning aircraft.[9]

A surprise night attack by the 2nd Battalion, 119th Panzergrenadier Regiment, on 12 February out of the Küstrin corridor, reached as far as the main railway line near Kietz, but was then driven back to its start line by heavy artillery fire with considerable losses.[10]

Meanwhile the 309th "Berlin" Infantry Division, having been formed at Döberitz, was dispatched overnight by rail to arrive on the morning of the 13th at Werbig, from where it was immediately fed into the line between Letschin and Genschmar.[11]

Heavy fighting resumed in the northern sector during the period 13-14 February where these newly arrived 303rd "Döberitz" and 309th "Berlin" Infantry Divisions, less the 300th Grenadier Regiment of the 303rd, were pitted against the 266th and 248th Rifle Divisions near Kienitz. But for the remainder of the month, heavy rain on top of appalling muddy conditions restricted all further activity in this sector.[12]

Then, at about 0900 hours on 2 March, the 8th Guards Army, now complete following the fall of Posen, suddenly launched a major attack westward from the line of the railway between Neu Manschnow and Reitwein on Rathstock and Hathenow, using a rolling barrage behind which appeared the 11th Tank Corps with an estimated 120 tanks, including T-34/85s, KV-2s and Stalin IS-1s, extended along a broad front. This barrage destroyed the German front line, but a German counterbarrage then effectively separated the accompanying Soviet infantry from their tanks. The Soviet tanks crossed the Manschnow-Podelzig highway (Route 112) and advanced another two kilometers before coming up against the German antitank defenses at about 1100 hours. About ten Soviet tanks were destroyed in this action by the defenses, which included the "Brandenburg" Panzer Regiment's 1st Hetzer Battalion and a company of General Vlasov's anti-Soviet Russian troops equipped with Panzerfausts, who particularly distinguished themselves in this action. Meanwhile the Soviet infantry were kept back on the east side of the highway by the German artillery fire.

The "Brandenburg" Panzer's 2nd Panther Battalion, supported by two companies of APCs from the "Kurmark" Armored Reconnaissance Battalion, mounted a counterattack that afternoon, only to be checked by Soviet artillery fire, which enabled the Soviets to retain and consolidate most of the ground they had gained that morning.[13]

The Reitwein Spur

As a result of a reorganization within the 9th Army implemented on 7 February, the "Kurmark" Panzergrenadier Division, under its commander, Colonel Willy Langkeit, was transferred to the command of the XIth SS Panzer Corps under the energetic and abrasive SS-General Mathias Kleinheisterkamp, and allocated the thirty kilometer sector of the front between Kietz and the Burgwall, an ancient hill fort just north of Frankfurt. Divisional Headquarters were set up in the manor farm at Libbenichen, about 500 meters east of the Dolgelin-Schönfliess railway line. To the division's existing establishment of

1 Panzer Regiment ("Brandenburg").
   1st Battalion of 35 Hetzer tank hunters.
   2nd Battalion of about 50 Panther tanks.
1 Panzergrenadier regiment (2 battalions).
1 armored reconnaissance battalion.
1 armored engineer battalion.
1 signals unit.
1 armored artillery regiment (1 heavy battalion, 1 light battalion,
   1 light antiaircraft battery).
supply column

were immediately added the "Raegener" Division's units in a process of reinforcement that was to turn this formation for a while at the beginning of March into the strongest on the Eastern Front. Over the next ten days the infantry establishment was further boosted by the arrival in dribs and drabs of four grenadier regiments raised from officer and NCO candidates at the Dresden, Potsdam, Vienna-Neustadt and Wetzlar Kampfschule (KS) training establishments, which arrived on 6, 10 and 17 February respectively, and later in February by two Organisation Todt construction battalions.[14]

Major General Raegener moved to the area immediately south of the Frankfurt Fortress, where he formed the 286th Infantry Division from the remnants of the 433rd and 463rd Infantry Divisions, Volkssturm battalions from Würzburg and Upper Austria, and miscellaneous Ad Hoc units of police and army personnel.[15]

In the meantime the "Kurmark" was extremely stretched in meeting its commitments. For instance, on 8 February, for the primary tasks of clearing the

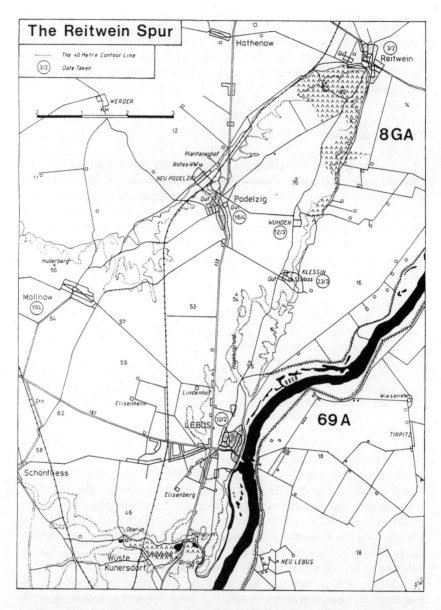

Reitwein Spur and the Göritz crossing points, it was still lacking the infantry and artillery resources to even consider mounting an attack. At about 2300 hours heavy infantry fire was reported coming from the area occupied by the Volkssturm battalion south of Lebus. It was subsequently discovered that two companies from the 69th Army had crossed the frozen river to form a bridgehead in the

Mühlental ravine leading to the hamlet of Wüste Kunersdorf.

The 2nd Battalion of the "Kurmark" Panzergrenadier Regiment was tasked with clearing this bridgehead, while part of the "Kurmark" Armored Reconnaisance Battalion checked the area between there and the Frankfurt garrison. The attack went in at 0400 hours and drove the Soviet troops back across the Oder, no further incursions being discovered.

However, this was the first encounter with the 69th Army west of the Oder, and its presence signaled a new danger for the "Kurmark"'s right flank, obliging a reconsideration of the division's deployment to meet this threat. Although there was considerable Soviet activity on the northern tip of the spur throughout that night up to company strength, where the German lines were now only thinly manned, it was decided that the major threat now lay at Lebus. The 2nd Battalion of the "KS Dresden" Grenadier Regiment was therefore ordered to take over from the RAD battalion in Lebus with responsibilty for the sector with the northern boundary of Schonfliess railway station/Lindenhof/Height 55/the Wiesen Farm, and the southern boundary of Schonfliess village/southern edge of Elisenberg/Oder. The 2nd Battalion of the "Kurmark" Panzergrenadiers was ordered to take over the Volkssturm battalion's sector astride the Mühlental and absorb that unit into its ranks.[16]

The arrival of the 1st "KS Potsdam" Grenadier Regiment on the 10th enabled an attack that evening, supported by a company of Panthers, that succeeded in reaching as far as the edge of the woods capping the northern tip of the Reitwein Spur before being checked.[17]

So the fighting continued in the Reitwein Spur area in a series of desperate counterattacks that rocked to and fro along the eastern side of the escarpment as both sides sought to gain and retain advantageous ground.

Then, without any warning by artillery preparation, at about 1600 hours on 12 February, the 69th Army launched a strong surprise attack with about two divisions across the still-frozen Oder into Lebus, scattering the thinly deployed elements of the "KS Dresden" Grenadier Regiment in whose sector the town lay. Leading elements broke through to the line of the Küstrin-Frankfurt railway and crossed it in several places. Some thirty to fifty T-34/85 tanks were brought across the river to help expand the new bridgehead north and south of the town.

During the night the 8th Guards Army stepped up its pressure on the Podelzig-Wuhden-Klessin sector with attacks of up to battalion size, in what appeared to be a deliberate attempt to draw the "Kurmark"'s reserves, but the "Kurmark"'s artillery were able to hold these in check. This was just as well, for Colonel Langkeit had decided that his priority lay at Lebus and had sent his only reserve, the 2nd Battalion of the "Kurmark" Panzergrenadiers, from Podelzig to block the Soviet advance by occupying the western part of Lebus. There the battalion seized the Elisenheim and drove the Soviets back across the railway line. However, there was now a two-kilometer gap between the 2nd Battalion and their 1st Battalion at Klessin, leaving exposed the divisional artillery deployed either side of Mallnow. The 1st Battalion was therefore tasked with keeping this area under observation.

The division's armored reserve, the 2nd Panther Battalion of the "Brandenburg" Panzer Regiment was at Sachsendorf behind the thin infantry screen in the Oderbruch (one battalion of the 1st "KS Potsdam" Grenadier Regiment and the "Kurmark" Engineer Battalion) and could not have reached Mallnow before 1900 hours, by which time an attack in the dark and without infantry support would have been futile. The Hetzer companies of the other battalion of that regiment were already individually deployed in support of the infantry battalions on the Reitwein Spur, and so were not available as a counter-attack force.

Contact with the "KS Dresden" was reestablished at 1730 hours. Small pockets of the regiment were maintaining a fierce resistance all over the area, but contact with many of its platoons had been lost and the casualties were unknown. Those subunits still under control were located mainly southwest of the town. Colonel Langkeit placed the 2nd Battalion of the "Kurmark" Panzergrenadiers under this regiment's command and sent a Hetzer company in support of its southwest sector. However, the confused situation meant that artillery fire could only safely be directed on the Soviet crossing points in east Lebus.

Early next morning a driver-training tank, a Mark I Tiger from the divisional field workshops, with only five shells for its 88mm gun but plentiful machinegun ammunition, was dispatched to take up position on the railway north of the 2nd Battalion of the "Kurmark" Panzergrenadiers in an attempt to block the gap. The "KS Dresden" was able to reorganize itself during the course of the day and was allocated the APC company of the reconnaissance battalion and the 11th (Infantry Gun) Company of the "Kurmark" Panzergrenadiers in support. Later that day a rocket-launching battalion arrived in the divisional area and was also allocated in support of this regiment. The 69th Army attacked northwest-ward out of the town with tanks and infantry, but these attacks were held. German counterattacks were equally unsuccessful. Although the 69th Army had left its artillery on the east bank, the troops on the west bank were strongly supported by antitank guns and mortars.

In appraising the situation on the 16th, the staff of the "Kurmark" noted that the Soviets obviously did not realize the weakness of the division's position, and that, assuming that the Soviet aim was to prize the division off the Reitwein Spur, the 1st Byelorussian Front had failed to coordinate the efforts of the 8th Guards and 69th Armies effectively. The boundary between those two armies was seen to run south of Klessin.

At midnight the newly constituted 712th Infantry Division took over responsibilty for the Wüste Kunersdorf-Burgwall sector, easing some of the pressure on the "Kurmark."[18]

The unblooded "KS Wetlar" Grenadier Regiment arrived on the evening of the 16th, enabling a slight redeployment within the "Kurmark." Attacks on the

17th by the depleted "Kurmark" Panzergrenadiers with the 2nd Panther Battalion of the "Brandenburg" Panzer Regiment on the northern outskirts of Lebus proved of no avail, for the Soviet artillery concentrations beat them back each time. Next day the "KS Wetzlar" Grenadier Regiment replaced the infantry element in these attacks with the following orders:

> Push through both sides of the Podelzig-Lebus road as far as the Lebus crossroads and split the enemy bridgehead.
> The main thrust of attack to be east of the road, where the tanks will be deployed.
> Preparation and support for the operation will be provided by the mass of the "Kurmark"'s artillery and mortars, as well as by a squadron of Me-109s.

The attack began at 1000 hours on 18 February afer a thirty minute artillery barrage, but was immediately met by an even stronger Soviet barrage that forced the infantry to dig in, while the tanks pushed on for about 1,500 meters until they came up against strong antitank defenses. Under these circumstances, Colonel Langkeit was obliged to call off the attack, and the troops returned to their start lines.

That evening the 69th Army carried out a counterattack of about regimental strength that drove in the "KS Wetzlar" Grenadier Regiment's lines and resulted in the taking of the Lindenhof. Next morning the "Kurmark" mounted a counterattack that regained the territory lost the night before, but Soviet reinforcements prevented any further advance.[19]

Meanwhile the Soviets had found fifty to sixty fishing boats stored in the little town and used them to form a pontoon bridge across the river, smashing the ice, which in any case had begun to melt on the 16th. With supplies flowing across it day and night, this bridge became a prime objective for the Germans.

The artillery strength available to the "Kurmark" was substantially increased over the second half of February and the beginning of March. Reinforcements included a 100mm gun battalion, a heavy antiaircraft regiment for use in the antitank and field artillery role, a rocket-launching battalion, two howitzer batteries, a mortar battalion with thirty-six 120mm mortars, two long-range K5 280mm railway guns and some heavy SPG units. With "on call" facilities to the locally deployed 404th Volks Artillery Corps, the "Kurmark" could eventually summon up to 250 guns in its support, and cooperation in providing defensive fire for the infantry worked extremely well. With unusually plentiful supplies of ammunition readily available, these resources could lay up to 8,000 shells on an area of 11,000 square meters to support or quell an infantry attack. Bombardment conditions on the Reitwein Spur from the artillery of both sides were described by some First World War veterans as comparable to that experienced at Fort Douaumont at Verdun in 1916.

Especially introduced to deal with the bridge at Lebus were two heavy artillery batteries, one equipped with two 210mm and the other with two French 200mm mortars, and great care was taken to prevent the Soviets from locating them. It took three days to set them up in the railway cuttings 1.5 kilometers west of Lebus without making any noise. Whenever they fired, which was roughly every two hours, it was under cover of artillery and lesser caliber mortar fire so as to avoid location by sound detectors or aircraft. Direct hits on the bridge planking were scored one to three times a day, but the Soviet engineers promptly made good the damage and the bridge remained in constant operation.

One night the 9th Army sent in naval frogmen, who entered the Oder upstream at Frankfurt to try and blow up the bridge, but they were spotted in the water by the Soviets and shot. None reached the bridge. Later an attempt was made from near Wüste-Kunersdorf to float down oil drums containing inflammable oil and explosives, but one blew up prematurely and the others were destroyed by small-arms fire before they could reach the bridge. Similar attempts to float explosives downstream to the pontoon bridge at Kalenzig from Küstrin also failed.[20]

On the night of 2 March, thirty-six Soviet tanks broke through to Mallnow on the corner of the escarpment between the Reitwein Spur and the line of the Seelow Heights, where the "Kurmark"'s artillery was concentrated, but most were destroyed, and the next day some of Colonel Rudel's tank-busting Stukas engaged the Soviet armour and managed to destroy some more of it.[21]

The fighting for the Reitwein Spur continued unabated, with the hamlets of Wuhden and Klessin as the key positions on the eastern edge being especially hard fought over. On 6 March a night attack by the Soviets sweeping down south along the Spur forced the German lines back to the eastern edge of Podelzig, leaving the battalion of the 1st "KS Potsdam" Grenadier Regiment isolated in Wuhden, where it had to set up an all-round defense. A counterattack the next day stalled under Soviet artillery fire and failed to get through. A Führer-Order was then issued declaring Wuhden a fortress, for which it was totally unequipped, its only supply resources being a potato store and a single well. Air supply was decided upon and a transport aircraft allocated for making night drops, but the Soviets promptly brought up their antiaircraft artillery and rendered this means of supply impracticable. The Corps Commander, SS-General Kleinheisterkamp, then ordered an armored thrust to relieve the hamlet, but this met such a hail of antitank gunfire that the tanks hardly got across their start line. A subsequent dash at night by three of the "Brandenburg"'s Panthers along the Podelzig-Wuhden road was more successful, for although one tank was knocked out and another damaged, the latter got through with the third tank, which was a communications vehicle manned by radio operators, and thus able to provide good communications for the beleaguered garrison. However, the first message out reported the majority of the officer cadets and subalterns forming the battalion as either dead or wounded and a combatant strength of only 150-160 men. They had no medical officer with them to attend to the wounded, were under frequent attack by Soviet infantry and were being heavily shelled day and night.

Attempts by the "Kurmark" to obtain approval for a breakout were dismissed by Corps Headquarters as being contrary to the Führer-Order declaring Wuhden a fortress. Eventually Colonel Langkeit decided of his own responsibility to order a breakout, by which time the potato store and well had been destroyed and only 80 of the original 400 men were left on their feet for the attempt on the 12th March. The wounded had to be abandoned. The "Kurmark" continued to report Wuhden occupied for another four days until permission was at last received from the OKW for its evacuation. That day the surviving officer cadets were commissioned second lieutenants by a special Führer-Order and all the Wuhden survivors were given fourteen days rest in the divisional rear area.[22]

Later in the month a similar fate was to befall Klessin, which had been held since 7 March by elements[23] of the 2nd Battalion, 1242nd Grenadier Regiment (formerly the "KS Wetzlar" Grenadier Regiment) under its commander, Lieutenant Schöne, when on the 10th the Soviets reached the Podelzig-Klessin road from the sunken road to the south of the hamlet with the help of some supporting armor, cutting it off. That night a counterattack by the 1242nd Grenadier Regiment, also supported by tanks, reestablished contact with the hamlet and destroyed a T-34. The following noon the Soviets in battalion strength attacked the German positions north of the hamlet and after some bitter fighting to and fro effected a breach in the line, which could only be cleared by using the last of the reserves. On the night of the 11th-12th the Soviets broke through the German lines on the boundary between the 1242nd and 1235th Grenadier Regiments west of Wuhden, then thrust south and cut off Klessin once more, forcing the troops fighting north of the hamlet back into it. Only a weak, and by day untenable, line of positions now remained between the main German positions on Height 54.2 and Klessin.

Under cover of darkness on the night of 12-13 March two tanks and two APCs were able to bring forward supplies and evacuate the wounded, although the APCs came under heavy enemy fire on the return journey.

A counterattack the following evening by the 1242nd Grenadier Regiment, supported by the "Feldherrnhalle" Battalion and intended to free and resupply the Klessin garrison, stalled with heavy losses. Although no serious fighting took place during the next few days, casualties continued to mount from the constant mortar fire directed on the hamlet, as well as tank fire from Wuhden. The wounded were having to be accommodated in the battalion command post and the cellar beneath, where the medical officer worked tirelessly in appalling conditions. Radio communication was maintained on both the command and artillery networks, the latter enabling the calling down of fire on Soviet forming-up points or on the attacks themselves to great effect in maintaining the defense.

During the night of 15-16 March the 1242nd Grenadier Regiment launched another attack on the Soviet blocking positions west of Klessin, and in a daring thrust through the minefields, two tanks commanded by Second Lieutenant Eimer of the "Brandenburg" Panzer Regiment broke through carrying twelve infantrymen as reinforcements, bringing the garrison strength up to 195 all ranks. The Soviets immediately counterattacked from the north and south, cutting Klessin off once more.

The problem of supply was partly relieved by the consumption of local resources, including some sheep, potatoes and a sack of peas. Then at 1600 hours on 17 March the Luftwaffe attempted their first air supply drop, but this failed as the entire load of containers fell into the Soviet trenches immediately east of the manor. However, two days later the Luftwaffe tried again and dropped thirteen supply containers right on the central roadway, but Soviet tank and machinegun fire prevented their recovery until nightfall. This event provided a great boost for morale.[24]

On the 18th March troops of the 69th Army at Lebus penetrated as far as Schönfliess railway station, but were then driven back to their start line on the Küstrin-Frankfurt railway.[25]

At 0515 hours on 20 March the 300th Grenadier Regiment (on detachment from the 303rd "Döberitz" Infantry Division) advanced toward Klessin behind a heavy artillery barrage. The regiment had been given two or three days to prepare this operation, in which it was supposed to relieve the garrison and establish a secure connection from the lines of the 1242nd from which it set off, but at the last minute the promised armored support was withdrawn. The commander of the 2nd Battalion of this regiment, Captain Böge, managed to break through along the track to the hamlet with some of his men and some sappers from the "Kurmark" Armored Engineer Battalion within fifteen minutes. Losses were considerable and only forty-five men actually got through to Klessin, where Lieutenant Schöne handed over command to him. The Soviets then counteracted with heavy artillery barrages, coupled with attacks from both north and south, and soon regained their blocking positions while systematically destroying the 300th's troops in their path. The 300th was obliged to launch another attack at 2330 hours with its few remaining resources, but this was again stalled by heavy Soviet artillery fire with heavy loss.[26]

All day on 22 March Klessin lay under heavy artillery, mortar, tank and machinegun fire. The combatant strength of the garrison fell sharply, both tanks were knocked out and the Soviets managed to occupy the eastern part of the manor.

Next morning the Soviets increased their hold on the manor and the garrison were constrained to form a blocking line immediately to the west of it. Two Soviet tanks, an antitank gun and several heavy machineguns then proceeded to dominate the hamlet from the cover of the manor, shooting up the German trenches throughout the day, so that casualties continued to mount alarmingly. Two breaches in the German lines on the northern side of Klessin were cleared with the limited forces available, but now nearly every soldier in the garrison had been wounded. At about midday the fifteen to twenty unwounded survivors took up defensive positions around the battalion command post in the western part of Klessin, into which they carried a number of the wounded. The Soviets then drove their way deeper into the hamlet, splitting the garrison into several isolated groups.

That evening the signal was received from Division: "Mission completed; fight your way out!" Captain Böge gave the order to assemble in the potato barn on the western edge of the hamlet for a breakout under cover of darkness. As many as possible of the wounded were brought to the assembly point while Lieutenant Schöne took a group to hold off the Soviet pressure from the east. However, heavy mortar and machinegun fire resulted in contact with Schöne's group being lost.

With the aid of a well-directed concentration of fire, the main body were able to reach the gully to the south of Klessin in thick smoke and dust just as twenty to thirty Soviet troops entered it from the southern end with their weapons ready to fire. Fortunately, in the gully the Germans came across some Panzerfausts that the Soviets had captured and so were able to turn them against the Soviets, killing many of them. Then, under cover of the smoke and fumes from a German artillery barrage, Captain Böge's group fought their way through the blocking positions and twenty-six of them reached the German lines, to be followed some time later by Lieutenant Schöne's group, thirty to thirty-five of whom got through.[27]

The Southern Flank

On 13 February Reichspropaganda Minister Josef Goebbels visited the Frankfurt garrison, accompanied by General Busse, whose nominee as Commandant, Colonel Ernst Biehler, a fellow native of the city, was appointed two days later. Eventually the garrison was to comprise an estimated 30,000 troops, 100 guns, twenty-two mobile and twenty-five dug-in tanks.[28]

The purpose of Goebbels's visit was to see the situation at the front for himself and to exhort the troops to greater efforts in holding the bridgehead as a basis for a thrust on Posen. (Posen fell on 22 February after five weeks of siege, releasing more Soviet troops for the Oder front.) These exhortations resulted in the mounting of an attack next day by Ad Hoc, Police and Volkssturm units on the Eichwald bridgehead from Güldendorf and Lossow, but this attack foundered under Soviet artillery fire from the opposite bank, during the course of which a chance shell caused the demolition of the road tunnel under the northern railway embankment, burying an SPG and fifty men sheltering there.[29]

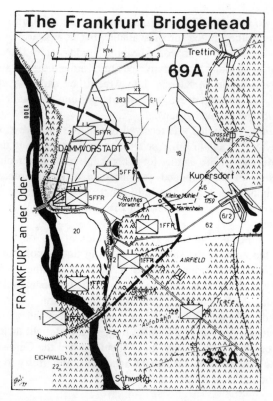

Further south, near Fürstenberg, Ernst-Christian Gädtke's SPG unit was redesignated the 1st Company, 32nd SS Tank-Hunting Battalion, as part of the newly formed 32nd SS Volunteer "30. Januar" Grenadier Division, on 10 February. This new battalion consisted mainly of former members of the 16th SS "Reichsführer-SS" Panzergrenadier Division, which had been evacuated from Corsica and Sardinia with their more modern SPG IVs, some of which were issued to the 1st Company to replace the obsolete equipment.[30]

On 28 February, the Germans succeeded in retaking most of Vogelsang, but successive attempts to clear the rest of the village failed with heavy losses, mainly through lack of support from heavy weapons. Meanwhile the Soviets were also attempting to take the village and close up to Fürstenberg, but neither side had sufficient resources to meet its aims.[31]

The Cost of Attrition

The 9th Army's task of destroying the bridgeheads can be seen as having been far beyond its capabilities. Despite further reinforcement, the personnel strength continued to dwindle from casualties sustained in the constant fighting.

By the middle of March most of its divisions were down to an infantry strength of under 4,000 men. The 712th Infantry and the "Kurmark" Panzergrenadier Divisions alone lost over 2,000 men in the period from 6 February to 11 March, while the 9th Army as a whole lost 35,000 men dead, wounded or missing between 1 February and 19 March.[32] The dramatic scale of these losses can be seen when compared with the overall strength of that army, which on 11 March mustered only 50,516 men, having sustained particularly heavy losses in the first half of February.[33]

Soviet casualties had been equally heavy during this period. Major General I.P. Rosly later compared the losses of 971 in dead and wounded of his 9th Rifle Corps (5th Shock Army) in the Vistula-Oder Operation with the 3,154 lost in the first ten days of February out of a total loss of 6,177 between 1 February and 15 April 1945.[34]

A typical example of conditions among the German troops in the valley bottom is given by Fritz Kohlase, who had been posted to the 303rd Fusilier Battalion, which had been engaged in the Neu Lewin-Kienitz sector. He wrote:

> The Fusilier Battalion had been in the Oderbruch since the beginning of February. It was only used for either a night or a day engagement at a time and otherwise lay several kilometers behind the front line awaiting orders for the next attack. Although only short, these engagements were costly. Each engagement brought about 50 percent casualties. The losses in weapons and equipment were also considerable. The intervals between engagements were not used for replenishment with men and equipment.
>
> When I arrived at the 2nd Company at the beginning of March it had a fighting strength of only about 30 men. By the middle of the month it had risen back to 50 men.
>
> It was much the same in the other companies. They had been at full strength at the beginning of February, that is, with a good 100 men when they went to the front. Their losses reflected the hard nature of the fighting on the Oderbruch front.
>
> The three infantry companies were at first predominantly equipped with the 44 assault rifle, now at the most only one man in four had one. There was a lack of essential items like entrenching tools, verey pistols and also tent-halves, pistols and field glasses. Only the bicycles remained, making the battalion mobile without having to use up motor fuel.[35]

The failure to reinforce the 9th Army adequately while at the same time demanding a constant sacrifice of manpower in futile attempts to drive the Soviets back across the river inevitably caused General Busse to switch from the fruitless battering of the bridgeheads to concentrate on the holding of the corridor between them to the Küstrin garrison and to preventing further Soviet encroachment on the Reitwein Spur.

The German Deployment

By 15 March the 9th Army was masking the Küstrin bridgeheads with the CIst Corps on the northern flank from the Hohenzollern Canal to Kienitz with the 606th, the 309th "Berlin" and the 303rd "Döberitz" Infantry Divisions. From there the XIth SS Panzer Corps was responsible for the sector down to four kilometers south of Lebus (i.e., the Burgwall) with the 25th Panzergrenadier, the "Müncheberg" Panzer, the "Kurmark" Panzergrenadier, and the 712th Infantry Divisions, plus the Küstrin Fortress. All these formations, apart from the 25th Panzergrenadier Division, were newly raised. As previously mentioned, the 9th Army also had two Volks artillery corps either side of Seelow and was supported by the 4th Air Division of the 6th Air Fleet with some three hundred aircraft, as well as the 23rd Flak Division.[36]

Then at the very end of March the 9th Parachute Division arrived on attachment to the 9th Army and was inserted between the 309th and 303rd Divisions, taking over the latter's positions astride Zechin. The 25th Parachute Regiment on the left flank had its command post in Letschin, the 27th on the right in Neu Langsow, while General Bruno Bräuer's divisional headquarters were set up in Neuenhäuser, just outside Platkow.[37]

CHAPTER 7

The Küstrin Corridor
and Fortress

The Fortress Besieged

While throughout February and early March the 5th Shock, 8th Guards and 69th Armies had been able to retain and gradually expand their bridgeheads in the Oderbruch and on the Reitwein Spur, Marshal Zhukov's declared wish of 4 February to have these two bridgeheads unite had still not been met, and the key position of the Küstrin Fortress, with the Warthebruch extending beyond it, continued to split the Soviet effort in the Oderbruch like a deep wedge.

Over the centuries Küstrin had developed from a fortified town with its castle standing at the junction of the Warthe with the Oder into a massive fortress encompassing the old town, Küstrin-Altstadt, with suburbs across the Warthe, Küstrin-Neustadt; and the Oder, the Oder-Insel (island), Küstrin-Kietz and Küstrin-Kuhbrücken-Vorstadt. Defensive outworks, or bastions, had also been established on the approaches to the bridges leading to the fortress.

The Warthe originally flowed around the southern edge of the town, but a channel dug to relieve the pressure of the Warthe's floodwaters on the eastern side eventually became the main course of that river. The original mouth silted up, turning the land on which the town stood into a peninsula with two roads and two railways merging from the south and southeast at the southeastern corner of the fortifications. The road and railway then continued outside the Altstadt, crossing each other on the peninsula before traversing the Warthe into the Neustadt on separate bridges.

The main road from Berlin, Reichsstrasse or Route 1, first crossed the Oder-Insel on the bend in the Oder opposite the fortress, and then curved round the Altstadt along the line of demolished bastions to the road bridge leading into the Neustadt. Also cutting across this island was the main railway line from Berlin, which spanned the Oder 150 meters further north and then crossed the Warthe on the third bridge.

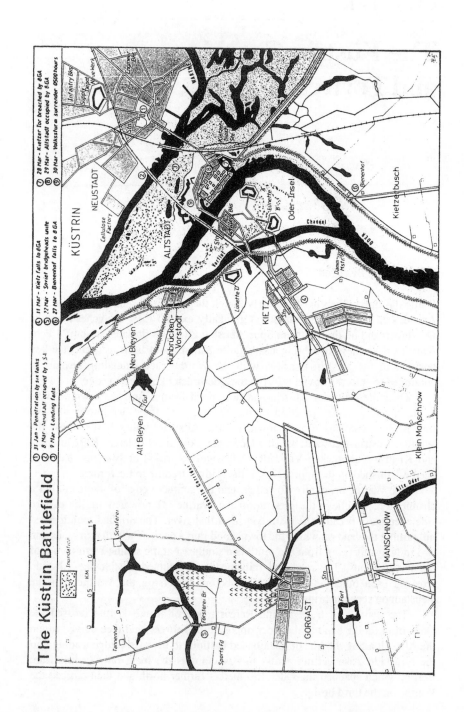

The Küstrin Battlefield

KÜSTRIN

NEUSTADT

ALTSTADT

Oder-Insel

KIETZ

Kuhbrücken-Vorstadt

Neu Bleyen

Alt Bleyen

Schäferei

Tannenhof

Försterei Br

Sports Fd

GORGAST

MANSCHNOW

Klein Manschnow

Kietzerbusch

Benenhof

Cellulose Factory

Lünette D

Lünette D

Damm-Mstr-Gut

Channel

ODER

WARTHE

Infantry Bks

Supply Depot

Engineer Bks

Alle Oder

Fort

Stn

Stn

Stn

Stn

Inundation

0 5 KM 10 15

① 31 Jan - Penetration by six tanks
② 8 Mar - Neustadt occupied by 5 S A
③ 9 Mar - Landing fails
④ 11 Mar - Kietz falls to 8GA
⑤ 12 Mar - Soviet bridgeheads unite
⑥ 27 Mar - Benenhof falls to 8GA
⑦ 28 Mar - Kietzer for breached by 8GA
⑧ 29 Mar - Altstadt occupied by 8GA
⑨ 30 Mar - Volkssturm surrender 0500 hours

Although by 1945 the original fortifications were no longer effective in the manner experienced at Posen, having been partially dismantled and allowed to decay during the previous half century, the fortified Altstadt lay on the Oder bank with a belt of woodland fringing the remains of its outer bastions on the eastern side, merging into extensive water meadows separating it from the Warthe and extending right up to the northernmost tip of the Oder. Deliberate flooding had inundated not only part of these meadows but also the whole Warthe estuary to the southeast. The Neustadt was a modern industrial town, the Oder-Insel an artillery barracks precinct with the Altstadt railway station, Kietz a railway junction adjoining what was essentially a rural village with a separate, modern "Deutschland-Siedlung" to the south of individual houses catering for the specially large families urged by the Nazi regime, and Kuhbrücken-Vorstadt a tiny hamlet nestling in a hollow formed by surrounding dikes.

On the last day of January, when Soviet tanks had made a surprise penetration of the Neustadt suburb, Küstrin was totally unprepared for its fortress role. Not only were there inadequate troops to defend it, but also a basic lack of arms and ammunition, all of which would subsequently have to be brought through the gap between the two Soviet bridgeheads at night.

Himmler's nominee as fortress commandant, SS-Lieutenant General Heinz-Friedrich Reinefarth, did not arrive until 2 February, by which time the town was all but completely surrounded. As an army sergeant Reinefarth had been awarded the Knights' Cross, and then had transferred to the Waffen-SS, where he gained rapid promotion and the addition of the Oak Leaves to his Knights' Cross. Undoubtedly a brave soldier, he was also known as "the Butcher of Warsaw" for his work in the ruthless suppression of the Polish Home Army uprising the previous year.

Construction of defenses was immediately begun in and around the town. While the military garrison formed a screen around the Neustadt incorporating the outer bastions with three lines of trenches, the Volkssturm prepared the Altstadt with fire trenches on the old bastions of the citadel. Other Volkssturm built and occupied defenses on the meadows below the ancient fortifications. A big antitank ditch with flanking ramparts was prepared in front of the Kietzer Tor (Kietz Gate) at the southern end of the Altstadt. This had been proved necessary when two Soviet tanks advanced several hundred meters along the Göritzer Chaussee before the garrison could engage them. Some captured guns were sited at either end of the Oder and Warthe bridges as part of zigzag antitank obstacles, and the trees in one street were cut down to make a landing strip for light aircraft, although none actually came. Antitank barriers were also erected on the southern exits from Kietz.[1]

Meanwhile the vital access and supply corridor, known as the "pipeline" to the Germans, was kept open by the 21st Panzer Division up to 9 February and thereafter by units of the 25th Panzergrenadier Division until relieved on the night of 19-20 March. With the exception of one short interruption on 13 March, the Germans were able to keep this route open until the 22nd of that month. Fully under Soviet observation, some six kilometers long from Gorgast to the railway bridge over the Vorflut Channel, and passing through an area from three to five kilometers wide, this route went via the Alt Bleyen manor farm position and was only usable at night by tracked vehicles.[2]

Bombardments by "Stalin-organs" on 5 and 7 February created considerable damage in the Neustadt, and a major conflagration reduced a large area to ashes. From then on the town came under sporadic artillery and mortar fire. The inhabitants had long since become accustomed to the thunder of the guns and to bursts of machinegun fire, even the nightly bombing raids by single aircraft.

On 18 February the road bridge over the Warthe was damaged by artillery fire, so engineers working at night laid planking for motor traffic on the railway bridge before repairing the damaged one. However, the water mains carried by the latter had been severed and from then on water in the Altstadt could only be obtained from the old pumps there.

As hopes for the relief of the garrison began to fail, orders were given for the evacuation of the civilian population, the Neustadt being cleared on the night of 19-20 February and the Altstadt and Kietz the following night, but all men capable of bearing arms had to remain. The evacuees were loaded onto trucks and driven off along the single track of the "pipeline" to Gorgast. None of these night moves appear to have attracted Soviet attention.[3]

In mid-February Marshal Zhukov issued instructions for the taking of Küstrin. The 5th Shock Army was reinforced with two heavy howitzer regiments, an independent tank brigade, a Guards rocket launcher regiment, a bridge-building regiment and a pontoon-bridging regiment, and its divisions were brought up to strength. With these additional resources, General Berzarin planned an attack by the 32nd Rifle Corps for 28 February but, in the event, bad weather was to delay execution until 8 March.[4]

The fighting for Küstrin increased in intensity as the days went by, the shelling and mortaring increasing with it. Casualties mounted daily but the will to fight on remained. The Soviets received some reinforcements and tried to push their way forward. Especially fierce fighting occurred at the "Bienenhof", an inn and cluster of houses defended by elements of the 500th Infantry Battalion on the east bank of the Oder opposite Kietz, at the northern tip of a strung-out hamlet known as Kietzerbusch and commanding the road running south to Göritz. The Soviets tried time and time again to take this establishment and each time were repulsed with heavy losses, as occurred on 14 February when they used eight tanks and two infantry battalions. Similarly all the earlier attacks on Kietz itself proved unsuccessful, for there the German infantry were strongly backed by flak artillery in the ground role, which rejected all Soviet tank attacks, either in mass or individually in support of infantry attacks.[5]

The Soviets also tried to fight their way into the Neustadt and in one of these earlier attacks the cellulose factory was lost with its defenders, a platoon of the Küstrin 16th/186th Volkssturm Battalion, whose survivors were shot as "partisans." Thereafter the two combatant Küstrin Volkssturm battalions (a third battalion was engaged in the construction of defences) were provided with proper army uniforms and paybooks, their Volkssturm armbands and civilian clothes thrown away. The factory was later retaken by the Germans and held until 9 March.[6]

The fortress garrison eventually comprised members of all arms of the army and Waffen-SS mixed with flak, police and gendarmerie units. By the end of February it had reached its maximum ration strength of about 16,800, of which only about 10,000 were actually combatants. These numbers included some 900 local Volkssturm. In heavy armament the Soviets reckoned the garrison had 102 fieldpieces, thirty antiaircraft guns, twenty-five SPGs, ten rocket launchers and fifty mortars, with an estimated fighting strength of 10,000 men. At 1200 hours on 16 February the fortress, which hitherto had come directly under Headquarters 9th Army, was delegated to Headquarters XIth SS Panzer Corps.[7]

On 7 March three regiments of Colonel General Chuikov's 8th Guards Army started a sustained attack on Kietz with a view to cutting off the fortress. This included an attack by a battalion of Seydlitz-Troops reported on the 9th. After some extremely hard fighting most of the suburb was secured by the 11th but the Soviets failed to reach the Vorflut Channel bridges, the Oder-Insel remaining in German hands. These attacks were supported by diversionary attacks on the southern edge of the Küstrin corridor.[8]

At about 0230 hours on 7 March a raiding party of sixty men from the 1038th Rifle Regiment coming down the Warthe in twelve boats attempted a landing on the south shore of the Neustadt, but were betrayed by an unexpected exposure to moonlight and had to withdraw under heavy fire.[9]

Then at about noon on 8 March, the 32nd Rifle Corps launched its attack on the Neustadt, which was defended by about three-fifths of the entire garrison under Feldgendarmerie-Colonel Franz Walter. Following a heavy artillery and bombing attack, the Soviet troops broke through the perimeter defenses in three places and eventually reached the near end of the main railway bridge at about 2300 hours that evening. The Germans were then obliged to blow the bridges across the Warthe, isolating a considerable number of their troops in the Neustadt, some of whom continued to hold out in the northern part, where the Neue Werk bastion, garrison supply depot and von Stülpnagel Infantry Barracks were located.[10]

Next day the Soviets bombarded the Altstadt and then tried to storm it with troops crossing the Warthe in inflatable boats, but this attack failed. Although the Neustadt had been lost, the defense of the Altstadt was to continue for another three weeks. The fortress was now virtually cut off and under almost continual artillery and mortar fire, as well as bombing and machinegunning from ground-attack aircraft operating out of the Königsberg (Neumark) air base only ten minutes' flying time away.[11]

The remaining German troops in the Neustadt were finally overrun on the 12th, the Soviets reporting having taken some 3,000 prisoners, many of them wounded, and having counted 3,000 German dead. That evening Moscow Radio falsely claimed the taking "of the town and fortress of Küstrin, the important traffic junction and strong Fascist defensive position on the Oder covering the approaches to Berlin."[12]

That was not how Zhukov saw it, for on 13 March he issued fresh orders for the reduction of the Küstrin Fortress and the unification of the bridgeheads, just as the 32nd Rifle Corps (5th Shock Army) was attacking the Küstrin-Altstadt garrison in conjunction with another attack by the 4th Guards Rifle Corps (8th Guards Army) from Kietz. Neither of these attacks succeeded, and the plans for this operation had to be reviewed once more. The urgency of Zhukov's orders showed that he was not too involved with the East Pomeranian operation or with the operational control of his main forces to look ahead to the earliest resumption of the main operation on Berlin.

Closing the Corridor

The 5th Shock Army was now ordered to use two reinforced rifle divisions in a main attack on Golzow, with a subsidiary attack from the Alt Bleyen area on Gorgast. The stated aim was to break through the German defenses in the Genschmar/Alt Bleyen sector, take the area Genschmar/Golzow and Kuhbrück-en-Vorstadt, seize the 16.3 and 10.3 elevations, but not Golzow itself, and then go go over to the defense.

The 8th Guards Army was ordered, also using two reinforced rifle divisions, to break through the defenses in a northwesterly direction, complete the taking of Kietz, and then go over to the defense in the area Golzow/Alt Tucheband/Hathenow. The main attack was to be conducted toward Golzow with a subsidiary attack on Kietz as far as the Vorflut Channel.

The operation planned thus involved these two armies using only part of their resources, while the main forces had the task of defending the existing bridgeheads and of tying down the German troops with diversionary attacks by small groups. Close coordination between these two armies, and with the supporting elements of the 16th Air Army, was vital if the plan was to succeed, for it was appreciated that the fortress was well favored with natural obstacles, which would be extremely difficult to overcome.

The 5th Shock Army detailed the 32nd Rifle Corps, which in turn detailed the 60th Guards and 295th Rifle Divisions, for the main thrust. The 1373rd Rifle Regiment of the 416th Rifle Division was tasked with the subsidiary thrust,

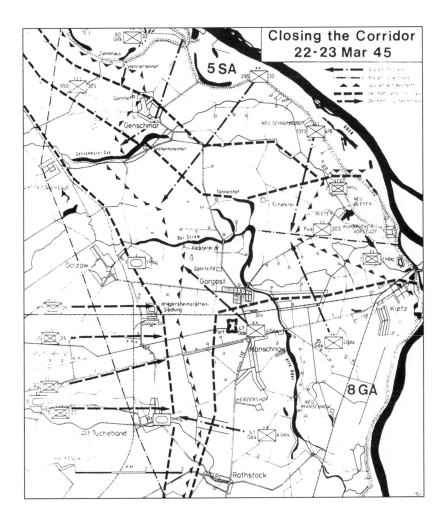

Closing the Corridor
22-23 Mar 45

while the other two regiments of that division were to secure the banks of the Warthe opposite the fortress.

The 8th Guards Army detailed the 4th Guards Rifle Corps, whose 47th and 57th Guards Rifle Divisions would be used for the main assault. Two regiments of the 35th Guards Rifle Division would be used for the subsidiary thrust, while its third regiment would secure the Oder embankment.[13]

Meanwhile, on the night of 19-20 March the 303rd Fusilier Battalion had relieved troops of the 25th Panzergrenadier Division at the Alt Bleyen manor farm, where the vital road from Gorgast connected with the Küstrin Fortress. On their way they had passed some tanks of the "Müncheberg" Panzer Division in Golzow and a battalion of the "Leibstandarte-SS Adolf Hitler," which had been sent to reinforce that division, about to take up positions on the flanks of the corridor. The garrison of this pocket between Neu Bleyen and Kuhbücken-Vorstadt now also included the 2nd Battalion of the 1st "Müncheberg" Panzer-grenadier Regiment and the 1st and 2nd Battalions of the 2nd "Müncheberg" Panzergrenadier Regiment.[14]

The Soviet operation commenced with an air attack, involving four days of systematic bombardment of the fortress. The land attack by both corps then began at 0715 hours on 22 March, and that afternoon the 295th and the 47th Guards Rifle Divisions met on the Förster Bridge over 'Der Strom' (Alte Oder) north of Gorgast, thus completing the encirclement of the Küstrin Fortress.

By the evening of the same day the rifle divisions operating on the outer sweep of the encircling operation had reached the line one kilometer southwest of Genschmar/the eastern exit of the Wilhelminenhof/two kilometers east of Golzow/the eastern edge of Alt Tucheband, although the 309th "Berlin" Infantry Division continued to hold on to positions a few hundred yards west of Genschmar until relieved by the 9th Parachute Division at the end of the month. The Soviet troops on the inner sweep had also been successful, having reached the line Alt Bleyen/the Gorgast Schäferei (sheep farm)/the west bank of "Der Strom" as far as Gorgast/the northern edge of Kietz.[15]

However, the ground gained had only been taken at considerable cost. When the attack began, Captain Horst Zobel's 1st Battalion of the "Müncheberg" Panzer Regiment was deployed with his 2nd Company of mixed SPGs and Mark IV tanks at Gorgast, less one platoon that had gone forward to Alt Bleyen and was subsequently taken over by the Küstrin garrison, his 3rd Tiger Company at Golzow and his 1st Company of Panthers at Alt Tucheband. Skillfully camou-flaged and handled, this battalion claimed to have destroyed fifty-nine Soviet tanks alone that day, including some Stalin tanks, but not counting others hit and immobilized, at a total cost of a little material damage and only two men wounded. The overall claim by the 9th Army for that day was 116 Soviet tanks.[16]

The 25th Panzergrenadier Division, then held in Army Reserve and refit-ting in the Friedersdorf area, was put on alert and placed under temporary command of the XIth SS Panzer Corps. By 1800 hours the division was mount-ing a counterattack eastward from Werbig on the "Müncheberg" Panzer Divi-sion's right. The 25th Panzergrenadiers were deployed with the 119th Panzergrenadier Regiment on the left astride the Berlin-Küstrin railway, backed by the division's armored combat team and the 292nd Army Flak Battalion, and the 35th Panzergrenadier Regiment on the right astride the Seelow-Küstrin highway (Route 1). Despite strong resistance, the division retook Golzow railway station and destroyed many Soviet armored vehicles before having to dig in.[17]

Further south, Sergeant Wolfdieter Waldmüller, radio operator in a brand-new Mark IV tank of the newly formed 8th Panzer Battalion of the 20th Panzer-grenadier Division, described his experience on the night of 22-23 March:

> We drive forward to a start position left of the main road to Küstrin.
>
> 2200 hours night attack to the relief of the German troops in Küstrin.
>
> My first time in action. All hell has broken loose. Lacking experience and unable to see what is going on, I have to concentrate on operating the radio. As radio operator I make several mistakes in the procedures, forgetting to switch from "Receive" to "Send" at the right moment, or forgetting to use the correct code word in my transmissions and sometimes using clear text.
>
> Our breakthrough has no luck. There are enormous losses on both sides, especially Russian. Next morning I see for the first time many abandoned and burnt-out Russian T-34s with wooden boxes for seats, as well as destroyed Stalin tanks. But also shot-up German tanks. I have had my first taste of action, and seen my first fallen comrades.[18]

The Soviet attack was resumed next morning and during the course of the 23rd their troops reached the line one kilometer west of Genschmar/the eastern edge of Amt Friedrichsaue/1.5 kilometers east of Golzow/the eastern edge of Alt Tucheband, but then had to go over to the defense as a result of the heavy casualties they had sustained. Those on the inner sweep reached the line of the northern edge of Neu Bleyen/one kilometer west of Kuhbrücken-Vorstadt/Kietz railway station by the evening.[19]

However, the latter encountered increasing resistance, the Germans stubbornly continuing to hold on to a narrow strip on the west bank of the Oder encompassing the Alt Bleyen manor farm, the tiny Kuhbrücken-Vorstadt hamlet, Lünette "D" (a moated outwork of the original fortress on the west bank opposite the Oder-Insel) and the immediate approaches to the Vorflut Channel bridges.[20]

Similarly, Captain Zobel with four Tigers, two of which the batallion's command tanks, held on to a farmstead some 150 meters northeast of the bridge across "Der Strom" and due east of Golzow that he had identified as vital to the commmand of the bridge and for mounting a possible counterattack. During the course of the morning his infantry support was reduced from 200 to 7 men from the heavy Soviet fire concentrated on his position. He later discovered that radio interception had picked up an admonition to the Soviet commander opposing him for not taking the position and a later claim from this Soviet commander that he had identified eight Königstiger dug in at the farmstead.[21]

The 25th Panzergrenadiers' armored combat team attacked at midnight on the 23rd from Gorgast but was eventually obliged to withdraw due to overwhelming Soviet strength. Nevertheless, in three days of fighting the Germans could claim a defensive victory in that they had destoyed some 200 Soviet tanks.[22]

Major von Lösecke, commanding the 90th Panzergrenadier Regiment of the 20th Panzergrenadier Division, describes his unit's role in this battle:

On 23 March we took up a reserve position in the Pismühle area, 1,500 meters southeast of Seelow, but had to march back to Werbig in the early morning. At noon I was summoned to Divisional Headquarters. This sunny spring afternoon drive made one think of times of peace, although noise of combat could be heard in the distance. From Division I received the task of sending a battalion that evening to northwest of Alt Tucheband and, in combination with the 76th Panzergrenadier Regiment on the right and another infantry regiment on the left, of attacking the enemy positions at Manschnow and pushing forward as far as the "Alte Oder" east of that village and, if possible, establishing a bridgehead east of the "Alte Oder." In order to minimize the effects of the enemy air and artillery capabilities it was necessary to attack only at night.

During the drive to the assembly area my APC drove into a soft, clayey field and stuck fast. As all the radio communications equipment was on this vehicle, I could not leave it and had to wait. It was an unpleasant delay. The 3rd Battalion's assembly area northwest of Alt Tucheband was shared by the 8th Panzer Battalion, which had been allocated to my support. As the tank commander had better radio communications with Division and the artillery, I climbed into his tank. My APC followed close behind.

At the beginning of the attack we crossed the causeway forming the forward edge of the assembly area. We moved smoothly at first and soon crossed the road leading northward from the eastern end of Alt Tucheband, and the battalion broke through the first enemy positions. Shortly afterward the tanks reported a minefield and stopped. The leading company of the battalion reached the western farms of Manschnow and encountered strong enemy resistance. While our right-hand neighbor was advancing only slowly the left-hand one did not even appear to have left its assembly area. Through its brave attack the 3rd Battalion had become a wedge thrust into the enemy front line and was now receiving fire from both flanks. The enemy artillery started bombarding the whole of our assault area, while our own artillery only fired the odd shot into Manschnow. As the enemy minefields could not be cleared in the dark, the tanks had to remain where they were.

Despite courageous attempts the attack had stalled and casualties were mounting. Just before dawn I decided to curtail the taking of casualties by withdrawing the battalion to the start line without waiting for instructions from Division. The attack, which had been carried out with insufficient means to shatter the strong enemy bridgehead west of Küstrin, had foundered.

I set up my regimental command post in some buildings at Neu Tucheband. Shortly afterward the Divisional Commander, Colonel Scholze, arrived with another colonel and I made my report about the battle without holding anything back, describing the weak support from our own artillery, the strength of the enemy's defensive fire, the difficulty with the fire from the flanks, and the consequent heavy casualties sustained by the battalion. To the question why I had withdrawn the battalion, I explained that in that completely flat and open country the outbreak of day made all movement absolutely impossible. Consequently the withdrawal of the battalion had been a tactical necessity. To some quite sharp comments from my side about the higher command that could order such an attack with inadequate means, neither of the gentlemen replied. They were apparently convinced of the correctness of my conduct. Shortly afterward they excused themselves and climbed silently into their vehicle. While I had been addressing myself principally to Colonel Scholze, I had paid little attention to the other colonel, but as my adjutant informed me, it was in fact the Corps Commander who had been really listening to my account of my conduct and my views on the battle. Nevertheless, I am of the opinion that neither he nor Colonel Scholze had been responsible for giving the orders for this attack. These orders had come from the very highest level. Soon after this encounter we packed up and overtook the brave soldiers of the 3rd Battalion on their march back to Werbig.[23]

The Regimental Signals Sergeant of the same 90th Panzergrenadier Regiment, Fritz-Rudolf Averdieck, saw the action from a slightly different angle:

On 22 March we carried out duties and training in Döbberin. We were woken up that morning by Russian artillery fire and drove to a reserve position near Seelow. Strong Russian air activity drew extensive antiaircraft fire, which brought down seven bombers and fighters that day.

Next evening (the 23rd) we drove in the dusk as Russian air activity died down to an assembly point for a night attack in the Oderbruch near Seelow. A Volks Artillery Corps was supposed to be supporting us with 500 guns, and the attack was supposed to be conducted by several divisions from all sides and push forward to the Alte Oder. There was feverish activity on the roads as night fell. Infantry companies marched along widely spaced from each other, while tanks and armored personnel carriers (APCs) rolled forward in long columns. The attack was to commence at midnight, following an hour-long barrage. However, it soon appeared that nothing had been properly prepared. The Volks Artillery Corps officers were hardly trained, and only a few guns gave sporadic fire.

Then there was a delay in getting the attacking units under way while the tanks waited for the infantry and the infantry for the tanks. Eventually, some twenty minutes after the last shell, they started, but the Russians had had sufficient warning and the barrage of mortar and artillery fire that fell on them left our grenadiers with 50 percent casualties, and once a few of the tanks had driven over some openly laid mines, the advance stopped.

Then as the dawn approached (the 24th) we had to dig in and camouflage as the flat landscape gave long-range visibility and we could also expect strong air attacks. However, the day did not turn out to be as hot as expected, for our own air force was very active and shot down two enemy aircraft. That evening we were pulled back and put into Corps Reserve near Seelow.[24]

The German Counteroffensive

Meanwhile there were conflicting opinions over the conduct of operations between Headquarters 9th Army and Army Group "Weichsel" on one side, and the Army General Staff (OKH) and the Armed Forces General Staff (OKW) on the other. The former wanted, with a new but limited attack, to facilitate a breakout by the garrison, to hold the line established on 23 March, and to put the divisions available to the task of eliminating the 5th Shock Army's bridgeheads in the Kienitz-Gross Neuendorf sector. However, the OKH and OKW, at Hitler's insistence, wanted the fortress to be relieved and ordered an attack to be launched from the Frankfurt Fortress's bridgehead on the east bank northwest to Küstrin, which, it was hoped, would shatter the communications and forces of the 69th Army and 8th Guards Army holding this sector. This latter plan was known as "Operation Boomerang." It depended on getting the five divisions concerned across the single bridge at Frankfurt, which could not possibly have gone unobserved, thus eliminating the essential element of surprise if the operation was to have any chance of success. The controversy over this matter eventually was to contribute to the causes for Colonel General Heinz Guderian's dismissal as Chief of the General Staff on the 28th.[25]   When Colonel General Gotthardt Heinrici took over Army Group "Weichsel" on 22 March, the 25th Panzergrenadier Division was supposed to be about to move to the Frankfurt bridgehead in preparation for the attack on the east bank, although the Küstrin Fortress had just been encircled. Heinrici visited Führer Headquarters on 25 March and managed to persuade Hitler to change the plan to a reopening of the Küstrin corridor. The orders to SS-Lieutenant General Reinefarth commanding the Küstrin Fortress were to hold out at all costs, so the reopening of the corridor with the added but unrealistic goal of reducing the Kienitz bridgehead was an acceptable alternative to the original plan of attack for Hitler, although Heinrici regarded both proposed attacks as an unnecessary waste of manpower. The date for the revised attack was set for the 27th.[26]

To conduct this attack General Karl Decker's Headquarters XXXIXth Panzer Corps was given the 25th and 20th Panzergrenadier Divisions, the "Führer" Grenadier Division, the "Müncheberg" Panzer Division, the "1001 Nights" Battle Group and the 502nd SS Heavy Tank Battalion.[27]

These formations had the task of breaking through the Soviet defenses in the sector formed by the Küstrin-Werbig railway line as far as the Oder dike on the Kalenzig meadows. The 20th Panzergrenadier Division and Major General Mäder's "Führer" Grenadier Division in the middle were to thrust through to the fortress and, together with the forces on the flanks, enlarge the strip up to the line Küstrin/the Küstrin-Werbig railway/as far as the Oder near Neu Bleyen/the Oder dike at the Kalenziger Bunst/the Kalenziger Wiesen (meadows).[28]

The attack began at 0400 hrs on 27 March and after a few hours got halfway to Gorgast, and as far as the Wilhelminenhof and Genschmar before the

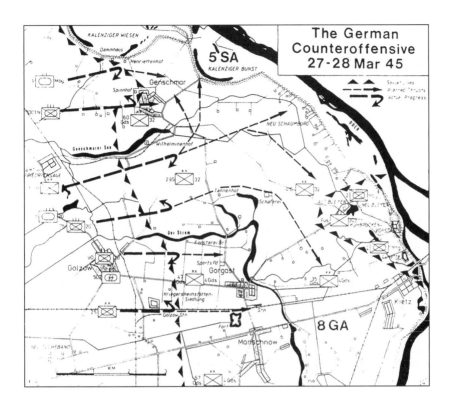

German divisions were driven back to their start points with heavy losses. According to the 9th Army's situation report of 27 March, five commanding officers, 68 officers and 1,219 enlisted men had been lost. The reasons given were the minefields, heavy mortar and antitank fire with accompanying artillery fire, well-constructed strong points in the individual barns and the lack of ground cover. In fact the Germans had given the Soviets far too much time in which to consolidate their positions in a greatly enlarged bridgehead.[29]

On the northern flank, with flanking protection from the 1st Battalion of the "Müncheberg" Panzer Regiment, the "1001 Nights" Battle Group, which had started the attack with three infantry companies and a total strength of 390 men and 49 Hetzers, was reduced to only 40 men per infantry company, having lost 51 killed, 336 wounded, 32 missing, and having had 25 Hetzers destroyed. According to Captain Zobel, the Hetzers were late getting into their start position, having first to negotiate a railway underpass, by which time the Soviet artillery had been fully alerted. One infantry company of this elite battle group reached as far as the western edge of Genschmar, but with daybreak came under such heavy artillery, tank and antitank fire from the Henriettenhof, Genschmar village, the southern edge of the Genschmarer See and the Wilhelminenhof (the latter having fallen to the Soviets in the meantime), that it was forced to withdraw.[30]

Despite the XXXIXth Panzer Corps's initial lack of success, the same day at 1730 hrs the "Führer" Grenadier Division and part of the "Müncheberg" Panzer Division made a fresh attack on the Wilhelminenhof strong point and the wood 700 meters northwest of it, making some progress before having to go over to the defense.[31]

Detailed information on this battle in the 20th Panzergrenadier Division's sector is available from the accounts of the commander of the 90th Panzergrenadier Regiment, Major von Lösecke, and his Regimental Signals Sergeant as given below. The map itself shows how hopeless this particular action was from the start, with the water obstacles and defended localities boxing in the area of attack. Surprisingly, neither side mentions the old fort, an outpost of the Küstrin Fortress surrounded by a water-filled moat halfway between Gorgast and Manschnow, which must have provided a most effective strong point for whoever held it. Major von Lösecke wrote:

> As there were still some isolated German units in action between Alt and Neu Bleyen, once more orders came from the highest level to launch an attack on the enemy bridgehead. This was to be from the Heimstätten settlement by the troops stationed there, from Golzow by the 90th Panzergrenadier Regiment, from north of Golzow by the 76th Panzergrenadier Regiment, and north of it by the "Müncheberg" Panzer Division with its new tanks. I was given the task of driving hard south out of Golzow as far as the "Strom" ditch, then on southeast to the sports field one kilometer northwest of Gorgast, and then to attack Gorgast. The 76th Panzergrenadier Regiment was to attack via the Tannenhof to the sheep farm two kilometers north-northeast of Gorgast and then to press on in a southeasterly direction. As no significant participation by the Luftwaffe could be expected, the whole attack would have to be conducted at night.
>
> I went with my battalion commanders on a reconnaissance of the land to be attacked across, which we viewed from a building due east of Golzow. The countryside was completely open and flat, dropping a little away to the north toward the brook, on which there were a few trees and bushes. The farmstead immediately south of the bridge 500 meters north of Golzow was still in our hands, while the other farmstead east of Golzow was occupied by the enemy, although lying north of the brook. In the distance one could see the colorful roofs of Gorgast, the greenhouses on the western edge and the tall clump of trees in the manor park.
>
> I decided to split the regiment into widely separated echelons to advance in the order 2nd, 1st then 3rd Battalions. The 2nd Battalion would lead the main attack and was given the task of going via the sugar factory and the farmstead south of the bridge 500 meters northeast of Golzow, attacking in an easterly direction, of taking the farmstead near Point 11.5 (1,000 meters east of Golzow station) and the "Am Strom" farmstead two kilometers east of Golzow station, and of securing the Förster Bridge 1400 metres north of

Gorgast, in order to enable a continuation of the attack southeastward on Gorgast.

The 1st Battalion would follow deployed to the right, while the 3rd Battalion would remain in its assembly area west of Golzow at the disposal of the Regiment. A Tiger battalion would be available to support us in our attack and cooperated with the Regiment. The forward observers of the Infantry Gun Company and the 2nd Battalion of the 20th Artillery Regiment were also given their tasks on this reconnaissance as far as the artillery had not been given their own targets on divisional orders. Several artillery units would work on Gorgast, for which an allocation of 1,000 shells had been made.

On 26 March the regiment moved forward into the area west of Golzow. The move took place at night in order to conceal the preparations for attack from the enemy, and by morning everything had disappeared into the few farmsteads and barns.

On the 27th March the 2nd Battalion moved into the assembly area east of Golzow station while the 1st Battalion remained on the western edge of the village ready to follow deployed to the right. The Tiger battalion rolled forward at 0300 hours and the attack began. I had my command post in the building immediately east of Golzow station as it was the most practical from a communications point of view, for from here I could best reach all parts of the regiment, as well as the artillery, the tanks and Division while combat was in progress.

Our artillery bombarded Gorgast. Infantry weapons opened up. Soon came a message from the 2nd Battalion that they had broken through the first enemy lines. Further reports said that the right-hand company of the 2nd Battalion was engaged with the enemy in a strongly defended farmstead 1,000 meters east of the railway station, and that the left-hand company was under heavy enfilade fire from the sector north of the brook, where the 76th Panzergrenadier Regiment were attacking. One could hear heavy fire coming from there too. Finally the right-hand company of the 2nd Battalion took the farmstead, where the tanks remained in position. The left-hand company was also unable to advance as the enemy north of the brook were firmly ensconced in their buildings and were maintaining a constant enfilading fire on the regiment's whole front of attack. Our own tanks could not progress further because of enemy mines. The fighting came to a halt. In answer to the obviously nervous calls from Division, I could only repeat that enemy resistance had stiffened to such a degree that one could no longer expect a breakthrough before dawn. This gave me great concern for my 2nd and 1st Battalions. The latter had meanwhile been drawn into the fighting and had taken part in the assault on the farmstead, but needed to be got back under worthwhile cover so that when daylight came they would not be exposed to enemy fire without protection of any kind in completely open ground. However, I could not withdraw my troops without the tanks, as the tanks could not stay there without infantry protection.

The day began to dawn and what I feared occurred. As soon as the morning mist lifted, the enemy began to fire at the stationary tanks, which presented an easy target on the plain. At 1100 hours a bombardment by all calibres began, including "Stalin-organs." The soldiers, receiving no support from either their own artillery or the Luftwaffe, began to leave their positions, at first individually and then in groups. It was a panic. I stopped them near the command post and led them forward once more. In a short while the the old front line was regained. The enemy had not moved forward. In the evening we shortened the line so as to start making a line of defense. The tanks were towed away during the night of 28-29 March and the enemy artillery fire died down.[32]

Again it is interesting to see this action through the eyes of the Regimental Signals Sergeant, Fritz-Rudolf Averdieck:

After a full day's rest we prepared for another attack on 26 March. The aim was to push through to Küstrin via Golzow and Gorgast and relieve the hard-pressed garrison of this fortress. In view of the exposed nature of the terrain we could only occupy our assembly areas and attack under cover of darkness. We reached the assembly area at midnight. There were some Tigers to support us and so I established radio contact with them. Our confidence mounted considerably as at 0300 hours a barrage burst forth from a number of guns and went on for an hour, after which we attacked. We drove through Golzow and soon attained our first objective. Then our company came under a terrible mortar barrage and suffered 50 percent casualties.

We drove back to the start line in our APC, which at least gave us cover from the sides. Three Tigers fell victim to mines, although there were still attempts, even as day broke, to carry the attack through to Gorgast.

During the morning attacks and counterattacks went on until they were finally abandoned, and we were happy to be able to hold on to our positions with the weak forces remaining. Then came endless rocket, artillery and mortar fire, as well as air attacks.

Following a bombing attack, some of our troops took to flight and had to be brought back into line by the regimental commander himself.

As the battalion command posts were only a few meters away from us, we used our manpack radios from the cellar of a building that was frequently badly rocked in these bombing attacks. The situation failed to calm down even when evening came. It was hardly dark when the "Lame Ducks" arrived and started dropping bombs and incendiaries on Golzow in a regular pattern, with several acting in unison. Bombs were exploding very close and soon most of the buildings were on fire from the incendiaries. Consequently, at midnight the commander decided to move his command post out of this inferno back about a kilometer to a farmstead. On our way our small convoy was attacked by a "Lame Duck" with incendiaries, the fire falling close around us.[33]

It is estimated that in this fighting between 22 and 27 March the Soviets lost more than 200 tanks and the Germans about 2,000 men.[34]

The Fortress Falls

Gradually hemmed in by encroaching Soviet units, the 303rd Fusilier Battalion, supported by a dug-in 88mm flak gun and three SPGs, finally abandoned the Alt Bleyen manor farm position and their heavy equipment on the night of 26-27 March and withdrew to the Kuhbrücken-Vorstadt, which was already under attack from Soviet troops now occupying Neu Bleyen village to the immediate north.[35]

Massive attacks on the fortress positions by ground-attack aircraft and bombers were resumed on 28 and 29 March. But the problem of tackling the Küstrin Fortress was a formidable one, as Colonel General Chuikov of the 8th Guards Army described:

> The citadel itself was set on an island formed by the Oder and Warthe rivers. The spring flood had submerged all the approaches to the island. The only links between the citadel and the surrounding land were dykes and roads fanning out towards Berlin, Frankfurt, Posen and Stettin. Needless to say, the enemy had taken care to block these roads securely, covering the dykes and embankments with dugouts, pillboxes, trenches, caponiers, barbed wire, minefields and other defences. Our small subunits managed to come so close to the enemy fortifications that hand grenade and Panzerfaust exchanges went on almost round the clock. But we were unable to deploy large forces here since a single tank took up the whole width of a dyke.

Chuikov went on to describe how he worked out a plan of attack with his artillery commander, General Pozharsky, and the commanders of the 35th and 82nd Guards Rifle Divisions, whose formations would be involved in the assault. While the air support could concentrate on the fortress itself, the land forces would have to deal with the individual obstacles confronting them.

To deal with the latter, they decided to bring forward three 203mm batteries, siting one on the dikes on either side of the Oder to engage targets on the opposite side in crisscross fire. To avoid hitting their own troops, the forward units would display distinctive markers. The third battery would engage the walls of the fortress from the south.

The 82nd Guards Rifle Division would conduct the attack on the east side of the Oder, spearheading its assault with a single company on each dike, while the 35th Guards Rifle Division would conduct the attack on the west bank, which would include a regimental assault across the Vorflut Channel onto the Oder-Insel.

Chuikov continued:

> Here is the plan of the assault. On the eve of the offensive, the 28th March, our ground-attack aircraft and bombers were to carry out precision bombing of the citadel and other permanent defences. This would compel the enemy to

abandon them and seek shelter in the field fortifications. The artillery was not to open fire except for the battery shelling the fortress walls point-blank.

In the morning of the 29th March our air force would hit the same targets. Let the enemy remain in the field fortifications believing he has outwitted us. But the moment the air raid ends, at 0800 hours sharp, guns of all calibers, including the heavy guns firing at point-blank range, were to start bombarding the field fortifications and keep firing for 40 minutes. Under this cover assault groups of infantry and sub-machinegunners would take to the boats and land on the island. The general assault would start at 0840 hours.[36]

On 27 March, the day of the 9th Army's last abortive attempt to relieve the Küstrin garrison, the Soviets finally managed to take the isolated "Bienenhof" position. Using barges and rafts they also managed to cross the flooded Warthe meadows and establish themselves on the railway tracks leading to the town from the southeast. There followed some intensive fighting in the limited area in front of the Kietzer Tor (Kietz Gate) in which the Kietzerbusch railway stop exchanged hands several times. This was a preliminary, a reconnaissance in force, leading to the main attack the next day, in which the Soviets broke through into the Altstadt despite all attempts to stop them and reached as far as the Schloss by 1800 hours. By then the defense were down to one 150mm infantry gun with only six rounds and two 75mm guns with about thirty rounds between them.[37]

On the afternoon of the 28th, SS-Lieutenant General Reinefarth decided to evacuate the Altstadt, but his orders were issued hastily and poorly executed, so that some troops and a considerable number of Volkssturm were left behind when the railway bridge, the last link between the Altstadt and the Oder-Insel, was blown by German engineers that evening between 2100 and 2200 hours.

As the defense could no longer expect to hope for relief, Reinefarth that night radioed for permission to break out with his garrison. His request led to a furious row in the Führerbunker, in which Colonel General Guderian, as Chief of the General Staff, tried to defend the actions of his field commanders before an apoplectic Hitler, only to be replaced by General Hans Krebs for his pains. General Busse had not refused Reinefarth's request, but Hitler wanted Reinefarth arrested and court-martialed.

Throughout the 29th, the remains of the garrison were confined to the Oder-Insel, where the Soviets closed in to within fifty meters of the Artillery Barracks, and a small strip of embankment between Lünette "D" and the Kuhbrücken-Vorstadt, where hand-to-hand fighting took place all day, leaving both sides exhausted and the Germans out of ammunition. A single trench ran the length of the connecting dike, the Vorflut Channel side being mined. Reinefarth's officers persuaded him to effect a breakout whether Hitler approved or not, for it was clear that the position was now untenable for more than a few hours. This was agreed, but with participation on a voluntary basis in view of Hitler's orders. That evening those electing for the breakout assembled on the dike west of the

Vorflut Channel and were split into four groups for the attempt. Roughly seven kilometers separated them from the German lines.

The breakout took the form of a sudden infantry attack at about 2300 hours on the nearest Soviet positions to the west and continued in desperation and disorder, each individual plunging forward in the darkness, ignoring Soviet fire, for to take cover meant giving up, splashing through the watercourses and attacking each line of trenches as they appeared. Beyond the three lines of Soviet trenches facing the Küstrin position they came across the burnt-out hulks of tanks destroyed in the earlier fighting, fought their way through another three lines of westward-facing Soviet trenches and eventually reached the German lines at dawn. Their unexpected approach to the latter at first also drew German fire, but 1,318 are said to have got through, including Reinefarth and 118 Volkssturm.[38]

Chuikov described the final assault on the Altstadt:

> On the morning of the 29th March the air attack was repeated. It was followed by an artillery preparation. From my observation post I could see heavy shells fired point-blank slamming into the enemy pillboxes and dugouts on the dykes. It was an impressive sight. Explosions hurled heavy stones and logs high into the air.
>
> At 0830 hours our assault groups disembarked from their boats on the island. Ten minutes later we heard the chatter of machine-gun and automatic fire and the explosions of hand grenades and Panzerfausts.[39]

Of the 135 Volkssturm still remaining on the Altstadt peninsula, a few managed to cross in the remaining inflatable boats and fishing craft, but the river was too swollen and fast-running to try and swim across and the whole area was now under heavy machinegun fire from the Soviets ensconced on the Kietzer Tor. A last conference was held in a bunker on the night of the 28th-29th and unit commanders given permission to try and break out with their units before the Volkssturm battalion commander, Reserve Captain Rudolf Tamm, negotiated surrender with the Soviets in the morning.

After the Volkssturm surrender the few troops still holding out in the ruins of the Altstadt and glacis outside that had not been party to the surrender were captured and shot. The 200 or so wounded in the Main Dressing Station were supposed to have been honorably treated by the Soviets in accordance with the terms of surrender, but it appears that some of those that could not walk were shot.[40]

It is estimated that the defence and attempted relief of the Küstrin Fortress cost the Germans about 5,000 killed, a further 9,000 wounded evacuated to their own lines, and 6,000, mainly wounded, taken prisoner, while the Soviets lost about 5,000 killed and 15,000 wounded.[41]

The Soviets now had a bridgehead about fifty kilometers wide and seven to ten kilometers deep, the vital nodal point at Küstrin had been secured, and preparations for the next phase of operations could proceed from a far stronger basis.

The Soviet engineers could get on with their extensive preparations for the Berlin Operation, including the rebuilding of the heavy capacity bridges at Küstrin.

Looking back on this period, Averdieck, Signals Sergeant of the 90th Panzergrenadier Regiment, commented:

> Several quiet days then followed (28 March to 1 April) as a result of the weather being misty. There were some sporadic air attacks by day and night, including incendiaries, and the Russian artillery participated with smoke shells, putting an end to any ideas of launching an attack. Then on Easter Sunday (1 April) we were assigned to some new positions. The expected attack had yet to occur. We set up our command post in a large farmstead, the Annahof. From 1 to 13 April we went through a completely quiet period, although the Russians fired their smoke shells repeatedly. During a visit to the 1st Battalion I had the opportunity to examine the Russian-occupied country-side and the place where we had stopped their attack. About fifty to sixty tanks stood shot-up in a small area. I listened to the radio a lot, including some beautiful opera, and also the catastrophic news from the Western Front. Reichs Marshal Göring drove past once on a visit to the neighboring para-chute division. Appeals and orders arrived to hold the Eastern Front at all costs, and to hold on to our positions, command posts and administrative areas to the last man. During this time 600 men managed to break through to us from the Küstrin Fortress, suffering heavy casualties from our own artillery. Then on the last evening we were offered something new. A Ju 88 with a fighter sat on top appeared under heavy Soviet antiaircraft fire. Suddenly the lower aircraft was released and dived on its target, and a massive explosion followed. As there was a shortage of fuel, the bomber had been filled with explosives and deliberately used in this manner. The soldiers dubbed this phenomenon "Father and son."[42]

CHAPTER 8

The East Pomeranian Operation

It is no good looking in Zhukov's memoirs for an informative account of the the East Pomeranian Operation, for he barely mentions it. It seems that this was merely an annoying distraction from his main aim, the taking of Berlin, and therefore this episode is almost entirely covered by a counterattack against Chuikov's allegations that the city could have been taken earlier.[1] He summarizes:

> Initially, the task of routing the enemy in East Pomerania was supposed to be the sole responsibility of the forces of the 2nd Byelorussian Front. However, their strength proved to be totally insufficient. The offensive of that Front, begun on the 10th February, proceeded very slowly; its troops covered only fifty to seventy kilometers in ten days.
>
> At that moment the enemy launched a counterattack south of Stargard and even succeeded in pressing our troops back, gaining some twelve kilometers southward.
>
> In view of the situation, the Supreme Command decided to move four field and two tank armies from the 1st Byelorussian Front in order to liquidate the East Pomeranian grouping, whose strength by then had grown to forty divisions.
>
> As is known, joint operations by the two Fronts to knock out the East Pomeranian grouping were completed only towards the end of March. You can see what a hard nut that grouping was.[2]

Clearly the sheer speed of the Vistula-Oder Operation had brought problems with it that made the conduct of this next phase extremely difficult. The railway bridges over the broad expanse of the Vistula were still in course of reconstruction, a broken link in the essential chain of supply. Consequently there was a serious shortage of ammunition, fuel and lubricants. The troops themselves were battle-weary, the units depleted, no reinforcements were coming forward, and there was the crisis over discipline with the arrival on German soil. In

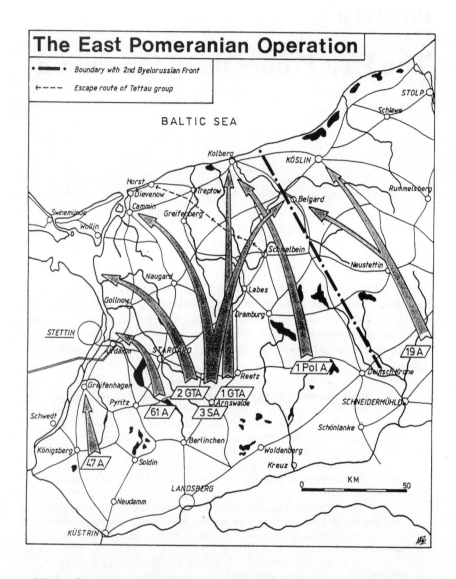

The East Pomeranian Operation

Boundary with 2nd Byelorussian Front

Escape route of Tettau group

BALTIC SEA

addition, the weather conditions were particularly bad with snow storms, rain, sleet, fog and mud impeding movement.[3]

Nevertheless, this operation, which had arisen out of Stalin's failure to award Rokossovsky's 2nd Byelorussian Front the additional army to help close the opening gap between Zhukov's troops speeding westward to the Oder and Rokossovsky's pushing northward to the Baltic, was an important development. Not only had Zhukov had to drop off troops to cover this flank as he advanced, but it had given the Germans the opportunity of bringing forward reserves to mount a counteroperation from the Stargard area.

Operation "Sonnenwende" (Solstice) was the idea of Colonel General Guderian, part of a plan that would tackle the Soviet forces from Stargard in the north and from the Oder between Guben and Glogau in the south. This, however, depended upon reinforcements from other fronts being allocated to the task, but as Hitler sent them off to Hungary instead, it was only possible to mount the northern thrust, and that with limited resources. In order to ensure the operation was properly conducted he managed to persuade a reluctant Hitler, who was outraged at the suggestion that Himmler and his staff might not be competent, after a two-hour tirade to accept the appointment of Guderian's chief assistant, Lieutenant General Walther Wenck, to take charge.[4]

SS-General Felix Steiner's 11th SS Panzer Army was detailed for the task, operating in three groups which would attack southward from a start line about fifty kilometers long. In the center the IIIrd (Germanic) SS Panzer Corps, consisting of the 11th "Nordland" and 23rd "Nederland" SS Volunteer Panzer-grenadier Divisions of Scandinavian and Dutch volunteers respectively, and the "Führer-Begleit" Infantry and the 27th SS "Langemarck" Grenadier Divisions, would attack from the line Jakobshagen-Zachan to relieve Arnswalde, then head toward Küstrin. On the right flank the XXXIXth Panzer Corps, consisting of the "Holstein" Panzer, the 10th SS Panzer, the 4th SS Police and 28th SS "Wallon-ien" Grenadier Divisions, starting from the immediate area of Stargard, would attack southward toward Dölitz. The left flank would be protected by a group consisting of the "Führer" Grenadier, 163rd and 281st Infantry Divisions, supported by the 104th Tank-Hunting Brigade, which would push toward Landsberg parallel with the advance of the other groups.[5]

Aware of their move across the Oder, Zhukov had the 2nd Guards Tank Army and the 61st Army deployed across their front from east to west, with the 1st Guards Tank, 47th and 3rd Shock Armies in reserve.[6]

The 11th SS "Nordland" Panzergrenadier Division opened the assault on the 15th February, achieving temporary surprise with their thrust on Arnswalde, where the besieged German garrison was relieved. The remaining German forces attacked on the 16th and achieved some limited success over the next two days despite persistent Soviet counterattacks and also coming up against strong antitank defenses of guns and mines.[7]

On the 17th Wenck was summoned to Berlin to brief Hitler on the progress of the operation. On the way back Wenck took over the wheel from his exhaus-ted driver, only to fall asleep himself and crash the car, hurting himself badly. General of Infantry Hans Krebs took over the operation the next day, but by then the initiative had been lost. The German units had all been forced to go on the defensive and that evening Army Group "'Weichsel" decided not to try and renew the attack.[8]

Zhukov decided to launch an attack toward Stettin on 19 February, using the 2nd Guards Tank Army, the 61st Army and the 7th Guards Cavalry Corps. Two corps of the 61st Army surrounded Arnswalde while one division went in to clear the town in bitter street fighting. However, the 2nd Guards Tank Army could make little progress against constant German counterattacks, so Zhukov called off the operation and switched to the defensive.[9]

Back from the Yalta Conference, between 17 and 22 February the Stavka issued fresh instructions to Zhukov and Rokossovsky calling for a combined attack that would split the German forces in half and then fan out to clear the area. In pursuance of these instructions Rokossovsky launched an attack on 24 February, spearheaded by the 3rd Tank Corps in a northerly thrust to the Baltic coast near Köslin, while the main body did a right hook toward Danzig and Gotenhafen. However, the newly arrived 19th Army failed to keep up with the 3rd Tank Corps (its commander was replaced as a consequence) and a gap opened up on Rokossovsky's left flank between himself and Zhukov.[10]

Zhukov did not start his operation until 1 March, aiming with the 1st Guards Tank Army on his right flank for Kolberg on the Baltic coast. This maneuver took the Germans by surprise, creating havoc in their rear areas, where the roads were already thronged with refugees. Kolberg was reached on 4 March and the siege of the ancient fortress town was undertaken by two divisions of the 1st Polish Army. The successful defense and eventual evacuation of the town was conducted under almost impossible conditions by an heroic colonial officer, Colonel Fritz Fullriede, who held out until the morning of 18 March, for which Hitler personally decorated him with the Knights' Cross a week later.[11]

Meanwhile the 1st Guards Tank and 61st Armies were having to fight their way through Stargard, which was taken on 4 March. They went on to line up against the German 3rd Panzer Army's Altdamm bridgehead, which spanned some eighty kilometers east of the Oder between Greifenhagen in the south and Gollnow in the north, and presented a formidable obstacle. The 47th Army went on to clear the east bank of the Oder up to Greifenhagen, which it reached on 6 March, while the 3rd Shock Army cleared the area to the north up to the coast, which was reached on the 9th.[12]

However, a group of up to 16,000 German troops under Lieutenant General Hans von Tettau, with about 40,000 civilian refugees accompanying them, managed to break out of encirclement just north of Schivelbein on 5 March to eventually reach the seaside resorts of Hoff and Horst, where they established a bridgehead in the hope of being evacuated by sea. As this did not materialize, they then fought their way westward along the cliffs to Dievenow, from where the navy ferried them across to the island of Wollin on 11 and 12 March.[13]

In the middle of this, Zhukov was summoned to Moscow for another discussion with Stalin and the General Staff on the forthcoming Berlin Operation. On this occasion, Zhukov is not sure whether it was the 7 or 8 March, he went straight to see Stalin at his dacha, finding Stalin looking extremely tired.

Before their more formal talks began they took a walk in the garden during which Zhukov ventured to ask Stalin a personal question about the latter's son Yakov, who was a prisoner of war of the Germans. Stalin eventually replied that he thought that the Germans would shoot him. Later Stalin briefed him on the outcome of the Yalta Conference. The next day Zhukov and Antonov did some more work on the plans for the Berlin Operation, their proposals being approved that night by Stalin.[14]

On 8 March the Stavka temporarily transferred the 1st Guards Tank Army to Rokossovsky's command to enable him to complete his mopping up eastward along the Baltic coast, which prompted Zhukov to telephone Rokossovsky and get him to promise to return the army in the state in which he received it![15]

Although the Altdamm bridgehead had to be tackled, for it presented a permanent threat of intervention on the east bank, Zhukov approached it cautiously, deciding on 12 March to keep it covered with the already-deployed 2nd Guards Tank, 47th and 61st Armies, but to withdraw the 3rd Shock Army into reserve in readiness for the Berlin Operation. He then brought forward four artillery breakthrough divisions to give him a density of 250-280 guns and mortars per kilometer of his selected breakthrough sector for when he resumed the offensive two days later on the 14th. The next day Hitler peremptorily ordered some of the 3rd Panzer Army's mobile units to reinforce the 9th Army opposite Küstrin, thereby seriously weakening the defense. Consequently, on 19 March the 2nd Guards Tank and 47th Armies succeeded in breaking through the German defenses, and General Hasso von Manteuffel, who had taken over the 3rd Panzer Army on the 10th, told Hitler that either they had to withdraw everyone across the Oder that night, or lose the whole lot the next day. Hitler gave his permission, and the Germans withdrew, blowing up the bridges behind them.

By the 21st the last remaining pockets of resistance in Altdamm had succumbed, and the Soviets could claim to have killed 40,000 Germans in the bridgehead area and captured 12,000 more, together with 126 tanks and SPGs, over 200 guns and 154 mortars. For Zhukov, however, the main achievement was that this diversion was over and they could now safely concentrate back in the Küstrin bridgehead and prepare for the Berlin Operation.[16]

With the collapse of German resistance on the east bank of the Oder, Guderian was able to engineer the replacement of Himmler as commander in chief of Army Group "Weichsel" with Colonel General Gotthardt Heinrici on 20 March. Guderian had found Himmler not at his headquarters in Prenzlau but in a sanatorium at Hohenlychen, where he was being treated by his private physician for a common cold. Guderian managed to persuade Himmler to allow him to apply to Hitler for Himmler's release from that appointment in view of the burden of all the others he held.[17]

Guderian lost his own post a week later, being "sent on six weeks' leave" by Hitler on 28 March following the previously related argument in which Guderian had supported Busse's conduct of the failed attempt to relieve the Küstrin garrison.[18]

Meanwhile Marshal Koniev had been busy clearing Silesia. His forces had closed up to the Neisse River on Zhukov's southern flank on 15 February, still leaving large areas of Upper and Lower Silesia to be conquered from a very active opposition, and, as he reported on the situation on 16 February:

> We assessed the situation and pointed out that the left flank of the Front was lagging very much behind; the troops had moved hundreds of kilometres away from the supply bases and were with great difficulty being kept going on a starvation diet of ammunition and fuel; the troops had sustained considerable losses in personnel, and the infantry divisions now numbered an average 4,600 men; of the 3,648 tanks and SPGs we had had on the 12th January (the beginning of the Vistula-Oder Operation) only 1,289 were now in commission; the bad roads in the wooded and marshy country were hindering the maneuvers of the armoured troops and they were suffering losses; the airfields were unfit and our air men could hardly be used; the enemy was continuously gathering strength, having reinforcements from the other fronts, and the fighting was becoming increasingly more stubborn.[19]

The great city of Breslau was surrounded on 18 February with a garrison of 45,000-50,000 troops, and the siege of this city was to tie down one of Koniev's armies until 6 May, a remarkable total of seventy-seven days.[20]

Although there was a lull for the 1st Ukrainian Front's troops on the Neisse from the end of the Lower Silesian Operation on 24 February to the opening of the Berlin Operation on 16 April, the majority of the Front's troops were actively engaged along their left flank until the end of March against the German 17th Army, and in the Upper Silesian Operation against Colonel General Heinrici's 1st Panzer Army. In securing the Oppeln and Ratibor areas, they sustained particularly heavy casualties in armor during the second half of March. Thus Koniev's situation was roughly on a par with Zhukov's when they met in Moscow for the final top-level planning conferences for the Berlin Operation.[21]

PART III

Launching
"Operation Berlin"

CHAPTER 9

Planning and Logistics

The end of March brought a review of the situation on both sides. For the Germans it was now clear that there was no hope of reducing the Soviet bridgeheads with the resources at hand, as the failure of the 9th Army's XXXIXth Panzer Corps's attack had proved. The collapse of the German effort in Eastern Pomerania meant that the Soviets could now switch their formidable resources to the Küstrin area for a direct thrust on Berlin. For the Germans, preparation for a defensive battle was of the utmost urgency.

With the East Pomeranian and Silesian operations successfully completed, Stalin summoned his "Berlin" front commanders to Moscow to finalize the planning for "Operation Berlin." Zhukov arrived first on 29 March, the day on which, to his great relief, the Küstrin Fortress was finally secured. He saw Stalin that evening and briefed him on his 1st Byelorussian Front. Stalin then gave him two days to sort out the final details of his plans with the General Staff. He and Koniev were to present their plans for Stavka approval on 1 April. The accounts of what actually happened in Moscow at this point differ in detail. All refer to their belief that, despite the agreements reached at the Yalta Conference in February about the zoning of postwar Germany, the Western Allies would try to get to Berlin ahead of them. Consequently time was of the essence in mounting this operation.[1]

Perhaps the account of General Sergei M. Shtemenko, Chief of the Operations Department of the General Staff, is the most objective. In a preliminary discourse on the planning, he related:

> The work of the General Staff in planning the culminating attacks was made extremely complicated by Stalin's categorical decision concerning the special role of the 1st Byelorussian Front. The task of overcoming such a large city as Berlin, which had been prepared well in advance for defence, was beyond the capacity of one front, even such a powerful front as the 1st Byelorussian. The situation insistently demanded that at least the 1st Ukrainian Front should be

aimed additionally at Berlin. Moreover, it was, of course, necessary to avoid an ineffectual frontal attack with the main forces.

We had to go back to the January idea of taking Berlin by means of outflanking attacks by the 1st Byelorussian Front from the north and north-west and the 1st Ukrainian Front from the south-west and west. The two Fronts were to link up in the Brandenburg-Potsdam area.

We based all our further calculations on the most unfavourable assumptions: the inevitability of heavy and prolonged fighting in the streets of Berlin, the possibility of German counterattacks from outside the ring of encirclement from the west and south-west, restoration of the enemy's defence to the west of Berlin and the consequent need to continue the offensive. We even envisaged a situation in which the Western Allies for some reason might be unable to overcome the resistance of the enemy forces opposing them and find themselves held up for a long time.[2]

Shtemenko then records the events of the 1945 Easter weekend in Moscow:

By this time the General Staff had all all the basic ideas for the Berlin operation worked out. In the course of this work we kept in very close contact with the Front Chiefs-of-Staff, A.M. Bogolyubov, M.S. Malin and V.D. Sokolovsky (later with I.Y. Petrov) and, as soon as the first symptoms appeared that the Allies had designs on Berlin, Zhukov and Koniev were summoned to Moscow.

On March the 31st they and the General Staff considered what further operations the Fronts were to carry out. Marshal Koniev got very excited over the demarcation line between his Front and the 1st Byelorussian Front, which gave him no opportunity of striking a blow at Berlin. No one on the General Staff, however, could remove this obstacle.

On the next day, 1st April 1945, the plan of the Berlin operation was discussed at GHQ. A detailed report was given on the situation at the Fronts, and on Allied operations and their plans. Stalin drew the conclusion from this that we must take Berlin in the shortest possible time. The operation would have to be started not later than the 16th April and complete in not more than 12 to 15 days. The Front Commanders agreed to this and assured GHQ that the troops would be ready in time.

The Chief of the General Staff considered it necessary to draw the Supreme Commander's attention once again to the demarcation line between the two Fronts. It was emphasised that this line virtually excluded the armies of the 1st Ukrainian Front from direct participation in the fighting for Berlin, and this might make it difficult to carry out the operation as scheduled. Marshal Koniev spoke in the same vein, arguing in favour of aiming part of the forces of the 1st Ukrainian Front, particularly the tank armies, at the south-western suburbs of Berlin.

Stalin decided on a compromise. He did not completely abandon his own idea, nor did he entirely reject Marshal Koniev's considerations, supported by the General Staff. On the map showing the plan of the operation he silently crossed out the section of the demarcation line that cut off the

Ukrainian Front from Berlin, allowing it to go as far as Lübben (sixty kilometres to the south-east of the capital) and no further.

"Let the one who is first to break in take Berlin," he told us later.[3]

So this operation was to become not only a race against time to beat the Western Allies to Berlin, but also a race between the front commanders for the glory of taking the enemy capital. Instead of three to four months to prepare for such an operation, as had been the case so far, only two weeks were allowed, calling for a logistical miracle. The operational timings too, presumably based on the unusual experience of the Vistula-Oder Operation, were highly unrealistic, expecting the main German defenses on the Seelow Heights to be breached on the first day so that the two tanks armies could rush ahead as they had to the Oder and take Berlin in a classic pincer movement by 21 April and reach the Elbe by 1 May.

Surprisingly, the Yalta Conference in February had not provided for proper liaison and coordination of effort between the Western Allies and the Soviet command, and Stalin had been able to take advantage of this to deceive both the Allies and his own front commanders. On 28 March he had received a signal from General Eisenhower, Supreme Allied Commander in the West, who, unilaterally and against the wishes of the British leadership, had decided to disregard Berlin and direct his main thrust on the Erfurt/Leipzig/Dresden area and the mythical "Alpine Redoubt."[4] Stalin had promptly replied approving these proposals and announcing his own intentions of a main thrust on Dresden with only subsidiary forces directed on Berlin. From German signal traffic the Allies had been alerted to the imminence of the Soviet offensive and had pressed Stalin for details, but it was not until the eve of the attack that he was to divulge the date to them, again emphasizing that his main thrust would be in the south.[5]

Stalin signed the directive approving Zhukov's plans for the 1st Byelorussian Front's operation on the night of 1 April and Koniev's the following day. The directive for Marshal Rokossovsky's 2nd Byelorussian Front was not issued for another week. He was still heavily engaged in mopping up the German forces remaining in East Prussia and was not expected to launch his part of the Berlin Operation until 20 April.[6]

Zhukov's orders gave him the primary task of taking Berlin and pushing on to the Elbe, for which he would receive further considerable reinforcements from the Stavka Reserve, while Koniev would support the Berlin operation by destroying the enemy forces to the south of the city, and would have the secondary task of taking Dresden and Leipzig, both important industrial cities in the future Soviet Zone of Occupation. The 2nd Byelorussian Front would engage the enemy forces north of the capital. In the meantime the other fronts to the south would maintain pressure on the Germans to prevent the redeployment of strategic reserves to the "Operation Berlin" theater.[7]

The main problem for Zhukov in the breakthrough battle would be the clearing of the enemy from the commanding Seelow Heights. He proposed doing this with a simultaneous attack from his bridgehead in the Oderbruch by four reinforced combined-arms formations; the 8th Guards, 3rd and 5th Shock, and 47th Armies. They would clear breaches in the enemy defenses that would enable the 1st and 2nd Guards Tank Armies to pass through. The 2nd Guards Tank Army was to penetrate to the heart of Berlin from the northeast, while the 1st Guards Tank Army would bypass Berlin and Potsdam to the south, pushing on to the west. To cover his northern flank the 1st Polish and 61st Armies would conduct river crossings across the Alte Oder and Oder and would press westward north of the city, while the 69th Army would cover the 8th Guards Army's southern flank and contain the Frankfurt-an-der-Oder garrison in conjuction with the 33rd Army. The latter, with the 2nd Guards Cavalry Corps, would break out of its own bridgehead, and together these two armies would push westward along the line of the autobahn with the objectives of Fürstenwalde and eventually Brandenburg. The 3rd Army would form the front's second echelon, the 1st and 2nd Guards Tank Armies the mobile groups, and the 7th Guards Cavalry Corps the Front Reserve.[8]

The operational plans having been agreed in Moscow, there then followed two weeks of intense preparation on the Oder-Neisse Front, with prodigious feats being accomplished in the bringing forward of the required manpower, equipment, ammunition and supplies.[9]

Units depleted in the winter fighting had had to be brought up to strength, and their equipment overhauled and replenished. The Soviets were scraping the bottom of their manpower barrel by 1945, and released prisoners of war were being promptly rearmed, fed and thrust back into the line. For the first time they even used air transport to bring forward reinforcements.[10]

The newly allocated formations from the Stavka Reserve had to be brought forward and deployed into position. A more complicated maneuver was the lateral transfer of the two armies allocated to Marshal Koniev from the 2nd Byelorussian Front across Zhukov's lines of communication.[11]

The development of the bridgehead as a base for the launching of the operation was begun immediately. The first priority was to establish sufficient crossing points into the bridgehead. Ultimately twenty-six bridges were constructed over the Warthe and Oder rivers, of which two supplemented Küstrin's destroyed but repairable bridges and three led into the 33rd Army's bridgehead south of Frankfurt. Of the twenty-one bridges into the Küstrin bridgehead, eight were of sixty tons capacity, three of thirty tons, eight of sixteen tons, one of ten tons, and one of five tons. However, because of the high floodwaters experienced throughout this period, the bridges had to be built from dike to dike and thus ranged between 500 and 1,107 meters in length. Flooding also caused some previously constructed bridges to be submerged. The Soviet engineers marked the line of these bridges with posts so that they could be continued to be used, giving rise to the myth that construction of underwater bridges was their particular skill! The bridges were supplemented by forty ferries of varying capacity. In all thirteen pontoon and twenty-seven engineer battalions, as well as six military construction units, were employed on this often hazardous task, as the bridges were priority targets for the Germans. The bridge at Göritz is said to have been destroyed twenty times, and that at Zellin involved the loss of 387 men in the seven days of its construction, 201 of whom died.[12]

With their passion for statistics, the Soviets give a total of 1,671,188 vehicles, 400,000 horse-drawn wagons and 600,000 individuals on foot having crossed over into the Küstrin bridgehead in preparation for "Operation Berlin."[13].

For instance, Lieutenant General Bokov describes how on 8 April the artillery started crossing into the bridgehead in the 5th Shock Army's sector using five bridges and three ferries under a strict traffic control system at a rate of a brigade per night. Then on 11 April it was the turn of the armor, using the sixty-ton bridges at 300-meter intervals. Within four days all were across at a rate of seventy-five to ninety heavy armored vehicles per night. Artillery was used to cover the noise of their movement, followed by smoke laid by the chemical warfare units at daybreak until they were all safely camouflaged.[14]

The arrival of the Dnieper Flotilla by rail and water at the end of March enabled a more expert protection of the bridges at water level. On 7 April the flotilla received orders to protect the crossing points from drifting mines, to strengthen the antiaircraft defenses and to generally safeguard the crossing points with their boats. The flotilla consisted of two brigades, each having eighteen armored boats, twenty minesweepers, six floating batteries, two gun-boats and twenty semihydrofoils.[15]

Within the Küstrin bridgehead altogether some 636 kilometers of fire and communication trenches were dug, 9,116 firing positions for machineguns, mortars and antitank guns were prepared, plus a further 4,500 firing positions for from two to four guns each, and twenty-five approach roads. Ten of these approach roads were required to enable the two tank armies to deploy. A further forty-eight kilometers of roads had to be repaired, twenty-four kilometers of new roads laid and 112 bridges built. In addition some 7,000 stands and more than 5,000 covers for tanks and other vehicles had to be constructed.[16]

This massive task, causing the bridgehead to seethe with activity, was undertaken by all units in the bridgehead with the support of 194 engineer battalions and 14 military construction units. Frequent rain and a high water table interfered with the work and made the completion of some tasks impossible. The fields were flooded and so muddy that vehicles had to keep to the roads available, although the ground was firm enough for tanks further west in the Tucheband-Golzow area. Also the previous fighting in the Oderbruch and on the Reitwein Spur had left these areas liberally strewn with the mines laid by both sides. Consequently the Soviet engineers had to lift over 70,000 of these mines and clear some 340 lanes through existing minefields to prepare for the coming operation.[17]

Deceiving the Germans as to Soviet intentions in this phase was an especially difficult task, especially as the sheer scale of activity made an alternative picture hard to portray. The direction of the main assault and further operational moves were not difficult to deduce, but the troops in the bridgehead were expected to carry out such camouflage and deceptive measures as were possible right up to the beginning of the attack. Transport and troop movements were only carried out at night, without lights, and under radio silence. Zhukov wrote:

> The positions looked deserted in the daytime, but they came alive at night. Thousands of men worked with spades, crow-bars and picks in complete silence. The work was made more difficult by subsoil spring waters and the beginning of spring mud. More than 1,800,000 cubic metres of earth were excavated during those nights. On the morning of every next day no traces of the tremendous night work could be seen. Everything was carefully camouflaged.[18]

However, Chuikov commented:

> It was impossible to ensure adequate concealment when the enemy had a good view over the bridgehead, and also the east bank of the Oder. When night fell German searchlights probed the surrounding territory. We did not open fire to put them out; the artillery was ordered to hold fire until the last minute and not betray its location. When the searchlights went off, reconnaissance aircraft would light up the valley with flares and the Germans could see all of it quite distinctly.
> As the trees were not yet in leaf, camouflage was difficult. Digging was out of the question on account of the spring floods and subsoil waters. As soon as you turned up the earth with a spade, the hole filled with muddy water.[19]

The front's camouflage and deception plan was detailed and extensive. For instance, rail transport bringing forward fighting equipment was disguised as loads of wood and hay, and the redeployment of forces from the East Pomeranian Operation was similarly conducted under cover. In order to conceal the concentration and location of armor, four trainloads of tanks and artillery were openly sent to the rear every day. With the aim of deceiving the Germans into believing that the forthcoming attack would be in the form of a vast pincer movement from the baselines Stettin-Gartz and Fürstenberg-Guben, dummy assembly areas were established behind dummy river crossing preparation areas there. In the northern dummy assembly area between Altdamm and Pyritz this was backed by radio transmissions from recognizable subunits of the 2nd Guards Tank and 5th Shock Armies, while in the southern one between Crossen and

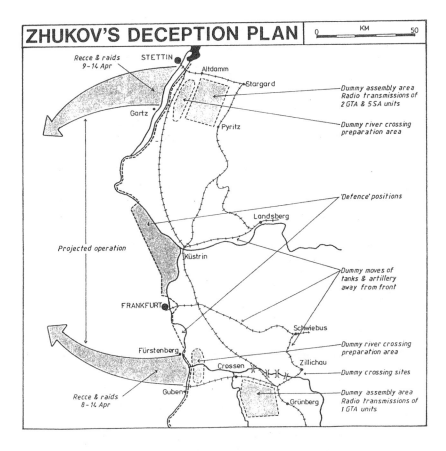

ZHUKOV'S DECEPTION PLAN

Grünberg similar radio transmissions were made by subunits of the 1st Guards Tank Army from 10 to 14 April. In this latter area four crossing points over the Oder were simulated. Then further authenticity was added to both projected assault areas by the infiltration of reconnaissance parties and repeated raids.[20]

One of the deception measures adopted was the distribution of documents and newspapers announcing the replacement of Marshal Zhukov by his Chief of Staff, General Vasili Danilovich Sokolovsky, thereby implying that the pressure was off this part of the front.[21]

Nevertheless, the arrival of all this manpower and equipment in the Küstrin bridgehead could hardly pass unnoticed. The 9th Army's daily situation reports of this time mention heavy vehicle traffic in the forward area, river-crossing traffic, attempts to remove minefields and barbed-wire entanglements, reinforcement of artillery in certain areas, even the conduct of ground appreciation exercises by officers using maps.[22]

The Rear Services had the complicated task of delivering the necessary supplies while some of the formations were still deploying. The size of the task is illustrated by the fuel and ammunition requirements to mount "Operation Berlin." There were 85,000 trucks, 5,000 aircraft, 4,000 tanks and 10,000 towing vehicles to supply with fuel, and the planned artillery consumption for the first day alone amounted to 1,197,000 shells out of a total stock pile of 7,147,000. In fact they were to consume 1,236,000 shells on the first day, an amount described as 2,450 railway wagon loads, or 98,000 tons. However, in terms of sets of ammunition per weapon, which was the way supplies were calculated, this was a considerable reduction of stocks from the Vistula-Oder Operation preparations, where from 3.1 to 9.8 sets were available for the various calibers, now only from 2.18 to 2.48 were available.[23]

Zhukov wrote of this:

> The nature of the operation required ammunition to be forwarded from Front dumps to the troops in an unending stream without the usual army and divisional dumps. The railway tracks were converted to the Soviet gauge and ammunition was carried almost to the very Oder. To provide an idea of the scale of these transport operations suffice it to say that if the trains supplying this operation were placed along a straight line one after the other, they would stretch for more than 1,200 kilometres.[24]

In fact the Rear Services regarded themselves as fortunate in having two main railway lines feeding the front at Küstrin and Frankfurt, the first with a capacity of twenty-four train pairs per day, and the second with a capacity of twenty-four to thirty train pairs. There were also four main routes available for supply by road.[25]

As the formations released from the East Pomeranian Operation arrived, a considerable amount of redeployment was necessary in and behind the bridgehead to accommodate them all. For instance, General Stanislaw Poplawski's 1st Polish Army had to redeploy between 8 and 13 April from Greifenburg in Pomerania, where it had been mopping up the coastal area, to Königsberg (Neumark) prior to slotting in between the 61st and 47th Armies on the east bank of the Oder. The 1st Polish Army's task in the forthcoming operation was seen as an opposed river crossing near the railway bridge between Alt Rüdnitz and Zäckerick; but General Poplawski found the river flooded to a width of nearly a kilometer in that sector, and a preliminary reconnaissance in force by the 2nd Polish Infantry Division foundered badly when their boats became stuck on a submerged dike in front of the German guns. He therefore asked Lieutenant General Perkhorovich for room to deploy two of his divisions in the 47th Army's bridgehead, a request later increased to three, and planned his major assault northward from there across the much narrower barrier of the Alte Oder.[26]

In the lineup for the forthcoming battle we find the following concentrations within the bridgehead:

The 47th Army (Karlsbiese-Ortwig sector)
    Eight of its nine divisions, plus three Polish divisions.
The 3rd Shock Army (Ortwig-Letschin sector)
    Six of its nine divisions, plus the 9th Tank Corps.
The 5th Shock Army (Letschin-Golzow sector)
    Eight of its nine divisions, plus the 9th and 12th Guards Tank Corps of
    the 2nd Guards Tank Army.
The 8th Guards Army (Golzow-Podelzig sector)
    All nine divisions, plus its 11th Tank Corps (now under command of
    the 1st Guards Tank Army) and a brigade each from the latter's two
    armored corps.
The 69th Army (Podelzig-Frankfurt sector)
    Seven of its nine divisions.[27]

With forty-one infantry divisions, 2,655 tanks and SPGs, and 8,983 guns and 1,401 rocket launchers, the Küstrin bridgehead was jam-packed full of troops, equipment, ammunition and supplies.[28] Colonel General Katukov of the 1st Guards Tank Army wrote:

> The roads in the 8th Guards Army area were completely full. Everywhere one came across trenches and dugouts. There was equipment and boxes of ammunition under every bush.[29]

In preparation for this coming operation, Colonel General Chuikov, commanding the 8th Guards Army, had a forward command post constructed on the spur overlooking the Oderbruch. The site chosen was at one of the highest points where a sandy cliff laced with young trees faced northwest toward Seelow. The whole area was densely wooded, providing excellent cover from enemy air observation. A jeep track led through the woods from Reitwein village along the northern side of the spur and then up a reentrant, connecting with other tracks from the rear. Slots were dug in the sandy soil to provide shelter for vehicles, signals and security posts, and a large U-shaped bunker tunnelled into the hillside just below the crest. This was about two meters in height and width, the legs being about nineteen meters long and the cross link about fifteen meters. From this command bunker communication trenches led to the observation post on the crest of the cliff. Although observation from this position, the only possible one, would certainly be obscured by distance and the murk of battle, it offered a distinct advantage for radio communication over the battlefield.[30]

To Chuikov's intense annoyance, Marshal Zhukov decided to position his forward command post at the same location, so Chuikov's had to be hastily extended to accommodate the Front Commander and his immediate entourage.

CHAPTER 10

Defense in Depth

A New Defense Philosophy

As a result of their experience with the Vistula-Oder Operation, the OKH made a thorough review of their defense philosophy in preparation for the battle for Berlin. In January the Soviets had been able to destroy both the frontline units and the mobile reserves with their preliminary artillery and air bombardments, eliminating much of the manpower and equipment essential for the conduct of the defense at one stroke. The Soviets had then broken through at high speed with their armored mobile groups to overrun the rear defenses before they could even be manned.[1]

A new philosophy was now evolved that involved the conduct of the defensive battle in considerable depth. This entailed the establishment of three consecutive defensive strips, each of two to three defensive lines. The bulk of the troops would be withdrawn from the forward lines immediately before the main enemy attack and then conduct an attritional battle in the area of the first two defensive strips, thus upsetting the assailant's initial plan of attack. The intent was expressed as being to

pull back the troops, above all the infantry, from the expected massive enemy
    artillery preparation and thus to preserve their fighting capability,
deceive the enemy as to the position and deployment of our own positions,
nullify the basic elements of the enemy's attack and fire plans, and to
    force the enemy into new and costly preparations for attack,
win time.[2]

This new philosophy was recognised by Hitler when he issued an order on 30 March that included the following:

I demand that the army group from commander in chief to the most junior soldier fully understands that the success of the coming battle can only be assured with the keenest defensive spirit and fanatical determination. The battle for Berlin must and will then end in a decisive victory for the defense. In particular I order:

1. The army group is to deploy those units still held back from frontline action to the defense so that sufficient depth can be achieved in every divisional sector.

2. About three to six kilometers behind the present forward edge of the battlefield a main battle line is to be defined and constructed, whose manning will be ordered by the commander in chief immediately before the timing of the enemy's main attack has been identified. On no account is the expected enemy's mass artillery preparation to hit the whole of our defenses.

3. The accelerated incorporation of Home Army and Luftwaffe training units into the eight to ten kilometers behind the forward edge of the battlefield is to be energetically enforced.

4. Commencing immediately, the artillery is to be deployed in such depth that the mass of the batteries can provide blocking fire in the area between the forward edge of the battlefield and the main battle line from positions in and *behind* the second position (eight to ten kilometers behind the forward edge of the battlefield).
    Permanently occupied battery positions are only to be located behind the main battle line. the mass of the flak artillery is to be similarly located in and behind the second position.

5. With the release of the 10th SS Panzer Division to Army Group "Mitte", all motorized units are to be withdrawn as counterattack reserves and hold themselves in preparedness behind the anticipated main points of the enemy attack so that they can counterattack without delay. Their state of readiness is to be repeatedly tested by means of exercises.[3]

Heinrici followed this up with instructions that included the following:

Special attention must be paid to the construction of defensive positions in the rear between the main battle line and the "Wotan-Stellung", the barrier zone and the preparation of bridges for demolition in the rear areas. Any soldier not engaged in combat is to work on the defenses.[4]

A further instruction was issued the next day for the artillery which laid down that every battery should have at least one alternative firing position and two dummy ones, with whose preparation officers from the camouflage service would assist.[5]

However, one aspect of defense philosophy that was not reviewed, although a modification was put into effect on this occasion, was the attitude toward antitank defense that persisted throughout the Second World War. Taking false lessons from their experience with tanks in the First World War, the Germans came to believe that tanks were ineffective once separated from their accompanying infantry. Troops in defense were therefore expected to concentrate on eliminating the accompanying infantry and either ignore or engage the enemy tanks with their close-range weapons, leaving a backstop of antitank guns to destroy any tanks that broke through the forward defences. This severely tested the courage of the frontline infantryman, who, as the war progressed, was encountering ever-growing concentrations of Soviet armored forces designed to smash through all opposition. In this final set-piece battle, although the backstop was still in place, other antitank guns were located as far forward as the foot of the Seelow Heights.[6]

The evacuation of the civilian population from the forward area was begun in February, but all men except for the sick and very old were expected to remain behind and work on the defenses. However, this seems only to have applied to the very forward area, for Lietzen on the "Stein-Stellung," the second line of the Second Defensive Strip, was still fully inhabited when the main Soviet assault began.[7]

Hitler continued to take a keen interest in the defense preparations, and on 4 April he summoned Heinrici to a meeting at which he reviewed the defense measures kilometer by kilometer and issued specific instructions for their improvement.[8]

Preparations for the defensive battle thus involved the construction of a defensive system of up to forty kilometers in depth to include three defensive strips, numerous fortified localities, and barrier zones, all backed by a large number of strong points.[9]

To make up for their deficiencies in manpower and equipment, the Germans concentrated on making the best possible use of the terrain, putting their main effort on the line of the anticipated Soviet main axis along the Küstrin-Berlin highway (Route 1), for the Küstrin bridgehead provided an obvious springboard for a direct drive on Berlin. However, the Soviets would first have to advance across the remainder of the Oderbruch, so to improve upon this obstacle, which was already riddled with streams, canals and irrigation ditches, the waters of an artificial lake some 200 miles upstream were released to flood the valley, turning part of it into a swampy morass and substantially raising the already high subsoil water table overall.[10]

General Busse later wrote:

> Despite the difficulties arising from the lack of cover and the limitations in the construction of positions there was an advantage with this terrain in which ditches and swamps precluded the use of armor. Attacks here could only succeed using great masses of infantry, strong artillery with plentiful ammunition and strong air forces. For the defense it was essential to destroy the attackers without the loss of too much ground. Should this occur and should they not be immediately rejected by local counterattacks, the loss of

such ground, if sustainable, should be permitted, for should the army be forced into a counterattack, there was a danger that lack of success would mean committing the weak reserves too soon in unsuitable terrain. A counterattack with armored forces would only be successful on the heights west of the Oderbruch. This would have to be done by hook or by crook before the enemy could establish himself, for the heights formed the critical point for the Russian armored forces. Their retention or loss, dependent upon the situation and strengths, would decide the result of the coming battle. The army was committed to this policy.[11]

All approaches to the Seelow Heights were mined in depth and covered with artillery and machinegun fire from numerous positions. Antitank ditches were dug three meters deep and up to 3.5 meters wide, and the forward edge of the main north-south irrigation ditch, known variously as the Haupt-Graben and the Seelake, was dug out to make a formidable tank trap. Special attention was given to the preparation of the third line of the First Defensive Strip immediately below the Seelow Heights.[12]

However, the main obstacle to a Soviet breakout from the Küstrin bridgehead was formed by the forward edge of the Seelow Heights escarpment, rising a minimum of thirty meters above the valley bed. Mainly too steep in its inclines for the tanks of that time, and containing some deceptive reentrants and twists of terrain behind which antitank guns could be concealed, it was indeed a formidable natural obstacle. Here the Second Defensive Strip began in considerable depth and then was linked to a Third Defensive Strip behind.

The First Defensive Strip, forming the Forward Combat Zone, was nevertheless still considered an important part of the defensive system. Using the conditions of the terrain to the best advantage, its first line of defense was to be between one and three kilometers deep, with concealed trench systems supported by numerous machinegun nests and other strong points to delay a Soviet advance. With a total depth of from eight to ten kilometers, the First Defensive Strip would enable the effective application of the new defense philosophy once the better positions some six kilometers from the forward edge became engaged. The Frankfurt Fortress with its fortifications, some of which incorporated tank turrets, was considered a powerful bulwark in the First Defensive Strip.[13]

The First Defensive Strip was to be manned by the equivalent of twelve divisions, most of whose troops, it was intended, would be withdrawn at the very last minute into the prepared positions of the second and third defensive lines of the First Defensive Strip and the first defensive line of the Second Defensive Strip.

The Second Defensive Strip, or Second Position, some ten to twenty kilometers behind the forward edge of the battlefield, would form the Main Combat Zone, and was afforded the same importance as the Forward Combat Zone for the first time in the Wehrmacht's defense philosophy. Again, as for the First Defensive Strip, an all-round defensive trench system would be supported by numerous interlocking strong points, in this case utilizing woods, villages and stretches of water, plus man-made abatis and antitank ditches. It also had to accommodate the field and flak artillery resources, part of the antitank resources (another innovation in Wehrmacht defense philosophy) and the reserves, as well as providing a launching position for fast-moving counterattack forces. Its depth and strength were designed to prevent any quick breakthrough from the Tactical Combat Zone as had occurred in the January fighting.

Its forward line, known as the "Hardenberg-Stellung," ran along the edge of the Seelow Heights and the Alte Oder and consisted of between two and three lines of trenches with commanding fields of fire and observation, and included a number of barriers of various kinds. Individual trench sections and artillery firing positions were located on the reverse slopes, which offered them far better cover than those in the Oderbruch. Seelow itself was turned into a strong point with its own battalion-sized garrison to block the highway to Berlin. An antitank belt was formed along the general line Müllrose-Biegen-Treplin-Carzig-Seelow-Gusow-Neu Trebbin, in which the majority of the five flak regiments of the 23rd Flak Division were deployed, with the 53rd and 185th in the Kunersdorf-Quappendorf area, the 7th between Gusow and Dolgelin, and the 35th and 140th concentrated near Schönfliess.[14]

The few approaches leading to the Seelow Heights through the boggy terrain of the Oderbruch enabled the Germans to have their artillery resources concentrate on relatively small target areas. The Heights provided good observation over these approaches while effectively concealing their gun positions on the reverse slopes from the Soviet artillery observers. These circumstances also helped compensate for their severely limited ammunition stocks. The field artillery were also augmented by the flak artillery deployed in the field role while at the same time providing an antiaircraft capability.[15]

In both the First and Second Defensive Strips all command posts, observation posts, gun emplacements and reserve locations were to be developed into strong points with the addition of machinegun emplacements.

The Army Reserve, should there be one, was to be deployed in depth between the "Stein-Stellung" on the second line of defense, which followed a natural fault running through the villages of Diedersdorf and Lietzen, and the third line of defense where the three antitank brigades were arranged in an open "V" along the line Neu Hardenberg/Müncheberg/Heinersdorf astride the anticipated main Soviet axis. The mobile counterattack forces, however, were deployed immediately forward of the "Stein-Stellung," ready to operate on the top of the Seelow Heights between the first and second lines, while the lighter tank-hunting units were initially deployed in the Oderbruch itself.[16]

Between the Second and Third Defensive Strips blocking positions were prepared covering both the Küstrin-Berlin highway (Route 1) and the Frankfurt-Berlin autobahn.[17]

The Third Defensive Strip was to prevent the operational breakout of the Soviet armor by means of a system of antitank barriers and barricades, with which the fire of the artillery, tanks, SPGs and hunting tanks would be coordinated to maximum effect. This was known as the "Wotan-Stellung," and ran along the general line of the western edge of the Scharmützelsee near Buckow and the eastern edge of Fürstenwalde. Because of the lack of defense stores and material for engineer preparation, this line consisted mainly of a chain of fortified towns and villages prepared for all-round defense and linked by barriers and fields of fire. The most important of these fortified locations were Fürstenwalde, Müncheberg, Sternebeck and Eberswalde.[18]

The deployment of antitank resources was of particular importance in the defense plan. These resources had two principal tasks: first of engaging the tanks supporting the Soviet infantry in the main assault, and second, of preventing the deployment and breakthrough of the tanks of the mobile groups into the operational depth. Consequently the antitank resources were deployed up to a depth of forty kilometers, that is, back to the Third Defensive Strip. In the Tactical Combat Area the divisional antitank resources, the artillery, antitank guns, tanks, SPGs and hunter tanks were tightly coordinated in a fire-plan system in which close-range engagement was the primary object.[19]

Manpower

Reinforcements had been found from the meager gleanings of Wehrmacht depots, various odd emergency and guard units provided from OKW resources, some Luftwaffe units, the Volkssturm battalions raised by the Gauleiters of Potsdam, Stettin and other places, and some field units raised by the police, customs and Reichsarbeitsdienst.[20]

General Heinrici had originally counted upon being allocated several armored formations to provide him with a strong counterattack capability should the Soviet armor succeed in breaking through his lines, but at the beginning of March Hitler had ordered an offensive in Hungary to relieve the only remaining oil fields. Temporary success had only been achieved at the cost of the last of the German armored reserves. According to Shtemenko, as early as November 1944 the Stavka had planned this distraction of the German armor to the flanks with the intention of weakening the resistance in front of Berlin.[21]

Lacking armored reserves, Heinrici had then asked for troops of any kind to help bolster his defenses. This request so enraged Hitler that in a tragicomic scene at the Führerbunker on 6 April, Göring, Himmler and Grand Admiral Dönitz hastened to appease their master by offering up all their remaining resources. They would turn out all depots, offices and service installations, dissolve their headquarters establishments and transform into infantry and gunners all those who had been rendered idle by the lack of ships and aircraft, thus producing enough manpower to form several new divisions. Göring promised 100,000 airmen, the SS would find a further 25,000 combatants, and the Kriegsmarine (navy) would send 12,000. However, this grandiose gesture eventually produced only 30,000 men totally unequipped and untrained for the role expected of them, for whom in any case Army Group "Weichsel" could only find 1,000 rifles.[22]

The 9th Army, which was expected to bear the brunt of the Soviet attack, was sent most of the reinforcements and resources available, including this allocation of various training units in an Army Group "Weichsel" document dated 5 April:

1. For the incorporation of personnel replacements and to absorb the Volkssturm units already allocated to the front it is proposed:
    a. 2,100 men of Wehrkreis III's training units' 5,300 to the Vth SS Mountain Corps.
    b. 2,300 men of Wehrkreis III's training units' 5,300 to the XIth SS Panzer Corps.
    c. 2,700 men of the Luftwaffe training units' 8,000 to the CIst Corps.
2. Incorporated personnel to be 75 percent equipped with hand weapons.
3. The remaining training units will be formed into reinforced regimental groups with the corps as corps field replacement regiments, for which the Corps HQs are to provide tactical leadership and ensure support for their training and supplies.
4. The commitment to battle as complete units of the remaining regimental groups is not foreseeable due to the present weapon and radio equipment state.[23]

The flux of units involved included a brief attachment of the 600th (Russian) Division of Lieutenant General Andrey Vlasov's White Russian troops, which had been raised, belatedly and with great reluctance on the part of the Nazi leadership, from anti-Stalinist prisoners of war who regarded themselves primarily as Russian nationalist patriots. The German forces had long used Russian auxiliaries both with and without the consent of the political leadership, but under General Vlasov there was an attempt to organize them formally. However, this particular division was diverted to Prague before the Soviet offensive began.[24]

Manning conditions at this stage of the war were very uneven. Infantry divisions (see Appendix IV for details of the establishment) were supposed to have 7,000-8,000 men, but the 9th Army's combatant strength return for 15 April (see Appendix VI) shows substantially less.[25]

Organization and Strengths

After a considerable amount of last-minute adjustment the 9th Army was finally organized basically as follows when the main offensive began on 16 April 1945.

1. CIst Corps, consisting of the 5th Jäger (Light), 606th and 309th "Gross-Berlin" Infantry Divisions, with the 25th Panzergrenadier Division in reserve.
2. LVIth Panzer Corps, with the 9th Parachute and 20th Panzergrenadier Divisions in the line, the latter backed by the tanks and remaining infantry units of the "Müncheberg" Panzer Division at Seelow.
3. XIth SS Panzer Corps, consisting of the 169th, 303rd "Döberitz" and 712th Infantry Divisions, with the "Kurmark" Panzergrenadier Division in reserve.
4. Vth SS Mountain Corps, consisting of the 286th Infantry and 391st Security Divisions, supported by the 32nd SS "30.Januar" Volunteer Grenadier Division.
5. Army Reserve, consisting of the 156th Infantry Division and Headquarters 541st Volksgrenadier Division commanding the tank-hunting brigades on the "Wotan-Stellung".[26]

The army's artillery came under the direction of Lieutenant General Kurt Kruse and included three Volks artillery corps, which were only slightly larger than a divisional artillery regiment (see Appendix V), the 406th commanded by Colonel Bartels being located near Wriezen, the 408th commanded by Lieutenant Colonel Adams north of Seelow and the 404th commanded by Colonel Vogt south of Seelow. There was also a heavy railway artillery battalion deployed between Seelow, Lietzen and Müncheberg.[27]

The sector of the front covered by the LVIth Panzer and the XIth SS Panzer Corps had the strongest artillery support within the 9th Army, with about 1,222 guns at its disposal, giving forty-five guns per kilometer of front. The German artillery had the advantage of overlooking a meticulously surveyed terrain with numerous aiming marks but, as previously mentioned, suffered from an acute lack of ammunition.[28]

It had been proposed forming a "Weichsel" Tank-Hunting Division from various resources, including a parachute tank-hunting brigade that was located near Müncheberg at the beginning of April and which had a complement of only 600 men, but planned to be increased to 1,000. On 11 April the "Weichsel" Tank-Hunting Division was reported to consist of the "D" ("Dorn"), "F", "P" ("Pirat") and "R" Tank-Hunting Brigades, each of three battalions. However, Headquarters 541st Volksgrenadier Division was given the command of those antitank units subsequently deployed on the "Wotan-Stellung" astride Müncheberg and gave its name to them.[29]

The "P" ("Pirat") Tank-Hunting Brigade together with one of the "D" ("Dorn") Tank-Hunting Brigade's battalions were deployed further back in the Buckow/Strausberg/Alt Landsberg area with the apparent role of engaging any Soviet tanks that broke through to there. The men of these units were equipped with Panzerfausts and Panzerschrecks for close-quarter fighting mainly at anti-tank obstacles and were mounted on bicycles for mobility.[30]

On the eve of the battle the combined strength c[f] the 9th Army approached overall some 200,000 men, with 658 batteries giving a total of 2,625 guns (of which 139 were flak batteries with 695 guns) and 512 operational tanks, SPGs and hunting tanks. The Luftwaffe's 23rd Flak Division included in these figures alone provided a total of 82 batteries between its five motorized regiments.[31]

Air support was provided by the 6th Air Fleet, commanded by Colonel General Ritter von Greim. The Germans still had about 3,000 aircraft available for service over the whole Eastern Front, of which 300 of the 4th Air Division were allocated in support of Army Group "Weichsel," but the scarcity of aviation fuel restricted sorties to the absolute essential and the number of serviceable airfields was also diminishing. Nevertheless, the Luftwaffe were able to acquit themselves well in the forthcoming battle. The Luftwaffe even included a *Kamikaze* unit based on the Japanese example and known as the Special Operations Unit, with thirty-nine volunteer pilots operating out of Jüterbog[32]

Deployment

Before the main battle commences, let us review the German forces deployed in the 9th Army's area in more detail. This deployment was by no means clear-cut, for the Germans appear to have deliberately blurred some of the divisional boundaries by overlapping, presumably in anticipation of the usual Soviet exploitation of such junctures.

Army headquarters were located at Bad Saarow, immediately to the south of Fürstenwalde. The chief of staff was Colonel Hölz, Ia (operations officer) Colonel Hoefer, Quartermaster, Lieutenant Colonel Schwanebeck, and Chief of Artillery, Colonel Schräpler.[33]

On the northern flank, the CIst Corps, whose headquarters staff had come from the Berlin-Brandenburg Wehrkreis III, was commanded by General of Artillery Wilhelm Berlin, with his command post at Schloss Harnekop.[34]

The 5th Light Infantry Division manning the line between the Finow Canal and the Alte Oder was commanded by General Friedrich Sixt with his command post in the Kurhaus at Bad Freienwalde. This was an old, well-tried, traditional South German formation, which bore the distinctive outline of Ulm Cathedral as its tactical emblem. The division had come from Pomerania in tatters and had been replenished west of the Stettiner Haff before taking over its sector along the Oder from some Luftwaffe, Police and Volkssturm units on the 1st April. Two weeks later the division received some combat-experienced reinforcements intended for the 28th Light Infantry Division, which had meanwhile been cut off in the Danzig area, as well as some Luftwaffe training units, whose keen young men, in defiance of Reichs Marshal Göring's specific orders, were absorbed into the division's battalions and were to acquit themselves well.

The division consisted basically of the 56th and 75th Light Infantry Regiments, each of three battalions, and the 5th Artillery Regiment of four battalions. Colonel Haidlen's 56th Light Infantry Regiment was deployed on the division's left north of Neu Glietzen. The Headquarters of Lieutenant Colonel Liebmann's 75th Light Infantry Regiment was at Sonnenburg, west of Alt Gaul, with the 2nd and 1st Battalions manning the line of the Oder from north to south, and the 3rd Battalion, augmented into the so-called "Sparrer" Combat Team commanded by Major Sparrer, in reserve but covering the regiment's southern flank along the Alte Oder. Confusingly, there were also some elements of the 606th Infantry Division in this area that were later to be absorbed by this combat team.

On 12 April the 5th Light Infantry Division repelled several river-crossing attempts near the destroyed railway bridge at Neu Glietzen. Then on 15 April similar attempts by Polish troops further south at the other railway bridge near Zäckerick were also defeated.[35]

The 606th Infantry Division, commanded by Major General Maximilian Rosskopf with his command post in Alt Gaul, was deployed mainly south of the east-west stretch of the Alte Oder in front of Wriezen, covering from Lietzegöricke to Ortwig. This division, with its Austrian headquarters staff, amounted to little more than a hotchpotch collection of odd units, including the 1st SS Guard Battalion of the "Leibstandarte-SS Adolf Hitler," the 3rd Panzer Depot Battalion, the "Brandenburg," "Potsdam" and "Spandau" Ad Hoc Battalions and the Bremen Police Battalion. These were organised into three regiments; Shadow Regiment "A" and the "Sator" and "Rhode" Regiments. Also temporarily under command was the 292nd Army Flak Battalion from the 25th Panzergrenadier Division.[36]

The 309th "Berlin" Infantry Division was under Major General Heinrich Voigtsberger, who had his command post at Neufeld, two kilometers north of Quappendorf, and covered the sector of the front from Ortwig to Zechin. It had been raised at the Döberitz Training Area west of Berlin on 1 February from Berlin-based honor guard and replacement troops and consisted of the "Grossdeutschland" (Field) Guard Regiment and the 365th and 652nd Grenadier Regiments, each of two battalions, the 309th Fusilier Battalion and the 309th Artillery Regiment of only one battalion. The division had recently been reinforced by the 1234th Grenadier Regiment, following the revision of the "Kurmark"'s establishment, together with the 4th and 5th Luftwaffe Training Regiments of the 1st Luftwaffe Training Division.[37]

The Corps Reserve consisted of the 25th Panzergrenadier Division under Lieutenant General Arnold Burmeister, which comprised the 35th and 119th

Panzergrenadier Regiments, each of three battalions, the 5th Panzer Battalion, and the 25th Artillery Regiment. Also available to the CIst Corps as mobile counterattack forces were the 111th SPG Training Brigade, located west of Bad Freienwalde, and the "1001 Nights" Battle Group, located west of Wriezen and led by the Knights' Cross holder SS-Major Blancbois. The latter consisted of the 560th SS Tank-Hunting Battalion (code-named "Soleika"), comprising a headquarters and a supply company, three tank-hunting companies (each with fourteen Hetzers), and four SPG companies, including several recovery tanks, plus the "Speer" Armored Reconnaissance Battalion from the Organisation Todt (code-named "Harem") with a motorcycle infantry company, antiaircraft quadruple machineguns, SPGs and 75mm guns pulled by motor vehicles. As escorting infantry, this combat group had a company from the 600th SS Parachute Battalion.[38]

Headquarters LVIth Panzer Corps under General of Artillery Helmuth Weidling, holder of the Knights' Cross with Oak Leaves and Swords, had only joined the 9th Army on the night of 12-13 April, taking over command of the 9th Parachute, 20th Panzergrenadier and "Müncheberg" Panzer Divisions from the XIth SS Panzer Corps, together with the sector of the front running from Zechin to just north of Sachsendorf at 1530 hours on the 15th. The Chief of Staff, Lieutenant Colonel Theodor von Dufving, and the Ia (operations officer), Major Siegfried Knappe, took over the command post of the Headquarters XXXIXth Panzer Corps at Waldsieversdorf, north of Müncheberg, where their predecessors had been taken out of the 9th Army's Reserve to join the 12th Army being formed east of the Elbe. The new arrivals suffered the disadvantages of being totally unfamiliar with the terrain and having only 50 percent of the field telephone wire and 35 percent of the radio equipment needed for their com-mand function.[39]

The 9th Parachute Division, under Luftwaffe General of Paratroops Bruno Bräuer with his command post in Platkow, covered the corps's northern flank down to exclusive Golzow. This division had been reformed in February from various parachute training and field units and consisted basically of the 25th, 26th and 27th Parachute Regiments, each of three battalions, and the 9th Parachute Artillery Regiment, also of three battalions, although the batteries' guns were down to a ration of only six shells per day. The 25th Regiment had fought in Pomerania, its 1st Battalion stemming from Skorzeny's Special Unit that had fought in the Ardennes, its 2nd Battalion coming from the famous "Brandenburg" Division, and the 3rd Battalion having been formed from fully trained parachutists.[40]

The 20th Panzergrenadier Division had experienced the Polish, French and Russian campaigns but was now considerably reduced in its fighting capacity, having been seriously depleted in the earlier fighting in the Oderbruch, where it had been engaged since the beginning of March. It was commanded by Colonel Georg Scholze with his command post in Gusow and consisted of Colonel

Reinhold Stammerjohann's 76th and Major von Lösecke's 90th Panzergrenadier Regiments, each of three battalions, plus the 8th Panzer Battalion and the 20th Artillery Regiment of three battalions. The 76th Panzergrenadiers stemmed from Hamburg and had been lately reinforced largely from the navy, whose sailors had hastily to be trained as infantrymen in the line. However, by 16 April the battalions of the 90th Regiment were down to about 300 men each, the 76th little better and the divisional fusilier battalion had been lost to the Küstrin garrison in March. Only the integral 8th Panzer Battalion remained subtantially intact.[41]

The "Müncheberg" Panzer Division had been formed in February from various training units and, since its first commitment in March, had been maintained at full strength in manpower and equipment as far as had proved possible. For infantry it had the 1st and 2nd "Müncheberg" Panzergrenadier Regiments, who had lost three battalions in the Alt Bleyen pocket at the end of March, but had since been reconstituted, the 2nd Regiment having been reinforced on 15 April by a new 3rd Battalion formed that day basically from two companies of officer cadets from Potsdam, one of two platoons of Volkssturm and one of Hitlerjugend. This 3rd Battalion was inserted into the line immediately below Seelow but lacked cohesion and was clearly of little military value. Earlier reinforcements received included elements of a "Leibstandarte-SS Adolf Hitler" SS Panzer Battalion and the 1st Battalion of the 1st SS Panzergrenadier Field Replacement Regiment. The armored element consisted of the "Müncheberg" Panzer Regiment of two battalions, the "Müncheberg" Armored Reconnaissance Battalion, and the "Müncheberg" Armored Artillery Regiment of two battalions. The Tank Battalions were equipped with the heavy Mark IVs, Mark V Panthers and Mark VI Tigers, some of those in the 2nd Battalion even having infra-red night sights, an innovation in tank warfare. The commander of this powerful formation was Major General Werner Mummert, who had his command post in Gusow.[42]

Although the 20th Panzergrenadier Division was supposed to have been replaced by the "Müncheberg" Panzer Division on the eve of the Soviet offensive, in fact elements of both divisions were mixed in the line in mutual support in front of Seelow for the main battle, together with a miscellany of odd units packed into the trenches below the town, including survivors from the Küstrin Fortress that had broken through as late as 14 April, and some recently arrived Luftwaffe personnel accredited to the 9th Parachute Division. However, part of the "Müncheberg," including the 2nd Battalion of the Panzer Regiment, was retained in Corps Reserve behind the "Stein-Stellung" near Diedersdorf.[43]

The corps had a mobile counterattack force operating in the Oderbruch in the form of Major Wolfgang Kapp's 920th SPG Training Brigade. There was also the improvised "Berlin" armored train operating out of the cutting south of Seelow station and consisting simply of an engine pulling five flatcars carrying tanks otherwise immobile for lack of fuel.[44]

Seelow had been declared a fortified location and allocated a garrison under a Captain von Wartenburg consisting of the 20th Panzergrenadier Division's Field Replacement Battalion of two companies plus two Volkssturm companies. Second Lieutenant Tams's company manning the forward edge of the town's defenses consisted half of sailors. Here, as a deception measure against the Soviet artillery, the town church spire was deliberately dropped one meter by demolition experts.[45]

Next in line came the XIth SS Panzer Corps under SS-General Mathias Kleinheisterkamp with its headquarters in Heinersdorf. This had a mixed army and Waffen-SS staff, the chief of staff being Colonel Giese, who rapidly transferred to the Waffen-SS when he encountered his commander's hostility to the army's General Staff officers, the Ia (operations officer) Major Thomas, and the Adjutant SS-Lieutenant Colonel Stadelbauer.[46]

The 303rd "Döberitz" Infantry Division, under Colonel Hans-Wolfgang Scheunemann, had its headquarters at Dolgelin railway station and was deployed either side of Sachsendorf. It had been raised at the Döberitz Training Area on 31 January and consisted of the 300th, 301st and 302nd Grenadier Regiments, each of two battalions, and the 303rd Artillery Regiment of four battalions. It too had lost its fusilier battalion to the Küstrin garrison in March. The regiments were deployed with the 300th around Hackenow, the 302nd astride Sachsendorf and the 301st near Werder.[47]

Within the 303rd Infantry Division's lines was Captain Udo Wenzlaff's 1st Battalion of the 26th Flak Regiment, originally the 755th Light Flak Battalion of the Home Defense at Flensburg, which had only been brought into the front line on 13 April. This battalion consisted of four batteries, three of which were equipped with 88mm guns, the 1st Battery deployed behind the Seelow-Frankfurt railway midway between Friedersdorf and Dolgelin, the 2nd Battery on the Heights between Ludwigslust and the Hugohof, and the 4th Battery on the Saumberg. The 3rd Battery, commanded by Captain Wilhelm Raisig, was equipped with 37mm guns and was deployed in a forward position in a field north of the Sachsendorf-Dolgelin road. Apart from a few Wehrmacht NCOs, the majority of this unit consisted of senior schoolboys and polytechnic students below normal military age that had been issued with Luftwaffe paybooks, been sworn in and had had their ranks changed from flak auxiliaries to gunners only three weeks previously, following a brief period of infantry training.[48]

The experienced 169th Infantry Division under Lieutenant General Georg Radziej, with a moose's antler as its symbol, had served in Finland from 1941 until 1944, then in Norway and, after a brief pause in Denmark, arrived in the Oderbruch during March. It consisted of the 378th, 379th and 392nd Grenadier Regiments, each of two battalions, and the 230th Fusilier Battalion. The divisional units all bore the number "230," as did the 230th Artillery Regiment, which had four battalions. Its command post was located in the manor farm at Neu Mahlisch. Since 14 April it had been allocated the 1235th Panzergrenadier

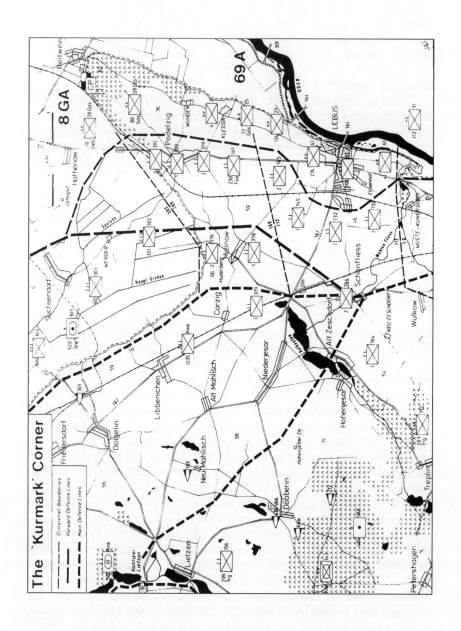

The 'Kurmark' Corner

Regiment of two battalions from the "Kurmark" Panzergrenadier Division as Divisional Reserve, this regiment being located on the escarpment in the Libbenichen-Carzig area.[49]

The 712th Infantry Division under Major General Joachim von Siegroth had been formed from regiments taken from the overexpanded "Kurmark" Panzergrenadier Division on 26 March and consisted of the 732nd and 745th Grenadier Regiments (previously the 1239th and 1241st Grenadier Regiments formed from the pupils and staff of the Dresden and Wetzlar Officer Cadet Schools respectively), and the 764th Grenadier Regiment, each of only two battalions, and the 1712th Artillery Regiment. Its command post was in the woods west of Alt Zeschdorf.[50]

The Corps Reserve, commanded by Colonel Willy Langkeit, consisted of his "Kurmark" Panzergrenadier Division with the 502nd SS Heavy Tank Battalion under SS-Major Hartrampf with its thirty Tiger IIs under command. The "Kurmark" now consisted of the "Kurmark" Panzergrenadier Regiment of two battalions, the "Brandenburg" Panzer Regiment with a battalion each of Panthers and Hetzer hunting tanks, and an armored reconnaissance battalion.[51]

Next came the Frankfurt Fortress with its garrison of about 14,000 troops under Colonel Ernst Biehler, who was to be promoted to Major General during the course of the battle. The Fortress area had only been brought under the command of the 9th Army as late as 10 April. The fifty-square-kilometer area involved included a large bridgehead manned by five so-called fortress regiments of miscellaneous army and Waffen-SS reserve units on the eastern bank extending as far forward as Kunersdorf, and on the western bank extended from the ancient Burgwall hill fort down to the village of Güldendorf (shown as Tzschetzschnow on some contemporary maps).[52]

The southern wing of the 9th Army was formed by the Vth SS Mountain Corps under SS-General Friedrich Jeckeln with his command post in the Heilstatte Müllrose sanatorium in some woods three kilometers southwest of the town.[53]

The 286th Infantry Division under Lieutenant General Emmo von Roden, whose command post was located in Kaisermühl, covered the first sector south of the Frankfurt Fortress down via Brieskow on the Friedrich-Wilhelm Canal to just south of Wiesenau railway station, thus mainly occupying heavily wooded high ground pocked by several large opencast mines between Lossow and Brieskow. The division consisted on paper of the 926th, 927th and 931st Grenadier Regiments, each of two battalions, and the 286th Artillery Regiment of three battalions, plus the 2nd Battalion of the 32nd SS Artillery Regiment. However, these so-called Grenadier Regiments were in fact just collections of odd units, including two Volkssturm and some civil police battalions strung together and consequently of little military worth. In view of this, the rear of the division was bolstered by two combat teams of the Corps Reserve formed from the 32nd SS Tank-Hunting Battalion. SS-Captain Paul Krauss's Combat Team

"Krauss," consisting of the unit's 2nd and 4th Companies, supported by a 250-strong army bicycle-mounted infantry company and a company from the 6th Frankfurt Fortress Regiment, covered the approaches to the Frankfurt-Berlin autobahn on the line Pagram Farm/Lichtenberg/Markendorf/Hohenwalde, a twelve-kilometer stretch that it was expected to hold with twelve combat vehicles and about 350 men. Further back, SS-Lieutenant Emil Schöttle's Combat Team "Schöttle," based on the unit's 1st Company equipped with 75mm SPGs and part of the 3rd Company with towed 75mm antitank guns, was backed by a company each from the divisional fusilier and engineer battalions as infantry. Both teams could call on artillery support from the 2nd Battalion of the 32nd SS Artillery Regiment.[54]

In the center opposite the Aurith bridgehead from the canal down to just north of Fürstenberg was SS-Colonel Hans Kempin's 32nd SS Volunteer "30. Januar" Grenadier Division with his command post at Riessen. This division consisted of the 86th "Schill," 87th "Kurmark" and 88th "Becker" SS Volunteer Grenadier Regiments, each of two battalions, and the 32nd SS Artillery Regiment with its remaining three battalions, each of two batteries. The division was well located, partly in three prepared lines of defense with flat meadowland before it, although that around Wiesenau was obscured by numerous bushes and there were also some patches of woodland near Vogelsang and the power station north of that village.[55]

Last in line was Lieutenant General Rudolf Sieckenius's 391st Security Division covering Fürstenberg and the river line down to the corps's boundary at Wellnitz, with the command post at Bremsdorf. This division consisted of the 95th Grenadier Regiment and the 1233rd Grenadier Regiment (officer cadets and Volkssturm from Potsdam), supported by some miscellaneous artillery and flak batteries. Again the so-called Grenadier Regiment was nothing more than a hotchpotch of various minor units, including Volkssturm.[56]

The remaining Corps Reserve consisted of SS-Captain Jakob Lobmeyer's 561st SS Tank-Hunting Battalion, equipped with the versatile Hetzer as the main combat vehicle, and supported by a maintenance company, a reconnaissance platoon and a platoon of infantry. Its command post was co-located with the Vth SS Mountain Corps's Headquarters at the sanatorium west of Müllrose.[57]

However, the German staff appreciation of the situation in the Vth SS Mountain Corps's sector was that no major Soviet thrust could be expected here, and it was therefore decided on 12 April that the 32nd SS "30. Januar" Grenadier Division would be transferred to the Army Reserve on the 18th, and be stationed behind the XIth SS Panzer Corps as a counterattack force opposite the expected danger point.[58]

Reserves

Two training divisions had been attached to the 9th Army. The sub units of the Luftwaffe training divisions located between Wriezen and Neu Hardenberg were apparently split up among the CIst Corps's formations in accordance with Army Group "Weichsel"'s previously quoted paper of the 5th April, in defiance of Göring's ban on mixing his Luftwaffe students with army units. General Siegfried von Rekowsky's 156th Infantry Training Division was deployed along the 'Stein-Stellung' south of Route 1 with its command post in Marxdorf and consisted of the 1313th, 1314th and 1315th Grenadier Regiments, each of three battalions. The division was manned by recent intakes from the upper and lower age brackets sent into the line to complete their training as a result of Hitler's order of 4 April, in which he had commented:

> So let us put these reserves in the second line, eight kilometres behind the first. Then these formations can get used to the first shock effects of preparatory fire and get used to combat. Should the Russians break through, they will come up against their positions. Then the Panzer Divisions will have to drive them out again.[59]

Just before the battle commenced this formation was renamed the 156th Infantry Division, but clearly was of little military value.[60]

In fact General Busse was relying on the release to him of the OKW's last reserve, the 18th Panzergrenadier Division, when the time came. This division was commanded by Major General Josef Rauch and consisted of the 30th and 51st Panzergrenadier Regiments of two battalions each, part of the 118th Panzer Regiment, and the 18th Artillery Regiment of three battalions.[61]

Morale

In addition to the whip and carrot propaganda methods used by Goebbels on the German population as a whole to maintain morale, the motivation of the troops on the ground included degrees of patriotism, a traditional sense of duty and obedience to orders, belief in the leadership and the Nazi system, but above all fear of falling into Soviet hands. Administrative units of the Nazi Party ensured the maintenance of discipline with draconian measures against anyone suspected of defeatism or cowardice. Allgemeine-SS and military police units covered the rear areas to prevent desertion, while others conducted summary courts-martial, hanging their victims on the roadsides with labels denouncing their crimes.[62]

On 14 April Hitler issued the following Order-of-the-Day, which was to take another two or three days to reach the troops for whom it was intended. It contained references to the fall of Vienna the previous day and the death of President Roosevelt of the United States on 12 April.

Führer's Order-of-the-Day

Soldiers of the Eastern Front!

For the last time our deadly enemies, the Jewish Bolsheviks, have rallied their massive forces for an attack. They intend to destroy Germany and to exterminate our people. Many of you eastern soldiers know well the fate that awaits above all German women and children; the old men and children will be murdered, the women and girls turned into barrackroom whores, and the rest marched off to Siberia.

We have been expecting this attack, and since January this year have done everything possible to build up a strong front. The enemy will be received with massive artillery fire. Gaps in our infantry have been filled by countless new units. Our front is being strengthened with emergency units, newly raised units and Volkssturm.

This time the Bolsheviks will meet the ancient fate of Asia, which means that they will bleed to death before the capital of the German Reich.

Whoever fails in his duty now behaves as a traitor to our people. Any regiment or division that abandons its position will be acting so disgracefully that they will be shamed by the women and children braving the terror of the bombing in our cities.

Above all, be on your guard against those treacherous officers and soldiers, who, in order to preserve their pitiful lives, fight against us in Russian pay, perhaps even wearing German uniform. Anyone ordering you to retreat, unless personally known to you, will be immediately arrested and, if necessary, killed on the spot, no matter what rank he may hold.

If everyone on the Eastern Front does his duty in these coming days and weeks, the last assault of Asia will crumble, just as the invasion by our enemies in the west will fail in the end, despite everything.

Berlin stays German, Vienna will be German again and Europe will never be Russian.

Form yourselves into sworn brotherhoods to defend, not just the empty concept of a Fatherland, but your homes, your wives, your children, and with them our future.

In these hours the whole German nation looks to you, my eastern warriors, and only hopes that by your resolution, your fanaticism, your weapons, and under your leadership, the Bolshevik assault will be drowned in a blood bath.

In this moment, in which fate has removed from the earth the greatest war criminal of all time, will the turning point of the war be decided.

Adolf Hitler[63]

On the evening of 15 April Hitler agreed to General Heinrici's request to withdraw all but a small skeleton force from the forward positions in readiness for the attack expected next day. First light was due at 0530 hours.[64]

For the whole of the Army Group "Weichsel" the ammunition and fuel states were perilously low. There was even a shortage of small arms ammunition, and the artillery had only enough shells for two and a half days' combat. These deficiencies, the weakness of the formations, the obligation not to give ground and the absence of worthwhile reserves, all gave the commanders cause for concern. The sum of all the measures taken for the defense was still inadequate in face of the impending storm, and although the Soviets would have to fight hard to effect a breach in the German defenses, success was only a matter of time. Once the 9th Army had been dislodged there would be no further opportunity for regrouping or avoiding the total and final collapse of the German Armed Forces and the Reich they were seeking to protect.[65]

CHAPTER 11

Orders and Reconnaissance

Zhukov's Conference

Between 5 and 7 April Marshal Zhukov held a conference at his headquarters in a school in Landsberg, which was attended by all his army and corps commanders, heads of arms and services, and their principal staff officers, as well as all the senior Political Department representatives. In a series of planning conferences and war games they discussed and thrashed out the problems of the forthcoming operation, which would involve not only the breakthrough battle but the subsequent taking of Berlin. The photographs taken on eight successive aerial reconnaissance flights over Berlin, captured documents and prisoner of war interrogations were used as an intelligence background, and engineers had prepared a scale model of the city to assist with their deliberations.

Colonel General Katukov of the 1st Guards Tank Army significantly commented:

> A look at the model and maps showed that we would not be able to repeat a variant of a deep breakthrough such as we had achieved between the Vistula and the Oder on this terrain. The conditions for a wide tank maneuver were lacking. With dogged, persistent fighting we would only be able to advance step by step and would have to bite our way through the enemy defences with bloody fighting.
>
> However, the victories of our troops in previous battles had given us much confidence. No one doubted that we would sweep aside the whole of the enemy fortifications on the approaches to Berlin.

The participants were filmed for posterity in their best uniforms with all their medals, as was the Soviet custom, sitting at school desks covered in maps, and then standing around a vast sand model table.

Following this session, Zhukov released his directives to the armies on the 12th with instructions for the commanders to submit their final plans for approval within thirty-six hours. Similar conferences and war gaming were then conducted by the armies down to corps level during the period 8 to 14 April.[1]

Chuikov claims that his 8th Guards Army had published manuals on street fighting and begun training cadres in these skills as early as February, but to what extent this had been exercised in reality and how far it had spread within the remainder of the front, bearing in mind the pressing problems they were subjected to throughout this period, remains open to conjecture. Indeed, from Chuikov's own comments at a later stage of the operation, it is clear that the preparation of the the troops for fighting under the very different circumstances they could expect to encounter in the city was not as thorough as has been claimed, although the recent storming of Posen and other fortified cities should have provided some useful experience in this respect.[2]

Part of Zhukov's overall plan was that surprise was to be attained by beginning the battle in darkness, two hours before sunrise. Illumination of the battlefield and the blinding of the enemy would be achieved at the beginning of the attack by means of 143 searchlights that had been taken from the now redundant Moscow antiaircraft defenses complete with their female crews and spread out over a distance of forty kilometers between the 3rd Shock (20), 5th Shock (36), 8th Guards (51) and 69th (36) Armies. These could also be used to designate axes of advance and boundaries and their light would provide an additional two hours to the time in which the troops had to accomplish their set tasks on the first day. The searchlights had previously been exercised to the satisfaction of the senior commanders in this role, but not in conjunction with an artillery bombardment.[3]

The overall plan envisaged an advance of 165 kilometers to be accomplished in eleven days. This entailed an average rate of advance of eleven to fourteen kilometers per day for the infantry and thirty-five to thirty-seven kilometres per day for the armor.[4] These figures themselves demonstrate some of the the false confidence provided by the success of the Vistula-Oder Operation that was to be reflected in the planning for this Berlin Operation.

Zhukov's Directives

As agreed in Moscow earlier on, Zhukov was intending to use three main assault thrusts to break through the German defenses, one each by the 47th and 3rd Shock Armies, and a strong direct thrust along the main axis by the 5th Shock and 8th Guards Armies acting in unison, while two armies operated on either flank. The allocation of resources released by the Stavka was made in accordance with the tasks given to these armies.[5]

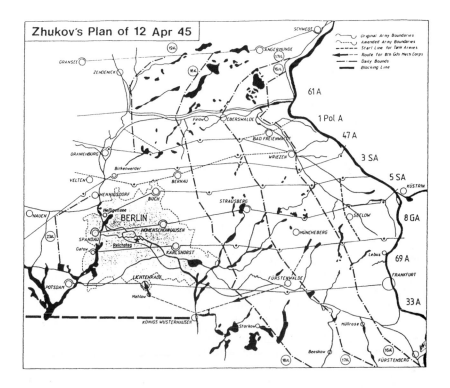

Rather than confuse the reader with a plethora of detail, the bounds and boundaries given in Zhukov's directives are plotted on the accompanying map. The entire concept deserves study, for it clearly reveals some of the premises upon which Zhukov's plans must have been based.

First, the daily bounds indicate that it was generally expected that this operation would be a repeat performance of the Vistula-Oder breakthrough battle, with the German defenses and reserves completely crushed in the opening barrage and onslaught. Thereafter it would be a race first to Berlin and then to the final river line of the Elbe, to be taken and reached by 21 April (D+5) and 1 May respectively, thus making May Day 1945 the most glorious in Soviet history.

Second, the bounds for the main assault group's first day defined as the line Wriezen-Lietzen, with the start line for the two tank armies drawn well before this, indicate that the Soviets had totally misread the German defense both as to layout and intent. Their aerial reconnaissance and intelligence services had failed to produce an accurate assessment of what lay ahead. Consequently, the armor, which was intended to be unleashed on Berlin only after the German defenses had been breached, was plotted in roughly halfway between the first and second lines of the Second Defensive Strip, exactly where the Germans expected to be able to give them a mauling.[6]

Third, Zhukov must have subsequently changed his mind about the fanning operation on the extreme flanks in favor of concentrating his forces within the framework formed by the Hohenzollern and Finow Canals in the north and the Friedrich-Wilhelm Canal in the south, for the front's situation report for 16 April reflects only minor activities outside these water boundaries, and the actual boundaries within which the 1st Polish Army fought vary considerably from those given in the 12 April directives.[7]

Fourth, the plan for the taking of Berlin envisaged the 5th Shock, 8th Guards and 69th Armies sweeping through from east to west, with the 8th Guards Army taking the Reichstag, while the 3rd Shock Army secured the suburbs and area immediately west of the Havel by D+7, and the 47th Army cleared the way to the Elbe. This appears to presume that the task of the main body would be completed with the taking of Berlin. In any case this aspect of the plan bears little resemblance to what was to actually occur.

Finally, Zhukov planned to block off any attempt by Koniev to intervene in the Berlin area by his orders to the 33rd Army to establish a blocking line from Königs Wusterhausen to Brandenburg, thereby cutting across the original boundary eradicated by Stalin that would have had Koniev as close as Potsdam.

These directives were issued under conditions of the greatest secrecy. Only the army commanders, their chiefs of staff, chiefs of the Operations Divisions (deputy chiefs of staff G3), and army artillery commanders were given access to the full directive. Others would only be informed of those areas of the plan necessary for the fulfilment of their specific tasks. The Rear Services and regimental commanders would only receive instructions by word of mouth, the latter not earlier than D-3, and junior officers and the rank and file only be told their tasks two hours beforehand.

Meanwhile all preparations for the operation were to be camouflaged to the utmost and the men told that they were preparing for a lengthy defense of their positions, a necessary precaution should any be taken prisoner beforehand.

The Artillery

In all the detailed planning that applied to this operation, considerable emphasis was given to the role the artillery were to play. The essence of the plan was the early destruction of the German defenses, reserves and will to fight, for which a powerful concentration of artillery was a necessary prerequisite. Recognizing this, Zhukov had taken personal charge of the artillery planning and amassed 14,628 guns and mortars of 76mm caliber and upward, plus 1,531 rocket launchers for the opening barrage and support of the tanks and infantry in the assault to follow.[8]

All this artillery was concentrated in the bridgeheads except for the 69th

Army's Army Artillery Group, which had to remain on the east bank of the Oder because of lack of space in that army's sector. To use the limited space in the bridgeheads to the best advantage, the normal regulatory spacing between pieces was ignored and some battery positions held more than a battalion's worth of guns.[9]

In order to be able to provide commanders from regimental level upward with artillery to call on when required, the arm was organized into regimental artillery groups (RAG) consisting of two to four artillery battalions with 60-80 guns, divisional artillery groups (DAG) consisting of one to three artillery regiments with 130-140 guns, corps artillery groups (CAG) consisting of two to four artillery regiments with 80-120 guns and some M-13 rocket launchers, and army artillery groups (AAG) consisting of four to twelve artillery brigades with about 250 guns.[10]

The additional artillery was allocated to the main assault force as follows:-

> The 47th Army had 1,360 guns and 122 rocket launchers in support, giving 345 to the kilometer.
> The 3rd Shock Army had 1,369 guns and 227 rocket launchers in support, giving 266 to the kilometer.
> The 5th Shock Army had 1,824 guns and 361 rocket launchers in support, giving 312 to the kilometer.
> The 8th Guards Army had 1,911 guns and 368 rocket launchers in support, giving 326 to the kilometer.[11]

Zhukov had accumulated a remarkable overall average of 84 guns per kilometer on the main line of advance and 295 per kilometer at the breakthrough points, plus 92 and 348 rocket launchers respectively, out of the 8,983 guns and 1,401 rocket launchers he had had deployed on the main line of advance.[12]

Targets to be engaged were allocated to the guns according to their range and type, the guns being deployed in depth between one and seven kilometers from the forward edge of the combat area and firing at target ranges of from 1.5 to sixteen kilometers.[13]

In the devastating opening barrage every gun available was to participate, even those of the already-deployed tanks and SPGs, and the guns of the Dnieper Flotilla and the antiaircraft and antitank defenses would also add their weight.[14]

The fire plan approved by Zhukov on 8 April provided for a ten-minute surprise concentration, followed by ten minutes of methodical fire and then another ten minutes of concentrated fire, a thirty-minute opening bombardment that would cover a depth of some ten to twelve kilometers. The attack by the infantry and armor immediately following this would be covered by a double creeping barrage for the first two kilometers and by a single creeping barrage for the next two. Then, for up to eight kilometers, the support would be in the form of successive concentrated barrages. The 8th Guards Army had an additional fifteen-minute barrage written into their fire plan for when its troops approached the line Werbig/Seelow station/Ludwigslust at the foot of the Seelow Heights.

However, as a result of the experience gained during the reconnaissance in force on 14 and 15 April, the set programme for the opening barrage was modified to suit the individual Army's sectors. For instance, in the 47th Army's sector the first phase was reduced to five minutes, giving an overall twenty-five minutes. In the 5th Shock Army's sector, where the reconnaissance in force had achieved the most progress, twenty minutes intensive shelling was to be followed by deliberate shelling with increasing density to a depth of eight kilometers. In the 8th Guards Army's sector, the pattern was altered to five minutes intensive, followed by fifteen minutes deliberate and then a final five minutes intensive shelling. The 8th Guards Army's single rolling barrage was reduced to a depth of 1.6 kilometers, and that of the 5th Shock Army to just one kilometer.[15]

As the attack would commence in darkness with the creeping barrage starting within 150-200 meters of their own troops, particular care had to be given to the laying of the guns, and the laying of fire was then carefully timed from sector to sector. Should the infantry be held up, the creeping barrage would return to the sector concerned.[16]

Colonel General V.I. Kazakov, the Front Artillery Commander, wrote of this:

The engagement of our artillery was preceded by a careful reconnaissance. Alone in the 1st Byelorussian Front's sector 7,000 firing positions and observation posts were deployed together with sixteen independent reconnaissance detachments, two artillery spotter aircraft squadrons and two observation balloon detachments, all for the necessary support of the artillery. Our spotter pilots flew 248 sorties, through which thousands of targets were identified, including 185 gun and mortar positions.

To defeat the enemy the strongest means had to be used, not only to break through the defensive positions but also to enable our infantry, motorized units and armored troops to make a rapid advance with the least losses.

To this end, the commander in chief of our front, Marshal G.K. Zhukov, demanded the substantial reinforcement of the artillery in the sectors of those armies on the main line of attack. The bringing forward of artillery into the sectors of these armies was particularly difficult, for it involved no less than ninety artillery and mortar regiments with 2,000 guns, mortars and rocket launchers (Katyushas), as well as 10,000 trucks and gun tractors being on the move. Road stretches of 200-280 kilometers were set aside for this. All these moves had to be carefully coordinated with the staff of other formations also redeploying their forces.

It so happened that on the instructions of our sector headquarters a further forty artillery and mortar regiments were brought forward by rail, which we also had to guide into their forming-up points. The preparations for the attack were carried out under conditions of great secrecy and carefully camouflaged. By the beginning of the operation our front disposed of about

20,000 guns and mortars of all calibers, including 1,500 rocket launchers. At the breakthrough points on the enemy defenses there were 300 guns and mortars for every kilometer of front. During the Berlin Operation my observation post was furnished with signals equipment like never before. I was in direct contact with the artillery chiefs of the armies, the commanders of the three artillery corps on the main line of advance, the commanders of the artillery divisions and also some lesser units too.[17]

The Armor

In comparison with previous major operations, the Berlin Operation offered very limited space for maneuver for armor. However, here a sharp distinction must be drawn between those tank and SPG units subordinated to the main strike force in the Oderbruch, and those assigned to the mobile groups. Roughly half of all the armor available (1,570 tanks and SPGs) was in the two tank armies or independent tank corps of the mobile groups, and 1,489 in the infantry support role, the latter comprising four tank brigades, seven tank and twenty SPG regiments, plus nine SPG battalions (nineteen tank regiments and sixty-nine SPG battalions).

The 1st Guards Tank Army was allocated Major General Yushtschuk's 11th Tank Corps from the 8th Guards Army, achieving an unprecedented strength of over 854 tanks and SPGs. Colonel General Katukov says that he included street fighting techniques in the preparatory training, for which the recent experience in the taking of Gotenhafen proved useful.[18]

The mobile groups were to exploit the tactical success of the main strike force by taking the attack on to Berlin. Between them the two tank armies had a total of 1,373 tanks and SPGs. Only the 3rd Shock Army had a mobile group of its own with the 9th Tank Corps, whose 197 tanks and SPGs were intended to reinforce its initial thrust in the tactical defense zone and which would then be used to develop the drive to encircle Berlin to the north at high speed in order to reach that army's designated bound west of the city by D+7.[19]

The start lines for the 1st and 2nd Guards Tank Armies were drawn on the roughly north-south line of Letschin/Gusow/Seelow/Dolgelin/Alt Mahlisch, on the presumption that by that point the German defenses would have been irretrievably breached and their tanks could sweep through unhindered to Berlin.

The commanders of the tank armies had different ideas on how to deploy their tanks, the 1st Guards Tank Army being deployed in one echelon and the 2nd in two. The 8th Guards Mechanized Corps on the southern flank of 1st Guards Tank Army had the special task of covering 28th Guards Rifle Corps's flank during the Oderbruch phase and then going on via Fürstenwalde, Neue Mühle (north of Königs Wusterhausen), and Mahlow to penetrate Berlin from the south.[20]

The Infantry

In order to be able to apply maximum weight to the points of attack, the assault units were allocated relatively narrow start lines and breakthrough points on which the supporting guns, mortars, rocket launchers, tanks and SPGs were concentrated. By the end of the first day these units were expected to have pushed through the First and Second Defensive Strips and be preparing to face the Third. In the 4th Guards Rifle Corps (8th Guards Army) for instance, the regimental start lines were only 600-700 meters, so that their battalions would be attacking in successive waves or echelons, followed in turn by the battalions of the regiments in the divisions of the corps's second echelon, and this was the pattern to be found elsewhere among the attacking formations.[21]

The 8th Guards Army had one tank brigade, three tank and seven SPG regiments, amounting to eighteen tank battalions and twenty-one SPG batteries, in direct support. Close cooperation between infantry and armor was ensured by linking each rifle battalion with either a tank company or an SPG battery, further split down to a tank platoon for each rifle company, giving each platoon the cover of an armored vehicle on which to ride or advance behind.[22]

Of Zhukov's seventy-nine infantry divisions, forty-one were concentrated in the Küstrin bridgehead for the initial assault with another four divisions of the 47th and 3rd Shock Armies on the east bank of the Oder ready to be brought across as soon as the others moved forward. The 5th Shock Army had five divisions, the 69th Army eight divisions, and the other armies six divisions each poised for the attack.[23]

The 3rd Army would form the front's second echelon, ready to follow up along the main axis, while the 3rd Guards Cavalry Corps would form the front reserve.[24]

The Air Arm

In addition to the 1st Byelorussian Front's own 16th Air Army, Zhukov had been assigned the 18th Air Army with a heavy bombing capacity and several independent air corps and divisions from the Stavka Reserve to support his operation. For the first three days of the operation he was also given the support of the 2nd Byelorussian Front's 4th Air Army and some of the Baltic Fleet Air Arm. These formations, together with the Polish Composite Air Corps, gave a total of 4,188 combat aircraft, of which the 16th and 18th Air Armies provided 1,567 fighters, 1,562 bombers, 731 ground-attack and 123 reconnaissance aircraft between them.[25]

Marshal A.A. Novikov had been tasked with the coordination of all air activity over the Oder-Neisse theater, that is, for both Zhukov's and Koniev's fronts, from a central headquarters based on the 16th Air Army. He located his command post at the headquarters of the 16th Air Army at Ludwigsruh, some twenty kilometers northeast of Küstrin, where he was also joined by an operations team from the 18th Air Army. An auxiliary headquarters was set up under his deputy some six kilometers from the northern edge of the combat area to supervise the bombing operations, while fighter operations were directed from three special air control centers. The 16th and 18th Air Armies cooperated closely, avoiding confusion over the battlefield by operating at different heights and times. These arrangements enabled them to maintain large forces in the air permanently, with the bombers of the 18th Air Army relieving the 16th Air Army at night.[26]

To accommodate these massive air forces some 290 airfields had to be prepared, the bomber formations of the 18th Air Army being located east of Posen, while the 16th Air Army had 165 airfields allocated so that the fighters were stationed some fifteen to forty kilometers from the battlefield, the ground attack aircraft thirty to fifty kilometers, the day bombers fifty and one hundred kilometers and the night bombers twenty-five to sixty kilometers.[27]

The main tasks of the air arm were first, close cooperation with the main strike force in the breakthrough battle, second, covering the advance of the mobile groups, and third, providing general air cover for the ground forces.[28]

Detailed planning was only made for the first day of the operation in connection with the breakthrough battle. During the opening barrage the night bombers (Po-2 biplanes) of the 16th Air Army would attack headquarters and communications centers in the First and Second Defensive Strips with the aim of disrupting the German command structure. The bulk of the air forces would then join in with the launching of the main attack. First 745 bombers of the 18th Air Army were to attack Letschin, Langsow, Werbig, Seelow, Friedersdorf and Dolgelin between 0407 and 0449 hours, then at daybreak about 1,200 bombers and ground-attack aircraft of the 16th Air Army would attack specific targets in support of the advancing ground forces.[29]

Three options were planned for the 16th Air Army: first, uninterrupted backing of the attacking troops in the Second Defensive Strip to help maintain momentum; second, should the rate of advance not be as fast as expected, attacks on targets in the First Defensive Strip; third, should the pace be faster than expected, attacks on targets further to the rear.[30]

The ground-attack formations were allocated in support of specific ground formations for the breakthrough battle, after which 75 percent of the 16th Air Army was tasked with the support of the tank armies. Katukov says that Major General I.V. Krupski, commanding the air corps in his direct support, actually directed his aircraft from 1st Guards Tank Army's headquarters.[31]

In order to enable continuing air support, the 2nd Guards Tank Army was to seize the German airfields at Alt Friedland, Werneuchen, Eberswalde and Strausberg by D+1 and secure them until relieved by the infantry.[32]

The Air Defense

The air defenses of the 1st Byelorussian Front were provided by the Front's antiaircraft artillery and fighter aircraft and by the 5th Home Air Defense Corps. In all there were four fighter corps, five independent fighter divisions, twelve antiaircraft artillery divisions from the Stavka Reserve, twenty-nine antiaircraft artillery regiments and twenty-two independent antiaircraft artillery battalions, which between them provided 1,567 fighter aircraft, 2,167 guns, 1,463 antiaircraft machineguns and 100 searchlights.[33]

These had the task of providing protection for the Oder crossing points, the troop concentration areas and the combat zone. The majority of the guns (58 percent) were allocated to the main strike force's troop concentration area, but the sixty-ton capacity bridges were also particularly well protected. For instance, the 8th Guards Army had two antiaircraft artillery divisions in direct support, each of one medium and three light regiments, and organized as that army's antiaircraft artillery group with 152 guns in all. These could provide cover with the engagement of up to twenty-four targets up to 3,000 metres and eight targets up to 8,000 metres.[34]

The antiaircraft defenses in the Küstrin-Göritz sector were reinforced by the 82nd Home Air Defense Division, a largely female formation, which arrived between 5 and 14 April with four antiaircraft artillery regiments, one antiaircraft machinegun regiment, one searchlight regiment and four independent antiaircraft artillery battalions. This gave the possibility of simultaneously engaging up to fifty targets at varying heights.

The fighter formations operated under the previously mentioned air control centers and were given set engagement areas, entry points and patrol areas to operate in. A system of ground-air recognition and target identification signals was also established.

It was important that intruding German aircraft be rapidly identified and the relevant antiaircraft resources informed. The 29th Air Signals Battalion provided six radio links to the 16th Air Army for informing the antiaircraft artillery units, but air observer posts with the various ground formations had only field telephones to relay such information.[35]

Morale

The Political Department in all its ramifications was responsible for the morale of the troops.

In the preceding operations the units and formations of the Red Army had suffered heavy casualties, in some cases up to 50 percent of their establishments, and it was imperative to replace them. Troop reinforcements came mainly from the middle of the Soviet Union, but also from the liberated territories and prisoner of war camps. Consequently the composition of the units became very uneven and demanded skillful handling by the political workers.[36]

The distribution of party and Konsomol members, whose numbers had also suffered severely, was reorganized to give a fairly even spread throughout the units and to provide a reserve of political activists to replace future battle casualties. By cross-posting where necessary, a nucleus of eight to twenty full or probationary party members was ensured in every unit of company size. The recruiting campaign for these organizations was remarkably successful, the 1st Byelorussian Front claiming 5,807 granted full and 5,890 granted probationary membership in the Communist Party in March 1945, the figures being 6,849 and 6,413 for the following month. With over 2,000 applications received for party membership on 15 April alone, it seems that many soldiers were anxious to ensure their future under the Soviet regime now that the Great Patriotic War had confirmed its supremacy. Another consideration was that the Red Army did not bother to inform next of kin of one's fate, but the party organizations did.[37]

Behind all this lay a major crisis in morale, which arose out of two principal factors, the exaction of revenge on the Germans for the terrible atrocities that had been committed in the Soviet homeland, and a growing reluctance among individuals to risks their lives in a war clearly about to end victoriously.

Ever since leaving Soviet soil the Russian soldiers had behaved abominably toward the civilian populations they had encountered, committing endless atrocities of murder, rape, looting, arson and willful damage, urged on by an official campaign of revenge put out by the Soviet press and radio. In the forefront of this campaign had been the writer Ilya Ehrenburg, and the soldiers, primitive peasants as most of them were, had responded with enthusiasm. The reason for this policy is uncertain, but it may have been designed to instill sufficient fear into the German population to cause them to abandon voluntarily the territory east of the Oder, and thus facilitate resettlement by the Poles in accordance with the predetermined postwar boundaries, or simply to provide motivation for the Red Army once the sacred task of clearing the enemy out of the Soviet Union had been completed.[38]

The fear that the Red Army inspired, involuntarily assisted by the Germans' own propaganda fomenting hatred of the enemy, was fully justified. In some places overrun by them, every town official and everyone in any kind of uniform, whether policeman, postman, railway employee or forester, was summarily executed. In some cases people were dragged to death behind horses, and there were incidents of the nobility being hunted down with great savagery, some being blinded, mutilated or hacked to death. Rape was widespread, and often accompanied by murder, and in some instances women were rounded up wholesale for use by the soldiers. Even card-carrying members of the Communist Party were not exempt from becoming victims of these outrages.[39]

The unparalleled extent of the devastation and the human suffering arising out of the German invasion of their country, quite apart from the atrocities of Himmler's extermination squads, had given the individual Soviet soldier ample grounds for seeking revenge. Many of them now were released prisoners of war and slave laborers with no love of their former masters.

Then, on 14 April, an officially inspired article in *Pravda*, the official organ of the Communist Party, had criticized Ehrenburg's views, thereby signaling a complete change of policy. From then on revenge against the Nazis and fascists would be pursued remorselessly, but the German people themselves would be wooed into the Soviet fold. However, it was far too late to stop the established trend, the Red Army was unable to accept such a volte-face overnight, and the atrocities were to continue unabated until the fighting was all over and the behavior of the troops could be constrained.[40]

The Political Department decided upon an extraordinary measure to combat the morale problem. This was the reintroduction of the carrying of battalion and regimental colors in battle, before which oath-taking ceremonies would be held at which the soldiers would be sworn to their duty. The standard-bearers were naturally appointed from the party faithful, who as usual were expected to set an example to the others. In addition, specially numbered red banners were issued to the individual armies to symbolize their forthcoming victories, one of which was destined to adorn the Reichstag building.

The carrying of banners into action thus became an unique feature of this battle. However, although the banners provided good propaganda material, they also tended to draw enemy fire, and the initial effect on the fighting troops was soon nullified by the heavy casualties exacted in the first phase of the operation. The reluctance to take risks, later to be camouflaged by somewhat bombastic accounts of minor episodes, was to have a strong influence on the conduct of the operation, despite all these measures.[41]

The Reconnaissance in Force

In order to confuse the Germans as to the impending main axes of attack, the reconnaissance in force ordered by Marshal Zhukov for 14 and 15 April was carried out along the entire front of the 47th to the 33rd Armies. Its intention was to identify the German artillery fire plan, the weaknesses and strengths of the German positions, and the actual forward edge of the German defensive system.[42]

According to Marshal Zhukov it also had another aim:

> It was in our interests to force the Germans to deploy more men and equipment on the forward line so that they would be hit by all the Front's

artillery and mortars during the artillery barrage before the offensive on April 16.[43]

Although not specifically included as an aim, it is clear that the acquisition of additional territory was a vital aspect of this preliminary operation, both to enable the sappers to clear routes through the minefields for the advance and to give more room for the preparatory deployment of units for the assault.

The reconnaissance was carried out by eleven battalions in the 47th Army's sector, six in the 3rd Shock Army's, twelve in the 5th Shock Army's and nine in the 8th Guards Army's. The 69th and 33rd Armies fielded a reinforced company from each of their divisions. The 3rd Shock Army does not appear to have been fully settled in, for it was the 5th Shock Army that fielded six battalions in the former's sector the first day, followed by six from the 3rd Shock Army on the 15th.[44]

Each battalion was generally supported by a company of medium or heavy tanks and a battery of SPGs, either ISU-152s or SU-76Ms, together with artillery and engineer support. During the night of 13-14 April the engineers cleared an enormous quantity of mines, preparing some eighty-seven paths through the minefields for the infantry and armor.[45]

The attack was launched at 0540 hours after a ten- to fifteen-minute artillery barrage on the German first line of defence. The advance was preceded by successive concentrated barrages, while the 8th Guards Army used a creeping barrage one kilometer ahead of its advancing troops. The Dnieper River Flotilla and ground-attack units of the 16th Air Army also added their support.

In the north of the area concerned the 5th Light Division had already repelled some river-crossing attempts by the 61st Army on 12 April, and did the same when the 1st Polish Army tried further south on the 15th, as mentioned in Chapter 10. The 606th Infantry Division held its ground until a second artillery barrage in the afternoon of the 14th shattered its forward positions. A Soviet attack supported by ten tanks reached the northern part of Karlsbiese, and another attack also backed by tanks breached the front line near Gieshof and reached as far as Neu Barnim. Further south the 309th Infantry Division was engaged most of the day but held its ground. In all the CIst Corps reported the destruction of five Soviet tanks that day.[46]

The 9th Parachute Division managed to hold on to their positions either side of Zechin, but at 1600 hours another artillery barrage preceded an attack supported by about eighty tanks and eventually Zechin had to be abandoned and the front line redrawn at Amt Friedrichsaue.

However, the main Soviet effort appears to have been directed at the 20th Panzergrenadier Division occupying the line between Golzow to Alt Tucheband, which received attacks from what appeared to the Germans to be several infantry divisions supported by two armored brigades along the axes of the Küstrin-Seelow highway (Route 1) and the railway line running parallel to it. The defense was ably supported by elements of Major Kapp's 920th SPG Training Brigade and the division was able to hold its ground all morning, although at some cost in manpower. The attacks were resumed in the afternoon after a thirty-minute bombardment, and this time the Soviet infantry, supported by sixty-five tanks, broke through as far as the southwestern corner of Golzow, then swung north to surround and take the village, although determined efforts by German tanks and SPGs prevented any further advance to the west. Another Soviet attack passing north of Golzow in conjunction with a thrust from the Genschmarer See area resulted in one of the 90th Panzergrenadier Regiment's battalions being cut off and virtually annihilated. The Soviets then launched an attack northwestward out of Golzow in support of the attacks on the 9th Parachute Division, which resulted in the 26th Parachute Regiment being forced out of Zechin and Amt Friedrichsaue back to Buschdorf by the evening. All subsequent attempts by the Germans to regain the Zechin salient failed.[47]

At the end of the day the "Müncheberg" Panzer Division was taken out of Army Reserve to support the badly mauled 20th Panzergrenadier Division, which was thought incapable of withstanding the main Soviet offensive expected on Seelow.[48]

Sergeant Averdieck described the events of the day:

> The bombardment starting at 0700 hours on the 14th April introduced the last phase of the war on the Eastern Front. The initial enemy attacks were all beaten back, the 76th Regiment shooting up twelve tanks, and by midday some small breaches in our lines had been eliminated. However, our own counterattack failed in the face of the second Russian bombardment, which was reinforced by simultaneous heavy air attacks. The companies fled back, naturally thereby incurring heavy casualties. They then occupied the main battle line about 200 meters in front of the Annahof. The Soviets could be seen hitting our surviving wounded with spades. At dusk the enemy closed in and the Annahof came under the fire of artillery, rockets and heavy weapons. We withdrew during the night and occupied the lines on the Seelow Heights above Werbig, in which we spent yet another quiet Sunday (15 April) under occasional disruptive fire. We had a magnificent view over the Oderbruch from these heights, except when the fumes of the explosions made everything hazy. I spent the night with my driver in a small, exceptionally weak bunker.[49]

The attacks on the 303rd Infantry Division in the valley bottom appeared to the Germans to involve three Soviet infantry divisions and an armored brigade. The German forward positions in the village of Alt Tucheband on the left flank were lost, as was the Hathenow Lehngut manor farm, 1,500 meters west of Hathenow on the right flank. The Soviets were able to push on with armored support as far as the Sachsendorf home farm before part of the 920th SPG Training Brigade deployed in a successful counterattack that cleared the village.

Further south on the Seelow Heights the 169th Infantry Division repelled several attacks supported by tanks along the line of the Reitwein-Podelzig railway. The neighboring 712th Infantry Division also held its ground against attacks along the whole of its front. A small breach west of Elisenberg was later cleared. The division claimed the destruction of eight Soviet tanks and counted 500 enemy dead.

Altogether that day the XIth SS Panzer Corps claimed eighty-one Soviet tanks destroyed and a further six immobilised, of which thirty-six and three respectively were attributed to Major Kapp's 920th SPG Training Brigade alone. The opening ninety minutes of artillery fire that morning had caused the Corps Reserve, consisting of the "Kurmark" Panzergrenadier Division and the 502nd SS Heavy Tank Battalion to be placed on alert, but their deployment did not prove necessary.

The Frankfurt Garrison too came under attack on the east bank of the Oder, where its defenses projected about three kilometers toward Kunersdorf, although apparently without serious intent other than to pin down the defenses.

South of Frankfurt in the Vth SS Mountain Corps's sector, strong Soviet artillery fire had fallen on the forward positions of the 32nd SS "30. Januar" Grenadier and 286th Infantry Divisions at dawn. This preceded six attacks of about battalion strength supported by ten tanks, flamethrowers and ground-attack aircraft. The latter appeared to be searching out the German artillery positions, attacking those antiaircraft guns that opposed them.

The 286th Infantry Division on the northern flank came under attack on its right wing in the valley bottom but held its ground. Next to it the 32nd SS "30. Januar" Grenadier Division repelled the Soviet attacks in the Ziltendorf-Vogelsang area, but a breach in the 87th Grenadier Regiment's lines took until the evening to clear, during the course of which a Soviet SPG was destroyed.

Throughout the day the 9th Army was provided with support from aircraft operating out of the Finow, Werneuchen, Strausberg, Eggersdorf, Fürstenwalde, Schönefeld and Oranienburg airfields.

A note on a telephone conversation between Lieutenant Colonel de Maizière and Colonel Hans-Georg Eismann at 1815 hours that day reads:

> The 9th Army is of the opinion that one must expect the main attack to take place tomorrow and has ordered the forward battle line to be drawn from Sachsendorf to southeast of Letschin. At the same time the "Müncheberg" Panzer Division is to enter the line and the 20th Panzergrenadier Division withdrawn as, according to the report of the general officer commanding the XIth SS Corps, as a result of today's fighting the 20th Panzergrenadier Division is no longer able to withstand a strong attack.[50]

General Busse later recorded:

On 14 April the enemy continued his attack with increased strength the whole extent of the line down to Lebus. The right wing of the XIth SS Panzer Corps [712th and 169th Divisions] rejected all attacks with heavy loss to the enemy. In the other sectors of the corps the enemy penetrated as far as the second line. Near Seelow such a crisis arose that the "Kurmark" Panzergrenadier Division had to be thrown into the fight to stop them from getting too far. Unfortunately they could not be evicted that evening. In the CIst Corps's sector the enemy advanced more than five kilometers toward Wriezen. The bridgehead in this sector thus achieved a depth of fifteen kilometers and was fully adequate for the deployment of strong forces. Losses in men and material were high on both sides, and ours could not be replaced, a serious matter. Concerned about this, that evening Army HQ again appealed for the 18th Panzergrenadier Division and the two Panzergrenadier brigades, but without success.[51]

However, Zhukov was not satisfied with the results of the 14th and for the next day ordered reinforcement of the units involved in the reconnaissance in force. For instance, in the 5th Shock Army's sector eight rifle regiments from the first echelon, a tank brigade and three independent tank regiments were committed with the support of five mortar brigades, three independent mortar regiments, seven artillery brigades, a heavy artillery battalion and three field and howitzer battalions, as well as some boats of the Dnieper River Flotilla.[52]

The 9th Army's situation report for that day describes events as follows:

Daily Situation Report

HQ 9th Army   15 Apr 45

The enemy did not start his offensive today as expected.

No noteworthy combat occurred in the sectors of the Vth SS Mountain and XIth SS Panzer Corps, presumably because of the enemy's previous high losses in men and equipment.

Against the CIst Corps's front the enemy conducted some uncoordinated attacks supported by a few tanks, which although causing some trouble east of Letschin and west of Ortwig, brought little local success.

In detail:

In the Vth SS Mountain Corps's sector there was an unsuccessful enemy attack of company size near Wiesenau. The clearing of the enemy from a small sector of trenches northwest of Wiesenau has yet to be completed.

Infantrywise, it was a quiet day in the Frankfurt Fortress area.

In the XIth SS Panzer Corps's sector, an enemy attack of battalion size took place against the 712th Infantry Division's forward positions near Elisenberg and down the Lebus-Schönfliess road, which was beaten back with a counterattack. The 169th Infantry Division rejected company-sized enemy attacks northeast and north of Podelzig, eliminating the breaches;

however, the farm 500 meters south of the Vorwerk Podelzig [500 meters north of Podelzig station] could not be retaken by our troops because of the fierce resistance put up by the enemy.

The forward positions on the right flank of the 303rd Infantry Division were pushed back to the Seelake stream.

The LVIth Panzer Corps, which took over command of the "Müncheberg" Panzer, 9th Parachute and 20th Panzergrenadier Divisions at 1530 hours, had to regain the forward positions in the "Müncheberg" Division's area.[53] Several unsuccessful enemy attacks of company size took place against the 9th Parachute Division's front. Countermeasures are in progress to eliminate a local breach. After some initial success our attack to regain Zechin fell through against fierce enemy resistance.

In the CIst Corps's sector the enemy attacked the front of the 309th Infantry Division with two divisions after a strong preparatory bombardment with the main thrust east and north-east of Letschin, as well as west of Kienitz. Following the successful breach west of the Freigut and Jesar-Graben ditch, an enemy regimental group with armoured support reached as far as the farmsteads 500 meters east of the Letschin rifle range. A simultaneous attack of regimental strength from Rehfeld was stopped by our artillery fire. An enemy force of two battalions and six tanks that had broken through west of Amt Kienitz was eliminated. The Vossberg sugar factory, which had been lost at about 1300 hours, was regained by counterattack. The 606th Infantry Division cleared the enemy out of the southern part of Ortwig and prevented a further enemy thrust northwest of Neu Barnim with a counterattack. Near Karlsbiese several enemy attacks of battalion size were driven back.

The 5th Light Infantry Division defeated an enemy attempt to cross near Zäckerick, destroying nine boats.

Our artillery brought lively disruptive fire and effective barrages to bear at night on enemy assembly areas and breaches, and by day supported our infantry's defensive fighting.

The Luftwaffe flew combat missions over the Oder bridges and attacked infantry concentrations and tanks to effect. Three tanks were destroyed.

The enemy air force attacked our front line with ground-attack aircraft and fighters, dropping bombs and machinegunning.[54]

On the central sector advances of from two to four, even five kilometers had thus been made during the course of the 15th, but neither the 69th nor the 33rd Armies had achieved anything that day. Nevertheless, the general results of this two-day reconnaissance in force had proved satisfactory. The basic bridgehead had been widened giving more space in which to deploy and some practice had been gained in liaison in combat between the newly grouped formations involved. The engineers continued to work frantically, clearing paths through the minefields laid by both sides that littered the valley bed, and ensured that two approach routes to the start lines were available for every armored corps.[55]

However, according to General Telegin, Member of the Military Council of the 1st Byelorussian Front, despite all the reconnaissance effort, resources and radio interception facilities available, it had still not been possible to plot the German defensive system accurately.[56]

On the evening of 15 April Hitler agreed to General Heinrici's request to pull back all but a skeleton holding force to the main defensive position in readiness for the attack expected next morning. First light was due at 0530 hours.[57]

PART IV

The Big Battle

CHAPTER 12

First Day of Battle

Let Battle Commence!

During the early hours of the night of 15-16 April, as the German forces withdrew from their forward positions where they could and prepared for the coming onslaught, the Soviet commanders ha.tily revised their operational plans in the light of the territorial gains of the past two days, while 330 night bombers of the 2nd Byelorussian Front's 4th Air Army attacked targets on their neighbor Zhukov's main axis.[1]

Then at 0120 hours, just two hours before they were due to attack, the battalion commanders and their officers were briefed on their forthcoming tasks. At the same time the political workers assembled the troops and read out to them their Military Council's appeal to all ranks of the 1st Byelorussian Front, signed by both Marshal Zhukov and Lieutenant General Konstantin Telegin, his Political Commissar. This exhortation contained the significant paragraph:

> Our victory flags wave over hundreds of towns and thousands of villages. We have freed millions of Soviet citizens from the fascist yoke. With our victories, but also with our blood, we have won the right to storm Berlin and be the first to enter the city. We shall [be the ones to] pronounce our people's strong condemnation over its German occupants.[2]

The political workers then went on with the oath-swearing ceremonies over the battle flags they had brought into the trenches with them, during which the soldiers committed themselves to perform their duty in the forthcoming battle.

Marshal Zhukov arrived at Colonel General Chuikov's headquarters shortly before 0300 hours and went to the observation post prepared for him with his senior staff officers. On his way from his headquarters in Landsberg, Zhukov had visited several command posts and was pleased with the state of preparedness shown.[3]

Promptly at 0300 hours the artillery barrage opened in unprecedented intensity. At the dispatching end, Chuikov described it:

> The second hand on the Front Commander's watch completed its sweep, and in an instant it became light as day. In the flashes of artillery fire we saw the unfurled Guards colours moving forward along the trenches to the assault positions.
> A volcanic rumble resounded as 40,000 guns began to fire. The Oder valley seemed to rock. Fountains of dust and smoke shot up into the air.[4]

The Front Artillery Commander, Colonel General Kazakov, wrote:

> On 16 April at 0500 hours Moscow Time a mighty salvo from our massed artillery ripped through the silence of the night, announcing the beginning of the artillery preparation for the attack on Berlin. It was an eerie picture, as along the whole front the muzzle-flashes of tens of thousands of guns and the flashes of exploding shells burst into light. Particularly effective were the Katyusha rocket salvos. The basic power of this spectacle, which was much more frightening by night than by day, left an indelible impression on us old gunners.[5]

At the receiving end Second Lieutenant Tams, on the forward edge of Seelow's defences, recounted:

> At 0300 hours on the morning of 16 April 1945 40,000 guns opened fire simultaneously. It seemed as if the dawn were suddenly upon us and then vanished again. The whole Oder valley bed shook. 40,000, a total known today, amounting to 333 to the kilometer. In the bridgehead it was as light as day. The hurricane of fire reached out to the Seelow Heights. It seemed as if the earth were reaching up into the sky like a dense wall. Everything around us started dancing, rattling about. Whatever was not securely fastened down fell from the shelves and cupboards. Pictures fell off the walls and crashed to the floor. Glass splinters jumped out of window frames. We were soon covered in sand, dirt and glass splinters. None of us had experienced anything like it before, and would not have believed it possible. There was no escape. The greatest concentration of artillery fire in history was directed immediately in front of us. We had the impression that every square yard of earth would be ploughed up.[6]

Another account comes from Gerd Wagner, who wrote:

> I, then a section leader in the 10th Company, 27th Parachute Regiment, had left the forward positions with my men in accordance with my orders only minutes before the opening bombardment to await it about a kilometer away near Gusow. Within a few seconds all the ten comrades of my section had

fallen, and I found myself in a still smoking shell hole, wounded, a fact that I did not notice until I reached the second line. As far as the eye could see were burning farms, villages, smoke and clouds of fumes. An inferno.[7]

And Friedhelm Schöneck, who was with the 309th Infantry Division at Sietzing, recounted:

It is 3 o'clock but still night. The night has gone mad. An ear-deafening din fills the air. In contrast to what we have experienced previously, this is no bombardment but a hurricane tearing apart everything in front of us, over us and behind us. The sky is glowing red as if it will crack open at any moment. The ground rocks, heaves and sways like a ship in a Force 10 gale. We crouch down in our defensive positions, our hands grasping our weapons in deadly fear, and our bodies shrunken into tiny crouching heaps at the bottom of the trench.

The bursting and howling of the shells, the whistling and hissing of schrapnel fills the air or what remains of it for us to breathe. Screams and orders are choked by steel, earth and the acrid smoke of the volcano that has suddenly opened up on top of us with incredible force.

One would like to be a mole and dig oneself in a flash into the protective earth, would like to find a solution in nothingness, but we lie as naked as earth-worms on a flat surface, exposed to a pitiless trampling, defenseless and without hope.

The infernal drumming continues. Into the middle of it dash hurtling furies, aircraft rushing in to attack right over our positions to complete the mad stirring of the whirling, bubbling witches' cauldron we find ourselves in.

Our trench system has disappeared, collapsed or been flattened by thousands of shells and bombs. The dugout we are sitting in has become even narrower, the walls driven inward, packing us together like sardines in a tin can. We tremble and pray, the beads of rosaries slipping through soldiers' dirty hands. We have lost all shame. Dear God, hear us calling to you from this hell! Kyrie eleison![8]

At 0320 hours the searchlights were switched as a signal for the advance to begin, and five minutes later the artillery switched to a double rolling barrage to precede the advance. However, the opening barrage had raised such a towering cloud of smoke, dust and debris that in many places the searchlights were unable to penetrate the murk, and where they were able to operate as expected they both caused night blindness among their own troops and attracted German fire. The Soviet infantry also felt exposed, silhouetted against the light as they advanced, for they had not practised this technique. All this caused considerable confusion on the ground. Requests from forward units for the lights to be switched off were promptly countermanded by the orders of superiors. In the end many units stayed where they were until daylight enabled them to find their way forward.

This was not how their front commander saw it:

The Nazi troops were virtually swamped in a sea of fire and metal. A thick wall of dust and smoke hung in the air, and in places even the powerful anti-aircraft searchlights were unable to penetrate it, but this troubled no one.[9]

However, we get a slightly different picture from Chuikov:

In the zone of the 8th Guards Army the glow of the artillery was so bright that from my command post we missed the moment when the searchlights were switched on. The Front Commander and I even asked what had happened, and were surprised to hear that the searchlights were already on.

I must say that though we admired the effect of the searchlights on the testing ground, we could not foresee how the ploy would work in practice on the battlefield. I saw the intense beams lighting up the swirling screen of fumes, dust and smoke whipping up over the enemy positions. The search-lights did not penetrate this screen, and it was difficult for us to watch the battle. To make it worse, there was a strong head wind. As a result, an impenetrable cloud of dust soon enveloped Height 81.5 where I had my command post. Visibility was down to nil and we had to rely on radio-telephone communications and liaison officers in exercising troop control.

The dense cloud of smoke and dust also handicapped the actions of the advancing troops.[10]

The devastation caused to the terrain by this tremendous bombardment must also have created considerable problems for the troops and vehicles having to cross it.

As this was going on, 743 heavy bombers of the 18th Air Army joined in the attack, bombing Letschin, Langsow, Werbig, Seelow, Friedersdorf and Dolgelin in the first two defensive strips with 884 tons of bombs, including phosphor and delayed-action types. They were relieved at daybreak by aircraft of the 16th Air Army, but these encountered some difficulties, for many of their airfields were fogbound and visibility was so poor over the battlefield as a result of the barrage that they were unable to find their designated targets and had to be switched to opportunity targets.[11]

One of these raids caught an ammunition train near Fürstenwalde, destroy-ing seventeen wagons containing a precious load of about 7,000 howitzer shells. During the course of the day the 8th Battery of the 100th Railway Artillery Battalion also lost all three of its huge 280mm guns deployed in the Seelow-Müncheberg area to air attack.[12]

For the infantry and their supporting tanks and SPGs the attack had got off to a faulty start, and Chuikov goes on to recount:

During the first thirty minutes of the offensive there was hardly any fire from the enemy whose command and observation posts and firing positions had been destroyed by our shelling and air force. Only a few machine-guns and artillery pieces sheltered in stone buildings and trenches responded to our fire.[13]

Although the progress of the 8th Guards Army was the most notable feature of the action, for that is where Zhukov's interest was mainly focused, we shall now turn our attention to the progress of the various formations in turn.

The Northern Flank

The 61st Army continued what now appeared to be little more than a deception plan by sending two reinforced rifle companies from the 80th Rifle Corps across the Oder on so-called reconnaissance missions which reached as far as the dikes on the west bank, one to near Niederkrönig, some three kilometers southeast of Schwedt, and the other to Niedersaaten.

The army's main effort of the day was to get two rifle battalions from the 89th Rifle Corps across the Oder either side of the combined rail and road bridge between Hohenwutzen and Neu Glietzen. Here they came up against Colonel Haidlen's 56th Light Infantry Regiment, which managed to force the northern battalion back across the river and to contain the other battalion's bridgehead to the eastern edge of Neu Glietzen. The 61st Army only claim was to have killed 150 German troops while, as usual with Soviet accounts, not stating its own losses, although the CIst Corps could claim having destroyed forty-one Soviet boats that day.[14]

The 1st Polish Army's operation began at 0415 hours when the 4th and 5th Regiments of the 2nd Polish Infantry Division joined the 3rd Division in effecting a northbound crossing of the Alte Oder from the 47th Army's part of the bridgehead opposite Güstebiese. At 0645 hours the remaining 6th Regiment of the 2nd Division crossed the Oder south of Alt Lietzegöricke and established a bridgehead on the west bank, then attacked southward to try and link up with the 5th Regiment. It was then reinforced at 1200 hours by the 2nd Division's training battalion.

The 1st Division's operation began at 0830 hours with the 2nd Regiment establishing another bridgehead across the Oder some 500 meters wide just south of the railway bridge, and repelling all German attempts to drive it back. This was followed by the 1st Regiment's crossing at 1500 hours with the assistance of the Soviet 274th Amphibious Vehicle Battalion and establishing another small bridgehead a bit further south opposite Zäckerick, again after some fierce fighting. Then at 1645 hours it was joined by the 3rd Regiment, enabling the division to go on to expand and connect its bridgeheads.

The 1st Division was later joined by the 6th Division from the second echelon, which began crossing at 1800 hours when the commander of the 1st Polish Army, General Stanislaw Poplawsi, became concerned about his right

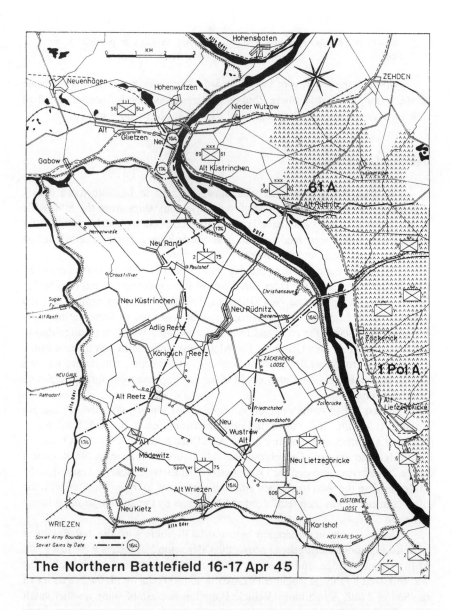

The Northern Battlefield 16-17 Apr 45

flank as a result of the 61st Army's failure to make any significant progress.

By 1700 hours units of the 1st Division had reached and taken the railway line near the hamlet of Binnenwerder, about a kilometer from the Oder, while units of the 2nd Division had occupied the hamlet of Zäckericker Loose and the village of Neu Lietzegöricke. The 3rd Division advanced on the main axis with the 4th Polish Tank Regiment. The 13th Polish SPG Regiment took Karlshof after a fierce fight and came up to Alt Wüstrow. Thus on this first day the 1st Polish Army had succeeded in crossing the Oder and smashing the German first and second lines of defense north of the Alte Oder, reaching the line of the railway bridge/Zäckericker Loose/300 meters west of Neu Lietzegöricke/eastern edge Alt Wriezen. In this fighting the 1st Polish Army claimed the destruction of four artillery batteries, seven mortars, thirty machineguns and fifteen vehicles, 500 German soldiers killed and twenty-three captured.

The 1st Battalion of the 75th Light Infantry Regiment on the 5th Light Division's right front had earlier rejected all attempts to effect a crossing near the hamlet of Zollbrücke, but when the Poles succeeded in establishing a small bridgehead opposite Zäckerick, thus threatening to cut the Germans off, the battalion was obliged to fall back. Meanwhile the "Sparrer" Combat Team continued to support those elements of the 606th Infantry Division in that area with combined counterattacks and flanking fire.[15]

However, the experiences of Lieutenant Erich Hachtel give some idea of the confusion that reigned behind the German lines that morning. As commander of the heavy weapons company (150mm howitzers and 120mm mortars) of the 75th Light Infantry Regiment, he had his command post close to the regimental command post in Königlich Reetz. He writes:

At 0930 hours I was summoned to the regimental command post. Lieutenant Colonel Liebmann turned to me: "Mr Hachtel, have you contact with the front?" I replied in the negative, adding that I had had no contact since 0900 hours. I discovered that the regiment also no longer had contact with the 1st Battalion and so no one knew exactly what was happening. Lieutenant Colonel Liebmann looked at me and said: "Take your tracked motorcycle combination forward, make contact with the 1st Battalion and report back to me what it looks like up front." With this task I raced first south to a dike and then along this to the 'Oder-Stellung' near Neu Lietzegöricke. Soldiers lying in their holes on the left side of the dike looked at us in amazement. We had driven along the front line and the area around us with its shell holes reminded one of a moon landscape. They must have been soldiers of the 3rd Battalion under its commander, Major Sparrer, who with his unit was known as "Combat Group Sparrer."

We reached the shattered village of Neu Lietzegöricke and found the command post of the 1st Battalion of the 75th Light Infantry Regiment on a big square in the middle of the village. The battalion commander reported that everything in his sector was in order and firmly in our hands. A breach in his 1st Company's sector had been cleared and the assailants driven back into the Oder with cold steel. As I then learned, they had been members of a Polish division, as one could tell from the dead left behind. With this message on as yet positive progress in the fighting, I returned to the regimental staff.

I then made my way to the left flank of our regiment to look at my platoon's firing positions. I drove alone on a motorcycle via Neu Ranft and then eastward along an arrow-straight road leading to Neu Küstrinchen. Suddenly

Russian aircraft appeared in the sky and attacked the convoy I was overtaking on the road. I saw how the machines wheeled to come over our road one after another, raking the road with their armament. People jumped madly aside seeking cover, horses broke loose, rearing up to collapse or gallop off the road with their wagons. I saw this distressing sight and accelerated away, seeing no other possibility of getting out of this mess. Once more I was lucky and so came to our firing positions safe and sound. Second Lieutenant Vogel came up to me straight away and reported that everything was in excellent order, being very pleased with our results. My visit to the observation post confirmed this. When I was about to leave, I noticed that my motorcycle had received two hits but, thank God, was still mobile!

So all attacks were repelled in our sector of the Oder and our front line remained firmly in our hands, although the situation to the south with our right-hand neighbor, the 606th Infantry Division, was threatening. Strong Russian tank units had broken through there, increasing the pressure already coming from the Küstrin area. Our 3rd Battalion under Major Sparrer's command was facing south and had to secure our right flank. This battalion was really meant as a reserve, but through the dangerous, obscure situation with our right-hand neighbor, the 606th Infantry Division, the battalion came to experience the enemy's full pressure and thus, with its attached elements, had to bear the main burden as Combat Team "Sparrer".[16]

By evening the situation here was judged sufficiently serious for the 2nd Company of the 111th SPG Training Brigade to be detached from the CIst Corps's reserve located west of Bad Freienwalde and sent to the support of the troops fighting north of the Alte Oder.[17]

The 47th Army

Lieutenant General F.I. Perkhorovich had managed to squeeze eight of the 47th Army's nine rifle divisions into his section of the bridgehead, as well as three divisions of the 1st Polish Army, and five of these were in the first echelon. His deployment from north to south ran as follows:

First Echelon	Second Echelon
77th Rifle Corps	
260th Rifle Division	328th Rifle Division
125th Rifle Corps	
60th Rifle Division	
175th Rifle Division	76th Rifle Division
129th Rifle Corps	
143rd Rifle Division	
82nd Rifle Division	132nd Rifle Division
Army Reserve	
	185th Rifle Division

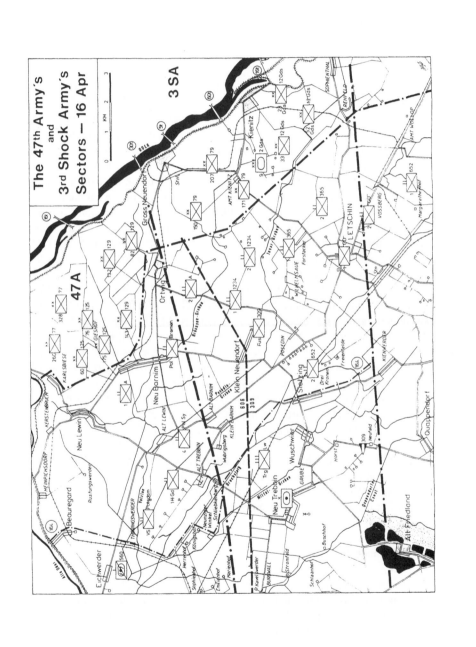

The 47th Army's
and
3rd Shock Army's
Sectors — 16 Apr

0 1 2 3 KM

47 A

3 SA

In direct support he also had one heavy tank, one heavy SPG and three other SPG regiments deployed on the ground.

The 47th Army was involved in heavy fighting all day with the mixed bag of German troops confronting it, for the line of advance was barred by a series of water obstacles, each in turn lending itself to the defense. Although the 47th Army failed to reach its objective of the line Wriezen-Kunersdorf, nevertheless this first day saw the end of the 606th Infantry Division as a viable fighting formation.

The village of Alt Lewin changed hands several times in the heavy fighting, with counterattacks being mounted by the 1st SS Guard Battalion and the 4th SS Police Security Battalion. The 292nd Army Flak Battalion, temporarily detached from the 25th Panzergrenadier Division, was in action all morning in support of a Luftwaffe officer cadet regiment outside Neu Trebbin but, after three hours of strafing by ground-attack aircraft, withdrew to new positions west of Kunersdorf.

As the situation deteriorated for the Germans, the "1001 Nights" Combat Group on standby north of Wriezen was first put on alert and then brought forward through Wriezen. As another precaution part of the 560th SS Tank-Hunting Battalion was deployed north and east of the town into positions that had been prepared beforehand. Then in the late afternoon reconnaissance troops sent forward along the Wriezen-Thöringswerder-Alt Lewin road reported that some twenty Soviet tanks had broken through. The gap in the German lines here was then plugged with some RAD troops supported by Hetzers of the 560th. On Hitler's instructions the 25th Panzergrenadier Division was then brought out of Corps Reserve southwest of Wriezen, where it had been subjected to bombing all day, and moved forward at dusk to form a line covering Wriezen to Kunersdorf.

The 47th Army advanced up to nine kilometers that day, reaching the line of the eastern edge of Beauregard/eastern edge of Thöringswerder/railway line 1.5 kilometers southwest of Thöringswerder/eastern edge of Herrenhof/eastern edge of Winkel (two kilometers west of Alt Trebbin). In their evening report the 47th Army claimed the destruction of three artillery batteries, two mortar batteries, and fifty machineguns, with some 3,000 German soldiers killed and over 300 captured, together with four artillery pieces, sixty machineguns and 2,000 Panzerfausts. As usual this report failed to mention their own casualties, but the Germans claimed twenty-eight Soviet tanks destroyed in this sector.[18]

The 3rd Shock Army

Colonel General V.I. Kutznetsov's 3rd Shock Army had been allocated the 9th Tank Corps as its own mobile force and, with the additional resources allocated to it, was fielding two heavy tank, one heavy SPG and four SPG regiments in support of the rifle divisions deployed in the following order from north to south:

First Echelon   **Second Echelon**
79th Rifle Corps
   150th Rifle Division
   171st Rifle Division   207th Rifle Division
12th Guards Rifle Corps
   33rd Rifle Division
   52nd Guards Rifle Division   23rd Guards Rifle Division
Army Reserve

                                7th Rifle Corps
                                 146th Rifle Division
                                 265th Rifle Division
                                 364th Rifle Division

Major General N.D. Vedeniev's 9th Tank Corps supported Colonel A.I. Negoda's 171st Rifle Division for the first day of battle, concentrating on taking the little fortified town of Letschin.[19]

Major General P.M. Safarenko's 23rd Guards Rifle Division must have been brought out of reserve at an early stage, for it is said to have taken part in storming the main defensive position and then that evening to have reached the line of the strongly defended railway embankment. During the ensuing action, following a short artillery bombardment, the female Communist Party organizer, Senior Sergeant L.S. Kravets, took over the 1st Company of the 63rd Guards Rifle Regiment when its commander was killed, earning for herself the title of Hero of the Soviet Union.[20]

Friedhelm Schöneck, who was with the 6th Company of the 652nd Grenadier Regiment, 309th "Berlin" Infantry Division, wrote:

> By late afternoon our position on the railway embankment was untenable. The ammunition was almost exhausted. The losses in dead and wounded were terrible. We were lying there, a forgotten outpost. There was no question of a command structure, everyone was fighting for himself alone without any set task or orders. But we were going to survive! Where the order actually came from, none of us could say. We got up and left that untenable position.
>
> Going through Sietzing, which we left burning behind us, we reached the road to Wuschewier, but it was no longer a road, only a cratered landscape over which we staggered. The village was just a single heap of rubble. Shattered vehicles were scattered about as if in a scrap yard, with ammunition boxes and equipment around. In between, dead and yet more dead.

Schöneck and his colleagues were surprised to find one of their company cooks hastily loading up his cart in a side street. They took some cold rations and coffee off him, and were issued copies of Hitler's Order-of-the-Day to read as they took a short break, only to be interrupted by Soviet machinegun fire from close by. Schöneck continued:

We abandoned our mess tins as we grabbed our weapons and ran toward the firing. A lone German SPG jolted screechingly to the village entrance to challenge the enemy. Machinegun salvos whipped across the street, and hand grenades exploded in doorways and cellar shafts; cries, shouts and groans. Behind us the cook's cart raced out of the village at full gallop, tins and ration boxes falling into the dirt on the street.

We had hardly finished clearing the houses, when clanking and explosions came from the other end of the village.

The whole night through we fought against an enemy who would allow us no rest. Time and again we were showered with splinters from a hail of mortar fire. Where exactly the enemy was located was impossible to establish in this confusion. Gradually the fighting drew toward the southwest corner of the village. It was increasingly obvious that the Russians had already surrounded us and that we, a colorful, thrown-together band of various units, were fighting our war in a lost outpost.[21]

The 3rd Shock Army claimed to have repelled five German counterattacks of company and battalion size that day and to have advanced up to eight kilometers, destroying 6 tanks, 4 SPGs, 17 artillery pieces, 7 mortars, 29 machineguns and 12 vehicles, killing 2,000 German soldiers and capturing 900 together with 20 guns, 12 mortars, 208 machineguns, 900 rifles, 10 vehicles and 16 stores of various kinds.

Major General S.N. Perevertkin's 79th Rifle Corps ended the day on the line of the road 500 meters south of Alt Trebbin/the northern edge Sietzing, while Lieutenant General A.F. Kazankin's 12th Guards Rifle Corps reached the line Sietzing/200 meters north of Kiehnwerder. Major General V.A. Sistov's 7th Rifle Corps was still in second echelon in the woods on the far side of the Oder east of Gross Neuendorf.[22]

The Soviets estimated that the 309th Infantry Division suffered about 60 percent casualties on this first day, and reported little organized resistance from the German defense during the opening phase of the battle.[23]

The 5th Shock Army

Colonel General N.E. Berzarin's 5th Shock Army was deployed with five divisions in the first echelon as follows:

First Echelon	Second Echelon
26th Guards Rifle Corps	
94th Guards Rifle Division	
266th Rifle Division	89th Guards Rifle Division
32nd Rifle Corps	
60th Guards Rifle Division	
295th Rifle Division	416th Rifle Division

9th Rifle Corps
     301st Rifle Division   248th Rifle Division
Army Reserve
                                 230th Rifle Division

The latter division was on the east bank of the Oder, but Berzarin's part of the bridgehead also accommodated the 12th Guards Tank Corps, the advance guard of the 2nd Guards Tank Army, the remainder of which started crossing the river as soon as the operation commenced. General Berzarin's own allocation of armor amounted to no less than six heavy and four other tank regiments, and two SPG regiments, one of them heavy.[24]

Lieutenant General F.E. Bokov, who was Berzarin's commissar (Member of the Military Council), later claimed that the 5th Shock Army's guns fired a total of 50,000 shells in the opening barrage, and that the army had thirty-six searchlights in its support.[25]

As Major Gerhard Schacht, commanding the 25th Parachute Regiment reported, part of the 9th Parachute Division was caught by the opening barrage while changing position and then suffered further heavy casualties from air attack. Worst hit were the two forward regiments, who put up a tremendous resistance, repeatedly counterattacking and suffering accordingly. The 3rd Battalion of the 26th and the 2nd Battalion of the 27th Parachute Regiments were almost totally destroyed during the course of this first day. Ammunition became so scarce that it had to be shared out to enable the parachutists to carry out their counterattacks. The divisional artillery supported the infantry as best it could, but it too was desperately short of ammunition. The 3rd Battalion of the 9th Parachute Artillery Regiment was equipped with some old Home Defense antiaircraft guns, whose sights for ground combat had had to be fastened to the barrels with wire. This battalion had taken up positions on a road near Buschdorf the previous day, but came under such heavy fire during the attack that it was obliged to withdraw to Platkow. Nevertheless, the flak played a large role in destroying the thirty Soviet tanks claimed to have been destroyed in the 9th Parachute Division's sector that day.[26]

Uniquely, a detailed description of the 5th Shock Army's progress that day is to be found in General Bokov's account. Major General P.A. Firsov's 26th Guards Rifle Corps was on the army's right flank. Its 94th Guards Rifle Division, commanded by Major General I.G. Gasparian, concentrated on the Vossberg sugar factory, where the 228th and 283rd Guards Rifle Regiments met fierce resistance from the 1st Battalion of the 652nd Grenadier Regiment (309th Infantry Division). Later the 286th Guards Rifle Regiment was brought forward from the division's second echelon to take the southern outskirts of Letschin, the town being a primary objective of the neighboring 3rd Shock Army. On the corps's left, Colonel S.M. Fomitchenko's 266th Rifle Division came up against part of the stubborn resistance put up by the 25th Parachute Regiment.

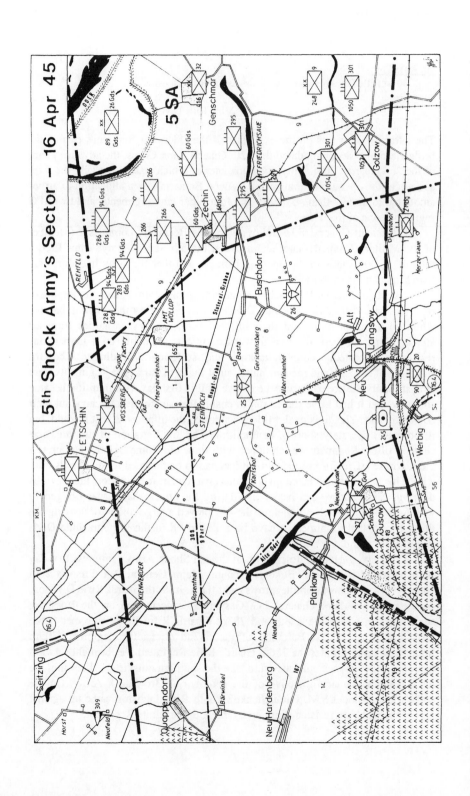

5th Shock Army's Sector – 16 Apr 45

In the center, Major General D.S. Zerebin's 32nd Rifle Corps was confronted by the bulk of the 25th and 26th Parachute Regiments with their front centered on Buschdorf. The attacking 60th Guards and 295th Rifle Divisions, commanded by Major Generals V.P. Sokolov and A.P. Dorofeyev respectively, were met by a counterattack mounted by a battalion of the 25th Parachute Regiment supported by ten to fifteen tanks at 0600 hours. This was checked by artillery and mortar fire, but remained an obstacle to the Soviet advance, so that the divisional second echelons had to be committed at 0700 hours, and it was not until about 1000 hours that the Buschdorf position was taken, the advance reaching the line of one kilometer west of Basta Farm/two kilometers northwest of Alt Langsow, where the 2nd Battalion of the 25th Parachute Regiment took up the defense.

There followed a two-hour delay while the Soviet troops regrouped for the next assault, then at 1210 hours a ten-minute artillery barrage, after which the 60th Guards and 295th Rifle Division resumed the attack. The one-meter-high railway embankment barring the line of advance was strongly defended and was not taken until 1400 hours.

It was at about 1400 hours that the 9th Tank and 12th Guards Tank Corps of the 2nd Guards Tank Army were introduced into the battle in the 5th Shock Army's area.

On the army's left flank, Major General I.P. Rosly's 9th Rifle Corps's 301st Rifle Division, commanded by Colonel V.S. Antonov, was opposed by part of the 26th Parachute Regiment and the 1st Battalion of the 2nd "Müncheberg" Panzergrenadier Regiment. Here the taking of the second line of defense led to the 1050th Rifle Regiment being brought forward from the second echelon to assist with the taking of the third line. Meanwhile, the corps commander became concerned at the failure of the 8th Guards Army's 4th Guards Rifle Corps to keep pace, and therefore called forward Major General N.Z. Galai's 248th Rifle Division from his Corps Reserve to fill the gap on the army boundary.[27]

Kurt Keller II with the 1st Company, 1st Battalion, 2nd "Müncheberg" Panzergrenadier Regiment, wrote:

During the night of 14-15 April we relieved a parachute unit between [Neu] Tucheband and [Amt] Friedrichsaue in front of Golzow. From this time onward the front line was only thinly manned.

My assault platoon lay between the embankment of the Berlin-Küstrin railway line and a road leading to Golzow. Until the Russian attack on the morning of 16 April the command post of the 1st Company, under Second Lieutenant Schuler, was in the since disappeared crossing-keeper's cottage west of Golzow near the Annahof farmstead. We were not fully surprised by that famous Red Army barrage, as one member of our platoon spoke perfect Russian and had already told the company commander on the evening of 15 April when the attack would begin. Here one should note that we were only thirty meters from the Russians opposite.

The volume of the bombardment, which lasted several hours, was like an earthquake. Once the barrage had passed over us the Russians attacked with the aid of tanks and searchlights. The smoke screen started by the Russians moved westward toward Langsow and Werbig, so we shot out some of the searchlights with rifle and machinegun fire and then moved back under cover of the Russian smoke via our command post to the Annahof, where the battalion command post was, to regroup, which was done at about 0800 hours.

The battalion commander, a captain, ordered us to set up a new line of defense and to clear the neighboring copse of the Russians that had penetrated it, which we were able to do. The Annahof position was vacated when the news arrived that Russian tank units had thrust past us and were moving on the Werbig railway junction, threatening to encircle us.

We then set off with our battalion commander to the regimental command post near a stream in Langsow not far from the goods station. On the way I was slightly wounded for the second time that day and was bandaged in the cellar of the regimental command post.

As the Russians were trying to surround us, the troops gathered at the regimental command post. Some of the soldiers decided to withdraw toward the Eberswalde-Seelow railway line. I myself with a larger group tried to get past the goods station in Werbig, where there were some Russian T-34 tanks, and to break through toward Seelow or Reichstrasse 1.[28]

Colonel Peshkov's 1052nd Rifle Regiment took Alt Langsow using a battalion supported by tanks and SPGs for a frontal atttack while his two other battalions enveloped the village from north and south, causing a hasty retreat.[29]

Sergeant Waldmüller of the 8th Panzer Batallion, now temporarily in command of his tank, which had been stationed between two farms on the edge of Alt Langsow the day before, wrote:

A farm near us is on fire. It is still dark and a bit foggy. Our infantry are streaming back toward us in the dawning light. It is difficult to distinguish between our own and the enemy soldiers in the mist. The Russians have hardly any tanks in our sector, but are attacking with masses of infantry and antitank guns. We pull back westward along the village street. I get the task of securing the village's northwesterly exit. Russian infantry are bypassing the village to the north. The sun comes through and the fog lifts a little. Russian antitank guns and infantry push forward to the eastern end of the village street. Our platoon leader, Second Lieutenant Scheuermann, gives the order for me to withdraw by the village's southwestern exit. We are the last vehicle!

In turning round our driver, an old Afrika Korps hand, drives into a heap of cobblestones, which cause our right track to come off. I radio for help. The vehicle in front of us, Sergeant Walter Bauer's SPG, comes back. Under fire from the Russian antitank guns and infantry, we attach his towwire to our tank and our towwire to our torn-off track. In this way, at the last second, he pulls out of the village for four kilometers to where we can fix our track again.

Meanwhile, some 200 meters away our platoon leader's tank has caught on fire inside, but once the fire has been extinguished, it is operational once more.

Staff Sergeant Schild is appointed the new commander of our tank. We withdraw to a position in the woods near Diedersdorf. Our company commander, Lieutenant Kaut, is reported to have been killed.[30]

General Bokov goes on to mention especially hard fighting at Werbig station, where the triangle of railway tracks surrounded by watercourses formed a strong defensive position, for here the north-south line has to rise in order to cross the east-west one, so that two sides of the triangle consist of high embankments penetrated only by narrow tunnels for the roads to pass through. Corps and divisional artillery were directed on this area and the railway line east of there, but it took two bombardments before the Soviet infantry could progress. The 220th Tank Brigade advanced under cover of the bombardments and participated in the attack at point-blank range. Werbig railway station changed hands three times.[31]

Kurt Keller described the road tunnels through the railway embankments as being choked with wrecked tanks and dead bodies, the slaughter of "thousands of Russian infantrymen" being assisted by the "Berlin" armored train. He described this train as consisting of about five flatcars carrying tanks equipped with 88mm guns and operating between Ludwigslust and Werbig. He also said that it was responsible for the destruction of about fifty-six Soviet tanks.[32] He continued his account:

After some of the fleeing troops had come under fire from about nine T-34s in breaking out via the goods station, the Russians shelled us with their artillery and other tanks for a further one and a half hours, so that we had to crouch down in shell holes between the goods station and the regimental command post as best as we could. We tried jumping from one shell hole to another back to the regimental command post to find better cover and then to break through via the farmsteads to Werbig. However, this did not work out, as we were taking heavy casualties from the Russian submachinegun and mortar fire, as well as machinegun fire. Sometime between 1100 and 1130 hours our last regimental commander, a major from Bruchköbel, surrendered with the remains of the regiment.

After the surrender the Russians shot all the wounded that were unable to march any more, as well as some soldiers that were not wounded, standing them up against the wall. I myself was stood up against a wall three times until an older Russian took me away, saying to me "You are not SS" and placing me in a group of prisoners being led away.[33]

By the end of the day the 5th Shock Army could claim to have advanced about ten kilometers, ending with the 26th Guards Rifle Corps on the Alte Oder near Quappendorf, the 32nd Rifle Corps on a line two kilometers north of

Platkow/one kilometer east of Gusow, and the 9th Rifle Corps occupying Neu Langsow and Werbig, and attacking Gusow. In the day's fighting they claimed to have destroyed over fifty guns and forty-three mortars, and to have killed 2,500 German soldiers and captured 400.[34]

General Bokov concluded:

> On the evening of 16 April the Army Commander and Member of the War Council analyzed the results of the first day of battle. This day the 5th Shock Army in some stubborn fighting had broken through the enemy's main defensive system and enabled the commitment of the 2nd Guards Tank Army. Naturally, this does not mean that everything had gone smoothly for us. As our analysis showed, several formations and units had shown themselves somewhat lacking in fighting ability, some commanders were incapable of maneuvering on the battlefield. Instead of going round strong points with their main forces and leaving them to be liquidated by the second echelon, they let them attack frontally in repeated, protracted actions and thereby delayed the speed of advance.
>
> Then our reconnaissance troops had not discovered the whole of the enemy fire system during the preparation for attack, and thus this could not be completely suppressed during the artillery preparation. Besides, not all the units had sufficient artillery support at the beginning of the attack. Deficiencies in engineer equipment resulted in the tanks and artillery remaining behind the infantry and the second echelon being delayed.
>
> A serious deficiency was established in the introduction of the tank army, its cooperation with the 5th Shock Army not always being precise and effective enough.[35]

His first paragraph seems to hint at attributing the blame for the high casualty rate suffered that day. His comment about the lack of sufficient engineer equipment demonstrates the effectiveness of the water obstacles across their path, and lastly his comment about poor cooperation shows how unexpected the commitment of the 2nd Guards Tank Army must have been.

The 8th Guards Army

Colonel General Chuikov's 8th Guards Army attacked with all three corps in line. Deployment is best visualized from the accompanying map, but from the north the 4th and 29th Guards Rifle Corps each had two divisions leading with a third in reserve, each division having two regiments leading with a third in reserve. In similar pattern the 28th Guards Rifle Corps, however, had only one division leading, a second in reserve and a third in Army Reserve. Although its 11th Tank Corps had been given to the 1st Guards Tank Army for this operation, the 8th Guards Army had been allocated six tank and four SPG regiments, four

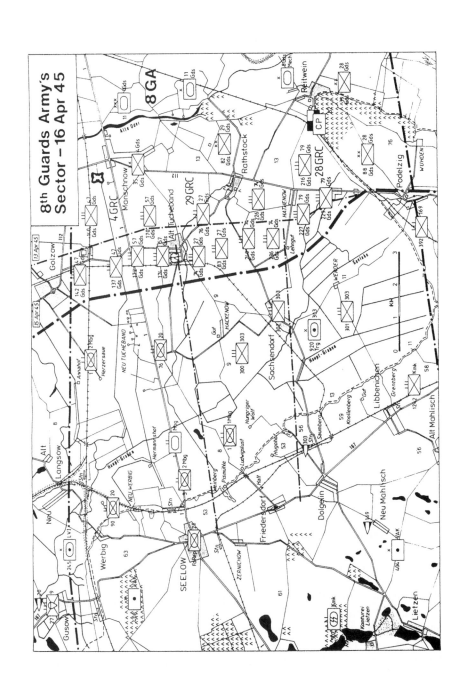

8th Guards Army's Sector – 16 Apr 45

and one of which respectively were classified as heavy. The formidably reinforced artillery resources are shown schematically in Appendix VIII.

The artillery preparation began as planned with a ten-minute bombardment. While the Army Artillery Group engaged the German artillery positions, the Corps and Divisional Artillery Groups shelled and mortared identified important strong points, and the Regimental Artillery Groups concentrated on destroying and suppressing resistance in the first lines of trenches. After five minutes of steady methodical fire, the second creeping barrage began sweeping over the German defenses. These barrages were reinforced by rocket launchers, effectively destroying all resistance within the First Defensive Strip, enabling the infantry and their accompanying armor to advance slowly over the first two kilometers or so.

The artillery then switched to a series of concentrated barrages and, where necessary, to engaging individual targets, while the leading divisions of the 4th and 29th Guards Rifle Corps were provided with a single creeping barrage to take them forward another one and a half kilometers.[36]

Lieutenant Colonel Helmut Weber, commanding the 300th Grenadier Regiment astride Hackenow, received orders to evacuate his forward trenches during the night, but several hundred unarmed reinforcements that had arrived around midnight and been divided up and sent forward to the various companies would have still been on the move when the bombardment started. The previous day his command post in the "Hungriger Wolf" Farm had been hit and consequently moved back 200 meters into some trenches, where it again came under fire and all communications were lost. Eventually his right-hand battalion reported being in new positions abreast of his old command post position, but nothing was heard of the left-hand battalion, so he sent his bicycle platoon to man some trenches behind it. Only the next day was contact reestablished with the remains of this battalion, whose commander had had to clear Soviet troops from on top of his bunker while still under artillery fire. When Weber went to seek artillery support for his right-hand battalion from his accredited artillery battalion he discovered that the latter had run out of ammunition the previous day and that there was a newly arrived regiment covering the boundary between himself and the 20th Panzergrenadier Division to his left.[37]

However, the German artillery, despite the acute shortage of ammunition, were able to put up a far more effective defense than the Soviets had anticipated, for the majority of their positions had not been discovered by Soviet reconnaissance, and Lieutenant General Kruse, the artillery commander, was able to bring into effect his carefully planned and coordinated fire plan, combining the efforts of the 404th and 408th Volks Artillery Corps astride Seelow with those of the divisional artillery units.[38]

The armor facing the 8th Guards Army in the valley bottom consisted of Captain Jaschke's 245th SPG Brigade operating out of Gusow, Captain Horst

Zobel's 1st "Müncheberg" Panzer Battalion directly in front of Seelow and Major Kapp's 920th SPG Training Brigade operating out of Sachsendorf.

Zobel was operating directly under command of General Mummert, his divisional commander, and had been in position a full day before the Soviet offensive began. His two remaining companies, one of ten Panthers and the other of ten Tigers, were deployed either side of Route 1 immediately behind the Haupt-Graben water obstacle, with four tanks of the right-hand company some distance forward in support of the 76th Panzergrenadier Regiment. As the morning mist cleared his well-experienced tank crews began engaging the Soviet tanks advancing toward them, knocking them out one after another. Later in the day he saw a solid column of Soviet armor moving towards Ludwigslust on his right flank, but he had strict instructions not to engage except to his front because of the shortage of tank ammunition. At dusk he received orders to withdraw to the Heights, by which time his unit had destroyed some forty to fifty Soviet tanks, his only losses being the four tanks out in front to the German flak, despite his warnings to the latter. The flak guns at the foot of the slopes had no tractors of their own, so Zobel's tanks tried to pull them out up the the gully north of the railway station, the Route 1 being blocked, but the guns proved too heavy and had to be abandoned.[39]

Meanwhile Second Lieutenant Tams's company on the forward edge of Seelow had experienced the horrific opening bombardment and then came under intermittent attack from bombers and ground-attack aircraft throughout the day, while his positions formed a catch line for stragglers making their way back from the fighting in the Oderbruch. In accordance with his instructions, Tams blew the waterworks at the foot of the hill and the Route 1 bridge over the railway. Then at noon the town came under a sudden, heavy artillery bombardment for half an hour, after which his company's positions were attacked by Soviet infantry that had percolated through. Tams's company held but only at a cost of 20 percent casualties. At dusk the attacks were intensified and Soviet infantry penetrated the cottages flanking the street leading to his barricade on Route 1, severing connection with his right-hand platoon. Some demoralized survivors of the Küstrin garrison that had been formed into Ad Hoc units deployed at the foot of the Heights came back reporting that the railway station was swarming with Soviet troops. He placed these stragglers on the left of his line at the junction with the neighboring Volkssturm company but they had disappeared when he checked his positions at dawn.

During the course of the night he was able to clear the cottages in front of his antitank barrier of Soviet troops and reestablish connection with his right-hand platoon. His company was now down to about eighty men.[40]

In the Neu Tucheband-Hackenow-Sachsendorf area the Soviets came up against a strong network of interlocking positions and barriers, and the fighting became vicious with the Germans counterattacking wherever and whenever they could, including an attack on the 8th Guards Army's southern flank by elements

of the "Kurmark" Panzergrenadier Division.[41] German resistance along the
Seelow escarpment, or "Hardenberg-Stellung", was particularly fierce, and the
antitank measures proved extremely effective.

Colonel General Chuikov said of this:

> For the first two kilometres our rifle units and tanks advanced under cover of
> the moving barrage successfully, though slowly. But then the machines,
> which had to get past the streams and canals, began to be left behind.
> Coordinated action between artillery, infantry and tanks was thus lost. The
> moving barrage, which had been carefully calculated for a certain length of
> time, had to be stopped, and the artillery switched over to support of the
> infantry and tanks by means of consecutive concentration of fire on different
> points. The enemy conducted a particularly stiff resistance at the Haupt-
> Graben, which skirts the foot of the Seelow Heights. The spring floods had
> turned it into an impassable barrier for our tanks and self-propelled guns. The
> few bridges in the area were kept under enemy artillery and mortar fire from
> beyond the Seelow Heights and from dug-in tanks and self-propelled guns, all
> well camouflaged.
>
> Our advance slowed down even more. The troops were unable to move
> until the engineers had set up crossings. Any kind of maneuvre by motor
> vehicles or tanks was impossible for the roads were jammed, and to try and
> move across country, in this marshy valley with its well-mined fields, would
> have been impossible.
>
> It was our Air Force that saved the day. Controlling the sky over the
> battlefield, our bombers, fighters and attack aircraft silenced the enemy
> batteries at the back of the German defence area. Finally the Haupt-Graben
> was crossed, and our troops began storming the Seelow Heights.
>
> By noon the 8th Guards Army had broken through the first two lines of
> enemy defences and reached the third, but failed to take it off the march.
>
> The slopes of the Seelow Heights were too steep for our tanks and self-
> propelled guns, so they had to search for more gentle ways up. They found
> them along the roads that led to Seelow, Friedersdorf and Dolgelin, but there
> the Germans had formidable strongpoints which could be suppressed only by
> accurate and very powerful artillery fire. This meant that our artillery had to
> deploy closer to the Seelow Heights.
>
> I issued an order saying that at 1400 hours [1200 hours local], after a 20
> minute artillery barrage, Seelow, Friedersdorf and Dolgelin were to be
> attacked and the Seelow Heights taken. For this purpose I ordered the artillery
> to move forward and establish cooperation with the infantry and tanks.[42]

Chuikov had become irritated by the fact that many of the forward German
positions had proved to be empty, suspecting a trap, and had thus lost valuable
time. If he was to achieve his objectives for this first day, which entailed
securing the Seelow Heights and reaching the line Alt Rosenthal/Neuentempel/
Lietzen so that the 1st Guards Tank Army would have a secure start line for its
breakthrough to Berlin, he still had a long way to go.[43]

More favorable progress was being made on his right flank, as Averdieck reported from his observation post on the rim of the Seelow Heights just south of Werbig:

> By midday, from the sounds of battle and rumors, the enemy were already past us on the left and right. The remains of the detachments deployed in front of us were caught in our positions [as they ran back]. Our troops were running from their trenches toward us as the Russian infantry appeared, and before we knew it the Ivans were already on our Heights. With some hastily assembled forces they were driven back halfway down again and the new positions held for the night.[44]

The Soviet troops involved were from Major General V.M. Chugayev's 47th Guards Rifle Division. Despite this incursion, the 27th Parachute Regiment continued to hold on to the hamlet of Werbig on the corner of the escarpment.[45]

Gunner Hans Hansen with the 3rd Battery, 1st Battalion, 26th Flak Regiment, 23rd Flak Division, which was deployed in a field west of the Sachsendorf-Dolgelin road, described his experience of the opening barrage and went on to write:

> This infernal, hellish storm continued with the break of day. The rays of the rising spring sun were unable to penetrate the thick haze of dust, smoke and mist that lay over the Oder landscape that morning. Instead an unusual twilight reigned when we dared to raise our heads from our holes as the fire subsided. But it was not peaceful. The barrage had only been a foretaste of the horror to come. The next act was staged by the Russian ground-attack aircraft, which, like unreal shadows, thrust throught the swirling clouds of dust and smoke and spat out death and destruction on everthing that still moved. One wave after another attacked our positions. We defended ourselves with an obstinate fury that partly arose from our fear, and achieved at least one being shot down, for our platoon had been spared casualties until then.
>
> The next act: We then came under bombardment from mortars and "Stalin-Organs." The infantry in the line in front of us retreated. Whether this was as a result of orders to do so, or the soldiers were simply going of their own accord, we did not know. Our troop now formed what one might call a forward strong point. The Russian infantry came on fast. In front of us Russian machineguns began hammering away in a row of bushes. The situation seemed precarious. Then we too received the order to withdraw. We had to leave our guns behind as there was no chance of towing them away.
>
> About a kilometer to the rear, the remains of shattered and scattered units were formed into a new defensive line along the Seelow-Dolgelin railway, in which we gunless flak soldiers were also inserted. The terrain was to our advantage, for the railway ran through a hill in a cutting, and from the upper slope one had a good field of fire over the ground to the east, while the foot of the cutting provided us with some cover from artillery fire.

The Russians kept up the pace. We had hardly settled ourselves down when the Russians appeared with mortars. To our right the head of the attack reached Dolgelin station, but was stopped there. We fired with the carbines and machineguns that we had been issued with, supported by the three guns of our 1st Platoon, which was located directly behind the railway and engaging in the ground battle with depressed gun barrels. The Russian attack stalled. Naturally the Russians were unhappy about this. Russian ground-attack aircraft flew up and down the railway, showing everything with a hail of steel.

Then, shortly after midday, there was another artillery bombardment, this being directed at the points of resistance at Seelow, Friedersdorf and Dolgelin. This time our casualties were worse than they had been from the morning bombardment, also among us Luftwaffe Auxiliaries. Our line of defense was critically thin, but then several tanks came up to our support behind the railway line.

The relevant reports speak of a twenty-five-minute bombardment. I had no watch in those days and had lost all sense of the time. Eventually the artillery fire broke off, and the Russian storm troops appeared immediately in front of our railway cutting out of the cloud of dust that hung over the land, as it had during the morning, and under cover of which they had worked their way forward. Now they attacked with their excited cries of "Hooray! Hooray!" Hand grenades flew into our railway cutting. We defended ourselves grimly and stubbornly, actually managing to defeat this attack, even if at severe loss to ourselves.

It gradually grew quiet at dusk in our sector. We Luftwaffe Auxiliaries then received the order to withdraw under cover of darkness and assemble in Friedersdorf. About thirty Luftwaffe Auxiliaries and some older soldiers assembled in this partly burning and destroyed village at about 2200 hours. (I use the title "Luftwaffe Auxiliaries" once more, although we were officially "Gunners", so as to distinguish ourselves from the older soldiers.) We then withdrew another six kilometers or so and spent the night in a bunker near Lietzen.

Ten or twelve of us Luftwaffe Auxiliaries had fallen on 16 April 1945, and about the same number had been wounded. Exact figures are not available.[46]

The first major crisis arose in the 303rd "Döberitz" Infantry Division's sector, when a large group of Soviet tanks managed to break through to the divisional command post at Dolgelin railway station. Colonel Scheunemann had already deployed all his resources and called for additional assistance from HQ XIth SS Panzer Corps before he was obliged to evacuate, and was then severely wounded while climbing into an APC outside the station. The Soviet tanks were unable to cross the railway because of the obstacles there, so turned north in an attempt to roll up the German lines.[47]

To counter this threat, the 2nd Battalion of the "Kurmark" Panzergrenadier Regiment, the 2nd Battalion of the "Brandenburg" Panzer Regiment and 1st

Soviet cavalry passing a sign that reads: "There's bloody Germany!" Courtesy of Chronos-Film GmbH.

A pensive Marshal Zhukov in his command post on the Reitwein Spur. Courtesy of Chronos-Film GmbH.

Refugees crossing over a bridge at Küstrin. Courtesty of Gedenkstätte / Museum Seelower Höhen.

German flak positions overlooking the Warthe River from the Altstadt in Küstrin. Courtesy of Gendenkstätte / Museum Seelower Höhen.

SS General Heinz Friedrich Reinefarth, Fortress Commandant of Küstrin. Courtesy of Gedenkstätte / Museum Seelower Höhen.

An unusually well-equipped Volkssturm unit marching off to the front. Courtesy of Gedenkstätte / Museum Seelower Höhen.

The vital road and rail communications across the Warthe and Oder Rivers at Küstrin in early April 1945. From top left can be seen part of the Neustadt, Warthe, Fortress and Altstadt, Oder, Oder-Insel with Artillery Barracks, Vorflutkanal, and Kietz. Note the extent of flooding and the two bridges top right still under repair. Courtesy of National Archives, Washington, DC.

Bridges blown by the Germans at Küstrin. Courtesy of Chronos-Film GmbH.

Hitler's visit to the CIst Corps headquarters at Schloss Harnekop on 3 March 1945. Courtesy of Gedenkstätte / Museum Seelower Höhen.

Soviet bridgebuilding techniques, using pile-drivers. The wooden construction was easily repairable. Courtesy of Chronos-Film GmbH.

A crowded Soviet ferry carrying a Studebaker truck–mounted rocket launcher and a Jeep. Courtesy of Chronos-Film GmbH.

A Soviet bridge and ferry landing stage in the early morning mist typical of the Oderbruch. Some of these bridges were up to a kilometer long in order to span the flooded Oder from dike to dike. Courtesy of Chronos-Film GmbH.

A battery of 122mm Soviet field howitzers set to fire across the Oder. Courtesy of Chronos-Film GmbH.

Colonel General Chuikov, commanding the 8th Guards Army, observes the progress of the battle for the Seelow Heights from his command post on the Reitwein Spur. Courtesy of Chronos-Film GmbH.

As part of Marshal Zhukov's deception plan, Soviet T-34/85 tanks being transported uncamouflaged to false assembly areas. Courtesy of Chronos-Film GmbH.

A Soviet T-34/85 tank emerging from flooded terrain. Courtesy of Gedenkstätte / Museum Seelower Höhen.

Soviet AA artillery in action guarding the bridges across the Oder. Courtesy of Chronos-Film GmbH.

Armaments Minister Albert Speer visiting Colonel General Gotthardt Heinrici at HQ Army Group 'Vistula.' Courtesy of Hartmut Heinrici.

General Helmuth Weidling, commander of the LVIth Panzer Corps in the center of the line. Courtesy of Gedenkstätte / Museum Seelower Höhen.

German 'Panthers' preparing for action in the Oderbruch. Courtesy of Gedenkstätte / Museum Seelower Höhen.

A Volkssturm machinegun position near Frankfurt/Oder. Courtesy of Gedenkstätte / Museum Seelower Höhen.

Soviet Petlyakov Pe-2 light bombers in mass formation. Courtesy of Chronos-Film GmbH.

Soviet infantry advancing across the Oderbruch. Courtesy of Chronos-Film GmbH.

Soviet antitank riflemen passing a wrecked German Panzer IV. Courtesy of Chronos-Film GmbH.

Soviet T-34/85 tanks attacking the Seelow Heights. Note that the auxiliary fuel tanks have been removed. Courtesy of Chronos-Film GmbH.

A German 88mm gun in the antitank role in the Oderbruch. Courtesy of Gedenkstätte / Museum Seelower Höhen.

German dead in their devastated trenches after the battle for the Seelow Heights. Courtesy of Chronos-Film GmbH.

Marshal Zhukov attending an Allied victory parade in Berlin, August 1945. Courtesy of Ullstein Bilderdienst.

The Allied commanders-in-chief gathered at Wendenschloss, Berlin, to discuss the setting up of the Allied Control Commission. From left to right: Field Marshal Sir Bernard Montgomery (UK), General Dwight D. Eisenhower (USA), Marshal Georgi Zhukov (USSR), and General Jean de Lattre de Tassigny (FR). Courtesy of Gedenkstätte / Museum Seelower Höhen.

Company of the 502nd SS Heavy Tank Battalion were deployed from Corps Reserve. It is possible that between them they were able to deal with the intruders, but it seems that some of the Soviet tanks helped to take the rear of the positions defending the Ludwigslust-Friedersdorf approach, where the Soviet breakthrough south of Seelow was eventually effected.[48]

The six Tiger IIs of the 502nd arrived at Dolgelin railway station at about 1030 hours and found themselves confronted by twenty Soviet tanks behind the antitank barrier blocking the Sachsendorf road, but could not immediately engage as their gun barrels could not be depressed far enough. Taking up a more favorable position, the Tigers then began engaging the Soviet tanks and soon destroyed eleven opposite them. Two of their own tanks were hit by Soviet tanks that they had failed to notice in a dip, but these two Tigers, despite track and hull damage, were able to remain in action. The Tigers then began firing at targets down in the Oderbruch, including the columns of Soviet armor approaching the Heights covered with infantry, whom they blew off with high explosive. However, not being equipped with night sights, which were then a rarity, the Tigers withdrew to the west of Dolgelin at nightfall for replenishment and safety as they were lacking in infantry cover. Later that evening Lieutenant Colonel Weber found his 14th Company guarding them and warned the tank commander that without the support of the tanks the position could not be held.[49]

Meanwhile Colonel General Chuikov was not the only one displeased at the lack of progress. According to Zhukov, at about 1100 hours he consulted with his army commanders and decided to commit his mobile force of two tank armies and the orders were given to move off at 1430 hours.[50] However, Colonel General Katukov of the 1st Guards Tank Army gives no indication of having been consulted, for he wrote that while consulting with his staff at his own headquarters:

> A telephone call interrupted our conversation. I recognized the voice of our front commander. He gave me the surprising order, even before the enemy resistance had been completely broken through, to take my 1st Guards Tank Army into the battle and complete the breakthrough of the tactical defense zone with 8th Guards Army.[51]

Chuikov's description of what then occurred is one of complete chaos as three tank corps ruthlessly pushed their way through on the few already fully congested routes leading forward in 8th Guards Army's sector. Conditions in much of the Oderbruch were such that movement off the roads was next to impossible for vehicles and difficult enough for those on foot. His own organization was ripped apart, the individual elements cut off from each other, the reserve formations unable to back up those in front and the artillery unable to redeploy.[52]

Again a policy of brute force was being applied. The battle had started with the junior commanders virtually unbriefed, the troops sent into action in such strength that the senior commander's plans would ultimately be achieved through sheer weight of numbers, rather than receiving specific tasks in combination with detailed reconnaissance. Even less finesse was now applied with the closed-down armor bulldozing its way through the infantry to try and punch a way through the German defenses. Coordination of effort in the front ranks stood little chance. For the Germans with clear fields of fire, it was a "field day." Soviet casualties in men and equipment mounted astronomically.

However, troops of the 47th Guards Rifle Division on the extreme north flank pushed through to the Wriezen-Seelow road (Route 167) south of Gusow that evening (as Averdieck had noted), thereby threatening Seelow from the north, and their grip on the lower slopes of the Seelow Heights above Werbig enabled the 57th Guards Rifle Division, the other forward division of the 4th Guards Rifle Corps, to reach Seelow railway station below the town at nightfall. Here they were engaged with the Ad Hoc units previously mentioned, and a determined effort was made to force a way into the town.[53]

By the end of the day the 4th Guards Rifle Corps could claim to be on the line of the southeastern edge of Werbig/Neu Werbig/eastern edge Seelow railway station/exclusive the Weinberg, while the 29th Guards Rifle Corps was on the line of the Weinberg/the railway stop northeast of Friedersdorf/Height 53, and the 28th Guards Rifle Corps was exclusive Height 53/eastern slopes of Height 59/lone building two kilometers northeast of Carzig, the latter's 88th Guards Rifle Division having taken the hamlet of Werder. The army was claiming to have killed up to 1,800 German troops and to have destroyed over 100 machineguns, 32 artillery pieces, 9 scout cars, 18 vehicles and 35 horse-drawn wagons, while having captured over 600 prisoners with 8 tanks and 12 SPGs.[54]

The 69th Army

The evacuation of the German front line of defense had apparently proceeded according to plan during the night and with it the key position of Podelzig, so that the advance of the 69th Army along the whole of its front on the Reitwein Spur had initial success and the defending 169th and 712th Infantry Divisions came under heavy pressure. An important goal on the right flank was the Hudenberg height outside Mallnow, from where German artillery observers had a commanding view over the Oderbruch. Backed by forty to fifty tanks, the infantry of the 25th Rifle Corps burst through the main German defenses south of Mallnow and reached as far as Niederjesar and the southern outskirts of Libbenichen before they could be held and turned back. Not only did Mallnow continue to hold out, but the 169th Infantry Division was able to regain its overnight positions during the course of the afternoon.

In the center, where the 61st Rifle Corps thrust down the Lebus-Schönfliess road, the main German positions along the railway embankment were similarly overrun and the village taken. An officer cadet battalion of the "Kurmark" Panzergrenadier Regiment and the 2nd Company of the 502nd SS Heavy Tank Unit were then brought out of Corps Reserve and placed under the command of Major General von Siegroth to restore the situation at Schönfliess. The German counterattack was launched at 1430 hours, the Tiger IIs leading the way along a gully that brought them into the village with their escorting infantry, causing the Soviets to flee. However, the tanks bogged down in the meadows on the far side of the village, bringing the advance to a halt, but the infantry were able to reach the railway embankment and restore the main line of defense by evening after some hard fighting.[55]

Whereas the armor available to the 69th Army had proved too weak to exploit the initial success, what seems to have gone unnoticed at senior Soviet level was the opportunity to effect Zhukov's alternative plan for the commitment of the 1st Guards Tank Army in the 69th Army's sector. In addition to the access routes to the plateau already held at Wuhden, Klessin and Lebus, the main road through Podelzig had been in Soviet hands from early morning and engineers could have been tasked to clear it of mines and obstacles. If the tanks were to be involved in the breakthrough battle, this would seem to have provided a more favorable opportunity for a successful launch on Berlin.

At the end of the day the army could only claim an advance of four kilometers, ending on the line of Height 66 (300 meters north of Mallnow)/the center of Mallnow/Height 68/Schönfliess/the railway junction three kilometres southeast of Schönfliess, but claimed having killed over 2,000 German troops, destroying up to 120 machineguns and 35 artillery pieces, and capturing 600 prisoners, 18 guns, 43 machineguns and over 800 rifles.[56]

The Frankfurt Fortress

The Frankfurt Fortress, with its large bridgehead on the east bank, was left virtually untroubled by the Soviets during the opening phases of the Berlin Operation as it was appreciated that the successful fulfillment of the main battle plan would obviate the need to attack the city, which would duly fall into their hands without any effort on their part. This had been decided at a meeting by the commanders of the 69th and 33rd Armies with the front's Head of Operations early in April.[57]

The Southern Flank

The terrain in the 33rd Army's sector did not offer a good operational basis, as the maps show. The bulk of the main bridgehead area was unsuitable for tanks, with swampy ground leading to the line of the Oder-Spree Canal, which itself presented a formidable defensive obstacle. The revised Soviet objective here seems to have been to tie down the Germans opposing them with about two-thirds of the forces available, while striking out to gain access to the Frankfurt-Berlin autobahn from the northernmost point of the arc Schwetig-Wiesenau.

Colonel General V.D. Svetaev had six of his divisions in the first echelon, plus the 119th Fortified Region formation screening the Fürstenberg sector and the 115th Fortified Region formation as his south-facing left flank. His deployment from north to south ran as follows:

First Echelon	Second Echelonn
38th Rifle Corps	
129th Rifle Division	
39th Rifle Division	64th Rifle Division
16th Rifle Corps	
383rd Rifle Division	
339th Rifle Division	323rd Rifle Division
62nd Rifle Corps	
49th Rifle Division	
362nd Rifle Division	222nd Rifle Division
Army Reserve	
	2nd Guards Cavalry Corps
	95th Rifle Division

His armor amounted to only one tank and two SPG regiments, all of which appears to have been devoted to his northern bridgehead.[58]

The latter strike was conducted from an extraordinarily small bridgehead fully exposed during daylight to German observers at close range. Aerial photographs taken a few days earlier show tank tracks on the west bank meadows south of the Eichwald, indicating that armor had been ferried across at night and concealed under the trees in preparation for this attack.[59]

The Soviet intent, however, was soon identified by their opponents, and the Vth SS Mountain Corps's reserves deployed to meet the contingency. The weak forces of the 286th Infantry Division facing the main Soviet assault stood little chance; the villages of Lossow and Brieskow were taken in the first hours. By noon the Soviet spearheads had thrust through the woods to breach the second line of defense along Route 87 in several places, and by 1700 hours some had broken through to the autobahn near Lichtenberg.

According to the 9th Army's situation report for that day, the strong points on the line of the opencast mines immediately to the south of Lossow, such as

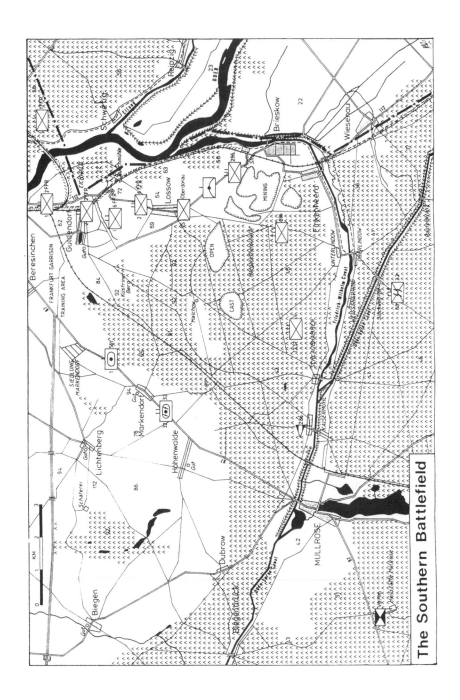

The Southern Battlefield

the Margarethenschacht, held out, but the Soviets pushed through along the banks of the Friedrich-Wilhelm Canal to take Finkenheerd, Unterlindow and Oberlindow, only to be driven out of these locations later in the day.[60]

As soon as the Soviet offensive began, SS-Captain Jakob Lobmeyer's 561st SS Tank-Hunting Battalion's three combat teams, based on the unit's company structure, automatically deployed in accordance with the defense plan. The 2nd and 3rd Companies went to the support of the 88th SS Grenadier Regiment in the Brieskow-Finkenheerd area and the 391st Security Division opposite Fürstenberg respectively. The 1st Company, under SS-Lieutenant Haukelt, headed north up Route 87, half to cover the approach to the autobahn, and half to go forward in support of the 286th Infantry Division. The latter group ran into the Soviets at the Malchow farmstead, this encounter causing the commander to call forward the northern group to the Güldendorf area so as be able to attack the Soviets simultaneously from either flank.[61]

SS-Captain Paul Krauss's Combat Team, consisting of the Hetzers and SPGs of his 32nd SS Tank-Hunting Battalion plus two Army infantry companies, was manning the second line of defence between Markendorf and Hohenwalde. It first came under attack during the morning from heavy Soviet artillery fire and aircraft, under cover of which some turncoat Seydlitz-Troops tried to penetrate its lines with cries of "Don't shoot, comrades!," causing considerable confusion, but when the Seydlitz-Troops started firing on Krauss's SPGs and antitank guns, the turncoats were gunned down. This incident was followed by a Soviet infantry attack of about regimental size, which was repulsed with the aid of the SPGs and antitank guns.[62]

Meanwhile the 88th SS Grenadier Regiment was heavily engaged around Wiesenau, the village changing hands twenty-one times in the course of a few days.[63]

The 33rd Army's claims for that day included an advance of up to 6 kilometers that took the line of the northwestern edge of the woods 3 kilometers west of Güldendorf/the western edge of the woods 0.5 kilometers east of Markendorf/Malchow/eastern edge of Unterlindow/eastern edge of Oberlindow/ Rautenkranz. However, in view of the 88th SS Grenadier Regiment's activities around Wiesenau, the last point seems questionable. Other claims included the killing of up to 2,000 German troops, the destruction of 50 SPGs and the capture of 23 artillery pieces, 14 mortars, 60 machineguns, 550 rifles and SMGs, 80 Panzerfausts, 2 locomotives with 100 railway wagons and their contents, 9 dumps of various kinds of stores, 7 loaded trucks, and up to 1,000 German troops.[64]

German countermeasures resulted in a change of boundary that afternoon, which led to the withdrawal of the Frankfurt Fortress Regiments to the north, so unifying the recognized area of operations under the 286th Infantry Division's jurisdiction. Reserves of the 286th Infantry and 32nd SS Volunteer Grenadier Divisions were then pushed into the gap from the south. That evening the 3rd

Battalion of the SS "Falke" Grenadier Regiment arrived in time to take part in SS-Lieutenant Haukelt's converging attack in the Güldendorf-Malchow sector, which resulted in the destruction of some Soviet troops trapped on open terrain. However, the Soviets kept pouring reinforcements into the Lossow breach, and fighting for access to the autobahn continued all night.[65]

The German Summary

General Busse wrote of this first day of battle:

> The 16th April was a great defensive success in view of the unequal strength. The state of the troops in the main attack sectors remained questionable. The losses in men and equipment were no longer comparable. The Luftwaffe had really supported the troops on the ground with all their might (about 300 machines) but could not stop the Russians from commanding the air. Their fuel stocks could only sustain two more days of such activity at the most.[66]

The Luftwaffe had fought bravely that day, doing their utmost to stem the Soviet onslaught with attacks involving fifteen to twenty aircraft at a time, the total number of flights involved being reckoned at 600 by the Soviets. These were mainly Focke-Wulf 190s attacking the bridgehead and crossing points. Then at dusk five flying bombs and four Ju-88 bombers were directed against the Soviet forces. Officer Cadet Ernst Beichl from a special volunteer Luftwaffe unit copying Japanese *Kamikaze* tactics, managed to destroy the pontoon bridge at Zellin with a 500-kilogram bomb attached to his FW-190 at about 1735 hours, as witnessed by his fighter escort.[67]

As flying conditions improved during the course of the day, the Soviet Air Force took a more active part in the battle, estimated at 2,000 sorties by the Germans, but the 9th Ground-Attack Air Corps had been unable to suppress the German artillery on the Seelow Heights.[68]

That evening Colonel Hans-Georg Eismann spoke by telephone to General Fiebig, commanding the IInd Air Corps. The main point of discussion, in view of the acute shortage of aviation fuel, was whether to give priority to tank-busting missions or to the destruction of the Soviet bridges. Then Colonel General Heinrici spoke to General Fiebig, as a result of which the latter undertook to have four bridges attacked that night, followed by an uniform attack on all the bridges the following afternoon by suicide missions.[69]

At 1645 hours the Chief of Operations of the 9th Army, Colonel Eismann, passed the following situation report to the OKH:

> The big attack on the 9th Army, involving a very stubborn and bitter struggle, has developed into an extremely tense situation at three points:

1 South of Frankfurt
2 Southeast of Seelow
3 East-northeast of Wriezen

The general situation is as follows:

Although the 9th Army has committed the whole of its reserves in immediate counterattacks everywhere to eject the enemy where he has broken through, the main battle line has not held in its entirety. Of all the reserves only the 25th Panzergrenadier Division has yet to be committed, and the way that the situation has developed means that they will have to be used for a counterattack.

Army Group has requested the release of the 18th Panzergrenadier Division to the support of the 9th Army. Army Group has decided to place this division in the area east of Müncheberg tonight in order to use it to prevent the enemy breaking through at Seelow.

He then went into some of the details already recounted, ending with:

Our own losses in armored vehicles are not inconsiderable, especially with the XIth SS Panzer Corps. Ammunition holdings are down to 54 percent of first-line issues. The infantry and armored troops have taken the most losses. Tomorrow will see the resumption of this attack, and our losses will be even heavier.[70]

As Colonel Hölz, the 9th Army's Chief of Staff, told Colonel Eismann at Army Group Headquarters, the German troops had been considerably affected by the devastating Soviet onslaught and a marked falling off in their performance had been noted.[71]

The request to the OKH for the release of Colonel Josef Rauch's 18th Panzergrenadier Division to the 9th Army was was received from Army Group "Weichsel" at 1910 hours. This division then immediately left its harbor area in the 3rd Panzer Army's sector and made for the Buckow-Müncheberg area.[72]

The Soviet Summary

The day could not have gone worse for Zhukov. He had fallen into Heinrici's trap, wasting much of his opening artillery barrage on vacated positions; his searchlight scheme had failed abysmally; his decision to launch his tank armies early had proved a tactical disaster; his losses in manpower and armor had been appalling; and now he was in deep trouble with Stalin. As he himself wrote:

By about 1300 hours [Moscow Time] It was clear to me that the enemy defensives on the Seelow Heights were still relatively intact and that we would be unable to take the Seelow Heights with the order of battle with which we had commenced the attack.

After seeking the advice of the army commanders, we decided to commit to battle both tank armies, in order to reinforce the attacking troops and ensure a breakthrough of the enemy defences.

At about 1500 hours I called Headquarters and reported that we had breached the first and second enemy lines of defence and that the Front had advanced up to six kilometres, but had encountered serious resistance from the Seelow Heights, where the the enemy defences appeared to be largely intact. In order to reinforce the all-arms armies, I had committed both tank armies to battle. I went on to report that in my opinion we would breach the enemy defences by the end of the next day.

Stalin listened attentively to me and then said calmly, "The enemy defences on Koniev's Front have proved to be weaker. He crossed the Neisse without difficulty and is now advancing without encountering any reistance of note. Support your tank armies' attack with bombers. Call me this evening and tell me how things develop."

That evening I reported to him the difficulties we were experiencing on the approaches to the Seelow Heights, and said that it would not be possible for us to take these Heights before next evening. This time Stalin was not as calm as during my first telephone call.

"You should not have committed the 1st Guards Tank Army in the 8th Guards Army's sector, but rather where the Headquarters wanted." Then he added: "Are you sure you will take the positions on the Seelow Heights tomorrow?" Forcing myslf to remain calm, I replied: "Tomorrow, on the 17th April, the enemy defences on the Seelow Heights will be breached by evening. I believe that the more troops the enemy throws against us here, the quicker we will take Berlin, for it is easier to defeat the enemy on an open field than in a fortified city."

"We will instruct Koniev to move Rybalko's and Lelyushenko's tank armies on Berlin from the south, and Rokossovsky to hurry his river crossing over the Oder and at the same time to strike past Berlin from the north," Stalin said.

I replied: "Koniev's tank armies are certainly in a position to make a rapid advance, and should be directed on Berlin. On the other hand, Rokossovsky will not be able to start his offensive from the Oder before the 23rd April, because he will not be able to manage the crossing of the Oder so quickly."

"Goodbye!" said Stalin dryly, and rang off.[73]

Stalin was not to speak to Zhukov again during the course of the breakthrough battle, an obvious sign of his extreme displeasure with the way things had gone.

In their memoirs both Zhukov and Chuikov claimed that the failure to gain their objectives on this first day was due to an underestimation of the strength of the German defenses.[74] But as General Babadshanian, commanding the 11th Guards Tank Corps, wrote:

Already during the conference on 5 April, several generals had drawn the front commander's attention forcibly to the fact that the main enemy defenses ran along the Seelow Heights, and that therefore the artillery and air strikes should be mainly concentrated on the Heights. Unfortunately their advice was not taken.[75]

CHAPTER 13

Second Day of Battle

The Northern Flank

On the extreme northern flank within the 3rd Panzer Army's sector, the 61st Army's 80th Rifle Corps reinforced its bridgehead on the dikes three kilometers southwest of Schwedt, thus continuing its deceptive role.

However, the 61st Army's principal move that day was to launch an attack with two regiments of the 89th Rifle Corps across the Oder at 0415 hours under heavy artillery cover and smoke screens to reinforce the Neu Glietzen bridgehead. Neu Glietzen was taken but the 56th Light Infantry Regiment managed to contain the slightly enlarged bridgehead and prevent any further expansion for the time being. The 9th Guards Rifle Corps also attempted a river crossing further south with two of its regiments and elements of the 89th Rifle Corps. Again the 5th Light Infantry Division was able to restrict the incursion to a small bridgehead. The 61st Army claimed to have killed 350 Germans and taken 4 prisoners from the 5th Light Infantry Division.

For the latter the main problem was where the 606th Infantry Division had collapsed on its southern flank the day before. The newly arrived 6th Polish Infantry Division kept up the pressure in the Alte Oder bridgehead during the night of the 16th-17th, and this second day of battle involved some especially bitter fighting as the Poles tried to expand their hold on that part of the Oderbruch. Nine Polish attacks of from battalion to regimental strength were thrown back by the "Sparrer" Combat Group and the 1st Battalion of the 75th Light Infantry Regiment in the area south of Alt Mädewicz and Alt Reetz, and also west of Neu Lietzegöricke.

The Poles claimed an advance of up to five kilometers that day and to have reached the line of a barn two kilometers southeast of Alt Küstrinchen/the eastern edge of Neu Ranft/the eastern edge of Neu Küstrinchen/Alt Reetz/Point 4.6 (four kilometers north of Wriezen)/up to the east bank of the Alte Oder opposite Wriezen. They also claimed to have killed 500 Germans, destroyed 23 artillery pieces and 30 machineguns, and captured 16 prisoners and two dumps containing engineer and medical stores.[1]

Again Lieutenant Erich Hachtel provides us with some insight into the battle from the German side:

> As information became even more uncertain and contact with the 606th Infantry Division had been broken, the situation to our south was really unclear.
>
> My regimental commander tasked me with making contact with the head-quarters of the 606th Infantry Division. I took a couple of men with me, armed with a machinegun and an SMG, and we raced south with our tracked motorcycle combination through our own lines toward the manor farmhouse at Alt Gaul, where according to the latest information the 606th Infantry Division's command post should be. We were well aware that we could come across the Russians at any moment and be shot at, but we had our mission to accomplish, come what may. We reached the manor at about midday. Defensive positions had been set up around it, occupied by infantry. We drove up to the manor and I went down the steps to a big cellar room that was the division's command post. I entered this room, in which several officers were sitting around a big, long table, at one end of which was a colonel, who was the commander of this division. I was looked at in astonishment when I reported my mission to the colonel. All appeared to be fixed in the belief that they were surrounded and only waiting for the Russians to arrive, for the colonel asked me in a friendly tone: "Comrade, how did you get through to us?" I explained the current situation to these gentlemen and suggested they to join me. They accepted my invitation and so we returned to our front line, while I drove on to report back to my regimental commander the fulfillment of my mission and give him the latest information.[2]

The 47th Army

The gap caused by the virtual collapse of the 606th Infantry Division on the first day was now filled by units of the 25th Panzergrenadier Division and the 2nd Battalion, 118th Panzergrenadier Regiment, of the 18th Panzergrenadier Division, which had been brought forward from Army Group Reserve during the night. Together these manned the line Wriezen/Bliesdorf/Kunersdorf.

The day started with the 47th Army launching a strong attack from the line Thöringswerder-Alt Lewin with infantry, armor and cavalry forces. Soviet aircraft then prevented effective German counterattacks, but the 47th Army still claimed to have repelled two of up to battalion strength supported by fifteen tanks and SPGs.[3]

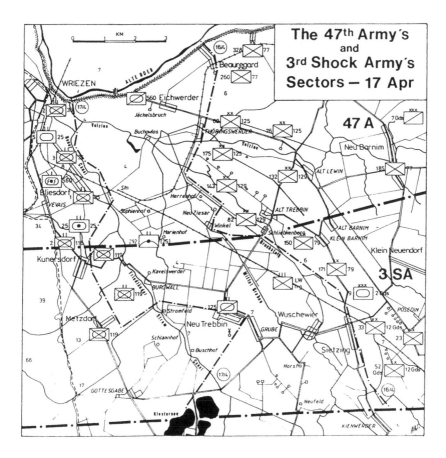

The 25th Panzergrenadier Division was now deployed with the 35th Panzergrenadier Regiment on the left, the 3rd and 2nd Battalions being on the outskirts of Wriezen, and the 1st Battalion at Bliesdorf. The 2nd Battalion was ejected from its forward positions during the day, but was able to regain them that night. The 119th Panzergrenadier Regiment was deployed further south in the path of the 3rd Shock Army, but all these units were supported by the division's 5th Panzer and 25th Tank-Hunting Battalions.

Meanwhile the divisional headquarters moved to Haselberg, eight kilometers west of Wriezen. The divisional history notes that at this stage it was still possible to maintain the supply of food and ammunition to their troops, and to evacuate the wounded at night.[4]

All day the Soviet artillery continued to pound the German lines and the nearer rear areas without pause. Following intensive artillery preparations, Soviet infantry repeatedly stormed the German positions until there was no further resistance to be met.

SS-Lieutenant Lirk's 1st Company of the 560th SS Tank-Hunting Battalion was engaged southeast of Wriezen, where strong Soviet armored forces were trying to break through. Daring action by the skilled Hetzer crews resulted in considerable damage being inflicted on the Soviet armor and infantry. When night fell, the last of the German infantry groped their way back to the Hetzers, under whose cover they made their way back to the new line of defense with a surviving 88mm antiaircraft gun and some APCs.[5]

The 1st Belorussian Front's daily situation report claimed for the 47th Army an advance of up to six kilometers ending with the 77th Rifle Corps on the line of the railway 500 meters northeast of Wriezen/a barn 500 meters east of Wriezen/the bend in the Friedländer Strom Canal one kilometer east of Wriezen. Elements of the 125th Rifle Corps forced the Friedländer Strom Canal and ended the day with its left flank on the line of the railway 1,500 meters southeast of Wriezen, while the 129th Rifle Corps ended on the line of the railway station two kilometers southeast of Wriezen/the northeastern edge of Kunersdorf. The 47th Army was credited with the killing of 500 Germans, the destruction of 11 artillery pieces and 38 machineguns, and the capture of 136 prisoners.

In preparation for the breakthrough phase, the 7th Guards Cavalry Corps crossed over to the west bank of the Oder and deployed in the area Ortwig/Neu Barnim/Posedin, although according to German reports, some cavalry were already in action that day.[6]

The 3rd Shock Army

Similarly for the 3rd Shock Army, this second day of battle was one of slow attrition with no spectacular gains. According to the 3rd Shock Army's official history, the advancing troops were supported by artillery concentrations of some 250-270 guns per kilometer, delivering thirty- to forty-minute barrages. They forced the Friedländer Strom Canal and by evening had reached the defended localities of Kunersdorf and Metzdorf, which were tackled by the 150th and 171st Rifle Divisions respectively, but it took some time to bring all the troops and supporting artillery forward. The 9th Tank Corps, supporting the latter division, had to wait until Captain V.M. Chemelyev's 221st Independent Engineer Battalion had built the necessary bridges to enable the tanks to cross the canal. Fighting was deliberately kept up all night in the hope of breaking through to the heights beyond, but this failed to materialize. The 7th Rifle Corps was brought across the Oder during the day to occupy a closer reserve position west of Letschin. The claim for the day amounted to 1,200 German troops killed and 287 captured, 5 guns, 15 mortars, 10 vehicles, 12 machineguns and 4 SPGs destroyed; and 47 machineguns, 7 mortars, 12 guns, 1 SPG, 12 vehicles and up to 500 rifles captured. The fact that German troops were still holding out in the village of Neu Trebbin, dead center in the army's line of advance, was omitted from the situation report.[7]

The defense in this area consisted basically of the 2nd and 3rd Battalions of the 119th Panzergrenadier Regiment plus the remains of the 4th and 5th Luftwaffe Training Regiments, ten Hetzers of the 25th Tank-Hunting Battalion and the 292nd Army Flak Battalion, which moved back from the area of the Marienhof farm to new positions five kilometers west of Kunersdorf, and remained all day in the ground-fighting role.[8]

Lieutenant Gerhard Hahn, commanding the 8th (Heavy Weapons) Company with the 2nd Battalion of the 119th Panzergrenadier Regiment recorded in his diary:

> At 0600 hours the battalion attacked in the flat valley bottom of the Oder near the Kunersdorf manor farm, five kilometers south of Wriezen, drove the Russians back over the Friedland Strom Canal. Under a heavy enemy artillery barrage the battalion took up defensive positions in the drainage ditches south of the Kunersdorf farm towards Metzdorf.
>
> Renewed enemy attacks with strong artillery and armored support were repulsed. The Russians and Germans are lying opposite each other in the parallel ditches. During the afternoon the enemy launched an attack against the battalion's front. Hardly any artillery fire, but losses from Russian snipers. Heavy casualties for the battalion today, especially in the 5th and 7th Companies. Company commander, 7th Company, severely wounded.
>
> The Russians have broken through to the Seelow Heights left and right of the battalion, enemy tanks pushing through to the west. By evening farms can be seen burning about five kilometers off.
>
> There is a danger that the battalion will be cut off. During the night of 17-18 April 1945, the companies can still be supplied with food and ammunition, and the dead and wounded taken back.
>
> The company commander of the 8th (Heavy Weapons) Company reprimanded by the battalion commander for wanting to give the order during the night for the companies to withdraw, as tomorrow will be too late and have catastrophic consequences. But the battalion commander cannot decide this without instructions from regiment or division.
>
> Toward morning, the radio links to the battalion's rear echelon and to regiment fail, the 8th Company's commander no longer has contact with the firing position of his heavy mortar platoon.[9]

Despite the shattering experience of the previous day, the German defense continued to put up a strong resistance. Friedhelm Schöneck, a survivor of the 652nd Grenadier Regiment, who, as related in Chapter 12, had reached Wuschewier during the night, goes on to describe his experiences on this second day:

> It was 0400 hours on 17 April when we assembled for the breakout at the western exit of the village behind the last houses. Grenade detonations ripped through the early morning air. We fired madly in the diffuse darkness to

where we supposed Ivan was. His reply came by return of post. Heavy machinegun fire forced us back into the village.

While a group returned fire from the village, some of us crept up to the Russian machinegun position from behind. Hand grenades exploded simultaneously on the left and right. The machineguns fell silent. We stormed ahead across the fields toward Grube.

We took a short breather between the few houses there, happy to have escaped the Russian pincers. Signal flares rose above Neu Trebbin, where there still appeared to be German troops.

We could sense the excitement with which orders were given out. The remains of various units were as mixed up here as the officer corps. There was no time for a breather. We picked up fresh ammunition at the corner of a building and then were directed to new defensive positions that ran in a northeasterly direction just outside the village. We were up to our ankles in water in the trenches.

The early morning cold crept through our uniforms with its dampness. We were tired and hungry. Shells exploded close by, flinging fountains of dirt out of the swampy ground high into the air. Ivan seemed to be everywhere. His machinegun bursts cheeped around our ears. Hardly anything could be seen from behind cover. Even the Russian "Duty NCO" was back, flying droningly like a giant insect over our positions and close enough to touch. We could not get him, and he knew it. Only the quadruple flak can do that, but they have been withdrawn to Berlin.

Exhausted we leaned against the side of the trench. My eyes, sore and inflamed, did not want to stay open. My comrades were the same. The last days had left their trace with deep lines on our faces.

I must have fallen asleep when suddenly the sound of something falling into the water brought me wide awake. Perhaps it was just a lump of earth falling into the bottom of the trench from a shell explosion.

A few minutes later, as if he had sprung out of the ground, a strange NCO stood near me. When he saw me pointing my assault rifle at him, he said appeasingly to me: "Man, what a firing position!" or something similar, and then: "In all this coming and going I seem to have forgotten the password!" An explosion in the immediate vicinity caused me to take cover for a second, and when I looked up again the stranger had vanished like a spook. His attitude had puzzled me. A little later a soldier from the heavy machinegun position came up to me and told me a similar story. We were both astounded by the similarity of our stories. Then we found the explanation: they were Seydlitz-Troops that Ivan had sent across to spy on our positions. We had found enough leaflets in the last few days calling on us to go across, and the loud-speaker propaganda had been a standing accompaniment to us on the Oder.

We suddenly received the order to leave our trenches. The Russians were trying to fall on us from the rear. We ran with our weapons right through the village, past the cemetery, to our next position, which was by the windmill. There was not much of the windmill left. Its roof was shot through and the sails torn and bent.

Exhausted from running, we sank down onto its stone base and on to the ground. Around me were unknown faces, infantrymen, members of the Luftwaffe and Waffen-SS soldiers.

Artillery fire flared up. The shells fell closer and closer to the windmill, which the Russians were using as an aiming mark. We sustained a lot of casualties in the few minutes before the Russian infantry began to attack. The Russian T-34 tanks came across country from the direction of Grube. Their shells struck the windmill and made the position untenable.

We had to abandon it and withdraw to the village. We dug ourselves in in a nursery garden. Only the skeletons of the greenhouses remained. The fighting went on all night. We bitterly defended literally every meter of ground. We successfully shot up several tanks with our Panzerfausts, but the Russian reserves seemed to be boundless. We held on to Neu Trebbin with our wild mob until the morning. Ivan was unable to advance a single step.[10]

In the fighting for Neu Trebbin the 125th Armored Reconnaissance Battalion is said to have fought to the last.[11]

The 5th Shock Army

The 5th Shock Army appears to have made the most significant progress of all Zhukov's armies on this second day of battle, which started with a twenty-minute artillery barrage along the whole of General Berzarin's front.

On the northern flank, the 266th Rifle Division made the first breakthrough across the Alte Oder southeast of Quappendorf and pushed forward to Neu Hardenberg, an action in which Guards Colonel Griniov of the 1028th Rifle Regiment is said to have particularly distinguished himself. Quappendorf was taken by Colonel Kondratenko's 288th Guards Rifle Regiment, which also captured 180 members of the 9th Parachute Division's Field Replacement and Training Battalion in a wood to the west of the village.

Although the 2nd Guards Tank Army's 1st Mechanized Corps was later able to cross the Alte Oder near Quappendorf and advance some distance into the woods beyond Neu Hardenberg, the lack of crossing places in this area resulted in the 12th Guards Tank Corps moving upstream to Platkow to cross over and then drive to Neu Hardenberg.

However, it was General Rosly's 9th Rifle Corps's progress on the southern flank that ensured the day's success. Here the 248th Rifle Division cut through on the extreme flank to surround Gusow from the rear, while Colonel Antonov's 301st Rifle Division conducted a frontal attack on the village. Gusow fell at about 1300 hours, and then, backed by elements of the 11th Tank Corps of the 1st Guards Tank Army, the 301st Rifle Division pushed through to Platkow, which was already being attacked frontally by the 1038th and 1040th Rifle Regiments of the 295th Rifle Division. In this manner, the German line of

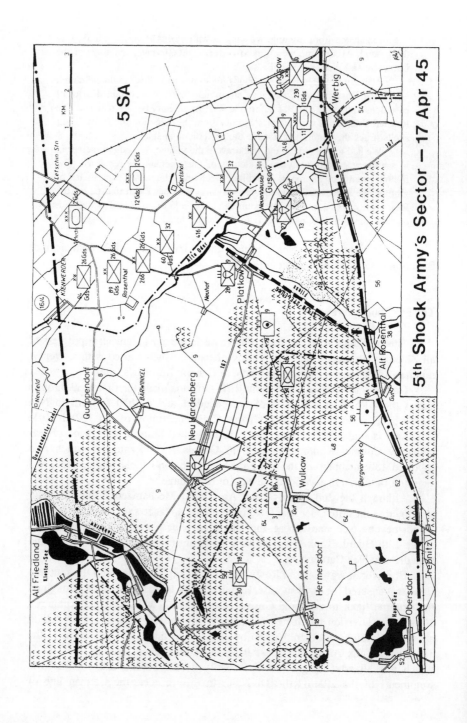

5th Shock Army's Sector — 17 Apr 45

defense was rolled up from the south, and once Platkow had been taken, the flank of the "Stein-Stellung" was turned.

The 27th Parachute Regiment defending this area suffered severely, its 2nd Battalion being virtually destroyed. The regiment's survivors fell back on Wulkow, where they regrouped, and the 3rd Battalion of the 9th Parachute Artillery Regiment, which had been in action near Platkow all day, withdrew at the same time to the Hermersdorf area.

The Soviet advance continued either side of Neu Hardenberg through the dense belt of coniferous forest that masks a gentle rise from the Oderbruch to a sudden ascent of thirty to forty meters, then giving way to undulating open countryside beyond. On the right, the valley of the Stobberow stream running past Alt Friedland led to the densely wooded, deep valleys and lakes of the Märkische Schweiz, a picturesque but labyrinthine area to be avoided if possible. But the road to the north of the stream led up to Ringenwalde and the plateau that was the next goal of the 2nd Guards Tank Army for the breakout to Berlin.

Meanwhile the 18th Panzergrenadier Division had arrived to fill the threatened gap behind the rapidly disintegrating 9th Parachute Division's defenses. The 30th and 51st Panzergrenadier Regiments had deployed in the woods either side of Wulkow, with the divisional artillery deployed behind them. As hastily fed-in reinforcements, they had the disadvantages of unfamiliarity with the terrain and no prepared positions to occupy. The dense woodland in which they were located could also be easily penetrated by the Red Army scouts. Consequently, although the 18th Panzergrenadier Division does not appear to have been engaged that day, its positions did not prove to be tenable.

The territorial gains claimed for the 5th Shock Army in the 1st Byelorussian Front's situation report for 17 April and by Lieutenant General Bokov in his book are clearly exaggerated, for the latter claimed that the army had reached the sector Ringenwalde-Hermersdorf-Obersdorf by 1800 hours. The other claims for the day included up to 1,500 officers and men killed; 10 guns, 12 mortars and 47 machineguns destroyed; and 250 enemy officers and men taken prisoner.[12]

The 8th Guards Army

The Soviet assault on the central sector of the Seelow Heights continued at full pressure all the second day. Dawn brought another formidable artillery barrage followed by a series of air attacks.

The early Soviet success at Gusow enabled the lines of the 20th Panzergrenadier Division, whose survivors had regrouped on the "Hardenberg-Stellung" astride Seelow during the night, to be turned from this northern flank, from where the Soviet tanks could scale the escarpment. Sergeant Averdieck of the 90th Panzergrenadier Regiment reported:

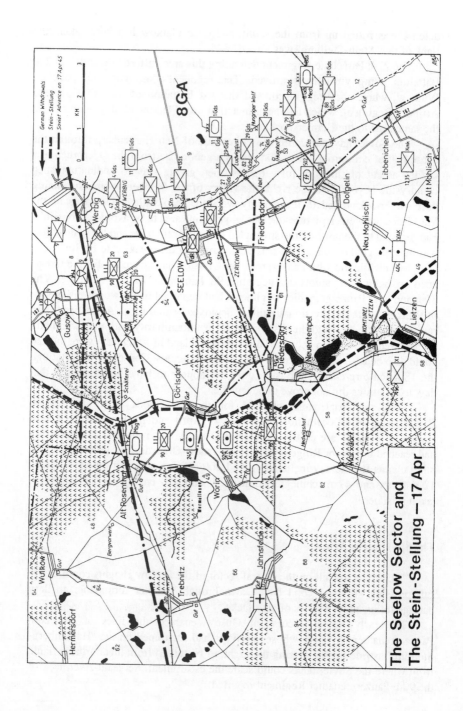

The Seelow Sector and
The Stein-Stellung — 17 Apr

At 0400 hours on 17 April our command post was moved back more centrally in our sector to Gusow railway station. We had hardly camouflaged the vehicle and moved into the cellar of the station when a tank alert was given. The tanks had come up the road without firing. At the same time the bomber squadron reappeared and started bombing a little to our rear. To add to our misfortunes, alarming reports were radioed from the battalions. The enemy was in the rear of the 1st and 2nd Battalions with tanks and infantry and the 3rd Battalion was falling back. At 0900 hours there was another bombardment on our forward positions, knocking out the radio APC of the 1st Battalion, and the crew of the 3rd Battalion's radio APC were injured by wood splinters. The section leader, although the most seriously wounded, nevertheless drove the vehicle back to the supply column himself.

The regiment was now in such disorder, for instance no communications or contact, that we had to withdraw under cover of some self-propelled guns (SPGs) and tanks to the next line of defense, the "Stein-Stellung" near Görlsdorf. It was none too soon, for we were already being fired at from the flank and were showered with wood splinters in the copse in which we stopped to assemble. When we arrived at midday with the remainder of the regiment at the "Stein-Stellung" it was already under shell fire and the Russians were assembling tanks and infantry opposite. Of our 1st and 2nd Battalions only a few scattered groups had come back, and these were now reorganized into a weak battalion. The command post was set up on the reverse slopes of the defense position. While the commanders were setting the sector boundaries, the enemy artillery and mortar fire steadily increased. Mortar bombs and salvos of rockets crashed down around us and it was getting more and more un-comfortable.

Suddenly there was another alarm. Somehow the Russians had got through our lines and were behind us. Before anyone knew what was happening our troops were leaving their positions. There was a mad rush by the staff to round up the soldiers and recover our positions with a counterattack. Soon machinegun and tank fire was coming from every direction. At dusk we went into the attack with the support of some 2cm antiaircraft guns and tanks, although these heavy vehicles were not very maneuverable in the woods. We formed a blocking position on the corner of a wood with our APC. The fighting went on into the night but the old positions were not recovered.[13]

Sergeant Waldmüller's tank of the 8th Panzer Battalion was engaged on the Heights near Seelow. He wrote:

The Russians attack in infantry masses, some drunk, and deployed in lines of up to three ranks deep. We defend ourselves with machineguns and high-explosive shells. Russian snipers aim at our driver's viewing slit, scoring six hits on it; a seventh hit enters the depressed muzzle of the gun just as it is being fired. Fortunately the result is only a swelling of the gun barrel due to the high-explosive shell detonating there. The heat causes the camouflage net to catch fire, and the gun is useless. We drive back to our field workshops at

Hoppegarten via Müncheberg, being stopped several times on the way by generals and high-ranking officers, who think that we are running away. We help ourselves to some food from abandoned houses. The workshops are in the woods. It rains and we sleep on the ground underneath our tank, still being disturbed by artillery strikes close by.[14]

In Seelow itself, Second Lieutenant Tams was informed that his company was now part of Combat Team "Rosenke" under the captain of that name commanding the 1st Battalion of the 76th Panzergrenadier Regiment, the remainder of this regiment now being south of the town, where it was to lose its commander, Colonel Reinhold Stammerjohann, killed in action that day.

Tams's No. 3 Platoon on the left flank had disappeared during the night, so Tams set off to ask for the services of the reserve platoon from the battalion command post, but Soviet tanks were already entering Seelow from the north and he was chased by their fire all the way, three of them actually entering the farmyard concerned behind him. The command post had been vacated, but Tams found the battalion commander near the narrow-gauge railway station taking stock of the situation. He ordered Tams to withdraw toward Diedersdorf. Meanwhile the remains of Tam's forward platoon had been driven back into the center of the town. He took these four men along with him, coming across another eight on the way. Only one man in ten had survived the battle so far, and these thirteen were now the strongest company in the combat team.

Near Diedersdorf they were ordered into the prepared positions of the "Stein-Stellung" south of Route 1 toward Neuentempel, where they found two 88mm guns dug in and well camouflaged some thirty to fifty meters deep in the woods. These were down to only five rounds apiece, but the gunners expected to get four tanks each with them and then to destroy their guns with the last rounds. Tams then received a few men as reinforcements and was also given the support of three Waffen-SS tank destroyers. At dusk the 88mm guns in front of them opened fire on approaching Soviet tanks and exacted their toll with seven destroyed, thus checking the Soviet advance for the night.[15]

The 4th Guards Rifle Corps, supported by the 11th Tank Corps, had thus had considerable success, ending the day on the line of the eastern edge of Alt Rosenthal/the northern bank of the Wermelinsee/Görlsdorf/the northern edge of Diedersdorf, with some of the armored elements as far north as Wulkow.[16]

The remains of the 303rd Infantry Division, supported by the 2nd Battalion of the "Kurmark" Panzergrenadier Regiment, held on to the area immediately to the north and east of Dolgelin but were gradually forced to form a front to the north as Soviet forces poured onto the plateau from the breach at Friedersdorf.

From his position close to Route 1, Captain Zobel of the 1st Battalion of the "Müncheberg" Panzer Regiment had seen the column of Soviet tanks following the narrow, tree-lined, cobbled track across the fields to the hamlet of Ludwigslust at the foot of the escarpment below Friedersdorf the previous afternoon, but direct orders from General Mummert and lack of ammunition had obliged him to concentrate his fire on the Soviet armor immediately to his front. The German position at Ludwigslust was a naturally strong one, for the paved track leading up to Friedersdorf climbed a narrow reentrant, whose lower end was blocked by a massive brick railway bridge with only a tunnel-like opening in it, and the steep-sloped high ground on either side was well fortified. However, it is possible that this position was turned by the Soviets with the help of some tanks that had reached as far as the railway near Dolgelin the previous day and were reported to have turned north toward Seelow.[17]

At dawn on 17 April the six Tiger IIs of the 1st Company, 502nd SS Heavy Tank Unit, were bombarded by rockets and then came under attack from Soviet infantry. The latter were successfully repelled by the flak platoon with its 20mm four-barreled guns, an extremely effective weapon when used against massed infantry in the direct fire role. With such a concentration of firepower, the company was able to hold its ground all day, despite repeated air attacks, but by late afternoon the concentration of strong Soviet infantry and armored forces to their north caused them to retire slowly to the west.[18]

Although they had been able to repel attacks all morning, a forty-five-minute barrage in the afternoon preceding a major Soviet assault forced the Germans back at Friedersdorf, Dolgelin and Libbenichen. The 1st Battalion of the 1st "Kurmark" Panzergrenadier Regiment supported the remaining elements of the 303rd "Döberitz" Infantry Division along the line of the railway astride Dolgelin. A counterattack during the morning succeeded in establishing a new defense line running west of Friedersdorf and through the center of Dolgelin.[19]

Lieutenant Colonel Weber of the 300th Grenadier Regiment wrote:

On the morning of the 17th there was the usual artillery fire. We kept the enemy at bay from our cellar entrance with machinegun fire. During a pause in the fighting, our visiting battalion staff left the cellar, and shortly afterward I too left with my staff. Our tanks and their escorting infantry had been turned away by the barrage. Behind the farm, about seventy meters away, we saw a Soviet rifle section advancing like skirmishers parallel to the village. They paid no attention to our rifle fire. We had to get ahead of them fast, and as the village street was under artillery fire, we went across the farmyard, and luckily there was a hole in the wall for us to get through. The land rose to the west. A Soviet tank was driving along the track to our right, loaded with infantry sitting on top. At a range of 600 meters it was difficult to tell friend from foe, so we disguised ourselves by pointing our rifles westward as if we were Russians. About a kilometer further on we came across the Tigers sitting on a rise surrounded by their own infantry support platoon. These tanks were supposed to retake the village. The visiting battalion staff had passed through ahead of us. We were asked to provide frontal protection for the tanks, which we did under my direction. After firing all round for a long while the Tigers had to break off their attack. Meanwhile a battle panorama had appeared on the horizon. Like a mirage in the desert, I saw a tremendous mass of troops to the northeast moving westward toward the Seelow breach.

That evening at divisional headquarters there was much news. Communications had been reestablished with the artillery. My left-hand battalion commander appeared and I was able to speak briefly to him. I also discovered that our neighboring regiment was supposed to have either flown or relieved itself on my orders. I was able to refute this immediately with the help of my liaison officer. The corps commander, who was also at the divisional headquarters, wanted to court-martial me. Filthy dirty as I was, I sought to justify myself before him, and the chief of staff only managed to hold me back with difficulty. The consequence was that the unknown neighboring regiment was stripped of all its awards and decorations, and the regimental commander shot himself. I do not know what he had been accused of. I stayed on at divisional headquarters on special assignment.[20]

The 29th Guards Rifle Corps was able to report having reached the line of the northeastern edge of Diedersdorf/the northern bank of the Weinbergsee/the northern edge of Dolgelin, while the 8th Guards Mechanized Corps was reported to be on the move from Friedersdorf to Diedersdorf, where a major thrust could be expected next day. South of Diedersdorf the artificially flooded valley effectively prevented any armored exploitation in that direction.

On the 8th Guards Army's southern flank, the 28th Guards Rifle Corps had made less progress, only reaching the line of Dolgelin/the eastern edge of Libbenichen/the copse two kilomcers southeast of Libbenichen, but this was not unsatisfactory in the circumstances of comparative strengths and keeping the Germans on that part of the "Hardenberg-Stellung" tied down and so prevented from interfering on the line of the main thrust.

Between them, Chuikov's 8th Guards Army and Katukov's 1st Guards Tank Army claimed for the 17th up to 3,200 German officers and men killed; 18 guns, 86 machineguns, and 48 tanks and SPGs destroyed, 16 guns, 60 machineguns and 4 tanks captured; and 450 German officers and men taken prisoner.[21]

The 69th Army

The 69th Army resumed its offensive on 17 April at 0830 hours after a thirty-minute bombardment, despite being handicapped by the reallocation of its heavy artillery support to the 8th Guards Army for the day. The 25th Rifle Corps, backed by some sixty tanks, managed to push the 169th Infantry Division out of Mallnow and its posiitons of the day before. However, the 61st Rifle Corps's efforts at Schönfliess were less effective, for the 712th Infantry Division, still supported by the Tiger IIs of the 2nd Company of the 502nd SS Heavy Tank Battalion, resisted numerous attacks in which twenty-five Soviet tanks were destroyed and all local penetrations eliminated.[22]

The 69th Army was credited with a tally of 1,200 German officers and men killed; and forty machineguns destroyed that day, plus 56 prisoners taken.[23]

The Southern Flank

The elimination of the Soviet troops attempting to reach the autobahn in the Güldendorf-Malchow pocket the previous day had failed to reduce pressure in that sector. Throughout the night Soviet reinforcements were pumped into the Lossow bridgehead, constantly thrusting forward. Supported by some thirty tanks, these forces managed to push through to the Frankfurt-Müllrose railway north of Markendorf, where they were engaged by SS-Lieutenant Haukelt's 1st Company of the 561st SS Tank-Hunting Battalion, whose Hetzers, despite repeated counterattacks, were unable to stem the Soviet advance unaided.

The "Krauss" Combat Team was severely depleted in the fighting around Markendorf village during the day. A company of the 32nd SS Field Replacement Battalion and the 3rd Company of the SS "Falke" Grenadier Regiment were hastily deployed in this area, but were unable to close all the breaches in the German lines.

The Soviet thrust along the Friedrich-Wilhelm Canal was renewed on the 17th. Unterlindow fell and Schlaubehammer came under pressure on the north bank, but south of this the Weissenspring-Oberlindow triangle formed with the Oder-Spree Canal remained in German hands.

During the night of 16-17 April there was a surprise encounter by German and Soviet troops on the bridge at Rautenkranz, for which no defence preparations had been made. Eventually the Germans forced the Soviets off and blew the bridge. There was a strong Soviet push in this direction westward from Wiesenau during the day, but this was held by the 88th SS Grenadier Regiment.

The 1st Byelorussian Front's daily situation report for 17 April could claim no more for the 33rd Army's progress that day, and that all attributable to the 62nd Rifle Corps. The lack of success of the 16th and 38th Rifle Corps had enabled half of the 32nd SS Grenadier Division's resources to be redeployed to meet contingencies elsewhere.

Nevertheless, the 33rd Army was ascribed a tally of over 900 German officers and men killed; twelve machineguns, two guns, three mortar and two artillery batteries, and four SPGs destroyed; and eighteen guns, two armoured cars and two dumps of fuel and ammunition captured, plus 54 German officers and men taken prisoner.

Meanwhile the 2nd Guards Cavalry Corps concentrated in the woods south and southeast of Pulverkrug east of the Oder in preparation for its insertion in the breakthrough.[24]

The German Summary

At his forward command post at Danmühle, west of Strausberg, Colonel General Heinrici reviewed the situation at the end of the second day of battle with his close staff, discussing all the defensive possibilities, but the prospects of success appeared thin. In a telephone conversation between Colonel Eismann of Army Group "Weichsel" and Major Schwarz of the OKH, the former said: "The 9th Army's battle has reached its climax, as identified by the appearance of both tanks armies [1st and 2nd Guards] and several infantry armies. The 9th Army has conducted itself bravely." Army Group "Weichsel" reported the destruction of 721 armored vehicles since the beginning of the battle, but did not mention German losses.[25]

The Luftwaffe's *Kamikaze* pilots had resumed their attacks on the Soviet bridges that day with thirty sorties, claiming seventeen bridges destroyed, including one of the Küstrin railway bridges, for a loss of twenty-two pilots and their machines.[26] In fact they had destroyed both the Küstrin railway bridges, as Lieutenant General N.A. Antipenko, chief of Zhukov's Rear Services, later wrote:

> On the night of 17-18 April, just as the work on the railway bridges over the Oder and Warthe was finished, the enemy made a strong air attack and destroyed both bridges. Troops of the 29th Railway Brigade and Moskaliov's bridge-building unit restored both bridges under continuous bombardment within a week, so that they were ready by 25 April. So the first train carrying heavy artillery was able to make its way to Berlin-Lichtenberg simultaneously with the entry of our troops into Berlin at 1800 hours on 25 April.[27]

Heinrici's original intention of using the 18th and 25th Panzergrenadier Divisions as the main counterattack force had been overridden by Hitler, who had ordered their redeployment near Seelow and Wriezen respectively, where, as a result of Russian air superiority and blocked roads, they both had reached their new deployment areas very late and found themselves immediately confronted by the advancing Soviets.[28]

With army group approval, General Busse called for further reserves in order to overcome the crises at Wriezen and Seelow. At first Hitler was not prepared to release the "Nordland" and "Nederland" SS Panzergrenadier Divisions from the Army Group Reserve, however, after further pleas, these divisions were eventually released to the 9th Army later in the day. They set off from the 3rd Panzer Army's sector at midnight, the "Nordland," which brought the 503rd SS Heavy Tank Battalion with it, being assigned to the XIth SS Panzer Corps and the "Nederland" to the Vth SS Mountain Corps.[29]

In order to strengthen the defenses on Route 1 in the Müncheberg area, several emergency battalions on standby in Berlin were taken by Berlin busses during the night of 17-18 April to the Buckow area, where they were placed under the command of the LVIth Panzer Corps. Still further reinforcements of dubious quality arrived. As General Busse wrote:

> Several hundred Hitlerjugend that had turned up against the Army's wishes, and without prior warning, were divided up among experienced engineer units in the wooded areas as guards in order to fulfill Hitler's orders committing them to battle.[30]

General Busse was also concerned with the developments on his southern flank, where Marshal Koniev's troops were smashing their way through General Fritz-Herbert Gräser's 4th Panzer Army. He later wrote:

> On the evening of 17 April there was already a threat to our own far southern flank, which in a short time became such as to cause a withdrawal. Again HQ 9th Army, fully supported by Army Group, tried to reach the OKH with the plea that because of the 9th Army's situation and in order to be able to hold on firmly to the boundary with the 3rd Panzer Army, it would be necessary to pull back before the front collapsed. All that the 9th Army got back was Hitler's sharp order to hold on to its front and to reestablish the position at the criticial points with counterattacks.[31]

The Soviet Summary

Despite the overall advance that could be claimed, the second day of battle had been as disastrous for the 1st Byelorussian Front as the day before. The casualty toll had continued to mount alarmingly. The rear areas had to be combed for any personnel capable of being redeployed as infantry to fill the gaps in the forward units, and concern at the consequences of the errors made in the planning and execution of this operation grew.[32] It seems that the realization was growing that the traditional tactics of attack in mass could no longer be sustained with the limited resources available. In this context, the comments of Colonel A.H. Babadshanian, commanding the 11th Guards Tank Corps of the 1st Guards Tank Army, about General Telegin, Marshal Zhukov's right-hand man, are particularly significant:

> During the night of 17-18 April, after the Second Defensive Strip had been breached and our troops were pursuing the attack, General N.I. Gerko appeared at my command post. He told me that I had to drive back to Seelow with him to attend a conference with Telegin, the Member of the Military Council. I told him what I thought about leaving my men in the middle of an attack, but found no sympathetic ear. General Gerko shrugged his shoulders and said that orders were orders.
> We drove along a badly damaged and distorted road to Seelow, in which no stone seemed to remain upon another. After a long search we found

the seemingly miraculously only remaining undamaged building in which the meeting was supposed to take place.

The feeble light from several trenchlights fell on the faces of those assembled. Telegin's expression was determined but could not disguise his depression. I had known him since 1942. In complicated situations Telegin had remained for me an example of party rectitude and principle. And now this depression. No doubt he too had been blamed for the delay at the Seelow Heights.

Most of those assembled there came from the armored units. It almost seemed, I thought, as if they were finally to blame for not having had the necessary movement in depth for their tanks.

It was well past midnight before we finally received permission to rejoin our units. We drove back to my command post in silence.[33]

Some more light on the Soviet armored effort comes from the account of General Katukov of the 1st Guards Tank Army. He wrote that it was not until the end of the day that Colonel Babadschanian reported his 11th Guards Tank Corps were through the second line of defense and pushing foward, having bypassed Seelow from the north. Katukov immediately ordered the 64th Guards Tank Brigade, a couple of SPG regiments and some other units forward out of his reserve to help reinforce this success. However, Babadshanian's left flank then came under attack from the south, so Katukov ordered Major General Dremov of the 8th Guards Mechanized Corps to leave just one brigade behind as security and to bring his main forces forward to secure Babadshanian's flank.[34] Consequently, the next day the bulk of both these armored corps were to be found streaming westward from either side of Seelow.

The Red Army's air effort that day had been disappointing, due to poor flying conditions. The 16th Air Army recorded 1,597 takeoffs, but half of these had been night flights by the old Po-2 biplanes, dropping their light loads of phosphor and high-explosive bombs. Eight aircraft had failed to return from combat missions against claims of nine German aircraft shot down, and two had been wrecked in landing accidents.[35]

CHAPTER 14

Third Day of Battle

For those who were able to notice it, 18 April 1945 was a beautiful, warm spring day, which meant that the Soviet Air Force was able to use all its available resources to pound the German defense.

Reinforcements for the 9th Army

The SS "Nordland" and "Nederland" Panzergrenadier Divisions had begun moving out of the 3rd Panzer Army's sector to reinforce the 9th Army from midnight on the 17th onward, hoping to reach their destinations before daylight. Two roughly parallel routes were available. One via Niederfinow, Harnekop, Prötzel and Müncheberg was dangerously close to the battlefront, while the second via Eberswalde, Heckelberg, Gielsdorf and Strausberg gave a safer margin, but both routes were equally difficult because of crowded roads and broken bridges.

The move was further handicapped by lack of transport for the infantry, so that some had to march, lack of fuel for the vehicles they had (part of the "Nordland" actually ran out of fuel between Heckelberg and Tiefensee) and the fuel available having been contaminated while being salvaged from sunken tankers in the Stettiner Haff, so that the drivers were constantly having to stop and clean their carburetors.

Consequently, the move became so disrupted that order was soon lost and eventually the individual vehicles arrived piecemeal at their destinations. Meanwhile the battle situation had changed and with it the orders for these divisions. The LVIth Panzer Corps was allocated the 11th SS "Nordland" Panzergrenadier Division, which consisted of:

11th SS Panzer Regiment.
    11th SS "Hermann von Salza" Panzer Battalion.
    503rd SS Heavy Tank Battalion.
23rd SS "Norge" Panzergrenadier Regiment.
24th SS "Danmark" Panzergrenadier Regiment.
11th SS Armored Reconnaissance Battalion.
11th SS Flak Batallion
11th SS Engineer Battalion

The XIth SS Panzer Corps was allocated the 23rd SS "Nederland" Panzer-grenadier Division, which consisted basically of the 48th SS "General Seyffarth" Panzergrenadier Regiment, which had only one battalion of two infantry companies, plus the regimental heavy weapon companies. The division's other Panzergrenadier regiment and the divisional artillery regiment had had to be left behind for lack of transport. Consequently the "Nederland" now only rated as a regimental combat group.[1]

The Door Swings Open at Wriezen

The situation now hinged on Wriezen more than ever, as 18 April saw the complete collapse of the CIst Corps's lines of defense in a hectic day of intense fighting. Not only was the 5th Light Infantry Division obliged to effect a major withdrawal that evening from the Oderbuch to the "Wotan-Stellung" overlooking the Alte Oder, but the "Hardenberg-Stellung" in the center and on the southern flank was breached in both the 606th and 309th Infantry Divisions' sectors.
Where the 1st Polish Army contested the 5th Light Infantry Division, villages changed hands several times and the cost in casualties was high on both sides. During the course of the day the Polish troops closed up to the section of the Alte Oder lying below the heights immediately north of Wriezen, but this obstacle, approached across waterlogged meadows, proved too daunting. Never-theless, the 1st SS Guard Battalion on the Alte Oder near Alt Gaul found itself so hard-pressed that it had to pull out to the west that night. In the northern sector opposite Bad Freienwalde, the 5th Light Infantry Division still held the ground between the two rivers all day, continuing to hold Alt Reetz, Neu Küstrinchen and Neu Glietzen, but by evening the division was in such danger of being outflanked and isolated in the Oderbruch that it had to withdraw.[2]
Lieutenant Erich Hachtel writes of this day:

On 18 April we were involved in some hard defensive fighting. The pressure came mainly from the south and there was the danger that our front on the Oder would be rolled up. Late that afternoon, I was driving along the road to Reetz, when I saw Sergeant Major Roth riding toward me on his horse, pulling a gun behind him. I stopped him and then saw brown masses coming across the fields toward us. I immediately ordered him to take up a firing position to the left of the road and he fired several richochets at minimum elevation that did not fail to take effect. The attackers were thrown into disarray and withdrew, so that we had peace for a short while. Sergeant Major Roth was ordered to a new firing position, and rode off.

On the evening of the same day I was summoned to a commander's conference in the regimental command post for a briefing on the situation and receive new combat orders. In the middle of this conference, a sentry ran in shouting that the Russians were right in front of our command post. Lieutenant Colonel Liebmann calmly ordered: "Everyone out to beat off the enemy!" They had come up to within twenty-five meters of the command post. After about ten minutes the enemy had been driven off and the situation was once more firmly in our hands. The conference was concluded without further interruption and orders were given for the withdrawal of the front line to the Wriezen-Bad Freienwalde road, which were immediately put into effect and thus began the orderly withdrawal west to the Elbe.

We drove by night through Wriezen, which was lit by burning buildings, to our designated area. It was a horrible scene that we had to drive through. The streets of this town were burning in a firestorm, and we had to find our way through a maze of collapsed house fronts.[3]

At the new command post at Neu Gersdorf, Lieutenant General Blaurock took over the command of the 5th Light Infantry Division from Lieutenant General Sixt, the latter replacing General Berlin as Corps Commander.[4]

Wriezen held out all day but was evacuated at nightfall. Only the 150-200 survivors of the 2nd and 3rd Battalions of the 35th Panzergrenadier Regiment under Captain Baumann remained ensconced in the Malz-Mühle (malt mill) on the town's northern exit.[5]

That evening, with the route through the town now controlled by the 47th Army, General Poplawski decided to outflank the Alte Oder obstacle and "Wotan-Stellung" defenses by passing the bulk of his troops through the town next day.[6]

The 1st Battalion of the 35th Panzergrenadier Regiment at Bliesdorf was attacked at 0400 hours and virtually destroyed. Only about fifty survivors struggled back over the heights via Biesdorf to Wollenberg.[7]

The Hetzers of the 1st Company of the 560th SS Tank-Hunting Battalion continued to fight all day south of Wriezen, losing their third company commander in three days, and eventually withdrawing under severe pressure only under cover of darkness.[8]

The 119th Panzergrenadier Regiment defended itself vigorously along the eastern edge of Kunersdorf and the drainage ditch leading south toward Metzdorf. Early morning counterattacks by the 3rd Battalion toward Bliesdorf and the 2nd Battalion toward the Friedländer-Strom Canal failed when met by heavy Soviet artillery fire. At 0800 hours the regimental commander gave the order by radio for the battalions to withdraw under cover of an artillery smoke

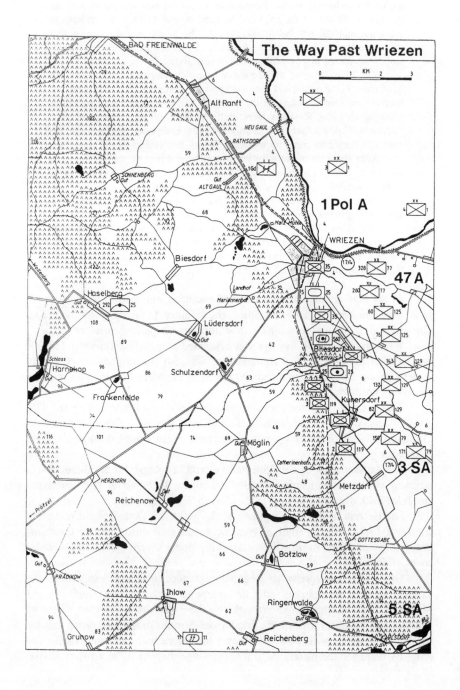

The Way Past Wriezen

0   1   KM   2   3

BAD FREIENWALDE

Alt Ranft

NEU GAUL

RATHSDORF

SONNENBERG
Gut

ALT GAUL

Malz Mühle

1 Pol A

WRIEZEN

Biesdorf

Haselberg

Landhof

Mariannenhof

Lüdersdorf
Gut

47 A

Schloss
Harnekop
Gut

Schulzendorf
Gut

Biesdorf
VERVAIS

Frankenfelde

Kunersdorf

Möglin
Gut

Catherinenhof

3 SA

HERZHORN

Reichenow
Gut

Metzdorf

Protzel

GOTTESGABE

PRADIKOW
Gut

Batzlow
Gut

Ihlow
Gut

Ringenwalde
Gut

5 SA

Grunow

Reichenberg
Gut

screen at 0900 hours. The supporting artillery failed to provide the expected smoke screen, but Soviet armored attacks on both flanks at 0900 hours, using Route 167 from Bliesdorf and Metzdorf respectively, obliged the individual battalions to withdraw of their own accord. However, three companies of the 2nd Battalion were either too heavily engaged, or failed to receive the order from their battalion commander, and were subsequently lost. The surviving company and battalion headquarters withdrew under heavy fire to the Möglin manor farm and dug in. There they came under further Soviet attacks, in which several T-34s were destroyed with the help of two SPGs. That afternoon the survivors pulled back another two kilometers toward Frankenfelde.[9]

For the 3rd Shock Army's 150th and 171st Rifle Divisions engaged against this regiment at Kunersdorf and Metzdorf, this too had been an expensive day, but at last they had gained the escarpment and were contesting possession of the villages of Möglin and Batzlow, a contest that again was pursued all night. Colonel V.M. Asafov's 207th Rifle Division was brought forward out of the 79th Rifle Corps's second echelon to assist with the breakthrough toward Sternebeck[10]

Meanwhile the 292nd Army Flak Battalion was subjected to continuous artillery and air attacks, including bombing by lend-lease Boston bombers, as a result of which it suffered considerable casualties. Battalion headquarters were obliged to withdraw from Haselberg, which then became the firing position for the battalion's guns.

That evening the 25th Panzergrenadier Division sought to establish a defensive front along the two-kilometer line of Lüdersdorf-Frankenfelde, hoping to establish contact with elements of the 18th Panzergrenadier Division supposed to be at Prötzel some eight kilometers away, but Schulzendorf was lost to the 47th Army.[11]

Further south, Friedhelm Schöneck, who with the remains of his company from the 2nd Battalion of the 652nd Grenadier Regiment, and remnants of other units, had defended Neu Trebbin throughout the night against the bulk of the 3rd Shock Army, fled with the survivors westward at dawn. Their first destination was the farmhouse in which the battalion command post had been located, but there they were told by a rear guard that the command post had moved back to Gottesgabe. They continued their flight, pursued by the fire of Soviet artillery, tanks, aircraft and machineguns, until they came to the wide expanse of the Friedländer Strom Canal. Some swam across, but Schöneck and some others used a fallen tree trunk to help propel themselves across. From the far side they then provided covering fire for the rest to cross just as the first Soviet tanks began emerging from Neu Trebbin, surrounded by swarms of infantry.

The German troops ran back to the Schlaanhof farm, where they desperately dug holes for themselves in a shallow depression, using their bare hands and bayonets. They counted twenty or more Soviet tanks approaching the canal, some of which turned south in search of a bridge, but the supporting infantry crossed the canal in front of them as they had done. The Soviet infantry continued their advance until checked by machinegun fire from the German position. The Germans then pulled back another 2,000 meters to Gottesgabe, where the houses were on fire, and the battalion command post was again not to be found.

Schöneck and a friend had become separated from the others in looking after a wounded comrade, for whom they were lucky enough to find an ambulance that would take him. In the woods west of Gottesgabe they came across an abandoned food dump, to which they helped themselves, and then fell asleep from exhaustion. During the night the Soviets pressed through the woods past them to the foot of the Heights.[12]

In fact elements of the 2nd Guards Tank Army, supported by the 5th Shock Army's 26th Guards Rifle Corps, broke out on to the plateau above, where fierce fighting took place with the 309th Infantry Division around Batzlow, which changed hands twice, Ringenwalde, which fell to the Soviets, and Reichenberg, which was attacked by an estimated sixty tanks.[13]

The Advance on Müncheberg

On 18 April, the third day of the offensive, the main Soviet thrust, coming primarily from the 5th Shock and 8th Guards Armies, developed on the approaches to Müncheberg, but at the same time the armored forces behind them, the 2nd and 1st Guards Tank Armies, were having to diverge on either side of the Märkische Schweiz obstacle.

During the morning, SS-Lieutenant Colonel Kausch, commanding the 11th SS Panzer Regiment, arrived and was briefed by officers of the 9th Parachute Division. The latter wanted him to take up a defensive position in a long gully with his tanks, but Kausch refused and instead placed his tanks into ambush positions as they arrived behind a high ridge west of Reichenberg, six kilometers north of Buckow. In order to get the maximum effective firepower, Kausch had organized and trained his tank units in the Russian way, forming small combat teams combining one or two Tigers of the 503rd SS Heavy Tank Battalion with three or four SPGs of the "Hermann von Salza" SS Tank Battalion, and securing them with companies or platoons of infantry. They had barely settled down in their ambush positions when about seventy Soviet tanks rolled out of the Ringenwalde area toward them. The Soviet tanks were caught out in the open and soon some fifty of them were destroyed.[14]

As they arrived, the first companies of the 23rd SS "Norge" Panzergrenadier Regiment were being deployed in the woods of the Märkische Schweiz to the northeast and east of Buckow, where they found themselves subject to constant harassment, for whenever they set up a new position, Soviet tank fire would threaten them from the rear or a flank. Soon no one knew where the front

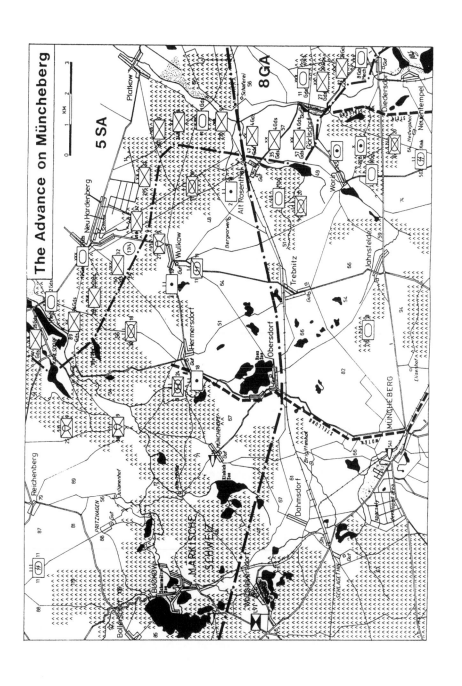

The Advance on Müncheberg

line was any more, as the dense woods and broken ground prevented any general overview.[15]

The 9th Parachute Division, now severely depleted, had mainly withdrawn into the wooded approaches to the Märkische Schweiz, with the 27th Parachute Regiment on the southern flank trying to defend the village of Wulkow, from where the roads and tracks spread west and south towards the town of Müncheberg and Route 1 leading through the belt of woods beyond to Berlin.

The 11th SS Armored Reconnaissance Battalion pushed forward to Wulkow as soon as it arrived in the combat zone, but then came under a massive artillery bombardment as the Soviets prepared to attack. It subsequently received orders to withdraw to a more tenable position. The commander of the 27th Parachute Regiment, Colonel Menke, was killed during an attack by Soviet tanks, and Captain von Majer took over the command.[16]

Soviet infiltration rendered the temporary positions of the 30th and 51st Panzergrenadier Regiments on either side of Wulkow untenable, thus making necessary a redeployment by the whole of the 18th Panzergrenadier Division. By 0900 hours, the divisional commander, Colonel Rauch, had to withdraw his headquarters from Münchehofe, which was already under threat of attack.[17]

Hermersdorf next came under attack. This lay on the "Wotan-Stellung" belt of antitank defenses, the Neu Hardenberg extension of which had already been turned by the 5th Shock Army's advance of the previous day, thus making Hermersdorf a key position. What effect the "Wotan-Stellung" had on the course of the fighting in this area is not known, but the elements of the 9th Parachute Division and an 88mm flak unit (possibly the 1st Battalion, 18th Artillery Regiment) defending the village were reinforced during the afternoon by part of the 3rd Battalion of the 24th SS "Danmark" Panzergrenadier Regiment, as the latter arrived in dribs and drabs to be deployed in the woods east of Buckow. However, by evening the flak unit had run out of ammunition and Hermersdorf had to be abandoned.[18]

By the end of the day, the 9th Parachute Division had become irretrievably split, the remains of the 25th Parachute Regiment and part of the 26th Parachute Regiment being forced off to the north, away from the LVIth Panzer Corps's control.[19]

The 1st Battalion of the "Müncheberg" Panzer Regiment had spent the second day of the battle out of the line replenishing its tanks in the woods west of Diedersdorf, its role having been taken over by the 2nd Battalion, and on the 18th the 1st Battalion was ready for action once more as it continued to secure its harbor area. Orders then arrived for Captain Zobel to take his tanks to recover the village of Trebnitz, which had just been penetrated by some Soviet armor. As they approached the village, it became apparent that Soviet infantry had already occupied it, and as the German tanks had no infantry accompanying them, they would be unable to attack the village. Instead the battalion took up a defensive position along the railway line immediately east of the village. As they did so a swarm of Soviet armor emerged from the woods north of them and began crossing their front. This was an ideal ambush situation, and within a short while the battalion could claim to have destoyed about fifty Soviet tanks, the senior Sergeant Major König's tank being responsible for seventeen alone before he was severely wounded in the face. The battalion then withdrew to its harbor area once more. That evening it came under massive artillery fire before orders arrived for it to pull back toward Müncheberg.[20]

The 90th Panzergrenadier Regiment of the 20th Panzergrenadier Division was in action closeby at Worin, as Sergeant Averdieck reported:

As tanks drove into our flank from the left on the morning of 18 April our APC and the remaining vehicles were sent back a kilometer to Worin. The small, deserted village looked so peaceful, but hardly had we set ourselves up in a house that a cannonade of tank fire broke out in our corner. As we were at a crossroads we came under fire from heavy weapons and artillery fire, in which several soldiers standing by a barn several meters behind our APC were wounded. In these two days our signals platoon had suffered seventeen casualties. During the morning the companies withdrew to Worin and the command post found itself in the front line. The Regimental Commander himself became a casualty. The divisional headquarters were only a few hundred meters away in the same village. To add to our misfortunes we had a mixture of petrol and diesel oil in our fuel tank so that the APC would only move very slowly and the engine had to be kept going. Our young Second Lieutenant, who had only been with the regiment a few days, had the daring plan to drive the APC over open country to the comand post, for as the route was downhill, should we fall into a hole we would quickly come out again. As we started off we came under a real mortar barrage. The vehicle speeded up, backfiring several times, and we were ready to give up the ghost. After minutes that seemed to last for hours we reached the cover of a sunken lane and followed it to behind a barn where all kinds of vehicles had assembled, oddly enough failing to attract the attention of enemy aircraft.

The Russians were bombarding the supply routes that we would have to withdraw over later. As their tanks penetrated Worin I decided to leave the place with my lame APC and with luck creep over the hill to the edge of the woods to await further events. Splintering trees forced us to move back further into the wood. There was some heavy antiaircraft artillery hidden in a commanding position on the edge of the woods. Everyone was to withdraw to in front of Müncheberg during the afternoon, but our division was to take up the rear guard once more. Convoys of vehicles rolled through the woods to Jahnsfelde to join the main road back to Müncheberg. However, a short while later the last convoy returned with the news that we were cut off. There were only about two kilometers of woodland track to the positions and tanks in our rear (Jahnsfelde was already occupied by the enemy) and we could hear machinegun fire from that direction. We knew that there had been fighting on either side of us for some time, and now there was no way out. The divisional radio vehicle, which tried to make a breakout on its own, fell into Russian hands as it emerged from the woods with three out of its five-man crew. With our APC almost lame from its fuel problem the situation was particularly uncomfortable, especially as there were none of our own positions behind us. We prepared for action and aimed our machinegun in the direction from which we expected danger, at the same time preparing the vehicle for demolition.

Toward evening our companies withdrew from Worin to redeploy to Müncheberg. Everyone assembled in the woods, infantry, armor and vehicles. The only possibility was to break through to our lines along a route unknown to the enemy. Our Regimental Commander, a lieutenant, organized those on foot, and our APC was put on tow by a Tiger. At dusk we took up positions along the edge of the woods. Firing behind us indicated that Ivan had followed us into the woods from Worin. As soon as it was dark enough, we broke out of the woods and encountered no resistance. We passed through the burning village of Jahnsfelde without incident and reached the main road to Müncheberg and then, a little later, our own lines, which we occupied immediately. Our APC was towed on into the town, where the fuel tank was emptied and refilled by our supply column.[21]

Second Lieutenant Tams was wounded in the right leg and foot during the fighting on the "Stein-Stellung", and was taken back to the Field Dressing Station at Jahnsfelde. Of his experience there, he wrote:

After I had been attended to professionally and bandaged, I was placed on a stretcher "outside." "Outside" was a place on the wide expanse of a football field, full of wounded lying in rows on stretchers. Suddenly, like lightning out of the sky, two Russian fighter-bombers flew low over the field dressing station and sawed lanes through the mass of helpless men with their machineguns. Filled with homicidal mania, the aircraft flew round a few times and attacked again and again.

Then, realizing how long it was taking to evacuate the wounded, as there were only four vehicles available, with the driver's agreement, I sat on the front left wing of a truck with my back to the direction of travel and hung on to the wing mirror. We were taken to a reserve hospital in Königs Wusterhausen.[22]

As expected, the main Soviet thrust was westward along Route 1, and it was here at the "Stein-Stellung" that the Germans temporarily brought the Soviet advance to a halt with the ferociousness of their resistance. Not only were the remains of the 20th Panzergrenadier and "Müncheberg" Panzer Divisions blocking the route, but the bulk of the "Kurmark" Panzergrenadier Division, including the 502nd SS Heavy Tank Battalion, was concentrated immediately south of the road around Marxdorf. As the Soviet armor and infantry came down the reverse slope from Seelow into Diedersdorf, much of the armor creeping along nose to tail along the road, completely blocking the highway, the Germans caught them in a hail of fire, in which the Luftwaffe also took part. The situation was so serious that Colonel General Chuikov had to call forward his reserve formation, the 39th Guards Rifle Division, to help force the way through, which was only achieved at a heavy cost in casualties.[23]

General Katukov of the 1st Guards Tank Army related how the 3rd Guards Cavalry Corps was introduced into the fighting on Route 1 as a result of the problems encountered:

> The counterattack did not ease off. The way things were going we could not count on the [8th Guards] Mechanized Corps making any headway. Something had to be done. I told Zhukov over the telephone what was happening, and asked him to send us some unit or other to secure our flank and take the pressure off Dremov's corps. Zhukov did not reply immediately. Apparently he was looking for a solution.
>
> "There is a cavalry corps in my reserve. I will give the order straight away. The cavalry will come to you. And one thing more; guard your flank stubbornly as you advance, otherwise it will not just go badly for the tank army, but for the rest of the Front's units too!"
>
> The cavalry corps did not keep us waiting long. Shortly afterward, it relieved the brigades of the Mechanized Corps deployed on the flank, thereby considerably easing the situation.[24]

Gunner Hans Hansen witnessed some of the action here:

> On the morning of 18 April it started again. We were thrown into a sector of the front line a bit further to the north, between Seelow and Müncheberg. One could hardly talk of a front line, for, apart from two heavy flak batteries from our battalion and several infantry stragglers, there was nothing else available. We were deployed in this gap with the task of providing infantry protection for the flak batteries. No sooner had we arrived than the Russians attacked head-on with a large armored force. It looked dangerous, as the fire-spitting monsters rolled slowly toward us, but the 88mm flak was superior, and the attack came to a halt in the concentrated fire of the heavy guns. Then the Russians changed their direction of attack further to our left, where they found no resistance worthy of the name, and rolled on past us. There was no doubt where they were going: to Berlin!
>
> We held on to the position, despite heavy fire, until nightfall, while the howling of tank engines and the rattling of their tracks could be heard deep on our left flank and almost in our rear. The danger of encirclement finally became too great, and we had to withdraw.[25]

Pressure on the XIth SS Panzer Corps's left flank increased considerably as the main Soviet thrust progressed toward Müncheberg. Sixteen Soviet tanks penetrated the woods south of Route 1 to create havoc in the Corps's rear area, but a mounted Cossack troop that had been held in reserve for such contingencies engaged and destroyed them all by evening.[26]

In the afternoon the German resistance began to wilt; those islands of resistance still holding out were either submerged or abandoned. The villages of Wulkow, Hermersdorf, Münchehofe, Alt Rosenthal, Trebnitz, Görlsdorf, Worin, Diedersdorf and Neuentempel were all lost during the course of the day, while Obersdorf changed hands three times, during the course of which twelve Soviet and four German tanks were destroyed.[27]

At General Helmut Weidling's LVIth Panzer Corps Headquarters, Colonel Hans-Oskar Wöhlermann, the newly appointed corps artillery commander, found the lack of information coming through by either telephone or radio extremely disturbing, and the location itself dangerously far forward for a command post. During the course of this day, Reichs Foreign Minister Joachim von Ribbentrop called on General Weidling for a briefing, and Weidling asked Wöhlermann, who had just returned from a tour of the front, to give an unvarnished description of the situation, which he did. Ribbentrop interrupted with one or two questions, but appeared completely crushed by the end of the account.

Shortly afterward, Reichs Youth Leader Artur Axmann appeared in the command post to report to Weidling on the preparedness for combat of the Hitlerjugend Tank-Hunting Battalion that he had deployed behind the front. Angered by this news, Weidling swore to the Reichs Youth Leader that he had no intention of committing the fifteen- and sixteen-year-olds to action. Axmann, who had lost an arm as an officer at the front, appears to have recognized the serious consequences of his plan and promised to withdraw his order committing them to action.

However, as Wöhlermann wrote:

> An especially shattering tragedy remained from this, that shortly afterward while the fighting troops were withdrawing to Strausberg, Hitlerjugend tank-hunting units were roaming about the countryside and in the Buckow woods, inadequately trained and sent into action by inexperienced leaders in a manner both unrealistic and unwarlike, to find their fate in death or captivity. I have no doubt that Axmann had given the promised counterorder. It seemed to me either that his counterorder did not get through in time, or that the enthusiastic young-sters could not be held back.[28]

Nevertheless, it had been Axmann that had exhorted the children of the Reich only the previous month with:

> There is only victory or annihilation. Know no bounds in your love of your people; equally know no bounds in your hatred of the enemy. It is your duty to watch when others tire, to stand when others weaken. Your greatest honor is your unshakeable fidelity to Adolf Hitler!

Reinforcements arrived that day for the LVIth Panzer Corps in the form of a Volkssturm battalion despatched by Goebbels overnight to the Oder front in

Berlin city transport busses after much debate in a somewhat dramatic but absolutely futile gesture.[29]

This day also saw the replacement of Luftwaffe General of Paratroops Bruno Bräuer as commander of the 9th Parachute Division by Lieutenant Colonel Harry Herrmann. The former appears to have been blamed for the failure of the division to hold its ground, and, according to Major Knappe, upon his arrival, Weidling had found Bräuer too old for the post and had asked for his relief.[30] However, a different reason is found in a recording by Colonel Eismann at HQ Army Group "Weichsel" of a telephone communication from Reichs Marshal Hermann Göring that day:

> Appraisal of the situation with the 9th Parachute Division has brought up the following: Divisional commander General Bräuer has not said that his division will quit the battlefield. Nevertheless, he reported that his units were completely disorganized and could no longer continue to keep up the hard fighting as they had so far. Then he asked the stupid question, whether he could stand down his division for twenty-four hours. I have sacked him and replaced him with Lieutenant Colonel Herrmann. The latter is an especially good leader. Apart from this I have sent the division reinforcements in the form of emergency units and had a special catch line established behind.[31]

Herrmann arrived that evening and had a long discussion with General Bräuer, whom he had known, served with, and deeply respected for many years. The division was indeed in a very poor state after all the pounding it had taken, but had accounted for itself well against all odds.[32]

The German Bulwark

While what remained of the front to the north of the XIth SS Panzer Corps crumbled away, this formation stayed relatively firm. The flooded valley running through Lietzen was enough of a deterrent to keep the bulk of the Soviet armor away, but the 8th Guards and 69th Armies still had the task of keeping up the pressure here and thereby preventing a redeployment of the German forces to the main line of advance. As the Soviet forces streamed through Friedersdorf, flanking units thrust southwest toward Lietzen.

On the XIth SS Panzer Corps's left flank the 303rd "Döberitz" Infantry Division's resistance weakened noticeably and the front line was breached in several places.[33]

The 2nd Battalion of the "Kurmark" Panzergrenadier Regiment, which had been attached to the 303rd Infantry Division since the 16th, held on to Dolgelin village until midnight, although surrounded on three sides. It was supported during the morning by the 1st Battalion of the "Kurmark" Armored Artillery Regiment, firing from near Lietzen. Then the latter received orders to withdraw to Hasenfelde, south of Heinersdorf, where it was needed to engage the Soviet tanks advancing on Neuentempel and Lietzen.[34]

At Lietzen, where the "Stein-Stellung" forked, the young trainees and First World War veterans of the 156th Infantry Division found themselves in action against unexpected opponents, as Helmut Altner wrote:

> The sergeant major burst in with a white face. "Everyone out! The Russians!" We grabbed our weapons. There were no sluggards, one could not dally. From the front came fleeing soldiers. Most had thrown their weapons away. Among them were Germans with black-white-red arm-bands and Russians. "Seydlitz-Troops" went up the cry along the line. And we took aim and fired as we had been taught, always at the body. From behind us came some tanks and reinforcements ran up. We advanced firing all the time. The Russians and Seydlitz-Troops started to pull back, slowly at first, then faster, finally fleeing. We could hardly see them to aim at any more. I emptied magazine after magazine. The chamber was soon red-hot.
>
> One of the wounded raised his hand: "Help, comrade!". The Iron Cross glinted on his breast, a foreign decoration next to it. He wore a black-white-red armband. We went on.
>
> We lay in the frontline trenches. We did not want to go any further. The reinforcements filled the trenches. There was the occasional lone shot. The company commander came and rounded us up. We went back.
>
> Dead lay among the shell craters. Many of them in field gray, nearly all German, some with the swastika on their chests, others with black-white-red armbands.[35]

The 69th Army, now with its heavy artillery support restored, continued to maintain heavy pressure on the 169th and 712th Infantry Divisions. The 25th Rifle Corps pushed forward on Niederjesar and the Germans were obliged to form a blocking front between that village and Carzig. However, the 61st Rifle Corps were unable to shake the 712th Infantry Division's hold on the Schönfliess area despite repeated attacks throughout the day.[36]

Nevertheless, the pressure now being exerted on either side of Frankfurt enabled the fortress commander, Colonel Biehler, to obtain permission to evacuate his bridgehead on the east bank of the Oder in order to reinforce his positions on the west bank. The troops were withdrawn that night and the sole bridge connecting the city with the Dammvorstadt blown at 0529 hours next morning.[37]

The Southern Flank

The 561st SS Tank-Hunting Battalion was now deployed on the Vth SS Mountain Corps's northern flank in the area between Rosengarten and the end of the autobahn, where it successfully blocked all Soviet attempts to break through.[38]

The positions of the newly arrived SS "Falke" Grenadier Regiment's command post and its 1st Battalion were overrun in the main Soviet attack that day, the battalion suffering severe casualties. The 3rd Battalion of this regiment was deployed in the Markendorf-Hohenwalde area, just short of Route 87, having approached from the direction of Lichtenberg. An attempt to move forward from this position drew heavy enemy fire and eventually this battalion ended up overlooking the road in the same positions that it had started from.[39]

The Soviets now attacked Markendorf in strength. SS-Lieutenant Krauss, whose combat team was defending the line near the village, became isolated in the fighting with some of his infantry. They were reduced to forming an isolated hedgehog around the village manor, which they had to retake three times, but they failed at the fourth attempt as the Soviets kept throwing in fresh reserves. Eventually he and nine survivors broke out at 2100 hours and found one of their Hetzers through which new radioed instructions were obtained for the combat team to withdraw to Line "C" near Hohenwalde and occupy new positions there. However, Line "C" proved to exist only on paper, although one and a half Ad Hoc companies were assembled there as a counterattack reserve under an SS-colonel, so together they started digging in on the prescribed line. Those Hetzers whose guns had been damaged were sent to the Lichtenberg sheep farm for workshop repairs, all being returned to duty.[40]

In their situation report at the end of the day, the 9th Army estimated that five Soviet infantry divisions, a tank corps and a cavalry corps were engaged in this sector alone. It could well be that the 2nd Guards Cavalry Corps had been brought across the Oder by this time to exploit the expected breakthrough.

The 12th Company of the 1st SS Panzergrenadier Training and Replacement Battalion advanced eastward along the northern bank of the Oder-Spree Canal until it came across the command post of the 2nd Battalion of the 88th SS Grenadier Regiment, east of Schlaubehammer. The company then supported the remains of this battalion in pushing into the area northwest of Rautenkranz. Soviet forces that had established themselves in the third German line of defense there were ousted and all further Soviet attacks repulsed.[41]

In order to gain the canal as a line of defense, the 1237th Grenadier Regiment (originally officer cadets), which had combined with elements of the 32nd SS Field Replacement Battalion the previous day, was tasked with closing up to the Oder-Spree Canal at the Rautenkranz bridge. A combat team based on the 32nd SS Engineer Battalion, to which had been attached part of the 32nd SS Field Replacement Battalion, including some recently attached Luftwaffe and navy personnel still in their old service uniforms, and some Hetzers of the 32nd SS Tank-Hunting Battalion were also involved.

The operation was launched at 1000 hours with the supporting fire of six light field howitzers, but this was met by strong Soviet artillery counterfire when the German troops were still 100 meters from the canal. While the German troops were pinned down by this fire, the Soviets were able to get more of their own troops across to reinforce their lines.

It was intended to resume the attack at 1500 hours but shortly before this the Soviets attacked in strength, driving the Germans back half a kilometer, while threatening to surround them with deep penetrations through the woods on either flank.[42]

The German Summary

The reluctance of Hitler to release reinforcements to the aid of the 9th Army had resulted in their arrival being too late to man prepared defensive positions, and now the few resources available were insufficient to create a new blocking line of defense in the center where the German first-line formations had been eliminated.

At 1230 hours Colonel General Heinrici, the army group commander, telephoned General Fiebig, the commander of the IInd Air Corps, asking for more air support against the Soviet armored concentration at Seelow. The Luftwaffe did what they could, but lack of fuel and the few units till flying could not do much in skies ruled by the Red Army's air forces. Nevertheless the Luftwaffe's claims for that day amounted to sixty-one Soviet tanks and seventy-eight aircraft destroyed, and the 9th Army's situation report claimed 157 Soviet tanks destroyed.[43]

The Soviet Summary

The day had seen considerable progress on the main Soviet lines of attack, but at considerable cost once more. The Diedersdorf episode in particular pointed up the command problems being encountered, and that evening Marshal Zhukov issued the following orders:

1. All army, corps, division and brigade commanders will visit their forward units and make a personal investigation of the situation, namely:
    a.   Location and nature of the enemy forces.
    b.   Location of own units and supporting arms, and exactly what they are doing.
    c.   Ammunition states of supporting arms and their fire-control organization.
2. By 1200 hours 19 April 1945 units will be put into order, tasks clearly defined, cooperation between units organised, and supplies of ammunition replenished. At 1200 hours a combined artillery and air preparation will commence and the enemy will then be attacked in conformity with the

artillery preparation, the advance being developed according to plan. Coordination of action in the 3rd Shock and 2nd Guards Tank Armies' sector will be the responsibility of the commander of the 3rd Shock Army, and in the 8th Guards and 1st Guards Tank Armies' sector that of the commander of the 8th Guards Army.

3.   A traffic-control service will be organized forthwith to ensure strict order on the roads.

4.   All transport vehicles of armored brigades and corps and those of corps and brigade rear services will be immediately taken off the roads and put under cover. In the future mechanized infantry will move on foot.

5.   In order to maintain coordination of action between the rifle divisions and tank brigades, the Military Councils of the 3rd Shock and 8th Guards Armies will have their own responsible officers, with means of communication, in each tank brigade of the 1st and 2nd Guards Tank Armies, and the 1st and 2nd Guards Tank Armies will have theirs in the rifle divisions.

6.   All officers who have shown themselves incapable of carrying out assignments and have displayed lack of resolution will be replaced by able and courageous officers.[44]

Chuikov was highly critical of these orders, writing:

This order arrived in our Army only on the morning of the 19th April, and by midday no one could have done anything. It was impossible to put into effect the recommendations on the organisation of coordination between the tank armies and the mixed armies within a few hours. It meant, after all, that everything was to be completely re-cast. This work should have been carried out by Front Headquarters when the operation was still in the planning stage, when there was plenty of time for it. And the main point was the question of what the tank armies were to do remained unsettled: were they operating independently, carrying out the Front Commander's order, or were they being attached as a supporting arm to the mixed armies?

Putting the responsibility for the coordinating action on the Army Commanders at a critical period in the development of the operation simply meant abdicating one's own responsibility and leaving it to be borne by others.[45]

Indeed, the fact that these coordinating instructions were issued so late in the operation points up Zhukov's original intention of using his armored forces independently of the main body of his 1st Byelorussian Front. Lack of properly organized coordination between armor and infantry on the battlefield during these first three days also indicates how confusing the situation must have been on the ground.

Another order issued by Zhukov that evening is quoted by Chuikov:

The Front Commander has ordered:

1.   The pace of the advance is to be increased without delay. Delay in the development of the Berlin Operation will result in the troops becoming exhausted and expending their ammunition without having taken Berlin.

2.   All army commanders will locate themselves at the observation posts of their corps commanders on the main axis. I categorically forbid them to remain behind their formations.

3.   The whole of the artillery, including the extra heavy, is to be brought up to the first echelon, not more than two to three kilometres behind the first echelon engaging the enemy. The artillery is to be engaged on those sectors decisive for the breakthrough. It is to be borne in mind that the enemy will resist all the way to Berlin, fighting for every bush and building. The tanks and SPGs must there-fore not wait until the artillery has eliminated all opposition before them before advancing over cleared areas.

4.   If we hit the enemy relentlessly and push forward on Berlin day and night, it will soon be ours.[46]

Colonel Babadshanian of the 11th Guards Tank Corps, while effecting his own liaison with the infantry, was witness to an interesting episode:

After some bitter fighting at the Seelow Heights our troops reached the Third Defensive Strip in the Müncheberg-Diedersdorf sector.

I drove to General Shemenkov's 29th Guards Rifle Corps command post with several officers of my own corps in order to coordinate further developments with him. His staff had set themselves up in a rather grand manor house. We went through several rooms until we finally came to the area in which this rifle corps's staff were working.

As soon as he greeted me, Shemenkov informed me that he would not be able to attack at 0800 hours as ordered. He had postponed the time of attack to 0900 hours.

"That must be reported to Chuikov!"

But Shemenkow paid no heed to me.

Early in the morning Chuikov and Katukov appeared. "Are the troops ready to attack?" asked Chuikov.

Shemenkow tried to explain why he had postponed the attack.

"What do you mean, postponed?" roared Chuikov.

How this exchange developed further, I cannot say, for Katukov took me aside and whispered: "There is nothing more here for you to do. Drive back to your troops as quickly as possible. The order must be executed according to schedule!"[47]

CHAPTER 15

Fourth Day of Battle

On this cool, cloudy, windy day the 9th Army was ripped apart by the powerful forward thrusts of the Soviet tank armies.

The army group commander, Colonel General Heinrici left his command post at Dammühle near Strausberg to return to his headquarters at Prenzlau behind the defenses of the 3rd Panzer Army. After three days of battle he knew that there was no chance of the 9th Army holding the Soviets back any longer. The only practical course of action now was to withdraw from the Oder immediately.

The command post of General Weidling's LVIth Panzer Corps had already moved back to Kolonie Herrenhorst, three kilometers south of Strausberg.[1]

The Northern Breach

During the night the 5th Light Infantry Division had withdrawn to the "Wotan-Stellung" on the orders of the CIst Corps, abandoning the so-called Insel (Island) and Oderbruch to the 61st and 1st Polish Armies.[2]

But General Poplawski ordered his 3rd, 4th and 6th Polish Infantry Divisions, with the bulk of the 1st Polish Army's armor, to pass through Wriezen on 19 April and strike out to the northwest, opening the way for the 2nd Division to cross the Alte Oder at Neu Gaul. This effectively turned the 5th Light Infantry Division's flank. Then, lining up in order from the north the 1st, 2nd, and 3rd Divisions, the 1st Polish Tank Corps, and the 6th Division, followed by the 4th Division in second echelon, the 1st Polish Army struck out due west, driving the retreating German forces before them. This drive also enabled the Poles to cross the Alte Oder near Alt Ranft, thus immediately threatening Bad Freienwalde from the south.[3]

Lieutenant Erich Hachtel, now also responsible for the 75th Light Infantry Regiment's rear guard, writes of this day:

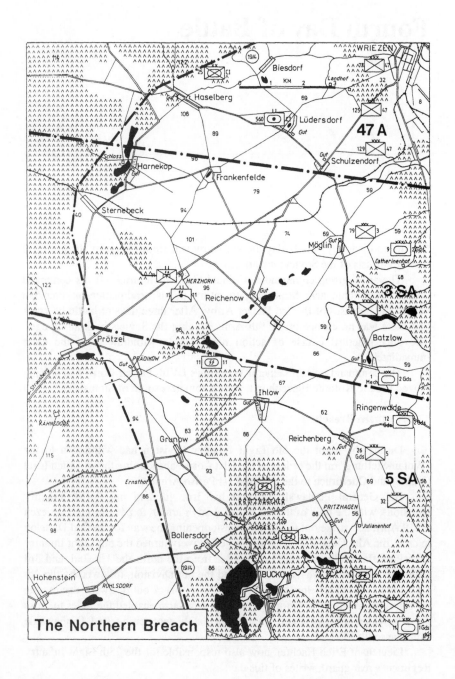

The Northern Breach

As the enemy had clearly broken through to the south with his overwhelming strength, even this new position was only of temporary duration, so that in the evening we withdrew to the line of the Bad Freienwalde-Werneuchen road and set up our company command post in Gersdorf. How confused the situation was is shown by the following incident. I had given my sentry orders to stop the tank company led by Knights' Cross-holder Lieutenant Kercher, as I wanted to speak to him about something. Shortly afterward the sentry reported that tanks were coming along the road. Expecting this to be Lieutenant Kercher and his tank company, we did nothing. The tanks rattled at full speed past our sentry, whom fortunately they did not recognize. The sentry returned breathlessly to our dimly lighted room to say that he had been lucky yet again for that had not been Lieutenant Kercher's company, but Russian T-34s. After half an hour these tanks came back through our location. It would seem that they had lost their way, thinking they were on the road to Berlin![4]

Headquarters CIst Corps was now at Tuchen, ten kilometers south of Eberswalde, organizing the retreat and intending to regroup in a bridgehead around Eberswalde. The rear guard was left to the 25th Panzergrenadier Division and the 560th SS Tank-Hunting Battalion.[5]

The 25th Panzergrenadier Division's headquarters moved to Kruge-Gersdorf, to where its fighting elements had been ordered for regrouping.[6] The 119th Panzergrenadier Regiment, hotly pursued, marched northwest via Haselburg and Wölsickendorf to Brunow, where it met up with the remains of the 1st Battalion of the 35th Panzergrenadier Regiment that evening. The latter's isolated 2nd and 3rd Battalions continued to hold out in the rolling mills at Wriezen, where there was some particularly hard, close-quarter fighting.

The 292nd Army Flak Battalion fought its way back to the Steinbeck area. Its batteries were involved in heavy fighting all day and suffered severe losses. That evening it deployed near Brunow, hoping to avoid the threat of encirclement from the south.[7]

Schöneck and his comrade reached Batzlow during the early hours and were allocated to the defenses with other survivors of the fighting so far and reinforcements in the form of sailors taken from their ships only days before; old men in civilian clothes with Volkssturm armbands, French carbines and fifteen rounds apiece, and Hitlerjugend, eager for the fight. According to the official Soviet histories, Batzlow was attacked in force by Lieutenant General A.F. Kasankin's 12th Guards Rifle Corps as early as 2100 hours on the 18th and taken at about 0300 hours the next day, but Schöneck says that the positions were good and that, despite only sporadic support from heavy weapons, they were able to reject attacks from one direction after another until the evening, by which time the ammunition was running out and casualties had been heavy. They then withdrew in some disorder to Ihlow, where they were rounded up by the Feldgendarmerie and reorganized into Ad Hoc units. This position, however, did not last long, and soon they were retreating once more toward Prädikow through the woods, where they were checked by troops of the 11th SS "Nordland" Panzergrenadier Division deployed there. Schöneck and his comrade were allowed through and reached Prädikow, where they came across the sergeant major commanding the 13th Battery of their divisional 309th Artillery Regiment, who recognized them and took them on as gunners.[8]

During the night and early hours of 19 April, elements of the 11th SS "Nordland" Panzergrenadier Division joined and strengthened the obvious danger point along the line Prötzel-Pritzhagen. By 0800 hours the leading elements of a seemingly endless column of Soviet tanks and motorized elements emerging from Wriezen reached the hamlet of Herzhorn, five kilometers from Prötzel. Here the Soviets came up against the left wing of the "Nordland," where the division's engineer and flak battalions were in ambush positions with some tanks and SPGs of the 11th SS Panzer Regiment. The fighting here lasted all day, but in the afternoon the Soviets prevailed, thrusting forward with strong forces to the west and southwest, and the German forces were obliged to withdraw to Strausberg under cover of darkness. By evening the 2nd Guards Tank Army had reached the line Frankenfelde/Sternebeck/Prötzel.[9]

It was at the latter village, an important traffic junction on the way to Strausberg and Berlin, that the Soviet armor encountered an old Panther tank from the 11th SS "Nordland" Panzer Regiment that had broken down on the way to reinforce the LVIth Panzer Corps. The crew were trying to get their vehicle going again when they saw the Soviet tanks approaching. The crew waited until the Soviet tanks were nearly on top of them before opening fire, destroying twenty T-34s in rapid succession, then wrecking their own tank with their last shell before abandoning it, but the Soviet advance had been effectively halted for the night.[10]

During the course of the morning Russian infantry and armored attacks made some progress in their main thrust along the Reichenberg-Pritzhagen-Bollersdorf road, where the 23rd SS "Norge" Panzergrenadier Regiment was deployed near Pritzhagen, with the 3rd Battalion on the right and 2nd on the left of the road. Pritzhagen had to be abandoned and the regiment then took up an interim position on the eastern edge of the Pritzhagener Forest, where it fought a delaying action, endeavoring to gain time.

When the Soviet tanks appeared, they kept back out of range of the Panzerfausts, which were the only antitank weapons the German troops had with them, and started firing at the treetops, showering the German troops with wood splinters and forcing them out of their positions. The Germans then withdrew through the woods down the Pritzhagen-Bollersdorf road by controlled bounds, with the Soviet tanks and infantry following, until they reached the prepared positions of the "Wotan-Stellung".

The Soviet tanks approached once more and were engaged by a solitary Hetzer, which they managed to destroy. Then a Königstiger came to the rescue,

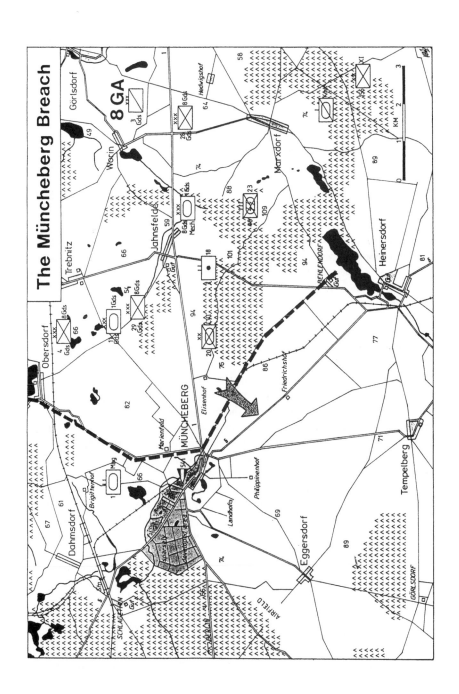

The Müncheberg Breach

8 GA

Görlsdorf · Wocin · Oberszdorf · Trebnitz · Jahnsfelde · Heidwigsdorf · Marxdorf · Heinersdorf

Dahmsdorf · MÜNCHEBERG · Marienfeld · Elisenhof · Friedrichshof · Behlendorf

Brigittenhof · Philippinenhof · Landhofs · Eggersdorf · Tempelberg

SCHLAGENTHIN · AIRFIELD · GÖRLSDORF

KM

destroying two of the T-34s and scaring off the rest. The position continued to hold out, but during the evening the Soviets broke through just north of Bollersdorf.

The 3rd Battalion of the 24th SS "Danmark" Panzergrenadier Regiment and some combat units of the Hitlerjugend were deployed in the woods east of Buckow. The woods were on fire and no one knew exactly where the front lay any more.

Other tanks and SPGs of the 11th SS Panzer Regiment were deployed in support of the infantry units along the division's front, while the 11th SS Armored Reconnaissance Battalion was on the right flank, supporting the remains of the 9th Parachute Division. Two companies of this unit were in position with a 75mm antitank gun on a road north of Müncheberg, their vehicles having been withdrawn to the west.[11]

The 9th Army was still asking for reinforcements, so five Berlin Volkssturm battalions were dispatched to Strausberg and Fürstenwalde. Additional reinforcements appeared in the form of three weak battalions from the revitalized 15th SS (1st Latvian) Grenadier Division, which went to the area west of Müncheberg, and an Ad Hoc infantry company formed from sailors from the cruiser *Blücher*.[12]

The Breach at Müncheberg

The 3rd Battalion of the 18th Artillery Regiment was caught on the move at daybreak as it was passing though Jahnsfelde on its way to Heinersdorf by a mass of Soviet tanks pouring through the village. The battalion hastily deployed into firing positions in front of a wood about a kilometer southwest of the village crossroads and engaged the Soviet tanks pursuing them. The ensuing battle cost the battalion the loss of 8 officers and 163 men killed, together with all its guns, against a claim of up to 100 Soviet tanks destroyed.[13]

On the 19th Erich Wittor's squadron of the "Kurmark" Armored Reconnaissance Battalion was ordered to withdraw from near Neuentempel to Marxdorf, but found the village already occupied by the Soviets and heavy fighting going on in the woods around. The squadron took up a position on the edge of the woods overlooking the village from the south. Wittor wrote:

> The Waffen-SS Königstiger had taken up a position at the corner of the wood on my squadron's right flank. How useful this was we were soon to find out. Late in the afternoon some T-34 tanks tried to push forward on Marxdorf from the woods on our flank. With incredible accuracy, the Tiger's 88mm gun shot up tank after tank. Each shell caused the tank hit to explode immediately, and all that remained of the still fast-attacking tank were the glowing remains. There were no misses and our delight was indescribable. The brilliant position

of our tank gave the Russians no chance to retaliate. It was only at nightfall that they were able to push through to Marxdorf with their tanks.[14]

A combat group of the 23rd SS "Nederland" Panzergrenadier Division, consisting of the divisional headquarters, several divisional units and the 48th SS Panzergrenadier Regiment, had reached the vicinity of Marxdorf during the previous evening. This group's given task of maintaining the link between the LVIth Panzer Corps and XIth SS Panzer Corps proved impossible, for already by 0900 hours, as the chief of staff of the 9th Army was reporting to Colonel Eismann at Headquarters Army Group "Weichsel" that the "Nederland" was engaged southwest of Marxdorf, the Soviets had pushed forward on Route 1 as far as the Elisenhof, a large farm just south of the main road and within two kilometers of Müncheberg.

The "Nederland" attacked northward towards Route 1. The "Trüger" Battalion of the 48th SS Panzergrenadier Regiment threw the Russians out of Marxdorf with a surprise attack and recaptured some German flak artillery with which they fought off attacks by Soviet tanks. Then the battalion pushed forward on the high ground north of Marxdorf, but then came under heavy defensive fire while still south of the main road. Eventually Soviet counterattacks caused the division to withdraw to the south into the XIth SS Panzer Corps's rear area.[15]

Although the antitank barrier based on Müncheberg held the Soviets in check for most of the day, by about 1700 hours sufficent Soviet forces had collected near the Elisenhof for them to punch their way through the last of the German defenses southwest toward Tempelberg and Buchholz, although at a cost of about sixty tanks, according to the report submitted by Army Group "Weichsel" for that day.

Then at about 1800 hours a strong Soviet force broke into Müncheberg from the northeast and soon gained control of this ancient little walled town, which had been subjected to heavy bombing and shelling all day. Within a short while this vital traffic junction, controlling access to the only route to Berlin through the woods beyond, was in Soviet hands.[16]

Colonel General Chuikov described the taking of the town:

The 242nd Regiment of the 82nd Guards Rifle Division did some fine fighting during the battle for Müncheberg. The regiment's commander, Colonel Ivan Sukhorukov, a veteran of the battle of Stalingrad, made a bold and carefully considered decision. His regiment approached Müncheberg by the road running form the Oder. The enemy had built numerous defence installations here. Leaving only one company in this sector, Sukhorukov ostensibly, in full view of enemy observers, pulled back his main forces, then swiftly entered the woods north of Müncheberg and from there attacked the town from the flanks and rear. His infantry operating in small groups was supported by tanks and self-propelled guns. Sukhorukov himself was with an infantry subunit in the centre of the regiment's battle order. House-to-house fighting lasted several hours. Carrying out their commander's orders, the troops tried to cut off the enemy's escape routes. They came to street intersections and, opening sudden fire, created the impression of having surrounded the place. The Germans panicked, which was exactly what Sukhorukov wanted. launching an all-out attack with his main forces, he finished off the enemy. The town was thus captured with our side suffering only minor losses.

When the fighting for Müncheberg was over, I learned from the regimental surgeon that Ivan Sukhorukov had been gravely wounded in the chest and leg. I had him promptly evacuated to a hospital. On the recommendation of the Army Command, Colonel Sukhorukov was made Hero of the Soviet Union.[17]

Sergeant Averdieck of the 90th Panzergrenadier Regiment described the situation around Müncheberg that day:

The 19th April had hardly begun when I was woken from a few hours of death-like sleep by the headquarters staff with orders to prepare for an immediate move. As a result of enemy tanks breaking through our lines we would have to pull back yet again. As there was enough fuel, the little APC whose crew had been wounded by wood splinters was remanned and sent on in advance. We reached the new supply column location in a pine forest at noon and prepared our vehicle for action once more. We were in touch with the little APC, which reported being unable to get through to the regimental command post and that the situation was completely confused. Then I failed to get any further response to my transmissions. Later the crew returned on foot, their APC having suddenly been attacked by a T-34, which chased them and shot them up. Then we had to drive on straight away, having received urgent orders to move as enemy armored spearheads were only a kilometer from our position. Apparently the Russians were no longer meeting any resistance, our enormous supply columns being in full flight without any thought of putting up any resistance. The journey to Rüdersdorf in the Berlin-Erkner area lasted until 0300 hours. Close by was the horde of refugees that had been forced to leave their homes in the middle of the night with their pushcarts.[18]

That evening an element of the 8th Guards Mechanized Corps reached as far as Fürstenwalde before being turned back. This probe had presumably been conducted in accordance with Zhukov's original orders for that formation, but now the losses in manpower, armor and time that had occurred during this four-day battle meant that all efforts had to be concentrated in a direct thrust on the capital.[19]

The Isolated Bastion

The survivors of the 303rd Infantry Division were formed into a battalion-sized combat team on the 19th, each regiment providing a company, under the overall command of the previous commander of the 301st Grenadier Regiment, and were tasked with securing the XIth SS Panzer Corps's northern flank. However, as described in Chapter 14, the latter was constantly extending and was being vigorously probed by the Soviets[20]

Gunner Hansen's unit, which had been providing infantry cover for one of their flak batteries, was relieved during the morning by two infantry companies and sent back to Heinersdorf to rejoin the battalion, but the situation was in such a state of flux that by the time they got there Soviet tanks had already got beyond them and the battalion had moved on. They set off in pursuit once more and eventually caught up the following day.[21]

Helmut Altner and his comrades with the 156th Infantry Division at Lietzen came under attack from mixed Soviet and Seydlitz-Troops once more. The fighting, during which they came under repeated artillery bombardments, lasted all day, but they were able to hold their ground with the support of some tanks of the 502nd SS Heavy Tank Battalion. The Seydlitz-Troops, who had fought savagely against them, then appeared to have been withdrawn at nightfall.[22]

That evening the men of Captain Vehse's 2nd Battalion of the "Kurmark" Panzergrenadiers defended Dolgelin until midnight, then destroyed almost all their vehicles and made their way unnoticed by the Soviets along the Dolgelin-Libbenichen railway line with the aim of rejoining the 1st Battalion and retreating together to Ahrensdorf. At Libbenichen the soldiers picked up the wounded from a field dressing station and carried them on to the 169th Infantry Division's lines at Carzig.[23]

The 69th Army was still trying to break through its opponents of the 169th and 712th Infantry Divisions near Lebus. This day Soviet troops penetrated as far as the Hohenjesar Farm two kilometers southwest of Alt Mahlisch, but were held up on the eastern edge of the latter village. The tiny village of Schönfliess was fought over once more, ending up in German hands.[24]

Increased pressure was reported on the flanks of the Frankfurt Fortress, where several minor attacks were successfully repelled.[25]

The Southern Flank

The point of the Soviet thrust in the area between Markendorf and Lichtenberg continued to be countered by the 561st SS Tank-Hunting Battalion, the SS "Falke" Grenadier Regiment, the remains of the 286th Infantry Division, and elements of the 32nd SS "30. Januar" Volunteer Grenadier Division.

That morning the 3rd Battalion of the SS "Falke" Grenadier Regiment launched an attack with the support of the "Krauss" Combat Team to recover the line of the Frankfurt-Müllrose railway but were met head-on by a Soviet attack coming from positions previously believed to have been occupied by the "AOK 9" Storm Battalion. The latter had just been ordered down to the Oberlindow-Finkenheerd breach by the 286th Infantry Division without informing their neighbors. Caught out like this, the 3rd Battalion had great difficulty getting back to its start point and then holding on to it.

Although the "Krauss" Combat Team had several vehicles damaged in this fighting, the supporting field workshops at Lichtenberg were able to restore them all to fighting condition.

Throughout this period the 2nd Battalion of the 32nd SS Artillery Regiment did its very best with the limited amount of ammunition it had available to support the German troops in this area, giving them the occasional breathing space while forcing the Soviet troops to dig in.

Early in the evening of the 19th, the armored element of the "Krauss" Combat Team was disengaged from its previous role and sent to the support of the XIth SS Panzer Corps, being replaced by the "Schöttle" Combat Team, which set up its command post at the Lichtenberg Sheep Farm.

A Hungarian Waffen-SS Battalion, which had been disarmed at the beginning of March on the instructions of the 9th Army and since employed in digging trenches, was rearmed by SS-Major Hengstmann with weapons discarded by fleeing German soldiers and incorporated into the group moving to the support of the XIth SS Panzer Corps.

South of the Friedrich-Wilhelm Canal, the lines of the 32nd SS Grenadier and 391st Security Divisions continued to hold against relatively weak Soviet pressure after another attempt to break out near Rautenkranz had been blocked by the combined efforts of the 1237th Grenadier Regiment and the 32nd SS Engineer Battalion.[26]

However, the situation with the XIth SS Panzer Corps was now so grave that those elements of the 32nd SS Grenadier Division that could disengage were sent to its support. These consisted of part of the divisional staff under SS-Colonel Kempin, the headquarters of the 86th SS Grenadier Regiment and one battalion, a battalion of the 87th SS Grenadier Regiment, elements of the divisional signals and tank-hunting units, and the Commander Signals and Commander Artillery. However, the roads were found to be completely blocked and by the time radio contact was eventually established with the XIth SS Panzer Corps, that headquarters was itself on the move. SS-Colonel Kempin then received the order to block off the line of the Spree between Fürstenwalde and the Müggelsee in Berlin with those units he had brought with him. This meant that from then on the division was completely split, for the units still facing the Aurith bridgehead were clearly unable to extricate themselves at this point.[27]

The remains of the "Kurmark", which was still between Marxdorf and Dolgelin, were then ordered to occupy a stop line along the autobahn between Berkenbrück and Kersdorf facing north and east, and to cover the withdrawal of other units through that point from the north. The "Kurmark" then began withdrawing in an orderly fashion via Steinhöfel and Berkenbrück to the designated position in dense woodland, where it was securely flanked by the waters of the Dehme and Kersdorfer lakes, and with the Spree behind.[28]

Defeat and Victory

The decisive battle for Berlin was over. The German 9th Army had just been shattered for the second time in three months, all the reserves had been burnt up, some 12,000 men had been killed in the four days of fighting, and there was now no chance of reestablishing any force capable of standing up to the Soviet onslaught.

Hitler's insistence that the 9th Army's right wing hold on to the Oder had prevented any flexibility in the handling of the formations facing the Soviet attack. The bulk of the 9th Army was now isolated south of the main Soviet thrust through Müncheberg and physically incapable of preventing the advance on Berlin. The remains of the CIst Corps were withdrawing northwestward into a bridgehead around Eberswalde south of the Hohenzollern Canal that would provide them temporary protection, while in the center General Weidling was conducting a fighting withdrawal via Strausberg to the bridges in the eastern suburbs of Berlin that would enable his LVIth Panzer Corps to rejoin the main bopdy south of the Spree. General Busse summarized this last day in his study:

> The fighting on 19 April brought about a further yawning gap in the army's front. It was impossible to close the gaps. The wrestling by the army group and the [9th] Army for approval to break off had no success. The army had decided that the LVIth Panzer Corps should withdraw toward the Spree west of Fürstenwalde and east of Erkner so as to cover the XIth SS Panzer Corps's left flank, and for the LVIth Panzer Corps to cut off from the Spree sector east of Fürstenwalde/Erkner so that with them as a flank guard the Oder front could swing away south of Berlin.[29]

Clearly none of the commanders involved had any intent of taking the battle to Berlin, of defending the city by street fighting. They had fought the decisive battle and lost; now they were primarily concerned with preserving their remaining forces and surrendering them to the Western Allies if possible. Fear of falling into Soviet hands remained the dominant factor.

The Soviets had won, had finally broken through the last of the German defenses on the Oder and were at last on their way to Berlin. But the cost had been horrific. An admitted 33,000 dead, but possibly more than twice as many, and 743 tanks and SPGs destroyed, that is, one in four, or the equivalent of an entire tank army. Moreover, the troops were exhausted.

Zhukov was obliged to revise his plans for the next phase, the taking of Berlin. The 1st Guards Tank Army and the 8th Guards Army would continue as a combined force on the direct line along Route 1 to the city and there swing south over the Spree and Dahme rivers to encompass the southern suburbs along an arc extending from the Spree to the Havel.

However, the 2nd Guards Tank Army would be temporarily split into its three component corps. The 9th Tank Corps would reinforce the 47th Army, together with the 7th Guards Cavalry Corps, to bypass Berlin to the north and then swing down to clear the far side of the Havel and block off the western approaches to the city. The 1st Mechanized Corps and the 12th Guards Tank Corps would approach the northeastern suburbs, acting as the spearheads of the 3rd and 5th Shock Armies respectively. The 2nd Guards Tank Army would then re-form with these two latter armored corps to take over the northern arc of suburbs, while the 3rd Shock Army took over the northeastern and the 5th Shock Army the eastern suburbs respectively. The 69th and 33rd Armies, together with his reserve 3rd Army, would converge on the remains of the 9th Army and destroy it.[30]

The primary objective was set as the Reichstag building, a distinctive, independently standing structure, still easily identifiable amid the chaos at the center of the ruined city. Fate would determine which formation would actually take the building, for all those surrounding the city, except the 47th Army, would be competing under front supervision.

Zhukov was aware that Stalin had given his rival Koniev permission to send his 3rd and 4th Guards Tank Armies toward Berlin on the night of 17 April, but still expected to have the city to himself, and part of Chuikov's task was to ensure this.[31]

The weakness of Zhukov's original plan for the use of his tank armies was to be demonstrated later in the fighting for the city when the 2nd Guards Tank Army literally ran out of supporting infantry. Zhukov had no Soviet infantry reserves left and had to call in the 1st Polish Infantry Division to help out.[32]

PART V

Beyond the Breakthrough

CHAPTER 16

The Fate of the German 9th Army

Although the subsequent fighting for Berlin lies outside the scope of this book, being covered in my other work on this subject, *The Battle of Berlin 1945*, some relevent aspects in connection with the fate of various elements of the 9th Army are covered below.

In the ensuing phase of "Operation Berlin", as Zhukov's troops advanced and closed in on the city, Seydlitz-Troops were particularly active, mingling among the retreating German units and passing on false verbal instructions to regroup at certain locations on the far side of Berlin. Captain Finckler of Headquarters Company, the 27th Parachute Regiment, recorded such an incident on 19 April:

> The sentries I had posted on the road reported that a paratrooper second lieutenant on a motorcycle combination had driven past and called out that the 9th Parachute Division was to regroup in Güterfelde, near Potsdam.
>
> However, as no written orders had been shown and the second lieutenant was not known, I stayed where I was with my command until the temporarily disrupted communications with the 9th Parachute Division could be reestablished that evening at Köpenick.[1]

The effectiveness of this Soviet ploy can be gauged by what happened separately to General Weidling and the 20th Panzergrenadier Division. Accounts vary as to exactly how and when Weidling learned that both Hitler and General Busse wanted to have him shot for directing the withrawal of his corps away to the west from a command post in Döberitz, but clearly this was a direct consequence of the passing of false instructions by the Seydlitz-Troops. Weidling was in fact then conducting a running battle through the eastern suburbs of the city in an attempt to rejoin the main body of the 9th Army via Königs Wusterhausen. A visit to the Reichs Chancellery on the evening of the 23rd clarified the matter, but resulted in Weidling being made responsible for the defense of Berlin on the arc Lichtenberg-Zehlendorf with his LVIth Panzer Corps, and then being appointed overall Defense Commandant of the city the following day.[2]

In this first new capacity, Weidling redeployed the 20th Panzergenadier Division to his right wing at Zehlendorf. On arrival on the morning of the 24th, it ran straight into Koniev's attack across the Teltow Canal and was driven back on to Wannsee "island," where it was effectively isolated for the remainder of the battle. However, Major General Scholze could now muster less than 100 men from his division when he arrived at Wannsee, for, in the confusion of the redeployment through the city, the majority of the survivors had headed for Döberitz, sufficient in number for reforming at Kyritz next day as the Armored Brigade of the 20th Panzergrenadier Division. This brigade, consisting of two infantry battalions, two artillery battalions, an armored company with eight SPGs, a flak and an infantry gun company, all fully motorized, managed to get through to the west without having to fight, and surrendered to the Americans just as it was about to be cut off by the Soviets.[3]

The fate of the city was already decided, and Weidling's belated appointment could have little effect on events when street fighting was already in progress and the system of defense predetermined. In conference with his senior commanders at Biesdorf on 22 April, all had agreed that to take the corps further into Berlin would be suicidal. None wished to bring the added misery of street fighting to the long-suffering inhabitants now trapped in the ruins. It was Hitler's and Goebbels's determination to fight on to the bitter end that decided their fate. Hitler's emulation of a pagan god, his *Götterdämmerung* would entail much unnecessary bloodshed, destruction and suffering, for if he went down, so would what was left of Germany with him.

Consequently, all Weidling's plans for breakouts to the west were rejected. Only when his own fate by suicide had been decided did Hitler agree to a breakout once ammunition supplies had been exhausted. However, shortly after Hitler's death on the afternoon of 30 April, his successor, Goebbels, countermanded this order in the forlorn hope of opening negotiations with the Soviets. Goebbels's emissary, General Krebs, failed to make any impact on the Soviets and on the following evening Goebbels and his wife committed suicide, having first murdered their six children.

By this time the situation had deteriorated to such an extent that a concerted breakout was no longer a viable proposition. At dusk on the evening of 1 May, Weidling conferred in the communications bunker at the Bendler Block with all those senior commanders that could be contacted. He told them that he would be surrendering at daybreak, giving all those who wished to do so the chance to break out during the hours of darkness. Many of his officers still felt bound by their personal oath of allegiance to Hitler to go on fighting, but Weidling felt very strongly that Hitler had betrayed them with his suicide, thus breaking the oath, and that was the point he stressed in his order of surrender to the garrison that was subsequently published by the Soviets on 2 May.[4]

Four major attempts at breakouts then took place in various parts of the city during the course of the night of 1-2 May, all greatly assisted by the inebriated state of the Soviet and Polish troops as they celebrated their May Day. The Red Flag had been hoisted on the Reichstag the day before, even though fighting was still going on inside the building, and victory, peace and the chance of returning home seemed very close. Just to have survived the war so far was sufficient cause for celebration.

The largest breakout was organized from the Zoo Bunker complex by Major General Otto Sydow of the 1st Flak Division and directed by Major General Mummert of the "Müncheberg" Panzer Division. Those on foot, soldiers and civilians alike, went through the U-Bahn tunnel towards the Olympic Stadium and then on to eastern Spandau, where the remaining armor and transport also converged, all passing under and through the Soviet lines without hindrance. At daybreak troops forced the two remaining bridges over the Havel at Spandau, with the recently-promoted Major Horst Zobel leading the armor into the ancient walled town in an APC, but this was against mounting opposition that turned the breakout into a bloodbath. Many got through to the Döberitz Training Area beyond the city limits, but the Soviet efforts to block them with aircraft, artillery, mortars and infantry fire, and their own lack of fuel and ammunition, all contrived to rapidly reduce the flood of survivors to a mere trickle, very few of whom actually reached the west.[5]

From Wannsee "island" the remains of the 20th Panzergrenadier Division and some elements of the Potsdam Garrison also tried to break out, initially eastward through the barricades manned by the Soviets at Wannsee station and then south across the Teltow Canal via Schenkenhorst, where they surprised elements of the 4th Guards Tank Army's headquarters, and on across the autobahn ring, heading for Beelitz and the lines of General Wenck's waiting 12th Army. On their way they suddenly emerged onto a fighter airstrip and became involved in a firefight, during which pursuing Soviet forces caught up and surrounded them in the open.[6]

SS-Brigadier General Mohnke organized a breakout from the Reichs Chancellery for those that wished to go. Ten groups set off at intervals via the U-Bahn and S-Bahn tunnels leading north as far as Friedrichstrasse station. The first group, which included the notorious Party Secretary Martin Bormann, crossed the Spree on a footbridge and made for Moabit, where some were captured and Bormann and his companion committed suicide. The others became involved in the breakout across the Weidendamm Bridge by elements of the 11th SS "Nordland" Panzergrenadier Division, with whom they were eventually trapped in the cellars of a brewery in Wedding and obliged to surrender.[7]

Another breakout attempt took place northward up Schönhauser Allee, the only apparently successful element of which was part of the "Grossdeutschland"

Guard Regiment, which broke out of the city with five tanks and sixty-eight men, causing alarm bells to ring at Zhukov's headquarters as various formations were frantically called upon to stop them. Nevertheless, these tanks were able to reach the vicinity of Oranienburg before running out of fuel. The party then split into four groups and continued on foot, all eventually reaching the Elbe and Schleswig-Holstein.[8]

Perhaps the most fortunate survivors of the original 9th Army came from the 5th Light Infantry and 25th Panzergrenadier Divisions. These first withdrew to the bridgehead being formed by the CIst Corps south of Eberswalde, thus screening the southern flank of General Hasso von Manteuffel's 3rd Panzer Army, which was not attacked by Marshal Rokossovsky's 2nd Byelorussian Front until 20 April.

However, on 25 April, the 25th Panzergrenadiers were tasked by General Hans Krebs to mount an operation southward across the Ruppiner Canal to the relief of Berlin, part of a wildly optimistic plan, conceived by Hitler, for SS-General Felix Steiner to save the city. The division broke through the thin Polish lines only to find itself pinned down in a small bridgehead at Germendorf, four kilometers west of Oranienburg, with no chance of proceeding further. Then on the afternoon of the 27th, the 2nd Byelorussian Front broke through the 3rd Panzer Army's lines at Prenzlau and the German front on the Lower Oder collapsed. Colonel General Heinrici decided to conduct a fighting withdrawal to surrender his troops to the Western Allies, ordering the 25th Panzergrenadiers to pull out of their bridgehead that night.

Side by side with the 5th Light Infantry Division, the 25th Panzergrenadiers then withdrew via Neubrandenburg to the Elbe south of Schwerin, where both divisions, closely pursued by the Soviets, surrendered to the Americans, having first discarded their weapons. The Americans then handed them over to the British, who allowed these formations to administer themselves and eventually organize their own disbandment that summer, unlike their comrades in Soviet captivity, who, if they survived, were unlikely to see their homeland again for another ten years.[9]

With the collapse of his final line of defense at Müncheberg on the 19th, General Busse had to take measures to secure the northern flank of his truncated 9th Army as best he could. The Soviet thrust toward Fürstenwalde threatened the rear of the 169th and 712th Infantry Divisions which, with the Frankfurt garrison, were still trying to hold on to their forward positions, as insisted upon by Hitler. To cover this exposed rear, which hinged on the 156th Infantry Division's position at Lietzen, and to counter the Soviet thrusts on his front, he had only the remains of the "Kurmark" and SS "Nederland" Panzergrenadier Divisions, the latter having been cut off from the LVIth Panzer Corps in the battle for Müncheberg. Inevitably the three infantry divisions began to reel back to the southwest as the situation deteriorated, with the Panzergrenadier divisions fighting to keep the escape routes open over the Spree east of Fürstenwalde. As previously mentioned, in order to cover the Spree west of this point, part of the 32nd SS "30. Januar" Grenadier Division had been pulled out of the line to establish a screen from Fürstenwalde to the Müggelsee along the Oder-Spree Canal/Spree River barrier.

On the evening of 21 April, scouts of the 3rd Guards Tank Army reached Königs Wusterhausen from the south, thereby effectively completing the encirclement of the 9th Army, although as they were on the other side of the water complex from the 8th Guards Army, the troops of the two Soviet fronts remained unaware of the proximity of each other. The orders from Moscow were to have the 9th Army surrounded by the 24th, so Marshal Koniev ordered forward the balance of the 28th Army to seal off the Spreewald pocket.[10] His orders to the 28th Army, which was allocated all the front's transport for the move, included placing two infantry divisions in the Baruth area as a counter-attack force in case of an attempted breakout. The screening force were to block off the exit routes with strong defenses against tanks and infantry to thwart any possible breakout to the west or southwest. Koniev was also very conscious of the vulnerability of his main communications route, the Dresden-Berlin autobahn.[11]

To comply with Moscow's instructions, Marshal Zhukov pushed forward the bulk of the 69th Army, together with the 3rd Army from his reserve, a move that not only applied pressure on the 9th Army from the north, but also served to protect the southern flank of his thrust on Berlin. By the evening of the 21st the 3rd Army had a bridgehead across the Spree west of Fürstenwalde in the area where part of the 32nd SS "30. Januar" Grenadier Division was hastily trying to establish a defensive screen.[12]

General Busse's Spreewald concentration now became a focus of attention for Air Marshal Novikov, who devoted a large part of the resources of the 2nd, 16th and 18th Air Armies to the harassment of the 9th Army "pocket" around the clock, with as many as 60 to 100 aircraft at a time.[13] With the 9th Army were tens of thousands of refugees from the eastern provinces who had been camping out in the woods since their arrival in the winter, their numbers now augmented by inhabitants of the combat zone that had fled their homes. Although there was sufficient food for everyone, internal communications rapidly deteriorated, and troops and civilians became hopelessly mixed in their predicament. Ammunition and fuel were in particularly short supply and when the artillery ran out of shells on the 21st, General Heinrici advised General Busse to find some means of disengaging from the enemy and to forget Hitler's orders about holding on to the Oder.[14]

Next day at 1100 hours General Heinrici telephoned General Krebs to say that unless the 9th Army was allowed to withdraw it would be split in two by nightfall. This time his words must have had some effect, for at 1450 hours Krebs telephoned back with permission for the Frankfurt garrison to abandon the city and fall back on the 9th Army, thus allowing some adjustment to the latter's overextended disposition.

At this stage the 9th Army's northern flank was still firm from Frankfurt to a bridgehead north of Fürstenwalde. From there it followed the line of the Spree to a point north of Prieros, where it cut down to the chain of lakes, with strong roadblocks across the Frankfurt-Berlin autobahn. On the evening of 19 April, General Busse had been given control of the neighboring Vth Corps, which had effectively been severed from its parent 4th Panzer Army to the south, and General Busse had immediately ordered it to leave only a light screen in the Neisse positions and to establish a line of defense from north of Lübben to Halbe. He had also taken its 21st Panzer Division under direct command of Army Headquarters and sent this division to establish a line of defense along the chain of lakes between Teupitz and Königs Wusterhausen, but the 21st Panzer Division had since been driven back from there to the next chain of lakes between Teupitz and Prieros, where it held out against all further attacks.

Hitler's orders for the 9th Army, which were received by Heinrici at 1720 hours, were to hold on to the existing line from Cottbus to Fürstenberg, and from there curve it back via Müllrose to Fürstenwalde. At the same time a strong front was to be established between Königs Wusterhausen and Cottbus, from which repeated, vigorous and coordinated attacks in cooperation with the 12th Army would be made on the deep flank of the enemy attacking Berlin from the south.

However, General Busse had already started making preparations for the breakout suggested by Heinrici. The redisposition of the Vth Corps was part of his plan. As soon as the Frankfurt garrison had withdrawn into his lines, the Vth and Vth SS Mountain Corps were to start a simultaneous withdrawal from their Oder/Neisse positions in two bounds back either side of Friedland to the line Straupitz/Beeskow/the junction of the Spree and the Oder-Spree Canal.[15]

On 24 April Colonel General A.V. Gorbatov's 3rd Army of the 1st Byelorussian Front linked up with the 1st Ukrainian Front's 28th Army at Teupitz, thereby completing the encirclement of the 9th Army in accordance with Stavka orders.[16]

Next day Colonel Biehler's Frankfurt garrison at last succeeded in breaking through to the 9th Army, a full three days after receiving Hitler's permission to do so. Thus by the evening of the 28th, General Busse was all set to break the 9th Army out of its "pocket". His formations were now all concentrated ready for the move in a small area roughly between Halbe and Märkische Buchholz, west of the Dahme River.[17]

Busse's intention was to save as many people as he could from the Soviets' clutches. Although he had lately received approval for his move from Hitler in the guise of the order instructing the 9th and 12th Armies to link up near Jüterbog to strike jointly toward Berlin, Busse, in his own words, "neither acknowledged, nor answered." He was in direct radio contact with General Wenck, who advised him of his secret line of march toward Beelitz, where the

Soviet lines were considered weakest, and as far as both generals were concerned, this was strictly a salvage operation.

The point of breakout suggested by reconnaissance was at Halbe, roughly on the Soviet interfront boundary, where coordination would be the least effective, particularly once the 9th Army had crossed the territory of one front, thus automatically checking the fire of the other. From there the proposed escape route ran some sixty kilometers through a wide belt of woodland running westward past Luckenwalde. They would have to move day and night to keep ahead of the inevitable countermeasures, but the trees would serve to hamper the effectiveness of the Soviet tanks and aircraft.

The 9th Army's preparations were both thorough and drastic. Anything not essential for the breakout was destroyed or discarded. Motor vehicles were wrecked and their tanks drained to provide fuel for the fighting vehicles. Artillery pieces lacking ammunition were rendered unserviceable and every soldier with a firearm, whatever his trade or employment, was organized into a combat unit.

It was planned to move in a tight wedge, for which the formations had been deployed as follows:

XIth SS Panzer Corps

Facing the breakout line near and north of Halbe with all the available armored vehicles, and tasked with effecting the initial breach and then taking over the northern flank of the breakthrough.

Vth Corps

Covering the southern flank of the breakout position, then responsible for following the XIth SS Panzer Corps through the breach and taking over the point for the breakthrough while also covering the southern flank.

Vth SS Mountain Corps

Covering the breakout from the east and northeast, thereafter covering the rear of the breakthrough.

21st Panzer Division

Covering the breakout from the northwest with orders to fall back on Halbe as soon as the Vth SS Mountain Corps were through the breach and to follow on as rear guard under command of that corps.

The remaining artillery were massed near Halbe with the few rounds that were left for them.

Between the military units swarmed tens of thousands of refugees opting to break out with the troops, although they must have realized how slim their chances of survival were. Having spotted some of the preliminary moves from the air, the Soviets knew where to concentrate their artillery and air efforts, including bombing the crossings over the Dahme River, and inevitably the toll exacted from these wretched refugees was high. Nevertheless, for most of them the conditions and prospects were now so bad that the breakout, however slender a chance it offered of getting safely across the Elbe, presented a worthwhile gamble.

As soon as dusk started falling, the operation began with a brief artillery barrage on the area selected for the breach, and the XIth SS Panzer Corps started a nightlong battle to clear the way.

Directly opposing them was the extreme right wing of the 3rd Guards Army, with the 21st Rifle Corps deployed in the woods between the front boundary on the Halbe-Teupitz road and the village of Teurow, where the Dahme River became the front line as far as Märkische Buchholz and was manned by the 120th Rifle Corps of the same army. The Dahme valley south of Teurow, where the forest had been cleared for cultivation, was crammed with Soviet artillery. In addition to their integral artillery support, the whole of the 1st Guards Artillery Division was assigned to this operation with the sole object of eliminating the 9th Army. The Soviet deployment was facilitated by the proximity of the Breslau-Berlin autobahn, serving as the main supply route for Koniev's troops in Berlin.[18]

After a night of desperate fighting a breach was opened by first light. Before it was full light the commanders had to get their people flooding through this breach. It was a hectic scramble, but the XIth SS Panzer Corps and the Vth Corps managed to get through and away. For the rear guard it was not so easy. It seems that the Soviets managed to close the breach before the Vth SS Mountain Corps could get through, and the latter then had to bear the brunt of the Soviet artillery fire in their own struggle to break through an area already strewn with the casualties of the preceding corps. Meanwhile the main body worked its way westwards through the woods, reaching the Soviet cordon on the Zossen-Baruth road by midday, and by evening had succeeded in breaking through this barrier.[19]

The survivors then rested in the woods west of the road prior to undertaking the next desperate stage of their breakout. The number of refugees managing to keep up with the wedge was diminishing rapidly. Contact had been lost with the Vth SS Mountain Corps and one assumes that the whole of the rear guard with the majority of the refugees had been caught in the Soviet trap and were in the course of being liquidated. In the obscurity of the woods the Soviets may well have been misled, at least temporarily, into thinking that they had caught the bulk of the 9th Army and later, having realized their error, were happy to prolong the myth.[20]

The Vth SS Mountain Corps and the 21st Panzer Division fought desperately to break out of the reinforced Soviet cordon and in so doing not only inflicted heavy casualties on the Soviets but also served to distract attention from the remainder of the 9th Army. Although they eventually managed to break out of the Halbe position, they were unable to break through the Soviet cordon and remained under a hail of shell and mortar fire. This bitter struggle continued for two days. The Soviets then claimed to have killed 60,000 and captured 120,000 prisoners, 300 tanks and self-propelled guns and 1,500 pieces of artillery. Shortly afterward a Soviet writer driving north along the autobahn found it littered for miles with wrecked vehicles and equipment, mingled with dead and wounded German soldiers whom the Soviets had not yet had time to remove.[21]

However, the state of the troops in the breakout party was now such that General Busse signaled General Wenck:

> The physical state and morale of the officers and men, as well as the states of ammunition and supplies, permit neither a new attack nor long resistance. The misery of the civilians that fled out of the pocket is particularly bad. Only the measures taken by all the generals have enabled the troops to stick together. The fighting capacity of the 9th Army is obviously at an end.[22]

Wenck immediately passed this discouraging information on to the OKW, who in the meantime had themselves put an end to any chances of relief from this direction by disclosing the 12th Army's disposition and intentions in their afternoon radio communiqué. This made it even more difficult for the 12th Army to hold on to their positions in a situation already precarious enough with the Soviets trying to cut off their line of retreat to the Elbe.

Wenck signaled the OKW again that evening:

> The Army, and in particular the XXth Corps, which has temporarily succeeded in establishing contact with the Potsdam garrison, is obliged to turn to the defensive along the whole front. This means that an attack on Berlin is now impossible, having ascertained that we can no longer rely on the fighting capacity of the 9th Army.[23]

During the night Wenck received a signal from Field Marshal Keitel which virtually acknowledged the inability of the two armies to relieve Berlin, leaving the choice of action to him.[24]

Meanwhile the remains of General Busse's 9th Army, guided by General Wenck's radio, were heading for the village of Wittbrietzen, six kilometers south of Beelitz. On the 30th they reached the village of Kummersdorf by noon and then had a brief rest in the woods on the artillery ranges northwest of the village before going on to the next stage. This involved breaking through yet another Soviet cordon on the Berlin-Luckenwalde road and then fighting their way westward through the night. The whole time they were being harassed by Soviet aircraft, artillery and mortar fire; attacks by infantry and tanks; and deception attempts and attacks by Seydlitz-Troops. In the early-morning darkness they had to make several detours in order to avoid pockets of Soviet troops and at dawn they came up against the 5th Guards Mechanized Corps's positions. They fought their way through this obstacle with the last serviceable Tiger tank in the lead, breaking through utterly exhausted into the 12th Army's lines on the morning of 1 May.[25]

Busse later estimated that some 40,000 men and several thousand refugees reached Wenck's lines. Other estimates are lower. Koniev says that about 30,000 of the 200,000 that broke out of the Halbe "pocket" reached the Beelitz area, but were then set upon again by his forces and that at the most only 3,000-4,000 could have got through to the 12th Army. In any case, when one considers the odds ranged against them, the unification of the 9th and 12th Armies was a considerable feat, for which both generals deserve full credit.[26]

That morning Wenck's 12th Army began withdrawing to the Elbe near Tangermünde, having held out as long as they dared. With them went the survivors of Busse's 9th Army and Lieutenant General Helmuth Reymann's Potsdam garrison with several hundred thousand refugees. Wenck sent General Maximilian Reichsfreiherr von Edelsheim to negotiate their surrender to the American 9th Army. Although the commander of the latter, Lieutenant General William Simpson, agreed to let as many soldiers as were able make their way across the river and offered assistance with the wounded, he absolutely refused to accept any of the civilian refugees. This extraordinary decision, which was presumably based on the problems of feeding, would have resulted in their involuntary abandonment to the vengeance of the pursuing Soviet forces on the east bank of the Elbe, had not the Soviets themselves intervened. Their air attacks on the German crossing points forced the Americans to withdraw sufficiently to enable the Germans to control their own crossings, which began on 4 May, using the XXth Corps as a covering screen, and were not completed until midnight on 7 May, by which time General Wenck reckoned some 100,000 soldiers and 300,000 civilians had been successfully evacuated.[27]

CHAPTER 17

Stalin Rules

In examining the reasons for Marshal Zhukov's out-of-character performance in planning and conducting his breakthrough battle for "Operation Berlin", one has to go back to his position and role in the order of things at the beginning of 1945. Despite all his previous success in turning chaos and disorder into victory for the Soviet arms time and again, his very success had ensured the enmity of others.

Stalin himself could stomach no rivals for popularity, and his notorious secret policeman, Lavrenty Berya, played on Stalin's paranoia by arousing suspicions about Zhukov's motivation and style of leadership from as early as 1942. That year he had V.S. Golushkevich arrested, Zhukov's former Chief of Operations with the Western Front, in an unsuccessful attempt to gain incriminating evidence against the popular hero. By 1944 Stalin had decided not to use Zhukov as a Stavka representative any longer, and charged N.A. Bulganin, then Deputy Commissar for Defense, with finding some error or omission with which Zhukov could be charged. Eventually two artillery manuals were found that Zhukov had personally approved, without first clearing them with the Stavka. An order was then distributed throughout the upper echelons of the command structure, openly warning Zhukov not to be hasty when serious questions were being decided. By the autumn of 1944 Stalin was becoming ever more openly critical of the directions Zhukov was giving to his subordinate fronts, culminating with Zhukov's effective demotion to the role of a front commander.[1]

With this worrying background, the Moscow planning conference at the beginning of April had then contrived to place him in direct competition with his rival, Marshal Ivan Koniev, for the highly prized conquest of Berlin. Further, the geographical features of his frontage seriously limited his tactical options exactly where the main German resistance could be expected to be concentrated, and the time for detailed planning and preparation for launching the operation was far shorter than normally allowed.

Under these circumstances, Zhukov's main discernible errors appear to have arisen from his own characteristics of impatience and dogged, ruthless determination in achieving his aim. These can be seen as:

1. Expecting a clear repetition of the Vistula-Oder Operation in both the success of the reconnaissance in force and the early destruction of the enemy reserves, enabling a rapid advance.
2. The initial tasking of his tank armies for the taking of Berlin.
3. The unrealistic use of searchlights.
4. The massing of men and armor into a small periphery resulting in heavy casualties to both.
5. The precipitate launching of his tank armies on the first day of battle.
6. The inflexibility of the mass means of attack, leading to heavy casualties and overall exhaustion.

On the other hand, his change of plan between 12 and 16 April concentrating his effort within the framework of the flanking water boundaries displayed a degree of flexibility in his planning, with the last-minute scrapping of the original flank operations that would have dissipated the efforts of the armies concerned.

The exchange with Stalin on the evening of 16 April, followed by three days of silence from the dictator, must have been unnerving for Zhukov, as was the realization that the casualties sustained were far greater than they could afford.

The next phase of the operation was to produce even more evidence of Zhukov's lack of favor with Stalin.

On the morning of 24 April, Colonel General Chuikov's advance formations of the 8th Guards and the 1st Guards Tank Armies, having crossed the Spree and Dahme Rivers on their way to span the southern approaches to Berlin in accordance with Zhukov's revised plans for the taking of the city, encountered elements of the 3rd Guards Tank Army of Koniev's 1st Ukrainian Front waiting for them on Schönefeld Airfield. According to Chuikov, Zhukov did not apparently learn of this encounter until the evening and then acted disbelievingly, insisting that Chuikov send officers to discover what units of the 1st Ukrainian Front were involved, where they were located and what their objectives were.[2]

If, as it appears, this was Zhukov's first intimation of Koniev's participation in the battle for the city itself, we can imagine the consternation this report must have caused. Apart from the blow to Zhukov's pride, this incident clearly demonstrated the lack of communication between the Soviet leaders and their continuing mutual distrust. Having had his hand revealed, Stalin then laid down the interfront boundaries, effective from 0600 hours on the 23rd (Moscow Time), which were to run from Lübben through Teupitz, Mittenwalde and Mariendorf to the Anhalter Railway Station. Within the city, this meant the line of the railway leading north from Lichtenrade. Any extension of that line left the Reichstag clearly to the west, and in Koniev's path.

Koniev was obviously aware of the GHQ order laying down the new inter-front boundaries when he issued his orders for the attack across the Teltow Canal for the 24th, which included instructions for the 71st Mechanized Brigade to cover the right flank and establish contact with the 1st Byelorussian Front. Somehow this GHQ order had been withheld from Zhukov, for his balance of forces and reported reactions to the news of this encounter on Schönefeld show how unprepared he was for this eventuality.[3]

However, although Koniev's attack across the Teltow Canal, supported by all the additional resources he could muster and under his personal supervision, was a full day ahead of Chuikov's, the latter's combined force was stronger and closer to the goal. During the next four days, as Koniev pursued his attack up through the southern suburbs, heading straight for the Reichstag, and using only one reinforced brigade to cover his open left flank, Chuikov took Tempelhof Airfield and then swung the bulk of his force left across the interfront boundary to line up to the Landwehr Canal from the Zoo to Kreuzberg. Consequently, when Koniev launched a massive attack on the morning of the 28th with a view to getting into the Tiergarten by evening, it was soon discovered that his troops were firing into the rear of Chuikov's, attacking territory already taken and occupied by the latter. It was Koniev's turn to be humiliated. Mortified, he left the 3rd Guards Tank Army commander to continue the battle on a modified line of advance approved by GHQ, and returned to his front headquarters.[4]

This left the field clear for Zhukov, whose immediate goal was to get the Red Flag hoisted on the Reichstag. This was accomplished shortly before midnight leading to 1 May, although German troops in the building continued to hold out until the afternoon of the 2nd, when the Defense Commandant of Berlin, General Weidling, finally surrendered the remains of the garrison.

Koniev's troops then withdrew from the city, leaving the 1st Byelorussian Front to close up to the line of the Elbe, where the American and British forces were waiting.

The fall of Berlin was shortly to bring Zhukov his third gold star as Hero of the Soviet Union, an honor that Stalin could not deny him.

In the early hours of 7 May, Colonel General Alfred Jodl signed the unconditional surrender of the German Armed Forces at General Eisenhower's headquarters in Reims. This was not good enough for Stalin, who wanted the surrender to be effected on his own ground, and as the Reims document had been a last-minute draft by Eisenhower's chief of staff, who had forgotten he already had in his safe the official surrender document that had taken the diplomats of the European Advisory Council six months to prepare, the Western Allies were obliged to agree to a second ceremony to be held in Berlin.

Stalin sent Andrei Vyshinsky, his First Deputy Commissar for Foreign Affairs, to organize the event, which would be presided over by Zhukov.

Vyshinsky was to remain as Zhukov's political adviser in Zhukov's new role as Commander in Chief of the Soviet forces in Germany and in his forthcoming role as the Soviet representative on the Allied Control Council for Germany. However, Vyshinsky's arrival brought a certain chill with it, for he had been the chief prosecutor in the trials that had purged the leadership of the Red Army in 1937-1938.

Eisenhower had no wish to repeat the surrender ceremony, and so sent his deputy, Air Chief Marshal Sir Arthur Tedder, to represent him, accompanied by General Carl Spaatz of the U.S. Strategic Air Force and General Jean de Lattre de Tassigny of the 1st French Army. The ceremony was delayed by one of Vyshinsky's diplomats having mislaid four lines of text, and also by the homemade French flag having to be resewn, having first been presented with horizontal red, white and blue bands in the Dutch style. Vyshinsky then raised objections about the Allied signatories. Zhukov and Tedder had already agreed to sign as principals, but Vyshinsky argued that although de Lattre could sign on behalf of his country, Spaatz could not, as Tedder was already representing the British-American forces. Finally agreement was reached and the Allied representatives assembled in Zhukov's office with a view to taking their places in the hall set for the ceremony at midnight (Moscow Time). The German delegation, headed by Field Marshal Wilhelm Keitel, Admiral Hans-Georg von Friedeburg and Luftwaffe-General Hans-Jürgen Stumpf, was then admitted. Within a short time it was all over, the German delegation withdrew, and the celebrations began. Major General John R. Deane, the head of the U.S. Military Mission in Moscow, who witnessed the ceremony, reported that Vyshinsky, seated on the far side of Tedder from Zhukov, was constantly getting up to whisper instructions into Zhukov's ear. Apparently Stalin later criticized Zhukov's reported speech as humdrum.[5]

Then on 5 June, General Dwight D. Eisenhower, Field Marshal Sir Bernard Montgomery and General Jean de Lattre de Tassigny flew to Berlin with the basic staff for founding the Allied Control Commission. Upon arrival they were driven to Wendenschloss, where Zhukov was occupying a villa on the banks of the Dahme River. General Eisenhower presented Zhukov with the American Legion of Merit. The Western delegations were then allocated villas but then were left waiting with growing impatience, presumably while Zhukov and Vyshinsky were consulting with Moscow. It was not until after they had threatened to leave that they were summoned to the yacht club, where the signing ceremony finally took place at 1700 hours. In the discussion beforehand, Zhukov told Eisenhower that the Allied Control Commission would not be able to begin work until the Americans and British had withdrawn to their proper zones from the temporary boundary on the Elbe. Montgomery estimated this would take three weeks to achieve, with which Zhukov agreed. The discourtesy shown by the Soviets on this occasion was such that the Western delegations declined an invitation to remain for a banquet arranged for them, flying back the same day.

Although President Truman told Stalin that he was prepared to start the withdrawal on 21 June, Stalin asked for a postponement, saying that Marshal Zhukov was needed back in Moscow for a meeting of the Supreme Soviet and for the victory parade scheduled for the 24th. Consequently it was 4 July before the Western Allies were able to take over their allocated sectors in Berlin.

The reviewing officer at the victory parade on Red Square should really have been Stalin as Commander in Chief, but Zhukov later learned from Stalin's son Vasily that Stalin had been unable to control the magnificent white Arabian stallion selected by Budenny for the reviewing officer to ride. Zhukov, of course, had no problem with the horse, and thoroughly enjoyed this moment of triumph. His parade uniform had to be reinforced with a metal plate to carry the weight of all his decorations, which included the three gold stars of a Hero of the Soviet Union, six Orders of Lenin, two Orders of Victory, the Order of the October Revolution, three Orders of the Red Banner and two Orders of Suvorov First Class, plus numerous foreign decorations. This parade was followed upon his return to Berlin by another with the Western Allies.[6]

The next big event was the Potsdam Conference in mid-July. Stalin's security was very much the responsibility of the NKVD, even the suggestion of a military guard of honor to greet him at the station being rejected. Zhukov escorted the dictator to his selected residence, but thereafter was merely an observer at the conference.

Later in the year, one of Berya's deputies, Viktor Abakumov, arrived in the Soviet Zone unannounced and started arresting some of Zhukov's staff. Zhukov summoned Abakumov and demanded to know why Abakumov had not presented himself upon arrival with an explanation for the arrests. Abakumov was unable to offer a satisfactory explanation, so Zhukov ordered the release of the arrested officers and sent Abakumov back to Moscow, a move that could not have improved relations with Berya.[7]

At a meeting in the Kremlin shortly afterward, Stalin accused Zhukov, who was not present, of claiming the credit for the Red Army's victories during the war and belittling the role of the Stavka. Some of the others present then joined in with critical comments: the knives were out for Zhukov.[8]

Then in March 1946 Zhukov was recalled to Moscow and appointed Commander in Chief of the Ground Forces. He promptly came into conflict with Nikolai Alexandrovich Bulganin, the First Deputy Commissar for Defense, whom Zhukov considered incompetent in military matters. The arguments between them resulted in a further deterioration in Zhukov's relationship with Stalin. In June Zhukov was summoned to a meeting of the Main Military Council, chaired by Stalin. Also present were Berya, Bulganin and Kaganovich from the Politburo, Marshals Koniev, Sokolovsky and Rokossovsky, and Generals Golikov, Rybalko and Kruhlev, with Shtemenko as secretary. Stalin gave Shtemenko a folder and asked him to read the contents. Inside was a letter signed by Air Chief Marshal Novikov, in which it said that Zhukov had often spoken unflatteringly about Stalin when discussing the Stavka and the government during the war. Further evidence obtained from over seventy arrested officers accused Zhukov of plotting against the party, the government and Stalin. When called upon to comment, Koniev said that, although Zhukov was difficult to work with, his conduct at the front had shown him to be honest and loyal, constantly going forward to ensure that the Stavka's orders were being carried out. The other commanders present commented similarly, only Golikov supporting the case against Zhukov. The Politburo members then spoke in turn, claiming that Zhukov was dangerous, conducting himself like a Bonaparte. When it was his turn to speak, Zhukov admitted that he had exaggerated his role in the victory over Germany but, as a Communist, had conscientiously fulfilled all that had been required of him by the party. The meeting concluded with the adoption of Stalin's proposal that Zhukov be assigned to the command of the Odessa Military District.

Novikov, who was rehabilitated after the death of Stalin, testified at the subsequent trial of Abakumov that he had been interrogated day and night about Zhukov from 22 to 30 April and from 4 to 8 May 1946, a process that left him a completely broken man, ready to sign the statement on Zhukov that had been prepared for him. Abakumov was shot.[9]

Relegated to the secondary Odessa Military District, which would normally be commanded by a colonel general, Zhukov was determined to maintain his normal standards. However, the humiliation continued, and in December 1947 he was called to a meeting of the Central Committee of the Communist Party, at which he found his was one of seven names being proposed for removal from the Committee. He refused to speak in his own defense, and once the vote was taken against him, he marched straight out of the room without uttering a word. He now fully expected to be arrested at any moment. Meanwhile others were being arrested in an attempt to gather more evidence against him, including Telegin, who had been his Member of the Military Council in the 1st Byelorussian Front. Telegin, tortured, was forced to retire from the army. He was then tried and sentenced to twenty-five years' hard labor, but was also rehabilitated after Stalin's death.

Under this pressure, Zhukov suffered a heart attack in January 1948 and after hospitalization was transferred to the command of the Ural Military District, another colonel general's appointment. His was not the only well-known name from the war that was no longer being mentioned by the propagandists. By the third anniversary of the fall of Berlin, *Pravda* managed to comment on the event without even mentioning Zhukov's name once.[10]

Two years later, fortune began to smile a little more kindly on him, as Stalin relented slightly. A local motorcycle factory elected Zhukov as their delegate to the Supreme Soviet, and then in June 1951 he was permitted to attend the Polish National Day celebrations in Warsaw as a member of the official Soviet delegation. This was followed by selection as a delegate to the Nineteenth Party Congress in October 1952, at which Zhukov was named a candidate member of the Central Committee.[11]

Then Stalin died in March 1953 and was succeeded by Nikita Khrushchev, who quickly appointed Zhukov First Deputy Minister of Defense and Commander in Chief of Ground Forces. Another early move of Khrushchev's was to organize the arrest of Berya at a meeting of the Council of Ministers. Because all the security at the Kremlin was in the hands of Berya's NKVD, Khrushchev got Zhukov to effect the arrest with the aid of some army officers that had no idea of their role until the very last minute. Berya was subsequently tried at a special court presided over by Koniev and shot.[12]

Zhukov became Minister of Defense and as such was in charge of the Soviet Armed Forces during the interesting and important period when the old conventional forces were being considerably reduced in size and the implications of nuclear warfare were being tackled for the first time.[13]

During this same period, Zhukov staunchly supported Khrushchev, and his support was appreciated. Instead of the usual Order of Lenin awarded on such occasions, in 1956 he received his fourth gold star as a Hero of the Soviet Union on his sixtieth birthday. Then in June 1957, Khrushchev had problems with the so-called Anti-party Group, who were proposing to depose him by means of a majority vote in the Presidium, but Khrushchev managed to get the decision postponed to a meeting of the entire Central Committee, and Zhukov helped to convene the latter quickly and get the decision reversed. The following month Zhukov was rewarded by becoming the first professional soldier ever to be appointed to the fifteen-man Presidium of the Central Committee.[14]

However, Khrushchev, Stalin-like, came to regard the strength of Zhukov's position as a threat to his own political leadership, and on 26 October of that year, upon Zhukov's return to Moscow from an official visit to Yugoslavia and Albania, it was announced that Zhukov had been relieved of all his duties. Some days later the reasons for this were published as accusations of having attempted to reduce the structure and role of the party organizations within the armed forces, encouraging the development of his own personality cult and the inflation of his role in the war, being inclined to adventurism in the foreign policy of the Soviet Union and in his leadership of the Ministry of Defence, and being lacking overall in party spirit.[15]

Deprived of his positions as a member of the Presidium and the Central Committee and as Minister of Defense, Zhukov withdrew to the dacha outside Moscow that Stalin had given him for life during the war. *Pravda* then published an article by Marshal Koniev that amounted to a scathing attack on Zhukov's role during the war and as Minister of Defense.

In March 1958 Zhukov was further humiliated by his contrived retirement as a Marshal of the Soviet Union, an unprecedented step, for marshals were normally transferred to the Group of Inspectors, whose occasional duties justified the continuation of their active duty perquisites, such as an aide-de-camp and a chauffeur-driven car.[16]

Zhukov was now fair game for his old antagonists, and in March 1964 Chuikov attacked Zhukov for not going on to take Berlin in February 1945, his book *The End of the Third Reich* being the first of the senior commanders' memoirs to be allowed to be published after the war.[17]

Shortly before he was deposed by a coup in October 1964, Khrushchev visted Zhukov in an attempt to mend fences, but Zhukov was not taken in.

The following year, under the Brezhnev regime, Zhukov was invited to attend a celebration of the twentieth anniversary of the victory over Germany, at which he received a great ovation. The next day he joined his old colleagues in reviewing the victory parade from the top of Lenin's mausoleum.[18]

A request then arrived from a French publisher for permission to include a book on Zhukov in a series of twenty books on commanders of the Second World War. Somehow this request managed to get through the system, resulting in Zhukov producing his memoirs, upon which he had been working since his retirement. There followed considerable delays in obtaining official clearance, during which Zhukov suffered a second heart attack, but then the manuscript was eventually approved by no less than General Secretary Brezhnev, and by the end of April 1968 the book was on sale in Moscow. Despite an official ban on any form of publicity, Zhukov's memoirs were an instant success, and the feedback from the readers, amounting to over 10,000 letters, encouraged Zhukov to start work on a second edition with his morale greatly enhanced.[19]

Then in 1971 Zhukov was elected as a delegate to the Twenty-fourth Party Congress, an event he looked forward to as a form of reinstatement, but, to his great disappointment, Brezhnev made it plain that he was not expected to attend.

Zhukov continued working on the revision of his memoirs. At one stage, Marshal Koniev visited him to apologize for his past conduct and to discuss what they had experienced during the war, in a spirit of reconciliation that Zhukov fully accepted.

In 1973 his second wife fell seriously ill and died in the November. Seven months later, on 18 June 1974, Zhukov also died, just prior to the publication of the second edition of his memoirs. He was cremated and his ashes buried with full military honors in the Kremlin wall.

He was survived by three daughters, two from his first and one from his second marriage, all of whom have proudly defended their father's name over the years.[20]

On the fiftieth anniversary of the end of the Second World War in Europe, Zhukov was finally honored by his countrymen with the erection of an equestrian statue in Moscow, symbolizing his great moment of triumph at the victory parade in 1945.

From this account, one can see how the blight of Stalinism affected not only its direct victims like Zhukov, but also how the portrayal of history within the Soviet Union and its satellites was warped to reflect the Communist Party line of the moment, leaving the unraveling of truth from fiction a monumental task for post-*glasnost* historians.

Abbreviations and Symbols

A	Army	Fd Rep	Field Replacement
AA	Antiaircraft	Flamethr	Flamethrower
Amb	Ambulance	FFR	Frankfurt Fortress
Amph	Amphibious		Regiment
APC	Armored personnel	F Gr	"Führer" Grenadier
	carrier	Fus	Fusilier
Armd	Armored	GCC	Guards Cavalry Corps
Arty	Artillery	"GD"	"Grossdeutschland"
Aslt	Assault	Gd	Guard
ATk	Antitank	Gds	Guards
B/Bde	Brigade	Gdsmn	Guardsman
Bbg	"Brandenburg"	Gen	General
BF	Byelorussian Front	Gp	Group
Bn	Battalion	GRC	Guards Rifle Corps
Br	Bridge/Bridging	GMRB	Guards Motor Rifle
C	Corps		Brigade
Capt	Captain	GRR	Guards Rifle Regiment
Cav	Cavalry	GTA	Guards Tank Army
Chem	Chemical	GTC	Guards Tank Corps
Col	Colonel	How	Howitzer
Constr	Construction	Hy	Heavy
Coy	Company	ID	Infantry Division
D/Div	Division	Ind	Independent
Def	Defense	Inf	Infantry
Det	Detachment	Jagdpz	Tank-Hunting
EM	Enlisted Men	Kmk	"Kurmark"
Engr	Engineer	L	Light
Fd	Field	LMG	Light machinegun

Lt	Light/Lieutenant
LW	Luftwaffe
Maj	Major
Mbg	"Müncheberg"
MC	Mechanized Corps
M/C	Motorcycle
Mech	Mechanized
Med	Medium/Medical
Mil	Military
Mine-Clg	Mine-Clearing
MMG	Medium Machinegun
MO	Medical Officer
Mor	Mortar
Mot	Motorized
MRB	Motor Rifle Brigade
Mtd	Mounted
Mtn	Mountain
1001 N	"1001 Nights" Battle Group
O/Cdt	Officer Cadet
Offr	Officer
Para	Parachute
Pl	Platoon
Pol	Polish/Police
Pol Sect	Political Section
Port	Portable
Pz	Panzer
PzGr	Panzergrenadier
PzGrD	Panzergrenadier Division
Regt	Regiment

RAD	Reichsarbeitsdienst
RD	Rifle Division
Recce	Reconnaissance
RL	Rocket Launcher
SA	Shock Army/
	Sturmabteilung
Sgt	Sergeant
Sigs	Signals
SMG	Submachinegun
SP	Self-Propelled
SPG	Self-Propelled Gun
SSgt	Staff Sergeant
Stn	Station
Sup	Supply
Svcs	Services
Sy	Security
TB	Tank Brigade
TC	Tank Corps
Tk	Tank
Tps	Troops
Tpt	Transport
Trg	Training
UF	Ukrainian Front
V	Volks
Vet	Veterinary
VGr	Volksgrenadier
Vol	Volunteer
VS	Volkssturm

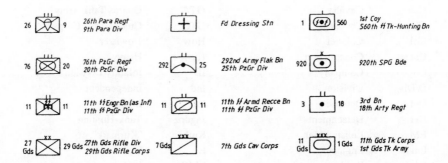

Appendices

Appendix I

ORGANIZATION OF A RED ARMY RIFLE DIVISION 1945

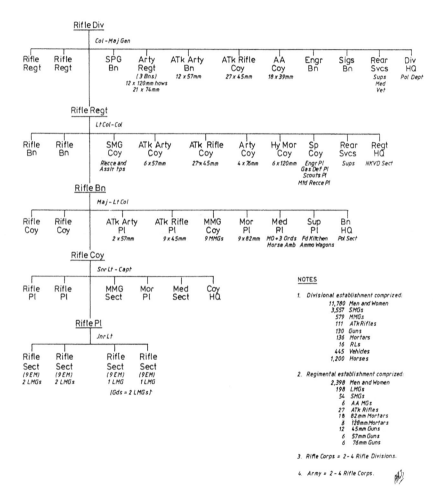

NOTES

1. Divisional establishment comprised:

11,780	Men and Women
3,557	SMGs
579	MMGs
111	ATkRifles
130	Guns
136	Mortars
16	RLs
445	Vehicles
1,200	Horses

2. Regimental establishment comprised:

2,398	Men and Women
198	LMGs
54	SMGs
6	AA MGs
27	ATk Rifles
18	82mm Mortars
8	120mm Mortars
12	45mm Guns
6	57mm Guns
6	76mm Guns

3. Rifle Corps = 2-4 Rifle Divisions.

4. Army = 2-4 Rifle Corps.

Appendix II

ORGANIZATION OF RED ARMY TANK AND MECHANIZED FORMATIONS IN 1945

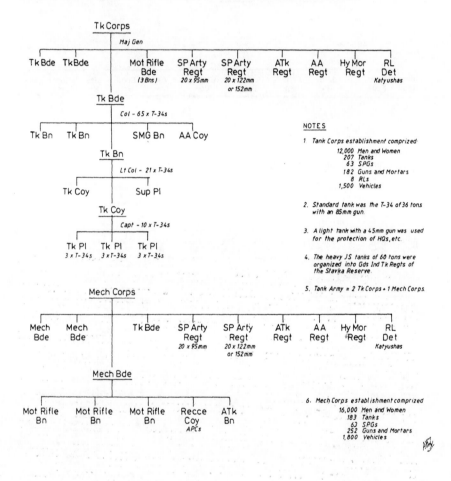

NOTES

1. Tank Corps establishment comprized:
   - 12,000 Men and Women
   - 207 Tanks
   - 63 SPGs
   - 182 Guns and Mortars
   - 8 RLs
   - 1,500 Vehicles

2. Standard tank was the T-34 of 36 tons with an 85mm gun.

3. A light tank with a 45mm gun was used for the protection of HQs, etc.

4. The heavy JS tanks of 60 tons were organized into Gds Ind Tk Regts of the Stavka Reserve.

5. Tank Army = 2 Tk Corps + 1 Mech Corps.

6. Mech Corps establishment comprized:
   - 16,000 Men and Women
   - 183 Tanks
   - 63 SPGs
   - 252 Guns and Mortars
   - 1,800 Vehicles

Appendix III

All-Arms Armies

47 A	3 SA	5 SA	8 GA	
9	9	9	9	Inf Divs
	11	14	8	Tk Regts
1	1	6	4	Hy Tk Regts
6	7	3	9	SPG Regts
1	1	1	1	Hy SPG Regts
	1	1		Armd Mine-Clg Regts
18	39	58	55	Arty Regts
	2	2		Hy Arty Units
7	12	19	13	ATk Bdes
12	9	11	13	Mor Regts
2	6	9	3	RL Regts
5	1	13	13	AA Arty Regts
1	1	1	1	Chem Tps Bns
3	1	3	5	Pontoon Bns
2		9		Ferry Bns
		2		Mot Engr Bns
2	1	2	1	Mil Constr Bns
1		1	1	Flamethr Bns
		1	1	Port Flamethr Bns

Flanking Armies

Northern Flank		Southern Flank		
61 A	**1 Pol A**	**69 A**	**33 A**	
9	5	11	7	Inf Divs
		2		Fortified Regions
	6	2		Tk Regts
	1	2		Hy Tk Regts
3	1	8	4	SPG Regts
	1			SPG Bn
1		1		Cav Corps
13	12	12	20	Arty Regts
10	6	7	6	ATk Arty Regts
1	2	8	5	Mor Regts
		5	2	RL Regts
5	1	9	13	AA Arty Regts
1		2	1	Chem Tps Bns
1	1	2	1	Combat Engr Bdes
2		2	2	Pontoon Bns
2				Ferry Bns
	3			Constr Bns
2		1	1	Mil Constr Bns
		1		Flamethr Bn
		1		Mot Flamethr Bn
1	1	1	1	Amph Veh Bn

Mobile Forces

1 GTA	2 GTA	
8	7	Tk Bdes
3	2	Hy Tk Regts
4	5	Mech Bdes
10	8	SPG Regts
3	3	Mot Rifle Bdes
7	7	M/C Bns
6	6	Arty Regts
3	3	Mor Regts
6	6	RL Bns
7	3	AA Arty Regts
1	1	Combat Engr Bdes

Front Reserves

3 A	Misc Units
7 Inf Divs	1 Cav Corps
3 SPG Regts	4 Mech Regts
1 Arty Regt	
1 ATk Arty Regt	
1 Mor Regt	1 Mor Bde
1 AA Arty Regt	16 AA Arty Regts
1 Combat Engr Bde	1 Combat Eng Bde
	1 Pontoon Br Bde

Appendix IV

ESTABLISHMENT OF A GERMAN INFANTRY DIVISION IN 1945

3 Gren Regts, each of 2 Bns.
    Each Bn of 3 Gren Coy (Nos. 1-3, 5-7)and 1 hy Coy (Nos. 4 & 8)
        with 4 lt inf guns and 6 med mors
    13th Heavy Company
        with 2 hy inf guns and 8 hy mors.
    14th Antitank company
        with 54 hy Panzerschrecks, plus 18 in reserve.

Fus Bn of 4 Fus Coys, mounted on bicycles.

Tk-Hunting Bn, consisting of
    Hy Tk-Hunting Coy, motorized,
        with 12 hy antitank guns
    SPG Tk-Hunting Coy
        with 14 SPGs.
    Med Flak Coy, motorized,
  with 9 x 37mm flak guns.

Arty Regt with
    3 Lt Arty Bns, each with
        2 Lt Fd How Btys (Nos. 1-2, 4-5, 7-8)
            with 4 x 105mm lt fd hows.
        1 Lt Fd Gun Bty (Nos. 3,6 & 9)
            with 6 x 75mm fd guns.
    1 Hy Arty Bn (Bty Nos. 10 & 11)
        each with 6 x 150mm hy fd hows.

Engr Bn of 3 Coys (Nos. 2 & 3 on bicycles),
    each with 2 HMGs, 2 med mors and 6 flame-
    thrs.

Sigs Bn, consisting of
    Fd Telephone Coy, partly motorized.
    Radio Coy, fully motorized.

Fd Rep Bn of 4 Coys, each with
    6 med and 4 hy mors
    1 lt inf gun and 1 lt fd how
    1 med and 1 hy antitank gun
    6 Panzerschrecks
    56 Aslt Rifles

Logistical Sp Regt.

(Source: Buchner, Alex: *Das Handbuch der deutschen Infanterie 1939-45*; Tessin, pp. 95-6)

Appendix V

ORGANIZATION OF A VOLKS ARTILLERY CORPS

Headquarters Battery.

Observation Battery.

75mm Field Gun Battalion,
   with 3 batteries of 6 guns each.

105mm Field Howitzer Battalion,
   with 3 batteries of 6 guns each.

100mm Field Gun Batttalion,
   with 2 batteries of 4 guns each.

122mm Field Howitzer Battalion,
   with 2 batteries of 4 captured guns each.

155mm Field Howitzer Battalion,
   with 2 batteries of 4 captured guns each.

170mm Battery.

Fire Direction Battery.

2 Heavy Mortar Batteries with 210mm mortars.

(Source: Müller-Hillebrand, *Das Heer 1933-1945*, Vol 3, p. 176.)

Appendix VI

COMBATANT STRENGTH OF THE 9TH ARMY ON 15 APRIL 1945

<u>CIst Corps</u>
5th Lt Div	4 970	
606th Inf Div	5 495	
309th "Berlin" Inf Div	5 926	
		16 391

<u>XXXIXth Panzer Corps/LVIth Panzer Corps</u>
25th Pz Gren Div	5 605	
"Müncheberg" Pz Div	1 986	
		7 591

<u>XIth SS Panzer Corps</u>
9th Para Div	6 758	
20th PzGr Div	4 848	
303rd "Döberitz" Inf Div	3 860	
169th Inf Div	5 956	
712th Inf Div	4 882	
"Kurmark" PzGr Div	4 370	
		30 654

<u>Vth SS Mountain Corps</u>
286th Inf Div	3 950	
32nd SS "30. Januar" PzGr Div	6 703	
391st Security Div	4 537	
		15 190

<u>Attachments</u>
Frankfurt Fortress	13 945	
600th Russian Inf Div	7 065	
		21 010

	TOTAL	**90 836**

(Source: MA DDR, WF-02/7061, Sheet 222 [Stich, p. 38]. The format of the original document has been altered to suit the conventions of this book.)

Appendix VII

ARMORED STRENGTH OF THE 9TH ARMY ON 13 APRIL 1945

Unit	Type	
CI Corps		
5th Light Div		
1005th Tk-Hunting Coy	Pz IV (L)	10
	SPG III	1
25th PzGrDiv		
5th Panzer Bn	Pz IV	1
	Pz V	30
	Pz IV (L)	7
	Pz IV (Flak)	2
25th Tk-Hunting Bn	Pz IV (L)	12
	SPG III	31
	Jagdpz IV	1
560th SS-Tk-Hunting Bn	SPG III	5
	Hetzer 38	37
"1001 Nights" Combat Gp	Hetzer 38	37
309th "Berlin" Inf Div		
"Berlin" Tk-Hunting Bn	SPG III	10
LVIth Pz Corps		
9th Para Div		
9th Para Tk-Hunting Bn	Hetzer 38	8
20th PzGrDiv		
8th Panzer Bn	Pz IV	15
	Pz IV (L)	16
	(Flak) IV	3
"Müncheberg" Pz Div		
"Müncheberg" Pz Regt	Pz III	1
	Pz IV	2
	Pz V	21
	Pz VI	10
	Pz IV (L)	1
	Jagdpz IV	1

XIth SS-Panzer Corps
303rd "Döberitz" Inf Div

'Döberitz' Tk-Hunting Bn	Pz IV (L)	7
	SPG III	17
303rd Armd Recce Bn	SPG III	2

169th Inf Div

1230th Tk-Hunting Coy	Hetzer 38	10
111th SPG Trg Bde	Pz IV (L)	6
	SPG III	33
	SPG III (How)	9

"Kurmark" PzGrDiv

"Brandenburg" Pz Regt	Pz V	28
	SPG III	12
"Kurmark" Tk-Hunting Bn	Pz IV	3
	Hetzer 38	16
502nd SS-Hy Pz Bn	Pz VI	29
	Pz IV (Flak)	4

Vth SS-Mountain Corps
32nd SS-Vol-Gr-Div

32nd SS-Tk-Hunting Bn	SPG III	20
	SPG 42	8

391st Sy Div

	Pz III	2
	Pz IV	-

Misc Units

1129th Tk-Hunting Coy	Hetzer 38	11
2nd Tk-Hunting Bn	Hetzer 38	24
15th Tk-Hunting Coy	Pz IV	1
	Hetzer 38	15
105th SS-SPG Bn	SPG (Italian)	10
105th SS-Pz Coy	SPG (Italian)	7
561st Special Troop	Pz IV	1
	Hetzer 38	16

LATER REINFORCEMENTS

18th PzGrDiv

"Schlesien" Pz Bn	Pz IV	26
"Schlesien" Tk-Hunting Bn	Hetzer 38	19
"Ostsee" Pz Trg Unit	Pz V	2
	Jagdpz IV	2

"Nordland" SS-PzGrDiv

11th SS-Panzer Bn	Pz IV (L)	10
	SPG III	22
503rd SS-Hy Pz Bn	Pz VI	10
	Pz(Flak) IV	7

"Nederland" SS-PzGrDiv

23rd SS-Tk-Hunting Bn	SPG III	4
	SPG 42	2
6th Tk-Hunting Bn	Pz III	-
	Hetzer 38	15

NOTES:

Pz IV (Flak) = "Möbelwagon" with 37mm L/60 gun, "Wirbelwind" with 4 x 20mm guns, or "Ostwind" with 37mm l/60 gun.

Pz IV (L) = Pz IV with long-barreled 75mm L/48 gun.

Pz V = "Panther."

Pz VI = "Tiger I" or "Tiger II"/"Königstiger."

SPG III = Sturmgeschütz III adapted as tank-hunter.

SPG 42 = Sturmgeschïz III with 105mm howitzer.

SPG (Italian) = Italian M 13/40 chassis.

(Source: MA DDR WF-03/5099 Sheets 303-4.

Adapted from HQ Army Group "Weichsel" return of 13 April 1945 as an indication of strengths as per the order of battle of 16 April 1945, plus the later reinforcements.)

Appendix VIII

ALLOCATION OF ARTILLERY RESOURCES IN SUPPORT OF THE 8th GUARDS ARMY ON 16 APRIL 1945

x = Units incorporated for the initial bombardment only.

xx = Units incorporated for the initial bombardment and support of the main attack only, without redeployment.

4 GRC

AAG 4
- 3 how arty regts
- 2 ex hy arty regts
- 6 mor regts

Reserve: 3 ATk arty regts

CAG 4
- 1 corps arty regt
- 1 mor regt

35 GRD

DAG 47
- arty 142 GRR x
- arty 35 GRD xx
- arty 140 GRR xx — 2 lt arty regts
- 1 lt arty regt xx — 1 arty regt
- 10 ATk arty regts xx
- 9 mor regts xx

47 GRD
- 142 GRR — 140 GRR
- 137 GRR
  - arty 142 GRR x / 2 arty bns / 3 mor bns
  - arty 137 GRR x / 1 arty bn / 3 mor bns

57 GRD

DAG 57
- arty 170 GRR x
- 12 ATk arty regts x — 1 lt arty regt
- 1 lt arty regt xx — 1 ATk arty regt
- 10 mor regts xx

- 172 GRR — 170 GRR
- 174 GRR
  - arty 172 GRR x / 2 arty bns / 1 mor bn
  - arty 174 GRR x / 1 arty bn / 1 mor bn

29 GRC

AAG 29
- 1 ex hy arty regt x
- 1 lt arty regt xx
- 3 mor regts xx
- 1 corps arty regt
- 3 hy arty regts

Reserve: 3 ATk arty regts

CAG 29
- 1 mor regt xx
- 3 mor arty regts
- 1 mor regt

82 GRD

DAG 27
- arty 76 GRR x
- 9 ATk regts x — 3 lt arty regts
- 1 mor regt

27 GRD
- 74 GRR — 76 GRR
- 83 GRR
  - arty 74 GRR x / 2 arty bns / 1 mor bn
  - arty 83 GRR x / 1 arty bn / 1 mor bn

DAG 74
- arty 82 GRD x
- arty 226 GRR x
- 9 ATk arty regts x — 1 lt arty regt
- 1 arty regt xx — 1 mor regt
- 2 ATk arty regts xx
- 1 mor regt xx

74 GRD
- 240 GRR — 226 GRR
- 236 GRR
  - arty 240 GRR x / 2 arty bns / 1 mor bn
  - arty 236 GRR x / 1 arty bn / 1 mor bn

28 GRC

AAG 28
- 1 ex hy arty bn
- 4 arty regts
- 3 hy mor regts
- 3 mor regts

CAG 28
- 9 ATk regts x
- 9 mor regts xx
- 3 how arty regts
- 3 ATk arty regts
- 1 mor regt

39 GRD

DAG 79
- arty 39 GRD xx — 1 how arty regt
- arty 216 GRR xx — 1 arty regt
- 9 ATk arty regts

79 GRD
- 227 GRR — 216 GRR
- 220 GRR
  - arty 227 GRR x / 1 arty bn / 3 mor bns
  - arty 220 GRR x / 2 arty bns

88 GRD

DAG 88
- arty 88 GRD x
- arty 266, 269 and 271 GRR's x
- 12 ATk arty regts x

---

arty GRD = 12 x 120mm / 21 x 74mm / 12 x 57mm ATk

arty GRR = 4 x 76mm / 6 x 57mm ATk / 6 x 120mm mor

277

Notes

Square brackets have been used throughout to denote the sources from which the reference given has been drawn, or to indicate which of several books attributable to an author is applicable.

CHAPTER 1. THE MAN

The content of this chapter is mainly drawn from Zhukov's own *Reminiscences and Reflections* augmented from Professor John Erickson's articles on Zhukov and Koniev in Field Marshal Sir John Carver's *The War Lords*, Colonel A.L. Sethi's *Marshal Zhukov: The Master Strategist*, and Colonel William J. Spahr's *Zhukov: The Rise and Fall of a Great Captain*.

1. Eric Larabee: *Commander in Chief*, p. 75, quoting Butov, *Tojo and the Coming of War*, pp. 127-28, and Ienaga, *The Pacific War 1931-45*, p. 82. The defeat was so humiliating that the Japanese did not release these figures until 1966!

2. Chaney, p. 307, quoting Nicolaevsky.

3. Spahr, pp. 88-89. In contrast to the Wehrmacht's 615,000 casualties in the same period, the Soviets had lost 2,204,000 men, of which 959,000 were in the drive on Moscow, 297,000 in the December 1941 fighting and 948,000 in Stalin's counter-offensive between 20 January and April 1942.

4. Preface to third Russian edition of Zhukov [Spahr].

5. Stich, Dokument 3.

6. Volkogonov, pp. 683, 706. Total Soviet deaths during the Great Patriotic War amounted to 26 to 28 million. Excluding these figures, between 1929 and 1953 a further 19.5 to 22 million victims can be attributed to Stalin's policies, a third of whom died either by execution, in the labour camps, or in exile in Siberia.

Colonel General G.F. Krivosheev's *Stamped Removed from Secrecy: Losses of the Armed Forces in Wars, Battles and Military Conflicts*, (Moscow Military Publishing House), pp. 219-20, gives the following casualty figures for the period 16 April to 8 May 1945:

	Killed	Wounded	Missing
2nd Bye Front	13,070	46,040	2,570
1st Bye Front	37,610	141,880	7,804
1st Ukr Front	27,580	86,245	4,949
1st/2nd Pol Armies	2,825	6,067	387

However, with the 33,000 killed admitted at Seelow and another 20,000 buried in Berlin, apart from those in between these two points, these figures appear dubious.

CHAPTER 2. THE SOVIETS

1. Seaton [*RGW*], pp. 588-9; Ziemke, p. 71; Wagener, Appx 2., *Tojo and the Coming of War*, pp. 127-8, and Ienaga.

Lend-lease supplies delivered included 1,900 locomotives and 11,000 railway flatcars, 427,000 trucks and jeeps, 35,000 motorcycles, 13,000 armored fighting vehicles (including 10,000 tanks) and nearly 19,000 aircraft.

2. Erickson, 1975-1983, II, p. 405.
3. Zhukov, pp. 358.
4. Mackintosh, p. 226.
5. Mackintosh, pp. 228-9.
6. Duffy, p. 343.
7. Duffy, p. 345.
8. Mackintosh, pp. 226-7; Duffy, pp. 322-3.
9. Erickson, 1975-1983, II, p. 405 [Duffy, p. 23].
10. Mackintosh, p. 226.
11. Duffy, p. 349
12. Mackintosh, pp. 224-5.
13. Mackintosh, pp. 222-4.
14. Spahr, p. 147; Tolstoy, pp. 281-2.
15. Mackintosh, p. 222. Comments on alcoholism from Oberst Harry Herrmann.
16. Tolstoy, pp. 143, 255.
17. Bokov, pp. 115-16, 146-47.
18. Komornicki, p. 79.
19. Duffy, p. 336.

CHAPTER 3. THE GERMANS

The description of Hitler is drawn from Joachim C. Fest's *Hitler*, Alan Bullock's *Hitler: A Study in Tyranny*, John Toland's *Adolf Hitler* and David Irving's *Hitler's War*; that of the Führerbunker from Trevor-Roper's *Last Days of Hitler* and James P. O'Donnell's *The Berlin Bunker*.

Georg Tessin's *Verbände und Truppen der deutschen Wehrmacht und Waffen-SS im zweiten Weltkrieg 1939-1945* in its numerous volumes provides a brilliant analysis of the German Armed Forces based on a study of the Field Post Office records. However, it is the accounts of Generals Heinrici and Busse on the situation on the Oder Front that have provided most of the detail given here.

1. Tieke, p. 22; Ziemke, p. 65; Erich Kempa's *Ich habe Adolf Hitler verbrannt* (Munich, undated), p. 76 and Hans Schwarz's *Brennpunkt FHQ: Menschen und Massstäbe im Führerhauptquartier* (Buenos Aires, 1950), p. 25, [Gosztony, pp. 91-93 and 91 respectively].

2. Rocolle, p. 13; Trevor-Roper [*LDH*], pp. 104-16.

3. Tieke, p. 62; Trevor-Roper [*LDH*], p. 135; Tully, p. 40.

4. Rocolle, p. 14.

5. Toland, pp. 1118-19. These bunkers later accommodated the Soviet Army High Command in East Germany.

6. Kuby, p. 86; Toland, p. 955.

7. Guderian, pp. 277, 305-6.

8. O'Donnell, pp. 40-43.

9. Guderian, pp. 323-6.

10. Trevor-Roper [*LDH*], pp. 65-66, 101.

11. Kuby, pp. 87-88; O'Donnell, pp. 197-98.

12. Tessin, with additional information on the Volksarmee from Tully. Note that the Germans used Roman numerals for their corps formation titles (including the unusual XXXX for 40) but not for their artillery corps. The Soviets did not use Roman numerals at all.

Wilke maintains that the XIth SS Panzer Corps HQ did not officially have the word "Panzer" in its title, but was so called because most of the staff wore the black uniforms of armored troops, and that the Vth SS Mountain Corps dropped the word "Mountain" from its title at the end of March; but contemporary documents all carry the titles used in this text.

13. Höhne, pp. 540-2. In Manvell and Fraenkel's *Heinrich Himmler* it is said that some senior SS officers were entertaining doubts about a successful conclusion to the war some two years earlier.

Additional material on the Waffen-SS is taken from the works of Burn and Quarrie, and also Clark, p. 386.

14. Marshall Cavendish's *Illustrated Encyclopedia of World War II* (New York: Marshall Cavendish, 1981), Vol. 11, p. 195.

15. LTC Timmons in *Parameters* (Journal of the U.S. Army War College).

16. Facts on German armor are taken from Campbell, p. 237; Foss, pp. 44-57; White, pp. 139-47.

Chuikov [1969], mentions seven "Ferdinands" encountered at Müncheberg, and on p. 150 is one of several mentions of the use of captured Panzerfausts by Soviet troops.

17. Report of Günther Labes to author dated 19 Deccember 1993. Problems with lacquered small arms ammunition confirmed by Wolfgang Schiller MBE.

CHAPTER 4. THE VISTULA-ODER OPERATION

1. Duffy, pp. 178-79; Tieke, p. 12.

2. Duffy, p. 249-51; BMA RH 19/XV/13K3.

3. MA USSR, Stock 333, List 396, File 396, Sheets 58 & 59 [Bokov, p. 101]; Chuikov, p. 159.

4. Chuikov, p. 160,Order No. 00172 of 27 January 1945.

5. Katukov, p. 329 ff; Spaeter, pp. 321-332.

6. Bokov, p. 85; Sokolov, p. 35 [Simon, p. 19].

7. *Die Handlungen der Artillerie operativer und taktischer Verbände nach der Erfahrungen des Grossen Vaterländischen Krieges 1941-1945*, Part II, p. 38 [Study material, "Friedrich Engels" Military Academy Dresden, Simon, p. 19].

8. Bokov, p. 102 f [Simon, p. 19].

9. Zhukov, p. 322. Repeated by many authors!

10. Bokov, p. 85. Lothar Loewe in coversation with the author. The villagers were evacuated by the Russians and held prisoner for five years before being returned to their village. Scheel article "Ein Dorf an der Oder."

11. One of these was a "Sherman" and another a "Valentine Mk III": Hermann Thrams in a letter to the author. Three of these were attributed to Uffz. Sommer's Tankhunting Platoon of the 1st Battalion, 25th Artillery Regiment using Panzerfausts. The advance guard of the 25th Panzergrenadier Division, consisting of the 2nd Battalion, 35th Panzergrenadier Regiment, and two companies of the 125th Armoured Reconnaissance Battalion, had just arrived at Küstrin-Neustadt station by train and had yet to unload (Boehm, p. 275).

12. Bokov, pp. 94-100; Chuikov, pp. 153-54. Chuikov goves all 3,000 inmates as having been executed, but Bokov, who goes into the war crimes investigation aspects, says that following an evacuation of most of the prisoners to Sachsenhausen concentration camp, the over 700 remaining were executed, except for four named survivors.

13. Von Hopffgarten, p. 475; Katukov, pp. 341-2; Schneider unpublished article "Die Festung Frankfurt (Oder) im Frühjahr 1945," p. 26.

14. Tiecke, p. 12; Scheel article.

15. Chuikov, p. 155.

16. Chuikov, p. 154-55.

17. Chuikov, p. 156; Brückl p. 13 [Simon, p. 22]; von Hopffgarten in correspondence with the author; Knüppel, *Ein leidgeprüftes Land*, pp. 21 & 42.

18. *Ljuki otkryli v Berline*, p. 257 [Simon, p. 22], in which it says that the 40th Guards Tank Brigade reached the Oder near Göritz at 2200 hrs on 1 February and that the 44th Guards Tank Brigade arrived the following morning.

19. Katukov, p. 343.

20. Zhukov, p. 332; Erickson, p. 474..

21. Bokov, p. 102; Chuikov, pp. 149 & 165. During the fighting to extend the bridgehead our artillery fired a total of 65,000 captured enemy shells, ranging in caliber from 105 to 150mm'; Erickson, p. 474; Zhukov, pp. 331-2 "As of the 1st February, infantry divisions were, on the average, 3,500 strong, but, for instance, the 8th Guards had only from 3,800 to 4,800 officers and men. The number of tanks in the two tank armies was 740, an average of 40 per brigade, whereas in fact many brigades had only 15-20 tanks."

22. Duffy, p. 123; Zhukov, pp 328-9

23. Zhukov, pp. 334.

24. MA USSR, Stock 233, List 2307, File 194, Sheets 100 & 101 [Bokov, p. 109]; Zhukov, p. 334.

25. Knüppel, p. 113.

CHAPTER 5. THE STRUGGLE FOR THE BRIDGEHEADS I

1. Simon, p. 10. The riverbed is now much shallower as a result of having not been navigated in this section since it became a national boundary at the end of the Second World War. With improved German-Polish relations the river was surveyed and buoyed for traffic once more in 1992.

2. Sokolov, p. 36 [Simon, p. 10].

3. The Oderbruch was drained and diked in the eighteenth century by order of Frederick the Great, who then invited settlers from all over the Continent. These brought with them their distinctively different styles of building and farming.

4. MA DDR, H 10.28.04./1, Sheet 765 [*1945*].

5. Von Lösecke MS, p. 210.

6. MA DDR, WF-03/5083, Sheet 863 [Simon, p. 32].

7. MA DDR, WF-03/5103, Sheet 412 f. [Simon, p. 33].

8. Busse, p. 151.

9. Von Hopffgarten; also Deutschland, pp. 525 f. [Simon, p. 34]. Based on the original 60th Infantry Division, the "Feldherrnhalle" was the only SA field formation.

10. Deutschland, p. 520 [Simon, p. 36].

11. MA DDR, WF-10/13257, Sheet 668; Groehler, p. 695 [Simon, pp. 35-36] and MA DDR, WF-03/5103, Sheet 403 [Stich, p. 38].

12. Groehler, p. 693 f. [Simon, p. 39].

13. *1945*, p. 211 [Simon, p. 39].

14. *Deutschland*, p. 517 [Simon, p. 39].

15. *1945*, p. 211 f; Seelower, p. 34 [Simon, p. 39]. Some details on the 'Mistel' are taken from *Die großen Luftschlachten des Zweiten Weltkrieges*, Klagenfurt: Neuen Kaiser Verlag GmbH (undated).

16. MA DDR, WF-03/17398, Sheets 461 & 488 [Simon, p. 351]; tanks in Knüppel, p. 104.

17. Schrode, p. 82. These Ju-87G Stukas were equipped with two 37mm cannon underslung from the wings outboard of the fixed undercarriage.

18. BMA RH XII/23, Sheet 352 and RH 19/XV/3 [Kortenhaus, pp. 105 & 107]; Schrode, p. 82.

19. Kroemer and Zobel to author.

20. Boehm, pp. 275-7.

21. Wewetzer to author.

22. Boehm, pp. 277-8; Schrode, p. 82.

23. Schrode, p. 82.

24. Scheel article.

25. Bokov, p. 86: Brückl, p. 11 [Stich]; Hahn, p. 6; Schrode, p. 82.

26. Schrode, p. 82.

27. Brückl, p. 11; MA DDR, WF-03/5083, Sheet 820 [Simon, p. 20].

28. Boehm, p. 278; Knüppel, pp. 94-95; Schrode, p. 85; Weber article.

29. Bokov, pp. 104 ff. [Simon, p. 36]; Scheel article; Zhukov, pp. 322-3.

30. Bokov, p. 106; Brückl, p. 11; MA DDR, WF-03/5083, Sheet 820 [Simon, p. 20]; Schrode, pp. 85-86.

31. Bokov, pp. 107-9; Schrode, p. 86.

32. Knüppel, p. 115.

33. BMA 10/159 gives the divisional strength as of 1 February [Kortenhaus, p. 106]; Kortenhaus, p. 107.

34. MA DDR, WF-03/5083, Sheets 27, 147 & 950 [Simon, p. 37]; Schrode, p. 88; Weber article.

35. BMA RH 19 XV/3 [Kortenhaus, p. 107]; Schrode, p. 88.

36. Hahn report, pp. 6-7; Schrode, p. 89. The 1st Platoon of t!.e 6th Company, twelve men commanded by a Second Lieutenant Valentin, was eliminated at 2100 hours.

37. Kortenhaus, p. 108.

38. Chuikov, p. 156.

39. Chuikov, p. 156; Knüppel, p. 114.

40. Knüppel, pp. 115-16.

41. Von Hopffgarten. The title of the "Kurmark", whether it was meant to be a Panzer or Panzergrenadier Division, was not officially determined until March, when the latter was decided upon.

42. Chuikov, pp. 157-58; von Hopffgarten.

43. Chuikov, pp. 158-59; von Hopffgarten, correspondence and maps to author; MA DDR, WF-03/5083, Sheets 875 & 950 [Simon, p. 37]. Chuikov says the Germans got to within 400 meters of the crossing point; von Hopffgarten's maps show otherwise.

44. Von Hopffgarten.

45. Knüppel, pp. 116 & 118; Herbert Tegeler in correspondence with the author.

46. Von Hopffgarten, from marked map sent to author.

47. Schrode, p. 90.

48. Schneider, p. 6, as amended by further notes, and Dr. H.-J. Teller in conversation with the author; Wilke.

49. Gädtke, pp. 3-4; Wilke disputes some of this.

50. Wilke in correspondence with the author.

51. *Oder-Zeitung* No. 31 of 7 February 1945 [Schneider].

52. Wilke.

CHAPTER 6. THE STRUGGLE FOR THE BRIDGEHEADS II

1. *1945*, pp. 152-6, quoting from *Das letzte Angebot des Teufels* by Hanns Baron von Freytag-Loringhoven.

2. Von Hopffgarten to author.

3. MA DDR, WF-03/5083, Sheet 360 f. [Simon, p. 34].

4. Kohlase, p. 26. (Kohlase references are to his unpublished manuscript, obtained prior to the publication of his booklet.)

5. Von Hopffgarten; Knüppel, p. 122; photographs in Seelow Museum.

6. Although varying dates in March have been quoted for this visit, confirmation comes from Goebbels's *Tagebuche 1945: Die letzte Aufzeichnungen* (Hamburg, 1977), pp. 100, 108 & 206 and Schenk's *Patient Hitler: Eine medizinische Biographie* (Düsseldorf, 1989), p. 159 [Dr. Raiber M.D. to the author], and Tieke, p. 22. Kohlase, p. 31, gives 9 March.

7. Although not mentioned in any of my military sources, the old fort between Gorgast and Manschnow clearly must have been of considerable value to the Soviet defense in this area. This fort and other outworks of the Küstrin Fortress appear to have been originally omitted from maps of the area for security reasons and the custom continued in later editions. They show up clearly on the 1945 aerial photographs. According to Knüppel, p. 159, the fort was taken by the Soviets sometime in February.

8. Kortenhaus, p. 108.

9. Hahn p. 7; Kortenhaus, p. 108, and correspondence with the author; Schneider re Rudel.

10. Bokov, p. 115; Hahn, p. 8.

11. Schöneck, pp. 11-12.

12. Hahn, p. 9.

13. Von Hopffgarten; Knüppel, p. 124.

14. Von Hopffgarten. According to Tessin, in February 1945 the infantry officer and NCO training schools (Fahnenjunkerschule der Infanterie) formed infantry regiments, each based on a 25 percent core of 400 cadets, the rest being made up of army and Volkssturm personnel, as follows:

    I - "Dresden": 1235, 1238, 1240, 1247, 1249 & 1256.

    II - "Vienna Neustadt": 1236 & 1239.

    III - "Potsdam": 1233, 1234, 1246, 1248 & 1250, and possibly 1243 & 1244.

    VIII - "Wetzlar": 1237, 1241 & 1242.

Of these regiments the 1234th, 1235th, 1241st and 1242nd had first served with the "Kurmark" Panzergrenadier Division, where they were known by their names as opposed to numbers. The 1234th was transferred to the 309th "Berlin" Infantry Division, the 1235th became the "Kurmark" Panzer-Fusilier Regiment, and the 1241st and 1242nd became the 745th and 732nd Infantry Regiments respectively of the new 712th Infantry Division.

These regiments consisted of only two battalions each and lacked the two heavy weapons companies of a normal infantry regiment.

Colonel Langkeit was promoted to Major General on 20 April 1945.

15. Wilke Archive.

16. Von Hopffgarten, marked map to author.

17. Von Hopffgarten, marked map to author; Knüppel, p. 30.

18. Von Hopffgarten, from comprehensive notes on command decisions taken at the time and later discussed with the divisional commander. The news of the fall of Lebus evoked a call from Goebbels demanding the "Kurmark" immediately retake the town, as Berlin's Middle East collection of cultural items had been stored there!

19. Lindner, p. 8.

20. Von Hopffgarten; Erich Wuttze re Küstrin [Eichholz].

21. Von Hopffgarten; Knüppel, p. 124.

22. Von Hopffgarten.

23. Von Hopffgarten the Klessin garrison on 12 March consisted of the 6th and 7th Companies of the 1242nd Grenadier Regiment and elements of its 2nd, 3rd and 5th Companies.

24. Von Hopffgarten.

25. Von Hopffgarten.

26. Von Hopffgarten; Weber article.

27. Von Hopffgarten from a report he wrote as Ia of the "Kurmark" on the 25th March and countersigned by Lieutenantt Schöne; MA DDR, WF-03/5086, Sheet 172 [Simon, p. 38]. A propaganda leaflet directed at the 1242nd Grenadier Regiment claimed that 300 German soldiers had been surrounded at Klessin and all had been killed except for 75 that had surrendered, none having escaped back to their own lines [Schneider].

28. Buwert, p. 25 [Schneider, p. 4]; Wilke contests these figures as excessive, claiming that many of the troops stationed in Frankfurt were dispatched eastward during late January to try and stem the Soviet advance.

29. Articles in the *Märkische Oderzeitung* of 13 February 1991 and 13 March 1991 [Schneider].

30. Gädtke, pp. 10-1.

31. Wilke in correspondence with the author.

32. MA DDR, WF-03/5086, Sheets 401, 725 & 993 [Simon, p. 40].

33. MA DDR, WF-03/5085, Sheet 993 [Simon, p. 40].

34. Bokov, p. 106.

35. Kohlase, pp. 25 & 29.

36. Busse, p. 154.

37. Wagner, pp. 44-45.

CHAPTER 7. THE KÜSTRIN CORRIDOR AND FORTRESS

1. Bokov, p. 119; Melzheimer, pp. 181-84, as amended by Hermann Thrams in correspondence with the author.

2. Hahn, p. 9; Kohlase, pp. 75-76.

3. Melzheimer, p. 183, as amended by Thrams.

4. Bokov, p. 123.

5. Melzheimer, p. 183; Thrams, p. 56.

6. Kohlase to author; Melzheimer, p. 183; Thrams, p. 38.

7. Bokov, p. 119; Kohlase, p. 75, as amended by Thrams, pp. 131-32.

8. Bokov, p. 119; Hahn, p. 8; Kohlase, p. 76; Thrams. Seydlitz-Troops mentioned in telephoned report to HQ 9th Army (exhibit in Seelow Museum).

9. Bokov, p. 123.

10. Kohlase, pp. 76-77; Thrams, pp. 85 & 94-105.

11. Bokov, pp. 130 f; Brückl, p. 15 [Simon, p. 43]; Melzheimer, p. 184; Thrams, p. 105, says 76 officers and 2,698 enlisted men.

12. Bokov, p. 129; Thrams, p. 105.

13. Brückl, p. 15 [Simon, p. 44]. The only elevation of 16.3 meters in the area is a hillock within the Kalenziger Wiesen, which was already occupied by the 60th Guards Rifle Division.

14. Boehm, p. 280; Kohlase, p. 33; Thrams, p. 113.

15. *Befreier*, p. 12; Kohlase, pp. 33 f; MA DDR, WF-03/5086, Sheets 242 & 292 [Simon, p. 44]; Schöneck, pp. 31-42.

16. Zobel to author.

17. Boehm, p. 280; Hahn, p. 9.

18. Waldmüller, p. 12.

19. *Befreier*, p. 12; MA DDR, WF-03/5086, Sheets 242 & 292 [Simon, p. 44]; Kohlase, pp. 33 f.

20. *Befreier*, p. 12; MA DDR, WF-03/5086, Sheets 242 & 292 [Simon, p. 44]; Kohlase, pp. 33f.

21. Zobel to author.

22. Boehm, p. 280; Hahn, p. 9.

23. Unpublished manuscript, courtesy of Dr. Averdieck.

24. Dr. Averdieck.

25. Busse, p. 154; Guderian, pp. 353-4: MA DDR WF-03/086, Sheets 262 ff. [Simon, pp. 48-49].

26. Duffy, pp. 243-5.

27. Boehm, p. 280; Hahn, p. 9; MA DDR W-03/5086, Sheets 170 & 223 [Simon, p. 49]. Rogmann to author, the 502nd SS Heavy Tank Battalion stemmed from the IInd SS Panzer Corps, the 503rd, which features later, from the IIIrd SS 'Germanic' Panzer Corps.

28. MA DDR W-03/5086, Sheet 261 [Simon, p. 50]; Thrams, p.115. Remer was the officer responsible for thwarting the 20 July 1944 plot against Hitler in Berlin.

29. MA DDR W-03/5086, Sheet 292 f. [Simon, p. 50].

30. Boehm, p. 281; MA DDR W-03/5086, Sheets 505 f. [Simon, pp. 50-51].

31. Hahn, p. 9; MA DDR W-03/5086, Sheets 292 & 313 [Simon, p. 51]; Zobel to author.

32. Unpublished manuscript, courtesy of Dr. Averdieck.

33. Dr. Averdieck, p. 107.

34. Kohlase, p. 78.

35. Kohlase, pp. 43-45.

36. Chuikov, pp. 167-69.

37. Kohlase, p. 79; Melzheimer, pp. 184-5; Thrams to author, and pp. 117-18.

38. Kohlase, pp. 49-51, 79, and Wewetzer, who participated in the breakout as a fusilier and an artillery NCO respectively, are the main sources here. Kohlase gives the Figures quoted, MA DDR, WF-03/17398, Sheet 521. Thrams, p. 121, gives 32 officers and 965 enlisted men.

39. Chuikov, p. 169.

40. Melzheimer, pp. 184-86, Thrams, pp. 117 & 120-22.

41. Kohlase, pp. 79-80; Thrams, p. 122, without quoting his source, gives 637 killed, 2,459 wounded and 5,994 missing.

42. Dr. Averdieck, pp. 107-8. This "Father and son" device was in fact the "Mistel" previously described (see Chapter 5, source note 15.)

CHAPTER 8. THE EAST POMERANIAN OPERATION

1. Zhukov, pp. 327-34.

2. Duffy, p. 188; Zhukov, pp. 330-1.

3. Duffy, pp. 181-82; Guderian, pp. 342-4; Zhukov, p. 337.

4. Duffy, pp. 182-83, as amended from Tessin.

5. Duffy, p. 183.

6. Duffy, pp. Erickson, p. 520.

7. Duffy, pp. 184-85; Erickson, p. 520; Guderian, p. 344.

8. Erickson, pp. 520-21.

9. Duffy, pp. 187-88; Erickson, p. 521.

10. Duffy, pp. 186-88; Erickson, p. 521.

11. Duffy, pp. 232-5; Erickson, p. 522.

12. Duffy, pp. 236-7; Erickson, p. 522.

13. Duffy, pp. 197-98; Erickson, p. 522.

14. Zhukov, pp. 339-41.

15. Erickson, p. 522.

16. Duffy, pp. 237-8.

17. Guderian, p. 350.

18. Guderian, p. 357.

19. Koniev, p. 61.

20. Duffy, pp. 127-47, 252-67; Koniev, pp. 58-60, 217.

21. Duffy, pp. 142-47; Erickson, pp. 524-6; Koniev, pp. 67-78.

CHAPTER 9. PLANNING AND LOGISTICS

1. Koniev, pp. 79-84; Zhukov, pp. 346-51. From the details given by Koniev, this was Field Marshal Montgomery's plan, and was presumably reported by the Soviet Mission at General Eisenhower's Headquarters, who may not have known that this plan had been rejected.

2. Shtemenko [*SGSW*], pp. 317-8.

3. Shtemenko [*SGSW*], pp. 319-20.

4. Eisenhower, pp. 397-403; Montgomery-Hyde, p. 525; Ziemke, p. 64; Seaton [RGW], pp. 562-5.

5. John Ehrmann's *Grand Strategy, October 1944-August 1945*, p. 142 [Gosztony, p. 122].

6. Shtemenko [*SGSW*], pp. 320-1.

7. Zhukov, pp. 346-51; *The Great Patriotic War of the Soviet Union* [*GPW*], pp. 376-8; Erickson, pp. 531-5.

8. *GPW*, pp. 88-9; Erickson, pp. 535-7. The role of the tank armies after the breakthrough is taken from a map used by General Ivanov in a 1993 briefing [Chronos-Film].

9. Zhukov, pp. 357-9; Novikov, p. 89.

10. Air transportation from Ryan, p. 237. The scraping of the manpower barrel did not, of course, involve the estimated over a quarter of a million NKVD troops guarding the Gulag camps containing over ten million prisoners. See Tolstoy, pp. 64 & 248.

11. Koniev, p. 81.

12. Antipenko, p. 279; Leosenia, pp. 281-3; Prosliakov, p. 42; Rotmistrov, pp. 45 ff. [Simon, p. 62-64]. Küstrin supplementary bridges from aerial photographs.

13. Antipenko, p. 278 [Simon, pp. 63-64].

14. Bokov, pp. 152-53.

15. Loktionov, pp. 203 f., 214 f. [Simon, p. 64].

16. Vorobe'ev, p. 89; Prosliakov, p. 43; Sovetskaya, Part 4, p. 550 [Simon, p. 65]; Leosenia, pp. 281 ff. [Stich, p. 96].

17. Leosenia, p. 284; Vorobe'ev, p. 85 [Simon, p. 65a].

18. Zhukov, p. 358.

19. Chuikov, pp. 176-77; Simon, p. 66.

20. Colonel Glantz's chapter on *Maskirovka*; Prosliakov, p. 43; Rotmistrov, pp. 44 f. [Simon, p. 66].

21. Kirian, p. 66 [Stich, p. 97]. Professor Earl F. Ziemke was also taken in by this: correspondence with author.

22. *Berlinskaya*, pp. 80 ff.; MA DDR, WF-03/5087, Sheet s 426, 500, 551, 614 & 629 [Simon, pp. 66-67].

23. Antipenko 1980, p. 335; *Berlinskaya*, p. 84; Vislo, p. 73 [Simon, pp. 67-8]; Zhukov, pp. 358 & 604. In the 1975 edition of his book, p. 327, Antipenko gives the comparative figures of consumption per kilometer of advance for the Vistula-Oder and Berlin Operations as 250 to 2,000 tons of ammunition respectively, and 333 to 1,430 tons of fuel.

24. Zhukov, p. 358.

25. Antipenko, p. 280.

26. Poplawski, pp. 289-94.

27. Simon, pp. 55-56.

28. *Berlinskaya*, pp. 80 ff.; *Die Handlungen*, Part I, p. 43; Poplawski, pp. 292 ff.; Vorobe'ev, pp. 116 ff., 126 [Simon, pp. 55-8, 60]; ViZ, 4/1965, p. 85 [Stich, p. 69].

29. Katukov, p. 362 [Simon, p. 68].

30. Chuikov's bunker was measured by Colonel Diebbert Lang and his son in 1988, shortly before the entrances were filled in as a safety precaution. The raw clay of the walls ceilings had been seared with flamethrowers and only one small working area, presumably Chuikov's, had been lined with timber. The remains of Zhukov's and Chuikov's observation posts and the communication trenches and bunkers that abound in that area are still clearly visible.

CHAPTER 10. DEFENSE IN DEPTH

1. Weier, pp. 145 ff. [Stich, p. 28].

2. MA DDR, WF-10/2601, Sheet 326 [Stich, p. 29].

3. MA DDR, WF-13433, Sheet 055 ff. [Stich, p. 32].

4. MA DDR, WF-03/5086, Sheet 366 ff. [Stich, p. 33]; Tieke, pp. 46 f.

5. MA DDR, WF-03/5086, Sheet 377 [Stich, p. 34].

6. Article by Colonel Timothy A. Wray: "German Antitank Tactics in Russia, 1941-5: A Case Study in Doctrinal Failure." (Draft to author.)

7. Altner, pp. 58-59; von Hopffgarten correspondence; MA DDR, WF-03/5083, Sheet 305 [Stich, p. 35].

8. Schwarz, pp. 23 ff. [Gosztony, pp. 91-93].

9. Stich, pp. 28-30.

10. Heinrici, p. 47 [Gosztony, p. 159]. According to Heinrici the dam used was at Otmaschau, but Stich, p. 23, refers to the Bobertal Dam, which had a capacity of 50 million cubic meters of water, and quotes a file note of 23 March in the Chief Engineer's records (MA DDR, WF-03/5086, Sheet 192) which reads: "The waters released from the Bobertal Dam have resulted in a general rise in the water level at Frankfurt between 17

and 21 March of 32cm, and at the Finow Locks between 18 and 23 March of 25cm. The water is beginning to fall." Perhaps both dams were used in a similar manner.

11. Busse, p. 158.

12. *Enzyklopädie GVK*, p. 287; MA DDR, WF-03/5087, Sheet 523 [Stich, p. 42].

13. Stich, p. 36.

14. Stich, pp. 36 & 43.

15. Stich, p. 41.

16. Stich, pp. 39 & 43.

17. Stich, p. 37.

18. Vorobe'ev, pp. 32 ff. [Stich, p. 36].

19. Stich, p. 42.

20. Thorwald, p. 31.

21. Shtemenko [*SGSW*], pp. 300-302; Ziemke, pp. 66-7.

22. Heinrici, pp. 36 ff. [Gosztony, pp. 91-93].

23. MA DDR, WF-02/7061, Sheet 222 [Stich article].

24. MA DDR, WF-003/5103, Sheet 403, and WF-10/13262, Sheet 616 [Stich, p. 38].

25. MA DDR, WF-02/7061, Sheet 222 [Stich, p. 38]. The format of the original document has been altered to conform with the conventions of this book.

26. Luethen, pp. 3,5 & 156-67, maintains that the XIth SS Panzer Corps changed its title to the XIth SS Corps on the 1st April, and that the Vth SS Mountain Corps changed its title to the Vth SS Volunteer Corps in mid March, but these changes are not reflected in contemporary documents.

27. Altner, p. 54, says the gun at Lietzen was 305mm, but he was no expert on that subject; Knüppel, pp. 55 & 159, re gun at narrow-gauge railway station in Seelow; Stich, p. 152; Tieke, p. 97.

28. Stich, p. 40.

29. MA DDR, WF-03/5100, Sheet 315 [Stich, p. 40].

30. Stich, pp. 43-4.

31. Artillery details from MA DDR, WF-03/5100, flak details from MA DDR, WF-03/5103, Sheet 403 [Stich, p. 38].

32. Rocolle, pp. 19-20; Thorwald, p. 32. Article on Special Operations Unit by "S.B." in *Alte Kameraden*.

33. Tieke, p. 18.

34. Tieke, p. 45.

35. Reinicke, pp. 355-7; Tieke, p. 110.

36. Keilig, p. 278; Dr. Hans-Werner Klement's notes to author; Sergeyev article; Tieke, pp. 45, 500.

37. Tessin, p. 99; Tieke, p. 45.

38. Tessin, p. 170; Tieke, pp. 78 & 108.

39. Knappe MS; Tieke, p. 78; Wagner p. 52. Von Dufving was later promoted Colonel in Berlin.

40. Wagner, pp. 6-16.

41. Averdieck MS; correspondence with the late Kurt Keller II; Tessin, p. 170; Tieke, p. 502. Keilig, p. 304. Scholz was promoted Major General on 20 April 1945.

42. Tessin, p. 139; discussions with Oberst Horst Zobel; research by Prof. Dr. Walter Kroemer. Report by Günther Labes on 3rd Battalion, 2nd "Müncheberg" Panzergrenadier Regiment.

43. Averdieck; Keller; Knappe MS; Tams; Zobel.

44. MA DDR, WF-03/17398, Sheet 490 f. [Stich, p. 152]; correspondence with the late Kurt Keller II.

45. Scheel article; exhibit at Seelow Museum; Tams article.

46. Von Hopffgarten; Tieke, p. 45.

47. Fritz Kohlase MS; Tessin, p. 99; Tieke, p. 45.

48. Hansen (1993), pp. 1-11; Wolfgang Schrader in correspondence with the author.

49. Von Hopffgarten: Keilig, p. 260; Tieke, p. 45. Tessin gives the 378th and 392nd Grenadier Regiments as having three battalions each, but a map giving the deployment on 15 April shows only two.

50. Keilig, p. 318; Tieke, p. 45.

51. Von Hopffgarten: Keilig, p. 191. Langkeit promoted Major General on 20 April 1945.

52. Tieke, p. 45; Weber article.

53. Tieke, p. 45.

54. Tieke, pp. 45 & 98; Wilke Archive.

55. Michaelis; Tessin, p. 399; Tieke, p. 45; Wilke Archive.

56. Keilig, p. 318; Tieke, p. 45; Wilke Archive.

57. Tieke, p. 102; Wilke Archive.

58. Wilke Archive.

59. Heinrici, pp. 36 ff. [Gosztony, p. 154].

60. Altner, pp. 35-57; Reinicke, p. 357.

61. Tessin, p. 170.

62. Altner, p. 38; exhibit in Seelow Museum.

63. Trevor-Roper [HWD], pp. 212-13.

64. Ryan, pp. 345 & 351; Erickson, p. 555.

65. Rocolle, pp. 19-20; Ziemke, p. 76.

CHAPTER 11. ORDERS AND RECONNAISSANCE

1. Katukov, pp. 359-60; Zhukov, p. 593. The model is now on display with other souvenirs of this battle at the former Soviet Army Museum, now "Gedenkstätte Berlin-Karlshorst."

2. Chuikov, pp. 126-27.

3. Artamanov, pp. 75 ff.; Vorobe'ev, pp. 129 ff. [Stich, p. 98].

2. Chuikov, pp. 126-27.

4. Panov, p. 361 [Stich, p. 51].

5. Stich, pp. 52-64.

6. Rotmistrov, pp. 45 f. [Stich, p. 74].

7. The 1st Polish Army's boundaries in "Operation Berlin" were displayed in an exhibit in the former Soviet Army Museum at Karlshorst.

8. *Berlinskaya*, p. 80 f. [Stich, p. 77].

9. *Die Handlungen*, Part I, p. 43 [Stich, pp. 76-77].

10. *Die Handlungen*, Part I, p. 44; Vorobe'ev, p. 72, the former giving 500 guns for an AAG, the latter 243. *Gen. Stab, Die Operationen*, p. 314, Table 45 [Stich, pp. 76-7].

11. *Gen. Stab, Die Operationen*, p. 314, Table 44 [Stich, p. 75].

12. *ViZ*, 4/1965, p. 85 [Stich, pp. 69 & 75].

13. *Die Handlungen*, Part I, pp. 43 & 75 [Stich, p. 76].

14. Simon, p. 64.

15. *Gen. Stab, Die Operationen*, pp. 315 f.; Matveyev article *Combat Artillery in the Berlin Operation*; Vorobe'ev, pp. 72f [Stich, pp. 77-78].

16. Stich, pp. 77-78.

17. Kazakov. The figure of 20,000 presumably includes all calibers and mounts of guns and mortars.

18. Katukov, pp. 357-8.

19. Panov, Table 56 [Stich, p. 72].

20. Rostmitrov, pp. 45 f. [Stich, p. 74].

21. *Entw. d. Taktik*, p. 151; *MAK Frunze, GdKK*, p. 421 [Stich, pp. 67-68].

22. *Entw. d. Taktik*, pp. 198 ff., ViZ, 6/1962, pp. 26 ff.; Vorobe'ev, p. 117, Table 5 [Stich, pp. 71].

23. *Berlinskaya*, pp. 80 ff.; Poplavski, pp. 292 ff.; Vorobe'ev, pp. 116 ff. [Stich, pp. 66-70].

24. *Geschichte der Kriegskunst*, pp. 360 f. [Stich, p. 51].

25. *ViZ*, 4/1965, p. 81, Table 2; Kozevnikov, p. 208 [Stich, p. 79]; Novikov, p. 89.

26. Zimmer, p. 33; Stich, pp. 83-84.

27. Novikov, pp. 88-89; Stich, p. 80; Wagener, p. 353.

28. Stich, p. 82.

29. Novikov, p. 90; Stich, pp. 81-82.

30. Stich, p. 82.

31. Katukov, p. 367; 16. *LA*, p. 330 [Stich, p. 83].

32. *Die sowj. LSK*, p. 109 [Stich, p. 82].

33. *Berlinskaya*, p. 80; Andersen, p. 110 f. [Simon, p. 60]; Vorobe'ev, p. 77, Table 2 [Stich 84-85]. I have translated "Luftverteidigungskorps der Westfront der Truppen der Luftverteidigung des Landes" simply as "Home Air Defense Corps."

34. Stich, p. 86.

35. *Entw. d. Taktik*, pp. 240 f. [Stich, p. 87]. Female antiaircraft gun crews seen by Fritz Kohlase, p. 60.

36. Radzievsky, p. 146 [Stich, p. 89].

37. Vorobe'ev, p. 107 [Stich, p. 91].

38. Bokov, p. 150; Katukov, p. 357; Klimov, p. 59; Werth, p. 644 [Gosztony, p. 58].
The role of Ehrenburg is also covered by Ryan and Tolstoy.

39. Red Army atrocities on German soil are well covered in Gosztony, Ryan and
Tolstoy. The latter, pp. 265-71, suggests that the Red Army was encouraged to behave in
this fashion in order to destroy or loot as much of the evidence of capitalist comfort as
possible and to create an irredeemable rift between the conquerors and their victims. See
also Toland [*LHD*], p. 9.

40. *GPW*, p. 383; Ziemke, p. 74.

41. Bokov, p. 160; Chuikov, pp. 140-41.

42. Vorobe'ev, p. 127 [Stich, p. 100].

43. Zhukov, p. 362.

44. Viasankin, pp. 36 f. [Stich, p. 101].

45. Prosliakov, p. 43 [Stich, p. 102].

46. Tieke, p. 87.

47. Wagner, p. 52.

48. Tiecke, p. 86.

49. Averdieck, p. 108

50. Washington archives T311/169/7221680. However, the 20th Panzergrenadiers
remained in the line, bolstered by various motley units, including Küstrin survivors.

51. Busse, p. 163. There is an error in this account, as it was the "Müncheberg"
Panzer Divison, not the "Kurmark" that came to the support of the 20th Panzergrenadiers.
The two Panzergrenadier brigades he refers to are the "Nederland" and "Nordland" SS
Panzergrenadier Divisions, both roughly down to brigade strength when they joined the
9th Army.

52. Bokov, p. 158 [Stich, p. 104].

53. Clearly there was some confusion at HQ 9th Army about whose divisional area
this was, for the 20th Panzergrenadiers were still in the line.

54. Washington archives T311/169/7221705.

55. Stich, pp. 104-6.

56. Telegin, pp. 67 ff. [Stich, p. 99].

57. Erickson, p. 555; Ryan, pp. 345 & 351.

CHAPTER 12. FIRST DAY OF BATTLE

1. Stich, p. 109.

2. Stich, Doc. 5.

3. Zhukov, pp. 362-3.

4. Chuikov, pp. 178-79.

Various times have been quoted for the start of the opening bombardment. The
Soviets were working on Moscow Time, and so record this at 0500 hours. The Germans
were on German Summer Time, which had been introduced in 1940, and in 1945 was due
to last from 1 April to 6 October, so for them this was 0400 hours, the time used in this

narration. However, Army Group "Weichsel's" morning report gives the time as 0350 hours, that is, ten minutes ahead of the hour in German Summer Time. This ten-minute advance occurs elsewhere in German reports, which also failed to distinguish the changeover from the opening barrage lasting twenty-five minutes to the creeping barrage, which went on for a further two hours, advancing at two kilometers per hour. Also, many contemporary German accounts confusingly use Central European Time.

5. Kazakov.

6. Tams article.

7. Wagner, p. 57.

8. Schöneck, p. 48-49.

9. Zhukov, p. 365.

10. Chuikov, p. 179.

11. Novikov, pp. 302 f.; *16. LA*, pp. 334 ff. [Stich, p. 112].

12. Altner, p. 61, re the gun at Lietzen; Tieke, p. 96.

13. Chuikov, p. 179.

14. Stich, Document 7; Tieke, p. 110.

15. Komornicki, pp. 102-7; Stich, Document 7; Tieke, p. 108.

16. Erich Hachtel in an article to the author dated 18 February 1945. On one of his visits to the Regimental Staff at Sonnenburg, where they were accommodated in a house belonging to Ribbentrop, Hachtel was shown a telegram from the German Ambassador in Tokyo, saying that even at the beginning of April the Japanese were seeking peace negotiations to end the war. (*"Die Japaner bereits Anfang April 1945 ihre Fühler zu Friedensverhandlungen ausgestreckt hatten und bereit gewesen waren, den Krieg von sich aus zu beenden!"*)

17. Tieke, p. 110.

18. Schrode, pp. 116-18; Stich, Document 7; Tieke, pp.108-12.

19. Glantz, p. 639; Stich, p. 58.

20. *Great Patriotic War of the Soviet Union 1941-1945*, 1974 English translation of abridged version, p. 379.

21. Schöneck, pp. 58-59.

22. Stich, Document 7.

23. *Geschichte des Großern Vaterländischen Krieges der Sowjetunion*, Band 5 [Schöneck, p. 54].

24. Glantz, p. 539; Stich, pp. 52-53.

25. Bokov, p. 161.

26. Tiecke, p. 121; Wagner, p. 58.

27. Bokov, pp. 161-66, 168.

28. Kurt Keller II in letter to author.

29. Bokov, pp. 161-66.

30. Waldmüller, pp. 14-15.

31. Bokov, pp. 161-66.

32. Kurt Keller II in letter to Prime Minister Stolpe of Land Brandenburg dated 27 March 1991. There is a photograph of the train in the Seelow Museum.

33. Kurt Keller II in letter to author. Keller escaped later that day and subsequently fought in Berlin.

34. Stich, Document 7.

35. Bokov, pp. 168-69.

36. Breddemann, pp. 62 f. [Stich, pp. 112-13].

37. Weber. The newly arrived regiment was probably in fact the 1st Battalion, 1st "Müncheberg" Panzergrenadier Regiment.

38. Tieke, p. 97

39. Tieke, p. 106, re SPGs; Zobel in conversation with the author. Location of the SPGs estimated by author.

40. Tams article.

41. MA DDR, WF-10/13256; Vorobe'ev, p. 131 [Stich, p. 113].

42. Chuikov, pp. 179-80. According to Vorobe'ev, p. 73, a further fifteen-minute bombardment had been planned for once the line Werbig-Seelow station had been reached.

43. Tieke, pp. 106-7.

44. Averdieck.

45. Wagner, pp. 58-59.

46. Hansen, pp. 10-13.

47. Tieke, pp. 104-6; Weber articles. Col Scheunemann was replaced by Col Albin Esch as divisional commander on the 21st.

48. Von Hopffgarten; Tieke, pp. 104-6.

49. Tieke, pp. 104-6; Weber articles.

50. Tieke, p. 107, says that the order for the commitment of the 1st Guards Tank Army came from Stalin, which would give a completely different complexion to the matter, but Zhukov recounts otherwise. There is some conflict about the time given for the tanks to move, but Rotmistrov, p. 294, and Vorobe'ev, p. 132, both confirm Zhukov's time of 1430 hours [Stich, p. 116.]

51. Katukov, p. 364-5.

52. Chuikov, pp. 180-81. The quotation from the 1967 English edition was omitted from later editions.

53. Chuikov, p. 181; Tieke, p. 107.

54. Stich, Document 7.

55. Von Hopffgarten; Schneider article, p. 6; Tiecke, pp. 103-4.

56. Stich, Document 7.

57. Report of B.M. Tichonrarov [Schneider, p. 6.].

58. Glantz, p. 539. With a strength of about 4,500 men, a Fortified Region (ukreplennyi raion) consisted of between four and seven artillery and machinegun battalions and was designed to tie down the non-operational parts of the front line.

59. Dr Teller.

60. Aktionbestände der Heeresgruppe Weichsel vom 1. März bis 28. April 1945 (National Archives, Washington, D.C.) [Gosztony, pp. 176-8].

61. Tieke, pp. 102-3.

62. Tieke, pp. 98-102.

63. Tieke, p. 97.

64. Stich, Document 7. The Soviet report mistakenly quotes Schwetig for Güldendorf.

65. Schneider, p. 24; Tieke, pp. 102-3; Wilke.

66. Busse, p. 163.

67. Article in *Alte Kameraden* taken from Oberstleutnant Ulrich Saft's *Das bittere Ende der Luftwaffe*, (Langenhagen: Verlag-Saft).

68. *16. LA*, pp. 336-9 [Stich, pp. 114-15].

69. Tieke, p. 112.

70. *Aktienbestände der Heeresgruppe Weichsel vom 1. März bis 28. April*, National Archives, Washington, D.C. [Gosztony, pp. 176-78].

71. Tieke, p. 111.

72. Tieke, p. 112.

73. Zhukov, pp. 366-7.

74. Chuikov, pp. 181-82; Zhukov, p. 368.

75. Babadshanian, p. 246.

CHAPTER 13. SECOND DAY OF BATTLE

1. Komornicki, p. 107-8; Stich, Document 8; Tiecke, p. 213.

2. Hachtel to author.

3. Tiecke, p. 121-23.

4. Boehme, p. 285; Schrode, pp. 119-20.

5. Tiecke, p. 122.

6. Stich, Document 8.

7. Stich, Document 8.

8. Schrode, pp. 119-20; Sergeyev article.

9. Hahn, p. 11.

10. Schöneck, pp. 59-61.

11. Tiecke, p. 122.

12. Bolkov, pp. 169-71; Stich, Document 8; Tiecke, p. 121; Wagner, pp. 59-60.

13. Averdieck, p. 109-10.

14. Waldmüller, p.16.

15. Tams, pp. 198-200.

16. Stich, Document 8.

17. Author's supposition from examination of the ground and report in Tiecke, p. 104.

18. Tiecke, pp 119-20.

19. Kroemer.

20. Weber article.

21. Stich, Docuemnt 8.

22. Von Hopffgarten; Schneider, p. 6; Tiecke, p. 119.

23. Stich, Document 8.

24. Stich, Document 8; Tiecke, pp. 116-17.

25. Tiecke, pp. 115 & 128.

26. Article in *Alte Kameraden* taken from Oberstleutnant Ulrich Saft's *Das bittere Ende der Luftwaffe* Verlag-Saft, Langenhagen.

27. Antipenko, p. 279.

28. Tiecke, p. 124.

29. Rogmann to author; Tiecke, pp. 124-25.

30. Busse, p. 162, The Hitlerjugend are also mentioned by Knappe, p. 13, although he dates the event as the 19th, but his account contains many obvious inaccuracies about this period.

31. Busse, p. 164.

32. Ziemke, p. 83.

33. Babadshanian, pp, 246-7.

34. Katukov, pp. 366-8.

35. Stich, Document 8.

CHAPTER 14. THIRD DAY OF BATTLE

1. Tieke, pp. 125-27.

2. Komornicki, p. 110; Reinicke, p. 357; Tieke, pp. 142-3.

3. Hachtel to author.

4. Reinicke, p. 357.

5. Boehm, p. 285; Dr. Schmook, Oderbuch Heimatmuseum, re mill; Schrode, p. 119.

6. Komornicki, p. 110.

7. Boehm, p. 285; Schrode, pp. 119-20.

8. Tieke, pp. 142-43.

9. Boehm, p. 285; Hahn, p. 11; Schrode, p. 120.

10. Official History of the 3rd Shock Army.

11. Klement to author; Schrode, p. 120.

12. Schöneck, pp. 61-70.

13. *Tagesmeldung der Obkdo der Heersgruppe Weichsel, Ia/Nr. 5885/45 geh.v.18.4.1945.*

14. Tieke, p. 140-41.

15. Tieke, p. 141.

16. Tieke, p. 140; Wagner, p. 58.

17. Tieke, p. 138.

18. Engelmann, p. 630; Tieke, p. 141; Wagner, p. 63.

19. Wagner, p. 62. Neither of these units subsequently took part in the Berlin fighting. The 25th eventually reached Schleswig-Holstein, where it surrendered to the British, while the 26th ended fighting the Americans south of Schwerin.

20. Zobel to author.

21. Averdieck, pp. 110-12.

22. Tams, p. 201.

23. Chuikov, pp. 149-51; von Hopffgarten; Zhukov, p. 607; Novikov, p. 92, says "With the help of the 16th Air Army, Soviet troops not only held their positions but even advanced a little." According to Tieke, pp. 136-37, the Luftwaffe claimed to have destroyed forty-three tanks, plus another possible nineteen, as well as fifty-nine aircraft.

In the 1967 English edition Chuikov says: "Not only had the tanks failed to make a forward break, even on the second and third days of the operation they remained behind the mixed armies."

24. Katukov, p. 369.

25. Hansen, p. 13.

26. Weber.

27. Knüppel, p. 181; Tieke, p. 136-37.

28. Knappe, pp. 13-14; Tieke, p. 139.

29. Von Ofen, p. 305 [Gosztony, p. 186.]

30. Knappe, p. 10; Tieke, p. 137.

31. *Aktennotiz, Ferngespräch Reichsmarschall mit Ia d.H.Gr.Weichsel. 18.4.45.*

32. Herrmann in correspondence with author. An extract from a letter of his quoted in Wagner, p. 60, reads: "General Bräuer was my company commander in 1934. After attending the War Academy in 1935 I was a platoon commander in the 3rd Company in the "General Göring" Regiment's 1st Battalion commanded by Major Bräuer, in the autumn 1937 his battalion adjutant, 1939 his regimental adjutant. In July 1940 I returned as commander of the 5th Company of the 1st Parachute Regiment commanded by Colonel Bräuer."

33. Tieke, p. 136.

34. Von Hopffgarten; Tieke, p. 136.

35. Altner, pp. 64-65.

36. Tieke, p. 136.

37. MA DDR, WF-03/5087 Sheets 1909 & 1911 [Buwert]; Schneider, p. 6.

38. Tieke, pp. 133-35; Wilke Archive.

39. Tieke, pp. 132-33; Wilke Archive.

40. Tieke, p. 132.

41. Tieke, pp. 130-31.

42. Tieke, p. 147.

43. Washington Archives T311/169/7221855.

44. Front Directive No. 00566/OP of 18 April 1945.

45. Chuikov (English edition of 1967) pp. 158-59.

46. Chuikov, pp. 185-86.

47. Babadshanian, pp. 247-8.

CHAPTER 15. FOURTH DAY OF BATTLE

1. Tiecke, pp. 147 & 151.
2. Reinicke, p. 357.
3. Komornicki, pp. 111-13.
4. Hachtel to author.
5. Schrode, p. 212.
6. Tieke, p. 156.
7. Klement to author.
8. Schöneck, pp. 69-79.
9. Tieke, pp. 152-53.
10. Tieke, pp. 140-41, wrongly attributed to 18 April.
11. Tieke, pp. 152-55.
12. Tieke, p. 156.
13. Engelmann, pp. 634-7.
14. Wittor to author.
15. Tieke, p. 150.
16. Tieke, pp. 150-52.
17. Chuikov, pp. 186-87. In the 1967 English edition Chuikov claimed that the Germans lost about 400 men, 8 tanks, 7 "Ferdinand" SPGs and 12 APCs at Müncheberg.
18. Averdieck, p. 112.
19. Tieke, p. 151.
20. Weber article.
21. Hansen, pp. 14-15.
22. Altner, pp. 63-69.
23. *Großdeutschland*, p. 632.
24. 9th Army situation report for 19 April.
25. Tieke, pp. 149-50.
26. Wilke Archive.
27. Tieke, p. 148.
28. Tieke, p. 149-51.
29. Busse, p. 165.
30. Skorodumov, p. 93.
31. Chuikov, p. 164; Koniev, pp. 701-2.
32. Korminicki, pp. 166-75.

CHAPTER 16. THE FATE OF THE GERMAN 9th ARMY

1. Wagner, p. 63.
2. Knappe, pp. 28-29; Kuby, p. 108; Tiecke, pp. 216-8; Weidling article, p. 42.
3. 'Mook Wi' veterans re Wannsee; Averdieck, pp. 115-19 re Armored Brigade.

4. Chronos-Film interview with von Dufving, 1993; Chuikov, pp. 241-4; Kuby, pp. 108 & 201-3; Tieke, pp. 216-7, 245 & 357; Weidling, pp. 115, 169-74.

5. Altner, pp. 210-45; Tieke, pp. 415 & 419. Possibly 10,000 took part in this breakout; Zobel in communication with the author.

6. Koniev, p. 189, who gives the date as 30 April; Schöneck, pp. 125-334

7. O'Donnell, pp. 217-8, 221-37, 256-61; Trevor-Roper [*LDH*], pp. 243-6.

8. Borkowski, pp. 136-37; Helmut Später's *Die Geschichte des Panzerkorps Grossdeutschland*, Vol. 3, p. 748 [Gosztony, p. 383].

9. Boehm, pp. 285-94; Reinicke, pp. 357-60.

10. *GPW*, p. 381.

11. Koniev, pp. 120-21.

12. *GPW*, p. 381.

13. Novikov, p. 95; Wagner, pp. 355-6.

14. Thorwald, pp. 88-89.

15. Busse, pp. 166-67.

16. Koniev, pp 161-62; Zhukov, p. 610.

17. Tieke, pp. 204-13.

18. Domank article & map; Koniev, p. 153.

19. Tieke, pp. 204-13.

20. Busse, p. 168.

21. *GPW*, p. 383; Kuby, p. 211; Ziemke, p. 110. The writer was Konstantin Simonov.

22. Thorwald, p. 190.

23. Gellermann, pp. 93-94; Wenck, p. 66.

24. Gellermann, p. 176.

25. Busse, p. 168: Tieke, pp. 309-45.

26. Busse, p. 168; Koniev, pp. 180-82; Wenck, pp. 68-69.

27. Gellermann, pp. 105-19.

CHAPTER 17. STALIN RULES

1. Spahr, p. 197.

2. Chuikov, p. 164; Koniev, p. 135, mistakenly says this was the 23rd; Kuby, pp. 52-53; Tieke, p. 201, in which the time of encounter as 0900 hours. Zhukov does not even mention it!

3. Koniev, p. 131.

4. Chuikov, pp. 183-85 & 196-97; Dragunsky, pp. 61-62, 93 & 120; Koniev, pp. 184-87.

5. Spahr, pp. 182-83.

6. Spahr, pp. 192-94.

7. Spahr, pp. 196-97.

8. Spahr, p. 198.

9. Spahr, pp. 200-203.

10. Spahr, p. 208.
11. Spahr, pp. 209-10.
12. Spahr, pp. 213-15.
13. Spahr, pp. 216-20.
14. Spahr, pp. 232-3 & 235.
15. Spahr, pp. 235-41.
16. Spahr, pp. 243-4 & 252-8.
17. Spahr, p. 165.
18. Spahr, pp. 259-60.
19. Spahr, pp. 260-3.
20. Spahr, pp. 263-4.

Bibliography

Altner, Helmut. *Totentanz Berlin: Tagebuchblätter eines Achtzehnjährigen*. Offenbach/Main: Bollwerk Verlag, 1947.

Artamaňov, I.D. *Prozektory i ich primenenie*. Moscow: 1957.

Averdieck, Dr. F.-R. "Das Ende der 20. Panzergrenadier Division." Unpublished MS.

Antipenko, Lt. Gen. N.A. *In der Hauptrichtung*. East Berlin: Militärverlag der DDR.

Averdieck, Dr. F.-R. "Das Ende der 20. Panzergrenadier Division." Unpublished MS.

Babadshanian, Col. A.H. *Hauptstosskraft*. East Berlin:Militärverlag der DDR, 1981.

Babadshanian, Col. A.H., N.K. Popel, M.A. Salin and I.M. Krachenko. *Ljuki otkryli v Berline*. Moskow: 1973.

Bieller, Seweryn. *Stalin and his Generals*. New York: Pegasus, 1969.

Blond, Georges. *Death of Hitler's Germany*. New York: Macmillan, 1954.

Boehm, Oberst a.D. Prof. Erwin. *Geschichte der 25. Division*. Stuttgart, undated.

Bokov, Lt. Gen. F.I. *Frühjahr des Sieges und der Befreiung*. East Berlin: Militärverlag der DDR, 1979.

Borkowski, Dieter. *Wer weiss, ob wir uns wiedersehen: Erinnerungen an eine Berliner Jugend*. Frankfurt-am-Main: Fischer Taschenbuch Verlag, 1980.

Breddemann, G. "Der Einsatz der Artillerie der Roten Armee zu Beginn der Berliner Operation." Thesis, "Friedrich Engels" Military Academy, Dresden, 1987.

Buchner, Alex. *Das Handbuch der deutschen Infanterie 1939-1945*. Friedberg: Podzun-Pallas Verlag, 1989.

Bullock, Alan. *Hitler: a study in tyranny*. Rev. ed. London: Penguin Books. (Originally published by Oldhams, London, 1952.)

Burkert, Hans-Norbert, Klaus Matussek and Doris Obschernitzki. *Zerstört Besiegt Befreit: Der Kampf um Berlin bis zur Kapitulation 1945*. Stätten der Geschichte Berlins, Bd. 7. Berlin: Edition Hentrich im Verlag Fröhlich & Kaufmann, 1985.

Burn, Jeffrey. *The Waffen-SS*. London: Osprey, 1982.

Buwert, Wolfgang. "Anmerkung zum Stand der DDR-Geschichtswissenschaft und zur Befreiung und Zerstörung Frankfurts 1945." In *Mitteilungen des Historischen Vereins zu Frankfurt (Oder) e.V.*, 1991

Campbell, Christy. *The World War II Fact Book*. London: Futura, 1986.

Carver, Field Marshal Sir John. *The War Lords*. London: Weidenfeld & Nicolson, 1976.

Chaney, Otto P. Jnr. *Zhukov*. Norman: University of Oklahoma Press, 1971.

Chuikov, Vasilii I. *The End of the Third Reich*. Rev. ed. Moscow: Progress Publishers. (Panther edition, London, 1969.)

Clark, Alan. *Barbarossa: The Russo-German Conflict 1941-45*. London: Hutchinson, 1965.

Die Handlungen der Artillerie operativer und taktischer Verbände nach der Erfahrungen des Grossen Vaterländischen Krieges 1941-1945. [Study material, "Friedrich Engels" Military Accademy, Dresden.

Doernberg, Dr. Stefan. *Befreiung 1945*. East Berlin: Dietz Verlag, 1985.

Dragunski, David Abramowitch. *Jahre im Panzer*. East Berlin: Militärverlag der DDR, 1980.

Duffy, Christopher. *Red Storm on the Reich*. London: Routledge, 1991.

Eichholz, Diedrich. *Brandenburg in der NS-Zeit*. Berlin: Verlag Volk und Welt GmbH, 1993.

Eisenhower, Gen. Dwight D. *Crusade in Europe*, London: Heinemann, 1949.

Engelmann, Joachim. "Geschichte der 18. Panzergrenadier-Division," Part IV. Unpublished MS, Oldenburg, undated.

Engelmann, Joachim. *"Lohn der Tapferkeit."* Unpublished MS, Oldenburg, undated.

Erickson, Prof. John. *The Road to Berlin*. London: Weidenfeld & Nicholson, 1983.

Fest, Joachim C. *Hitler*. New York: Harcourt Brace Janovich, 1973. (London: Weidenfeld & Nicolson, 1974.)

Fey, Willi *Panzer im Brennpunkt der Fronten*. Munich: J.F. Lehmanns Verlag, undated.

Foss, Christopher F. *World War II Tanks and Fighting Vehicles*. London: Salamander Books, 1981.

Gädtke, Ernst-Christian. *Von der Oder zur Elbe*. Unpublished MS, Berlin-Lichterfelde, 1992.

Gellermann, Günter W. *Die Armee Wenck - Hitlers letzte Hoffnung*. Koblenz: Bernard & Graefe, 1983.

Glantz, Col. David M. *Soviet Military Deception in the Second World War*. London: Frank Cass & Co., 1989.

Gosztony, Peter. *Der Kampf um Berlin in Augenzeugenberichten*. Düsseldorf: Deutscher Taschenbuch Verlag, 1970.

Great Patriotic War of the Soviet Union 1941-5, The, [*GPWS*]. Moscow: Progress Publishers, 1974.

Guderian, Col. Gen. Heinz. *Panzer Leader*. New York: Ballentine Books, 1965.

Hahn, Gerhard. Report dated 21 January 1978.

Hansen, Hans. *"...allzeit meine Pflicht zu tun."* Unpublished MS, Kropp, revised 1993.

Heinrici, Gotthard. "Die Abwehrvorbereitungen an der Oder." Unpublished MS, 1947.

Höhne, Heinz. *The Order of the Death's Head*, New York: Ballentine Books, 1971.

von Hopffgarten, GenLt. a.D. Hans-Joachim. "Der Kampf um die Oderbrückenköpfe Lebus und Göritz." In *Wehrkunde*, Nr. 11, 1955.

Katukov, Marshal Michail Jefremovitch. *An der Spitze des Hauptstosses*. East Berlin: Militärverlag der DDR, 1985.

Kazakov, V.I. *Always with the Tanks, Always with the Infantry*. Moscow, date unknown.) [Title translated from the Russian].

Keegan, John. *Waffen SS: The Asphalt Soldiers*. London: Pan/Ballentine, 1972. (Purnell, London, 1971.)

Keilig, Wolff. *Das deutsche Heer 1939-1945: Gliederung, Einsatz, Stellenbesetzung. Abschnitt 211: "Die Generalität des Heeres im 2. Weltkrieg 1939-1945 (Truppenoffiziere)*. Bad Nauheim: 1956-1970.

Kirian, M.M. *Vnezapnost v nastupatelnych operacijach Velikoj Otecestvennoj vojny*. Moscow, 1986.

Kitchen, Martin. *Nazi Germany at War*. London: Longman, 1995.

Klimov, Gregory. *The Terror Machine*. London: Faber & Faber, 1953.

Knappe, Siegfried. "Tagebuch-Aufzeichnungen." Unpublished MS, 1985.

Knappe, Siegfried and Ted Brusaw. *Soldat: Reflections of a German Soldier*. Shrewsbury, England: Airlife Publishing Ltd, 1993.

Knüppel, Fritz. *Kreis Lebus: Ein leidgeprüftes Land*. Heimatkreis Lebus, 1990.

Koch, H.W. *The Hitler Youth*. New York: Stein & Day, 1976.

Kohlase, Fritz. *Mit dem Fusilier-Bataillon 303 in Küstrin*. Berlin: Brandenburgisches Verlaghaus, 1993.

Komornicki, Stanislaw. *Polnische Soldaten stürmten Berlin*. Warsaw: Polish Military History Institute, Ministry of Defense, undated.

Koniev, Marshal I.S. *Year of Victory*. Moscow: Progress Publishers, 1969.

Kortenhaus, Werner. "*Lothringen, Elsass, Ostfront: Der Einsatz der 21. Panzer-Division*." Unpublished MS.

Kuby, Erich. *The Russians and Berlin 1945* New York: Hill & Wang, 1964.

Larrabee, Eric. *Commander in Chief: Franklin Delano Roosevelt, His Lieutenants and Their War*. New York: Harper & Row, 1987.

Leosenia, E.V. and V.P. Andreev. *Inzenernye vojska sovetskoj armii v vaznejsich operacijach Velikoj Ote-cestvennoj vojne*. Moskow, 1958.

Lindner, GenMaj. a.D. Rudi. "Der Tod war unser Begleiter." Unpublished MS, Frankfurt/Oder, 1993.

Luethen, Hanns and Horst Wilke. *Am Rande der Strassen*. "Arbeitsgemeinschaft Suchdienst-Archiv-Dokumentation, March 1991.

Mackintosh, Malcolm. *Juggernaut*. London: Secker & Warburg, 1967.

Melzheimer, Werner. *Die Festung und Garnison Küstrin*. Berlin: Landmannschaft Berlin-Mark Brandenburg, 1989.

Menvell, Roger and Heinrich Fraenkel. *Heinrich Himmler*. London: Heinemann, 1965.

Michaelis, Rolf. *Kampf und Untergang der 32. SS-Freiwillige-Grenadier-Division '30. Januar'*. Erlangen, 1993.

Montgomery-Hyde, H. *Stalin: the History of a Dictator*. London: Rupert Hart-Davis, 1971.

Nicolaevsky, Boris L. *Power and the Soviet Elite.* New York: Praeger Publications, 1964.

von Oven, Wilfried. *Mit Goebbels bis zum Ende.* Buenos Aires, 1950.

Panov, B.W., I.I. Kisselyov and A.G Charkov. *Geschichte der Kriegskunst.* East Berlin: Militärverlag der DDR, 1987.

Poplawski, Gen. Stanislaw. *Kampfgefährten.* East Berlin: Militärverlag der DDR, 1980.

Pykathov, B.V.K., K.S. Belov and S.S. Frolov. *History of 3rd Shock Army.* Moscow: Ministry of Defense, 1976.

Quarrie, B. *Hitler's Samurai.* Cambridge, England: Patrick Stephens, 1984.

Reimann, Viktor. *Goebbels.* New York: Doubleday, 1976.

Reinicke, Adolf. *Die 5. Jäger-Division.* Freidberg: Podzun-Pallas-Verlag, undated.

Rocolle, Col Pierre. *Götterdämmerung - La Prise de Berlin.* Indo-China, 1954.

Rotmistrov, P.A. *Ispolzovanie tankovych vojsk v berlinskoj operacii.* Moscow, 1985.

Ryan, Cornelius. *The Last Battle.* New York: Simon & Schuster, 1966. (Collins, London, 1973.)

Salisbury, Harrison E. *Marshal Zhukov's Greatest Battles.* London: Macdonald, 1969.

Scheel, Klaus. *Hauptstossrichtung Berlin,* East Berlin: VEB Deutscher Verlag der Wissenschaften, 1983.

Schneider, Joachim. "Die Festung Frankfurt (Oder) im Frühjahr 1945." Unpublished, 1993.

Schöneck, Friedhelm. "Die Zange: Tagebuch und Erlebnisberichte aus dem Jahr 1945.", Unpublished MS.

Schramm, Percy Ernst. *Kriegestagesbuch des OKW 1940-1945,* Vol IV. Frankfurt/Main: Bernard & Graefe Verlag für Wehrwissen, 1961.

Schrode, Wilhelm. *Die Geschichte der 25. Division: Die Wiederaufstellung der 25.* Panzergrenadier-Division, Herbst 1944 bis Kriegsende. Ludwigsburg, 1980.

Seaton, Albert. *The Russo-German War 1941-45.* New York: Praeger Publications, 1971. (Arthur Baker, London, 1971.)

Seaton, Albert. *Stalin as a Warlord.* London: Batsford,1976.

Sethi, Col. (Retd.) A.L. *Marshal Zhukov: The Master Strategist.* Dehra Dun: Natraj Publishers, 1988.

Shtemenko, S.M. *The Last Six Months.* [LSM] New York: Doubleday, 1977.

Shtemenko, S.M. *The Soviet General Staff at War.* [SGSW]. Moscow: Progress Publishers, 1970.

Simon, Hauptmann Manfred. *Die Bildung und Erweiterung des Küstriner Brückenkopfes.* Dresden: "Friedrich Engels" Military Academy, 1987.

Sovetskaja voennaja Enziklopedija. Moscow, 1976.

Spaeter, Helmuth. *Geschichte des Panzerkorps "Grossdeutschland", Die,* Part III. Friedberg: Podzun-Pallas-Verlag, 1968.

Spahr, Col. William J. *Zhukov: The Rise and Fall of a Great Captain.* Novato, California: Presidio Press, 1993.

Stich, Oberst a.D. Dr. (rer. mil.) Karl. *Der Durchbruch der Verteidigung der faschistischen deutschen Truppen an der Oder durch die sowjetischen Streitkräfte in der Berliner Operation im Frühjahr 1945.* Dresden: "Friedrich Engels" Military Academy, 1988.

Strawson, John. *The Battle for Berlin*. London: Batsford, 1974.

Strik-Strikfeld, Wilfried. *Against Stalin and Hitler*, London: Macmillan, 1970.

Subakov, W. *Der letzte Sturm*. Moscow: APN Verlag, 1975.

Suvarov, Viktor. *Inside the Soviet Army*. London: Hamish Hamilton, 1982.

Tessin, Georg. *Verbände und Truppen der deutschen Wehrmacht und Waffen-SS im zweiten Weltkrieg 1939-1945*. Osnabrück: Biblio Verband, 1977.

Thorwald, Jürgen. *Das Ende an der Elbe*. Stuttgart: Steingrüben Verlag, 1950.

Thrams, Hermann. *Küstrin 1945: Tagebuch einer Festung*. Berlin: Landesmannschaft Berlin-Mark Brandenburg, 1992.

Tieke, Wilhelm. *Das Ende zwischen Oder und Elbe: Der Kampf um Berlin 1945*. Stuttgart: Motorbuch Verlag, 1981.

Tiemann, Rolf. *Die Leibstandarte*, Part IV/2. Osnabrück: Munn Verlag GmbH, undated.

Tillery, Gerhard. "Hinter uns lag Berlin: Mein Fronteinsatz bei der 309. I.D. "Gross-Berlin." Unpublished MS.

Toland, John. *Adolf Hitler*. New York: Doubleday, 1962. (Futura, London, 1978.)

Toland, John. *The Last Hundred Days*. [*LHD*]. London: Arthur Baker, 1965.

Tolstoy, Nikolai. *Stalin's Secret War*. London: Jonathan Cape, 1981.

Trevor-Roper, Prof. H.R. *Hitler's War Directives 1931-45*, [*HWD*]. London: Sidgwick & Jackson, 1964.

Trevor-Roper, Prof. H.R. *The Last Days of Hitler*. [*LDH*]. London: Macmillan, 1972.

Tully, Andrew. *Berlin: Story of a Battle*. New York: Simon & Schuster, 1963.

Volkogonov, Dimitri. *Stalin: Triumph und Tragödie. Ein politisches Porträt*. Düsseldorf: Claasen Verlag, 1989.

Vorbey'ev, F.D., I.V. Propotkin and A.N. Shimansky. *The Last Storm*. 2nd Edition. Moscow: Ministry of Defense, 1975.

Wagener, Ray. *The Soviet Air Forces in World War II*. New York: Doubleday, 1973.

Wagner, Gerd. *Der 9. Fallschirmjägerdivision im Kampf um Pommern, Mark Brandenburg und Berlin*. Cologne: 1985.

Waldmüller, Wolfdieter. "Von Böbligen bis Magdeburg: die letzte 130 Tage." Unpublished MS, Geislingen/Steige, 1982.

Weier, K. "Die Entwicklung der Ansichten in den höheren Führungsorganen des faschistischen Heeres zur Rolle der Stellungsverteidigung an der deutsch-sowjetischen Front unter den Bedingung der strategischen Defensive." Dissertation, Militärgeschichtliches Institut der DDR, Potsdam, 1986.

Werth, Alexander. *Russia at War 1941-1945*. New York: E.P. Dutton, 1964.

Wewetzer, Horst. "Erinnerungen zum Ausbruch aus Küstrin." Unpublished article.

White, B.T. *Tanks and other Armoured Fighting Vehicles 1942-45*. Poole, England: Blandford Press, 1975.

Wilke, Horst. "Wilke Archiv." Unpublished MS.

Zhukov, Marshal Georgi K. *Reminiscences and Reflections*. Moscow: Progress Publishers, 1974. English translation 1985.

Ziemke, Earl F. *Battle for Berlin: End of the Third Reich*. London: Purnell, 1968.

Zippel, Martin. *Untersuchungen zur Militärgeschichte der Reichshauptstadt Berlin von 1871-1945*. Berlin, 1982.

Sundry articles from Soviet, East and West German magazines, including in particular:

"Berlinskaya operacija v cifrach." *Soviet Military History Journal*, Moscow, April 1965.
Busse, Theodor. "Die letzte Schlacht der 9. Armee." *Wehrwissenschaftliche Rundschau*, 1954.
Chernyayev, V. "Some Features of Military Art in the Berlin Operation." *Soviet Military History Journal*, April 1955.
Domank, A. "1st Guards Artillery Division Beats Off Counterattacks of the Enemy Attempting to Break out of Encirclement during the Berlin Operation." *Soviet Military History Journal*, March 1978.
Groehler, O. "Die faschistische deutsche Luftwaffe in der letzten Phase des zweiten Weltkrieges." In *Zeitschrift für Militärgeschichte*, East Berlin, 1971.
Matveyev, Col. Gen. A.I. "Combat Employment of Artillery in the Berlin Operation." *Soviet Military History Journal*, April 1985.
Novikov, A.A. "The Air Forces in the Berlin Operation." *Soviet Military History Journal*, May 1975.
Prosliakov, A.I. "Inzenernoe obespecenie vojsk 1-go Belorusskogo fronta v Berlinskoj operacii." *Soviet Military History Journal*, 1986.
Rotmistrov, P.A. "Ispolzovanie tankovych vojsk v Berlinskoy operacii." *Soviet Military History Journal*, September 1985.
Sergeyev, S. 'Battle of the 150th Rifle Division for a Fortified Stronghold." *Soviet Military History Journal*, June 1977.
Skorodumov, N. "Manoeuvres of 12th Guards Tank Corps in the Berlin Operation." *Soviet Military History Journal'*, March 1978.
Sokolov, S. "Sovetskoe operativnoe iskusstvo v kampanii 1945 goda v Evrope." *Soviet Military History Journal*, 1975.
Tams, Karl-Hermann. "Als Kompaniechef in Seelow im April 1945." *Militärgeschichte*, No. 6/90, pp. 565-76.
Telegin, K.. "Nad Berlinom: Znamja Pobedy." *Soviet Military History Journal*, May 1975.
Weber, Helmut. "Im Endkampf an der Oder 1945." *Greif-Rundbrief*, Nos. 93-8, 1990-1992.
Weidling, Helmuth. "Der Todeskampf der faschistischen Clique in Berlin aus der Erinnerung des Generals Weidling." *Wehrwissenschaftliche Rundschau*, 1962.
Wenck, Walter. "Berlin war nicht mehr zu retten." *Stern* magazine, April 1965.

Index

Abakumov, Viktor, 255-6
Adams, Lt Col, 124
Ahrensdorf, 235
Albania, 257
Allgemeine-SS 123, 133,
Allied Control Commission/Council, 254
"Alpine Redoubt," 109
Alsace, 49
Alt Blessin, 51
Alt Bleyen, 65, 82, 84-87, 92, 95, 128
Altdamm (Dabie), 40, 102-103, 113
Alte Oder Bridgehead, 219-21, 223, 259-
    61, 311. 313
Alte Oder River, 58, 64, 86, 88-89, 110,
    114, 121, 125-26, 161, 163-64, 173,
    191, 197, 210-11, 227
Alt Friedland, 146, 199
Alt Gaul 126, 192, 210
Alt Küstrinchen, 191
Alt Landsberg, 33, 125
Alt Langsow, 171-73
Alt Lewin, 166, 192
Alt Lietzegöricke, 161
Alt Mädewitz, 191
Alt Mahlisch, 144, 235
Altner, Helmut, 222, 235
Alt Ranft, 227
Alt Reetz, 191, 210
Alt Rosenthal, 178, 202, 220
Alt Rüdnitz (Starzya Rudnica), 114

Altstadt. *See* Küstrin-Altstadt
Alt Trebbin, 166, 168
Alt Tucheband, 53, 64, 84, 86-88, 111,
    149, 151
Alt Wriezen, 163
Alt Wustrow, 163
Alt Zeschdorf, 131
American Army, 19, 49, 242, 244, 253
American 9th Army, 250
"Am Strom" Farm, 92
Amt Friedrichsaue, 87, 149, 171
Amt Kienitz, 35, 49, 51, 153
Anhalter Railway Station, 252
Annahof Farm, 98, 150, 171
Ansbach, 63
Antipenko, Lt Gen N.A., 206
Antonov, Col V.S., 171, 197
Antonov, Gen A.I., 29, 39, 103
Ardennes, 127
Arnswalde, 101-102
Artillery Barracks (Oder-Insel), 96
Asafov, Col V.M. 213
Atlantic Wall, 34
Aurith, 37
Aurith Bridgehead, 60, 110, 132, 236
Austrian Army 37
Averdieck, Sgt Fritz-Rudolf, 89, 92, 94,
    98, 150, 179, 182, 199, 201, 217-
    18, 234
Axmann, Reichs Youth Leader Artur, 220

Babadshanian, Col A.K., 39, 189-90, 207-208, 226
Bad Freienwalde, 43, 126-27, 164, 210-11, 227, 229
Bad Saarow, 125
Bagramyan, Marshal Ivan C., 4
Baltic Area/Coast/Sea, 40, 101-103
Bartels, Col., 167
Baruth, 245, 248
Basta Farm, 171
Battle of Berlin 1945, The, 241
Batzlow, 213-14, 229
Bauer, Sgt Walter, 172
Baumann, Capt, 211
Beauregard, 166
Beelitz, 243, 246, 249-50
Beeskow, 246
Beichl, O/Cdt Ernst, 187
Belsky, Snr Sgt, 52
Bendler Block, 242
Berkenbrück, 237
Berlin, Gen Wilhelm, 53, 125, 211
Berlin, 9, 20-22, 29, 33, 35, 40-41, 43, 45-47, 49, 51, 58, 79, 84, 86, 95, 99, 107-110, 117-19, 121, 125-26, 137, 139-40, 143, 157-58, 171, 178, 183, 189, 196, 199, 206, 216, 219, 221, 226, 229-30, 234, 236, 238, 242-6, 248-9, 251-6, 258
Berlinchen (Barlinek), 32
Berlin Operation, *see* "Operation Berlin"
Bernau, 33
Berya, Lavrenty, 251, 255, 257
Berzarin, Gen Nikolai Erastovich, 34, 82, 169, 174, 197
Biegen, 121
Biehler, Col/Maj Gen Ernst, 75, 131, 222, 246
"Bienenhof" Inn, 82, 96
Biesdorf, 211
Biesdorf (Berlin), 242
Binnenwerder, 162
Blancbois, SS-Maj, 127
Blaurock, Lt Gen, 211
Bliesdorf, 192-93, 211, 213
Blücher, 316
Boehm, Col Prof. Erwin, 49

Bogdanov, Col Gen S.I., 36
Böge, Capt, 74-75
Bogolyubov, Gen A.M., 108
Bohl, Capt, 49, 63
Bokov, Lt Gen F.E., 111, 169, 174, 199
Bollersdorf, 232
Boneparte, Napoleon, 256
Boosen, 33
Bormann, Party Secretary Martin, 243
Brandenburg, 21, 108, 110, 125, 140
Brätz (Lutol Suchy), 32
Bräuer, Gen Bruno, 78, 127, 221
Bremsdorf, 132
Breslau (Wroclaw), 30, 104
Breslau-Berlin Autobahn, 248-9
Brezhnev, General Secretary Leonid, 258
Brieskow, 60, 131, 186
British Army, 19, 244, 253
British Government, 109
Bromberg (Bydgoszcz), 30-31
Bruchköbel, 173
Brunow, 229
Bryansk, 7
Buchholz, 233
Buckow, 33, 122, 125, 188, 206, 214, 216, 220, 232
Budyenny, Marshal Semyon M., 4-6, 255
Bulganin, Nikolai Alexandrovich, 251, 255
Bulgaria, 9
Burgwall, 63, 67, 70, 78, 131
Burmeister, Lt Gen Arnold, 126
Buschdorf, 150, 171
Buschmühle Restaurant, 60
Busse, Gen Theodor, 31, 38, 58, 63, 65, 75, 77, 96, 104, 119-20, 133, 151-52, 187, 207, 237, 241, 244-6, 249-50
Byelorussia, 5, 9, 29

Carzig, 121, 131, 182, 222, 235
Caucasus, 18
Chemelyev, Capt V.M., 194
Chugayev, Maj Gen V.M., 179
Chuikov, Col Gen Vassily Ivanovich, 14, 31, 37-39, 83, 95, 97, 99, 112, 115, 138, 157-58, 160-61, 174, 177-79,

181-82, 189, 219, 225-6, 233-4,
238, 252-3, 258
Clausewitz, 20
Communist Party, 9, 147, 167, 256, 259
Corsica, 76
Cottbus, 32, 246
Council of Ministers (USSR), 257
Courland Peninsula, 29
Crossen (Krosno Odranskie), 112

Dahlem (Berlin), 20
Dahme River, 237, 246-8, 252, 254
Dammvorstadt (Frankfurt/Oder)
(Slubice), 37, 222
Danmühle, 206, 227
Danzig (Gdansk), 102, 126
Deane, Maj Gen John R., 254
Decker, Gen Karl, 90
Dehmesee, 237
Denmark, 129
"Der Strom," 86-87, 92
Deutsch-Krone (Walcz), 31
"Deutschland-Siedlung," 81
Diedersdorf, 121, 128, 173, 202, 204,
216, 218, 220, 224, 226
Diehlo, 61
Dievenow (Dziwnów), 102
Dinkelsbühl, 63
Dnieper River, 8
Döbberin, 89
Döberitz Training Area, 65, 126, 129,
241-3
Dolgelin, 67, 121, 129, 143, 145, 160,
178-81, 202-204, 221, 235, 237
Dölitz, 101
Dönitz, Grand Admiral Karl, 122
Dorofeyev, Maj Gen A.P., 171
Dremov, Maj Gen, 208, 219
Dresden, 67, 109, 131
Dresden-Berlin Autobahn, 245
Drossen (Osno Lubuskie), 37
Dufving, Lt Col Theodor von, 127

Eastern Front, 22, 49, 67, 98
East Pomeranian Operation, 84, 99-104,
107, 112, 114

East Prussia, 29, 40, 109
Eberswalde, 122, 146, 172, 209, 229,
237, 244
Edelsheim, Gen Maximilian
Reichsfreiherr von, 250
Eggersdorf, 151
Ehrenburg, Ilya, 147-48
Eichwald, 60, 75, 184
Eimer, 2Lt, 74
Eisenhower, Gen Dwight D., 109, 253-4
Eismann, Col Hans-Georg, 151, 187-88,
206, 221, 233
Elbe River, 109, 127, 139, 212, 244, 247,
249-50, 253-4
Elisenberg, 69, 151-52
Elisenheim, 69
Elisenhof, 233
End of the Third Reich, The, 258
Erfurt, 109
Erkner, 234, 237
Erlenhof Farm, 61
European Advisory Council, 253

Falkenburg, 40
Fiebig, Gen, 187, 224
Finckler, Capt, 241
Finkenheerd, 186, 236
Finland, 6, 129
Finow, 151
Finow Canal, 32, 125, 140
Firsov, Maj Gen P.A., 169
First World War, 4, 10, 15, 22-23, 63, 71,
119
Flensburg, 129
Fomitchenko, Col S.M., 169
Förster Bridge, 86, 92
Fort Douaumont, 71
France, 4, 254
Frankenfelde, 213, 230
Frankfurt-an-der-Oder, 32-33, 37, 40, 43,
46, 58, 60, 63, 67, 69, 72, 90, 95,
110, 114-15, 129, 151, 188, 205,
222, 236, 246
Frankfurt-Berlin Autobahn, 110, 121,
132, 184, 186, 205, 223, 236, 246
Frankfurt Bridgehead, 37, 45, 58, 90, 222

Frankfurt Fortress/Garrison, 58, 63, 67, 69, 75, 90, 110, 120, 131, 151-52, 183, 186, 235, 244-6
Frederick II (the Great), 37
Freigut, 153
French Army, 49, 254
French Foreign Legion, 23
Friedeberg, 32
Friedeburg, Admiral Hans-Georg von, 254
Friedersdorf, 86, 129, 145, 160, 178, 181, 202-204, 221
Freidland, 236
Friedländer Strom Canal, 194-95, 211, 213-14
Friedrichstrasse Station, 243
Friedrich-Wilhelm Canal, 131, 140, 186, 205, 236
Führerbunker, 20-21, 96, 122
Führer Headquarters, 21, 45, 91
Fullriede, Col Fritz, 102
Fürstenberg (Eisenhüttenstadt), 37, 58, 60-61, 76, 111, 132, 184, 186, 246
Fürstenwalde, 35, 49, 110, 122, 125, 143, 151, 160, 232, 234, 236-7, 244-6

Gädtke, Ernst-Christian, 60-61, 76
Galadzev, Lt Gen S.F., 10
Galai, Maj Gen N.Z., 231
Gartz, 112
Gasparian, Maj Gen. I.G., 169
Genschmar, 52-54, 65, 84, 86-87, 90, 91
Genschmarer-See, 91, 150
Gerko, Gen N.I., 207
German Armed Forces. *See Armed Forces Index*
Germany, 4-5, 9-10, 13, 100, 107, 134, 242, 254, 256, 258
Germendorf, 244
Gersdorf, 229
Gestapo, 21, 36
Gielsdorf, 209
Giese, Col, 129
Gieshof, 53-54, 149
Glazunov, Gen, 37
Glogau (Glogow), 101

Goebbels, Joseph, 21, 29, 75, 133, 220, 242
Golikov, Gen, 255-6
Gollnow, 102
Golushkevich, Gen V.S., 251
Golzow, 38, 51, 54, 84-87, 92-94, 111, 115, 127, 150, 171
Gorbatov, Col Gen A.V., 246
Gorgast, 54-55, 65, 82, 84-87, 90, 94
Gorgast Shäferei, 86
Göring, Reichs Marshall Hermann, 19, 21, 98, 122-23, 126, 133, 221
Göritz (Górzyca), 33, 36-39, 46-47, 57, 68, 82, 111, 146
Göritz Bridgehead, 39, 43-44, 55-58, 64, 76-78
Göritzer Chaussee (Küstrin), 81
Görlsdorf, 201-202, 220
Gotenhafen (Gdynia), 102, 143
Gottesgabe, 213-14
Gräser, Gen Fritz-Herbert, 207
Great Patriotic War, 3, 7, 10-11, 14, 147
Greifenburg (Gryfice), 114
Greifenhagen (Gryfino), 102
Greim, Col Gen Ritter von, 23, 47
Griniov, Gds Col, 197
Gross Neuendorf, 35, 51-54, 90, 168
Grube, 197
Grünberg (Zielong Góra), 32, 113
Guben, 32, 101, 112
Guderian, Col Gen Heinz, 20-21, 90, 96, 101, 103
Güldendorf, 58, 60, 75, 131, 186-87, 205
Gusow, 51, 121, 127-28, 144, 159, 174, 177, 182, 197, 199, 201
Güstebiese, 53, 161
Güterfelde, 241

Hachtel, Lt Erich, 163-64, 192, 210-11, 227, 229
Hackenow, 129, 176, 177
Hahn, Capt Gerhard, 195
Haidlen, Col, 126, 161
Halbe, 246-8, 250
Hamburg, 128
Hansen, Hans, 179-80, 219, 235

"Hardenberg-Stellung," 121, 178, 199, 204, 210
Harnekop, 209
Hartrampf, SS-Maj, 131
Haselberg, 193, 213, 229
Hasenfelde, 222
Hathenow, 55, 57, 66
Hathenow Lehngut Farm, 151
Haukelt, SS-Lt, 184, 186-87, 205
Haupt-Graben, 120, 177-78
Havel River, 140, 238, 243
Heckelberg, 209
Heilstätte Müllrose, 131
Heimstätten Settlement, 92
Heinersdorf, 121, 129, 222, 232, 235
Heinrici, Col Gen Gotthardt, 90-91, 104, 118, 122, 134, 154, 187-88, 206, 224, 227, 244-6
Hengstmann, SS-Maj, 236
Henriettenhof Farm, 91
Hermersdorf, 199, 216, 220
Hero of the Soviet Union. *See* Order of Hero of the Soviet Union
Herrenhof, 166
Herrmann, Lt Col/Col Harry, 221
Herzershof, 58
Herzfelde, 32
Herzhorn, 230
Himmler, Reichsführer-SS Heinrich, 22-23, 31-32, 46, 64, 81, 101, 103, 122, 148
Hitler, Adolf, 19-21, 23, 31, 45, 64-65, 90-91, 96, 101-103, 117-19, 122, 133-34, 154, 166-67, 206-207, 220, 224, 241-2, 244-6
Hitlerjugend, 128, 207, 220, 229, 232
Hoefer, Col, 125
Hoff, 102
Hohenjesar Farm, 235
Hohenlychen, 104
Hohenwalde, 131, 186, 223
Hohenwutzen, 161
Hohenzollern Canal, 78, 140, 237
Hölz, Col, 125, 188
Hopffgarten, Maj Hans-Joachim von, 56-57
Hoppegarten, 202

Horst, 102
Hübner, Lt Gen Dr. Rudolf, 53
Hudenberg 182
Hugohof, 129
Hungary, 9, 101, 122
"Hungriger Wolf" Farm, 176

Ihlow, 314
Insel (Oderbruch), 227

Jahnsfelde, 217-18, 232
Jakobshagen, 101
Japan, 4
Japanese Army, 5
Jaschke, Capt, 176
Jeckeln, SS-Gen Friedrich, 131
Jelnya, 7
Jesar-Graben, 153
Jodl, Col Gen Alfred, 20, 253
Jüterbog, 125, 246

Kaganovich, L.S., 255
Kaisermühl, 131
Kalenzig, 53, 71, 90
Kalenziger Bunst, 52, 91
Kalenziger Wiesen, 91
Kaluga Province, 3
Kapp, Maj Wolfgang, 128, 150-51, 177
Karlsbiese, 54, 115, 149, 153
Karlshof, 162
Kasankin, Lt Gen A.F., 229
Katukov, Col Gen M.I., 37, 115, 137, 143, 146, 181, 208, 226
Kausch, SS-Lt Col, 214
Kaut, Lt, 172
Kazakov, Col Gen V.I., 142-43, 158
Kazankin, Lt Gen A.F., 168
Keitel, Field Marshal Wilhelm, 20, 249, 254
Keller II, Kurt, 171-74
Kempin, SS-Col Hans, 132, 236
Kercher, Lt, 229
Kersdorf, 237
Kersdorfer-See, 237
Kerstenbruch, 54
Kharkin Kol, 5
Khrushchev, Nikita, 257-8

Kiehnwerder, 168
Kienitz, 33, 35, 49, 52, 64, 66, 77-78, 90,
    153
Kienitz Bridgehead, 36, 43-44, 47-54, 58,
    64, 76-77, 90
Kietz. See Küstrin-Kietz
Kietzerbusch, 82, 96
Kietzer Tor (Küstrin,) 81, 96-97
Kiev, 7-8
Kleinheisterkamp, SS-Gen Mathias, 67,
    72, 129
Klessin, 46, 57-58, 69-70, 72-75, 183
Knappe, Maj Siegfried, 127, 221
Kohlase, Fritz, 64, 77
Kolberg (Kolobrzeg), 102
Kolonie Herrenhorst, 227
Kondratenko, Col, 197
Koniev, Marshal Ivan S., 5-9, 31, 104,
    107-110, 140, 144, 189, 207, 238,
    242, 245, 248-9, 251-3, 255-8
König, Sgt Maj, 217
Königlich Reetz, 163
Königsberg (Neumark) (Chojna), 84, 114
Königs Wusterhausen, 140, 143, 218,
    241, 245-6
Konsomol, 147
Köpenick (Berlin), 241
Köslin, 102
Krauss, SS-Capt Paul, 131, 186, 223
Kravets, Snr Sgt L.S., 167
Krebs, Gen Hans, 96, 101, 242, 244-5
Kremlin, 255, 257-8
Kreuzberg (Berlin), 253
Kriescht (Krzeszyce), 37
Kruge-Gersdorf, 229
Krüger, SS-Gen Friedrich-Wilhelm, 32,
    56
Krulev, Gen, 255
Krupski, Maj Gen I.V., 145
Kruse, Lt Gen Kurt, 124, 176
Kuhbrücken-Vorstadt. See Küstrin-
    Kuhbrücken-Vorstadt
Kummersdorf, 249
Kunersdorf, 121, 166 192, 194-95, 211,
    213
Kunersdorf (Nowe Biskupice), 37, 58,
    131, 151

Kursk, 18
Küstrin (Kostrzyn), 36-38, 40, 43, 46-47,
    51, 54-55, 64, 69, 72, 79, 81-82,
    86-87, 90, 94, 98, 101, 103, 107,
    110, 114, 119, 145-46, 150, 164,
    171, 206
Küstrin-Altstadt, 79, 81, 82-84, 96-97
Küstrin Bridgehead, 97, 103, 110-13,
    115, 119-20, 144
Küstrin Corridor, 84-91, 106-8, 110-12,
    119
Küstrin Fortress/Garrison, 43, 54, 65, 77-
    83, 90, 95-98, 104, 107, 128-29,
    177
Küstrin-Kietz, 54-55, 64-65, 67, 79, 81-
    84, 85-87
Küstrin-Kuhbrücken-Vorstadt, 79, 81,
    84, 86-87, 95-96
Küstrin-Neustadt, 36, 43, 49, 79, 82-84
Kuznetsov, Col Gen V.I., 166
Kyritz, 242

Lammerding, SS-Brig Gen, 31
Landsberg (Gorzów Wielkopolski), 32-
    33, 101, 137, 157
Landwehr Canal, 253
Langkeit, Col Willy, 63-64, 67, 69-71,
    73, 131
Langsow, 54, 145, 160, 171-72
Lease-lend, 15-16, 19
Lebus, 46, 58, 63-64, 68-72, 74, 78, 152,
    183, 235
Lebuser Plateau, 43
Legion of Merit, 254
Leipzig, 109
Lelyushenko, Col Gen D.D., 189
Leningrad, 4, 7-8
Lenin's Mausoleum, 258
Letschin, 49, 51, 53-54, 65, 78, 115, 143-
    45, 151, 153, 160, 167, 169, 170,
    194
Libbenichen, 57, 67, 131, 182, 203-204,
    235
Lichtenberg, 132, 184, 223, 235-6
Lichtenberg (Berlin), 206, 242
Lichtenrade (Berlin), 253
Liebmann, Lt Col, 126, 163, 211

Lietzegöricke, 126
Lietzen, 119, 121, 124, 139, 178, 180, 221-2, 235, 244
Lindenhof, 69, 71
Line "C," 223
Lirk, SS-Lt, 194
Lobmeyer, SS-Capt Jakob, 132, 186
Lodź, 30
Loose Meadows, 64
Lösecke, Major von, 45, 88-89, 92-94, 128
Lossow, 60, 75, 131, 184, 187, 205
Lower Silesia, 104
Lübben, 109, 246, 252
Lublin Government, 18
Luck, Col Hans, 55
Luckenwalde, 246, 249
Lüdersdorf, 213
Ludwigslust, 129, 142, 173, 177, 181, 202-203
Ludwigsruhe, 145
Lunette "D," 87, 96

Maginot Line, 44
Mahlow, 143
Maizière, Lt Col de, 151
Malchow Farm, 186-87, 205
Malin, Gen M.S., 108
Mallnow, 46, 58, 70, 72, 182-83, 204
Malz-Mühle, 211, 229
Manschnow, 54-55, 65-66, 88
Manteuffel, Gen Hasso von, 103, 244
Margarethenschacht, 186
Mariendorf, 252
Marienhof Farm, 195
Markendorf, 132, 186, 205, 223, 235
Märkische Buchholz, 246, 248
Märkische Schweiz, 199, 216
Marxdorf, 133, 218, 232-33, 237
Maybach I and II, 20
Mayer, Major von, 216
Menke, Col, 216
Meseritz (Miedzyrzecz), 32-33, 37
Metzdorf, 194-95, 211, 213
Ministry of Public Enlightenment and Propaganda, 26
"Mistel" Device, 47, 98

Mittenwalde, 252
Moabit (Berlin), 243
Möglin, 213
Mohnke, SS-Brig Gen, 243
Molotov, Vlateslav M., 6
Moltke, 20
Mongolia, 5-6
Mongolian Army, 5
Montgomery, Field Marshal Sir Bernard, 254
Morrell, Prof. Dr., 19
Moscow, 4, 6-9, 102, 104, 107-108, 110, 138, 245, 251, 254-5, 257-8
Moscow Radio, 84
Moskaliov, Engr, 206
Mostovoy, Gdsmn Sergei, 57
Müggelsee, 236, 245
Mühlental Ravine, 63, 69
"Mulberry" Harbors, 47
Müllrose, 121, 131-32, 205, 236, 246
Mummert, Maj Gen Werner, 49, 128, 177, 203, 243
Müncheberg, 64, 121-22, 124, 127, 160, 188, 202, 206, 209, 214, 216-19, 226, 232-4, 237, 244
Münchehofe, 216, 220

Nazi Party, 23, 133
Negoda, Col A.I., 167
Neisse River, 47, 104, 189, 246
Neu Barnim, 53-54, 64, 149, 153, 194
Neu Bleyen, 86-87, 90, 92, 94
Neubrandenburg, 244
Neue Mühle, 143
Neuendorf-im-Sande, 49
Neuenhäuser, 78
Neuentempel, 178, 202, 220, 222, 232
Neue Werk Bastion, 83
Neufeld, 126
Neu Gaul, 227
Neu Gersdorf, 211
Neu Glietzen, 126, 161, 210
Neu Hardenberg, 121, 133, 197, 199, 216
Neu Küstrinchen, 163, 191, 210
Neu Langsow, 78, 174
Neu Lewin, 64, 77
Neu Lietzegöricke, 162, 191

Neu Mahlisch, 129
Neu Manschnow, 38, 55, 58, 66
Neu Ranft, 163, 191
Neustettin (Szczecinek), 40
Neu Trebbin, 121, 166, 195-97, 213
Neu Tucheband, 88, 111, 171, 177
Neu Werbig, 182
"Nibelungen-Stellung," 46
Nicolaevesky, Boris, 6
Niederfinow, 209
Niederjesar, 182, 222
Niederkrönig, 161
Niedersaaten, 161
Normandy Beaches, 47
Norway, 129
Novikov, Marshal A.A., 144, 245, 256
NSKK, 49

Oberlindow, 186, 205, 236
Obersdorf, 199, 220
Obra River, 32
Oder Bridge, 61
Oderbruch, 36, 43-45, 53, 58, 64-65, 70,
    77, 79, 89-90, 110-12, 115, 119-21,
    127-29, 143-44, 150, 158, 164, 177,
    179, 181-83, 191, 195, 199, 210,
    227
Oderdamm, 64
Oder Front, 46, 64, 75, 220
Oder-Insel, 43, 79-81, 83, 87, 95-96
Oder Marshes, 78
Oder-Neisse Front/Theater, 110, 144, 246
Oder River, 32-35, 37-41, 43, 45, 47, 49,
    51-55, 57-58, 60, 64, 68-69, 79, 81-
    82, 84-85, 87, 90, 95, 101-104,
    109-10, 112, 114, 125-26, 137, 141,
    144, 146-47, 151, 153, 161-63,
    168-69, 189, 194-96, 205-206, 210,
    222-3, 227, 233, 237, 244-5
Oder-Spree Canal, 184, 205, 223-4, 245-
    6
"Oder-Stellung," 163
Olympic Stadium, 243
"Operation Bagration," 9
"Operation Berlin," 3, 98, 102-104, 107-
    11, 114, 138, 143, 183, 226, 241,
    251

"Operation Boomerang," 90
"Operation Sonnenwende," 101-102
Oppeln (Opole), 104
Oranienburg, 151, 244
Order of Hero of the Soviet Union, 5, 9,
    57, 167, 234, 253, 255, 257
Order of Lenin, 5, 255, 257
Order of Suvorov, 8, 255
Order of the October Revolution, 255
Order of the Red Banner, 4, 52, 255
Order of Victory, 8
Organisation Todt, 67, 127
Ortwig, 51-54, 115, 126, 152, 194

Pacific Ports, 13
Pagram Farm, 132
Perevertkin, Maj Gen S.N., 168
Perkhorovich, Lt Gen F.I., 114, 164
Peshkov, Col, 172
Petrov, Gen I.Y., 108
Pismühle, 88
Platkow, 78, 127, 169, 174, 197, 199
Podelzig, 46, 55, 58, 66, 69, 71-73,
    115, 151-52, 182-83
Poland, 13, 29, 32
Polenzig, 33
Polish Armed Forces. *See Armed Forces
    Index*
Politburo, 255-6
Pomerania, 31, 40, 114, 125, 127
Poplawski, Gen Stanislaw 114, 161, 211,
    227
Posedin, 194
Posen, (Poznan) 30-33, 40, 66, 75, 80,
    95, 145
Potsdam, 46, 67, 108, 110, 122, 128, 132,
    140, 241, 243
Potsdam Conference, 255
Potsdam Garrison, 243, 249-50
Power and the Soviet Elite, 6
Pozharsky, Gen, 95
Prädikow, 230
Prague, 166
Pravda, 148, 256-7
Prenzlau, 103, 227, 244
Prieros, 246
Pritzhagen, 230

Pritzhagener Forest, 230
Propaganda Ministry, 21
Prötzel, 209, 213, 230
Pulverkrug, 205
Pyritz (Pryzyce), 113

Quappendorf, 121, 126, 173, 197

Radom, 29
Radziej, Lt Gen Georg, 129
Raegener, Maj Gen Adolf, 46, 56, 67,
Raisig, Capt Wilhelm, 129
Rapallo Pact, 5
Rathstock, 58, 66
Ratibor, 104
Ratzeburg, 40
Rauch, Col Josef, 133, 188, 216
Rautenkranz, 186, 205, 223, 236
Red Square, 255, 258
Rehfeld, 153
Reichenberg, 214, 230
Reichsarbeitsdients (RAD), 35, 38, 52,
    55-56, 61, 69, 122, 166
Reichs Chancellery, 19, 21, 241, 243
Reichstag, 140, 148, 238, 243, 253
Reims, 253
Reinefarth, SS-Lt Gen Heinz-Friedrich,
    81, 90, 96-97
Reitwein, 38-39, 43, 46, 55-57, 66, 115,
    151
Reitwein Spur, 43-44, 46, 55-58, 64, 67-
    75, 77-78, 112, 182
Rekowsky, Gen Siegfried von, 133
Remer, Maj Gen Otto-Ernst, 90
Reppen (Rzepin), 37
Reymann, Lt Gen Helmuth, 250
Ribbentrop, Joachim von, 220
Riessen, 132
Ringenwalde, 199, 214
Roden, Lt Gen Emmo von, 131
Rokossovsky, Marshal Konstantin K.,
    4, 9, 39, 100, 102-103, 109, 189,
    244, 255
Roosevelt, Pres Franklin D., 134
Rosengarten, 222
Rosenke, Capt, 202
Rosly, Maj Gen I.P., 77, 171, 197

Rosskopf, Maj Gen Maximilian, 126
Roth, Sgt Maj, 210-11
Rothenburg-ob-der-Tauber, 63
Route 1, 38, 46, 54-55, 79, 86, 119, 121,
    133, 149, 172, 177, 202, 206, 216,
    218-19, 233, 238
Route 87, 184, 186, 223
Route 112, 66
Route 167, 182, 213
Rudel, Col Hans-Ulrich, 49, 65, 72
Rüdersdorf, 234
Ruppiner Canal, 244
Russia, 172
Russian Civil War, 4, 14
Rybalko, Col Gen P.S., 189, 255

Sachsendorf, 55, 58, 70, 89, 127, 129,
    150-51, 177, 179, 181
Safarenko, Maj Gen P.M., 167
Säpzig (Zabice), 38
Sardinia, 76
Saumberg, 129
Savelyev, Gds Snr Lt Afansi, 57
Schacht, Maj Gerhard, 169
Scharmützelsee, 122
Schenkenhorst, 243
Scheuermann, 2Lt, 172
Scheunemann, Col Hans-Wolfgang, 129,
    180
Schild, SSgt, 173
Schimpff, Col, 49, 53
Schivelbein (Swidwin), 102
Schlaanhof Farm, 213
Schlaubehammer, 205, 223
Schleswig-Holstein, 244
Schlieffen, 20
Schloss Harnekop, 65, 125
Schloss Küstrin, 96
Schneidemühl (Pila), 40
Scholze, Col/Maj Gen Georg, 89, 127,
    242
Schöne, Lt, 73-75
Schöneck, Friedhelm, 159, 167-68, 195-
    97, 213-14, 229-30
Schönefeld, 151
Schönefeld Airfield, 252-3
Schönfliess, 152, 183, 204, 222, 235

Schönfliess Railway Station, 67, 69, 74
Schönhauser Allee, 243
Schörner, Col Gen Ferdinand, 31
Schöttle, SS-Lt Emil, 132
Schräpler, Col, 125
Schuler, 2Lt, 171
Schulzendorf, 213
Schwanebeck, Lt Col, 125
Schwarz, Maj, 206
Schwedt, 40, 45, 191
Schwerin, 244
Schwerin (Skwierzyna), 37
Schwetig, 184
Schwiebus (Swiebodzin), 32, 37
Seelake Stream, 120, 153
Seelow, 38, 54-55, 64, 78, 86, 88-89,
    ·121, 124, 128-29, 142, 143, 145,
    149, 152, 158, 160, 172, 176-82,
    188, 199, 201-204, 206-208, 218-
    19, 224
Seelow Heights, 43, 72, 109-10, 119-21,
    129, 142, 150-51, 158, 177-79, 181,
    188-89, 195, 199, 201, 208, 214,
    226
Seredin, Gen, 38
Seydlitz-Troops, 83, 186, 196, 222, 235,
    241, 249
Shemenkov, Lt Gen S.D., 226
Shtemenko, Gen Sergei M., 107-108,
    122, 255-6
Siberia, 13, 134
Siegroth, Maj Gen Joachim von, 131, 183
Siekenius, Gen Rudolf, 132
Sietzing, 159, 167-68
Silesia, 30, 104
Simpson, Lt Gen William, 250
Sistov, Maj Gen V.A., 168
Sixt, Gen Friedrich 125, 211
Skorzeny, SS-Maj Otto, 127
Smolensk, 7
Sokolov, Maj Gen V.P., 171
Sokolovsky, Gen Vasili Dannovich, 108,
    113, 255
Sommer, Sgt, 51
Sonnenberg (Slonsk), 37
Sonnenburg, 126
Sophienthal, 35, 49

Southern Pfalz, 49
Soviet Armed Forces. *See Armed Forces
    Index*
Soviet Union, 3-6, 8-10, 13, 147, 257,
    259
Soviet Zone, 255
Spaatz, Gen Carl, 254
Spandau (Berlin), 49, 243
Sparrer, Maj, 126, 163-64
Spree River, 32, 236-8, 243-6, 252
Spreewald, 245
Stadelbauer, SS-Lt Col, 129
Stalin, Generalissimo Joseph, 3-10, 29,
    31, 39, 100, 102-103, 107-109, 140,
    188-89, 238, 251-7, 259
Stalin, Vasily, 255
Stalin, Yakov, 103
Stalingrad, 8, 14, 233
Stammerjohann, Col Reinhold, 128, 202
Stargard (Stargard Szczecinsky), 39-40,
    99, 101-102
Steinbeck, 229
Steiner, SS-Gen Felix, 23, 101, 244
Steinhöfel, 237
"Stein-Stellung," 119, 121, 128, 132, 199,
    201-202, 218, 222
Sternebeck, 12, 213, 230
Stettin (Szczecin), 40, 95, 102, 112, 122
Stettiner Haff (Zalew Szczecinski), 125,
    209
Stobberow Stream, 199
Straupitz, 246
Strausberg, 125, 146, 151, 206, 209, 220,
    227, 230, 233, 237
Strelkova, 3
Stülpnagel Inf Bks, von, 83
Stumpf, Gen Hans-Jürgen, 254
Sukhorukov, Col Ivan, 233-4
Supreme Soviet, 255-6
Svetaev, Col Gen V.D., 184
Sydow, Maj Gen Otto, 243
Sydowswiese, 49

Tamm, Capt Rudolf, 97
Tams, 2Lt Karl-Hermann, 129, 158, 177-
    78, 202, 218
Tangermünde, 250

Tannenhof Farm, 92
Tarnopol, 7
Tassingy, Gen Jean de Lattre de, 254
Tauerzig, 33
Tedder, Air Chief Marshal Sir Arthur, 254
Tegel (Berlin), 51
Telegin, Lt Gen Konstantin F., 10, 154, 157, 207-208, 256
Teltow Canal, 242-3, 253
Tempelberg, 233
Tempelhof Airfield, 253
Tettau, Lt Gen Hans von, 102
Teupitz, 246, 248, 252
Teurow, 248
Thomas, Maj, 129
Thöringswerder, 166, 192
Tiefensee, 209
Tiergarten (Berlin), 253
Timoshenko, Marshal S. K., 4
Tirschtiegel (Trzciel), 32-33
Tirschtiegel Riegel, 32, 34
Trebnitz, 216, 220
Treplin, 121
Truman, President Harry S., 255
Tuchen, 229
Tzschetzschnow. See Güldendorf

Ukraine, 8
Ulm Cathedral, 125
United Kingdom, 4
United States, 4, 134
Unterlindow, 186, 205
Upper Austria, 67
Upper Silesia, 30, 104
Upper Silesian Operation, 104, 107
Ural Mountains, 13
U.S. Military Mission, 254
U.S. Strategic Air Force, 254

Vasilevsky, Marshal Alexander M., 10
Vedeniev, Maj Gen N.D., 167
Vehse, Capt, 235
Verdun, 71
Vienna, 67, 134

Vistula-Oder Operation, 21, 37, 39, 77, 99, 104, 109, 114, 117, 138-39, 252
Vistula River, 9, 13, 29, 31, 39, 99, 137
Vlasov, Gen Andrey Andreyevich, 66, 123
Vogel, 2Lt, 164
Vogelsang, 37, 60-61, 76, 132, 151
Vogt, Col, 124
Voigtsberger, Maj Gen Heinrich, 53, 126
Volkssturm. See Armed Forces Index
Vorflut Channel, 82, 84, 87, 95-97
Voroshilov, Marshal K. J., 4, 7
Vorwerk Podelzig Farm, 153
Vossberg Sugar Factory, 153, 169
Vyazma, 7
Vyshinsky, Andrei, 253-4

Wagner, Gerd, 158
Waldmüller, Sgt Wolfdieter, 87, 172-73, 201-202
Waldsieversdorf, 127
Walter, Col Franz, 83
Wannsee (Berlin), 242-3
Warsaw, 9, 21, 29, 31, 81, 257
Warsaw-Lodź Operation, 30
Wartenburg, Capt von, 129
Warthebruch, 32, 37, 43, 79
Warthe River (Warta), 33, 43, 45, 79-83, 95-96, 110, 206
Weber, Lt Col Helmut, 176, 181, 203-204
Wedding (Berlin), 243
Weidendamm Bridge, 243
Weidling, Gen Helmuth, 127, 220-1, 227, 237, 241-3, 253
Weikl, Maj, 47, 49
Weinberg, 182
Weinbergsee, 204
Weissenburg, 63
Weissensee (Berlin), 33
Weissenspring, 205
Wellnitz, 132
Wenck, Lt Gen Walter, 101, 243, 246, 249-50
Wendenschloss (Berlin), 254
Wenzlaff, Capt Udo, 129
Werbig, 51-52, 65, 86, 88, 90, 142, 145, 150, 160, 172-74, 179, 182

Werder, 129, 182
Wermelinsee, 202
Werneuchen, 145, 151, 229
Western Allies, 13, 19, 107-109, 237, 244, 253, 255
Western Front, 98
Wetzlar, 67, 131
Wiesenau, 131-32, 152, 184, 186, 205
Wiesen Farm, 69
Wilhelminenhof Farm, 86, 90-91
Wilhelmstrasse, 19
Wilke, Horst, 61
Winkel, 166
Wittbrietzen, 249
Wittich, Lt Col von, 55
Wittor, Erich, 232-33
Wöhlermann, Col Hans-Oskar, 220
Wollenberg, 211
Wollin (Wolin), 102
Wölsickendorf, 229
Worin, 217-18, 220
"Wotan-Stellung," 118, 122, 124, 210-11, 216, 227, 230
Wriezen, 35, 49, 126-27, 133, 139, 152, 166, 182, 188, 191-95, 206, 210-11, 227, 229-30
Wuhden, 46, 57-58, 69, 72-3, 183
Wulkow, 199, 202, 216, 220
Wunsdorf, 20
Würzburg, 67
Wuschewier, 167, 195-96

Wuste Kunersdorf, 69-70, 72

Yalta Conference, 39, 102-103, 107, 109
Yeremenko, Marshal Andrey I., 4
Yugoslavia, 257
Yushtschuk, Maj Gen, 143

Zachan, 101
Zäckerick (Siekierki), 114, 126, 153, 161, 163
Zäckericker Loose, 162
Zechin, 49, 78, 126-27, 149, 153
Zehlendorf (Berlin), 242
Zellin, 51, 111, 187
Zerebin, Maj Gen D.S., 171
Zhukov, Marshal Georgi Konstanovitch, 3-11, 29, 31, 33, 35, 39-41, 52, 79, 82, 84, 99, 100-104, 107-10, 112-15, 137-42, 144-45, 149, 152, 157-58, 159-61, 181, 183, 188-89, 197, 206-207, 219, 224-6, 234, 238, 241, 244-5, 251-8
Ziebingen (Cybinka), 37
Zielenzig (Suleçin), 37
Ziltendorf, 151
Zobel, Capt/Maj Horst, 86-87, 91, 176-77, 202, 216, 243
Zollbrücke, 163
Zoo (Berlin), 253
Zoo Bunker, 243
Zossen, 20, 248

Armed Forces Index

GERMAN ARMED FORCES

OKW, 20, 73, 90, 122, 133, 249, 253
OKH, 20, 90, 117, 187, 206-207
OKL, 46
Wehrmacht, 20, 22-24, 31, 36-37, 121-22
General Staff, 19-21, 38, 129
Reserve or Home Army, 22, 118
Waffen-SS, 22-23, 81, 83, 123, 129, 131, 173, 197, 202, 231

Army:
    Army Groups:
"A", 31
"Mitte", 7, 31, 118
"Weichsel", 31, 45, 90, 101, 103, 123, 125, 133, 135, 187-88, 192, 206-207, 221, 224, 233
    Armies:
6th, 8
9th, 31, 46, 58, 63, 64, 67, 71, 76-78, 83, 86, 90-91, 96, 103, 107, 113, 123-24, 127, 131-33, 135, 151-52, 184, 188, 206-207, 209, 223-4, 227, 232-3, 236-8, 241-50
12th, 127, 243, 246, 249-50
17th, 104
1st Pz, 104
3rd Pz, 102-103, 188, 191, 206-207, 209, 227, 244
4th Pz, 65, 207, 246
11th SS Pz, 101
    Corps:
Vth, 246-8
XXth, 249-50
XXXIXth Pz, 90, 101, 107, 127
LVIth Pz, 124, 127, 153, 207, 209, 216, 220, 227, 230, 233, 237, 242, 244
CIst, 53-54, 64-65, 123-25, 127, 133, 149, 152-53, 161, 164, 166, 210-11, 227, 229, 237, 244
IIIrd SS 'Germanic' Pz, 101
Vth SS Mtn, 22, 32, 46, 56, 123-24, 131-32, 151-53, 184, 206, 222, 246, 247-8
XIth SS Pz, 22, 64, 67, 73, 78, 83, 86, 123-24, 127, 129, 132, 151-52, 181, 183, 188, 206, 210, 219, 221, 233-4, 235-7, 247-8
Wehrkreis III, 21, 123, 125
Frankfurt/Oder & Potsdam Garrisons
    see alphabetical list above
    Divisions:
5th Lt Inf, 124-25, 149, 153, 163, 191, 210-11, 227, 244
28th Lt Inf, 126
75th Lt Inf, 126, 163
156th Inf, 124, 132, 222, 235, 244
163rd Inf, 101

169th Inf, 124, 129, 151-52, 183, 204, 222, 235, 244
281st Inf, 101
286th Inf, 67, 124, 131, 151, 184, 186, 236
303rd 'Döberitz' Inf, 46, 53-54, 64-66, 74, 78, 124, 129, 150, 153, 180, 202-204, 221, 235
309th 'Grossberlin' Inf, 46, 53, 65-66, 78, 86, 124, 126, 149, 153, 159, 167-70, 210, 214
433rd Inf, 32, 67
463rd Inf, 32, 67
600th (Russian) Inf, 66, 123
606th Inf, 65, 78, 124, 126, 149, 153, 163-64, 166, 191-92, 210
712th Inf, 70, 77-78, 124, 131, 151-52, 182, 204, 222, 235, 244
"Führer-Begleit" Inf, 101
"Raegener" Inf, 46, 55, 57, 67
"Führer" Gr, 90, 101
9th Para, 78, 86, 98, 124, 127-28, 149, 153, 169, 199, 216, 221, 232, 241
18th PzGr, 133, 152, 188, 192, 199, 206, 213, 216
20th PzGr, 87-93, 124, 127-29, 149, 151, 153, 176, 199, 217-18, 241-3
25th PzGr, 49-54, 58, 65, 78, 81, 85-87, 90, 124, 126, 166, 188, 192-93, 206, 213, 229, 244
"Brandenburg" PzGr, 127
"Grossdeutschland" PzGr, 37
"Kurmark" PzGr, 32, 37, 46, 56, 58, 63-64, 67, 70, 73, 75, 77-78, 124, 126, 131, 151-52, 178, 181, 218, 237, 244
21st Pz, 49, 54-55, 65, 81, 246-8
"Holstein" Pz, 101
"Müncheberg" Pz, 49, 78, 85-86, 90-92, 124, 127-28, 150-51, 153, 218, 244
"Weichsel" Tk-Hunting, 124
391st Security, 124, 132, 186, 236
SA "Feldherrnhalle", 60
4th SS Police Gren, 101
10th SS Pz, 101, 118

11th SS "Nordland" PzGr, 23, 101, 152, 206, 209, 230, 243
15th SS (1st Latvian) Gr, 232
16th SS "Reichsführer-SS" PzGr, 76
23rd SS "Nederland" PzGr, 23, 101, 152, 206, 209-10, 232, 244
27th SS "Langemarck" Gr, 101
28th SS "Wallonien" Gr, 23, 101
32nd SS "30. Januar" Gr, 60, 76, 124, 132, 151, 186, 205, 235-6, 245
33rd SS "Charlemagne" Vol PzGr, 23
"Leibstandarte-SS Adolf Hitler" PzGr, 85, 126
541st VGr, 124
Brigades:
Armd Bde 20th PzGrDiv, 242
"Grossdeutschland Rep & Trg, 32
111th SPG Trg, 127, 164
245th SPG, 176
920th SPG Trg, 128, 150-51, 177
104th Tk-Hunting, 101
"D" ("Dorn") Tk-Hunting, 124-25
"F" Tk-Hunting, 124
"P" ("Pirat") Tk-Hunting, 124-25
"R" Tk-Hunting, 124
Regiments:
56th Lt Inf, 126, 161, 191
75th Lt Inf, 126, 163, 227
"Rhode" Inf, 126
"Sator" Inf, 126
Shadow Inf "A", 126
95th Gr, 132
300th Gr, 66, 74, 129, 175, 176, 203-204
301st Gr, 129, 235
302nd Gr, 129
365th Gr, 126
378th Gr, 129
379th Gr, 129
392nd Gr, 129
652nd Gr, 126, 167, 171, 195-97, 213
732nd Gr, 131-32
745th Gr, 131-32
764th Gr, 131
926th Gr, 131
927th Gr, 131
931st Gr, 131

1233rd Gr, 132
1234th Gr, 126
1235th Gr, 73, 129
1237th Gr, 223-4, 236
1239th Gr, 131
1241st Gr, 131
1242nd Gr, 74
1313th Gr, 133
1314th Gr, 133
1315th Gr, 133
"KS Dresden" Gr, 8, 67, 69-70
1st "KS Potsdam" Gr, 58, 67, 70, 72
"KS Vienna-Neustadt" Gr, 67
"KS Wetzlar" Gr, 67, 71, 73
30th PzGr, 133, 199, 216
35th PzGr, 52-54, 86, 126-27, 193, 211,
    229
51st PzGr, 133, 199, 216
76th PzGr, 88, 92-93, 128, 150, 177, 202
90th PzGr, 45, 87-89, 92-94, 98, 128,
    150, 199, 201, 217-18, 234
118th PzGr, 192
119th PzGr, 51-54, 58, 65, 86, 126-27,
    193, 195, 211-12, 229
125th PzGr, 54
192nd PzGr, 54
"Kurmark" PzGr, 57, 67, 69-71, 177,
    180-83, 202-203, 221, 235
1st "Muncheberg" PzGr, 86, 128
2nd "Müncheberg" PzGr, 86, 128, 171-
    72
25th Para, 78, 127, 170, 216
26th Para, 127, 150, 170, 216
27th Para, 78, 127, 158, 169, 179, 199,
    216, 241
"Grossdeutschland" (Fd) Gd, 126, 243-4
22nd Pz, 54
118th Pz, 133
"Brandenburg" Pz, 57-58, 67, 70-74, 131,
    180
"Müncheberg" Pz, 86, 91, 128, 176, 181,
    202, 216-17
6th Frankfurt Fortress, 132
5th Arty, 126
9th Para Arty 127, 169, 199
18th Arty, 133, 216, 232
20th Arty, 93, 128

25th Arty, 51, 127
230th Arty, 129
286th Arty, 131
303rd Arty, 129
309th Arty, 126, 230
360th Mor, 80
1712th Arty, 131
155th Armd Arty, 54
"Kurmark" Armd Arty, 67, 221
"Müncheberg" Armd Arty, 128
11th SS Pz, 210, 214, 230-2
23rd SS 'Norge' PzGr, 209, 214-16, 230
24th SS 'Danmark' PzGr, 209, 216, 232
48th SS "General Seyffarth" PzGr, 210,
    232-33
11th SS Pz, 286, 293, 315-6
86th SS "Schill" Vol Gr, 132, 236
87th SS "Kurmark" Vol Gr, 132, 151, 236
88th SS "Becker" Vol Gr, 132, 186, 205,
    223
SS "Falke" Gr, 187, 205, 223, 235-6
32nd SS Arty, 131-32, 326
SS Arty Trg, 60
Battalions:
203rd Ad Hoc Inf, 47, 49
345th Ad Hoc Inf, 47, 49
500th Inf, 82
"Brandenburg" Ad Hoc Inf, 126
North Caucasion Inf, 47
"Potsdam" Ad Hoc Inf, 126
"Raegener" Ad Hoc Inf, 57-58
"Spandau" Ad Hoc Inf, 126
230th Fus, 129
303rd Fus, 77, 85, 95
309th Fus, 126
"Truger" PzGr, 233
20th PzGrDiv Fd Rep, 129
9th Para Fd Rep, 197
"AOK 9" Storm, 236
Bremen Police, 126
3rd Pz Depot, 126
5th Pz, 52-53, 127, 193
8th Pz, 87-88, 128, 172-73, 201-202
25th Tk-Hunting, 53, 193, 195
200th Tk-Hunting, 54
21st Armd Recce, 53
125th Armd Recce, 197

"Kurmark" Armd Engr, 67, 70, 74
"Kurmark" Armd Recce, 66-67, 69, 70, 232
"Müncheberg" Armd Recce, 128
"Speer" Armd Recce, 127
292nd Army Flak, 86, 126, 166, 195, 213, 229
100th Railway Arty, 160
SA "Feldherrnhalle" Fd Rep, 46, 57, 73
1st Gd Bn "LSSAH", 126, 166, 210
1st Bn SS PzGr Fd Rep Regt, 128, 223
4th SS Police Sy, 166
600th SS Para, 127
32nd SS Fd Rep, 205, 223-4
11th SS "Hermann von Salza" Pz, 210, 214
11th SS Armd Recce, 210, 216, 232
11th SS Flak, 210
11th SS Engr, 210
32nd SS Engr, 223-4, 236
32nd SS Tk-Hunting, 76, 186, 223-4
"LSSAH" Pz, 128
502nd SS Hy Tk, 90, 131, 151, 180-83, 203-204, 218, 235
503rd SS Hy Tk, 206, 210, 214
32nd SS Tank-Hunting, 75, 131
560th SS Tk-Hunting, 127, 166, 194, 211, 229
561st SS Tk-Hunting, 132, 186, 205, 222, 235
3rd SS Arty Trg 46
Hungarian SS, 236
  Misc Units:
"1001 Nights" Battle Gp, 90-91, 127, 166
"Krauss" Combat Team, 131-32, 186, 205, 223, 236
"Rosenke" Combat Team, 202
"Schill" Combat Team, 60
"Schöttle" Combat Team, 132, 236
"Sparrer" Combat Team, 126, 163-4, 191
"Berlin" Armd Train, 128, 173
Feldgendarmerie, 229

Hitlerjugend Tk-Hunting, 300

Kriegsmarine (Navy): 102, 123, 128, 223
Blücher, 232

Luftwaffe: 19, 21, 23-24, 38-39, 46-47, 52, 55, 61, 74, 92-93, 118, 122, 125-26, 128-29, 132, 153, 166, 180, 187, 197, 206, 218, 223-4
6th Air Fleet, 23, 47, 78, 125
IInd Air Corps, 187, 224
1st Flak Div,, 243
4th Air Div, 78, 125
1st LW Trg Div, 126
23rd Flak Div, 46, 78, 121, 125, 179
7th Flak Regt, 121
26th Flak Regt, 129, 179
35th Flak Regt, 121
53rd Flak Regt, 121
140th Flak Regt, 121
185th Flak Regt, 121
211th Flak Regt, 51
755th Lt Flak Bn, 129
4th LW Trg Regt, 126, 195
5th LW Trg Regt, 126, 195
Special Operations Unit, 125, 187, 206

Volkswehr: 22
Volks Grenadier, 22
Volks Artillery, 22, 78, 89, 124
404th Volksartillery Corps, 71, 124, 176
406th Volksartillery Corps, 124
408th Volksartillery Corps, 124, 176

Volkssturm: 21-22, 32, 45-46, 52, 63, 67, 69, 75, 81-83, 96-97, 122-23, 125, 128-29, 131-32, 134, 177, 220, 229, 232
7th/108th VS Bn, 46, 63
16th/186th VS Bn, 83
Potsdam VS Bn, 46, 57
Würzburg VS Bn, 87
Upper Austrian VS Bn, 87

POLISH ARMED FORCES

Armies:
1st, 17, 32, 39-40, 102, 110, 114, 126,
140, 149, 161-64, 210, 227, 244
2nd, 21
Home, 181
Corps:
1st Tk, 227
Divisions:
1st Inf, 161-62, 227, 238
2nd Inf, 114, 161-62, 227
3rd Inf, 161-62, 227
4th Inf, 227
6th Inf, 161, 191, 227
Regiments:
1st Inf, 161
2nd Inf, 161
4th Inf, 161
5th Inf, 161
6th Inf, 161
4th Tk, 163
13th SPG, 163
Battalions
2nd Div Trg, 161

Air Force
1st Composite Air Corps, 17, 144

SOVIET ARMED FORCES

State Defence Committee, 6
Stavka, 6-10, 13, 32, 39, 99, 102-103,
107, 122, 138, 246, 251, 255-6
Stavka Reserves, 7, 13, 15, 109-110, 144,
146
General Staff (GHQ), 6-7, 29, 102, 107-
109, 189, 253

Red Army:
Military Districts:
Leningrad, 7
1st Byelorussian, 5
Kiev Special, 6
Odessa, 256
Ural, 256

Fronts:
Leningrad, 9
Reserve, 7
Southwestern, 7
Steppe, 8
Voronezh 8
Western 7, 251
1st Army Group, 5
1st Byelorussian, 9-10, 17, 29, 31-32, 37,
40, 70, 99-101, 107-109, 142, 144-
47, 149, 154, 157, 188-90, 194,
197, 199, 205, 207, 225, 245-6,
253, 256
2nd Byelorussian, 9, 29, 31, 39-40, 99-
100, 103, 109-110, 144, 157, 244
1st Ukrainian, 8-9, 29-31, 104, 107-109,
144, 207, 245-6, 248, 252
2nd Ukrainian, 8
3rd Ukrainian, 9
Armies:
3rd Gds, 248
8th Gds, 14, 31, 33, 37, 39-40, 55, 66, 69-
70, 79, 83-84, 90, 95, 110, 115,
138, 140-44, 146, 149, 160-61, 171,
175-82, 189, 199-204, 214, 221,
225, 238, 245, 252-3
1st Gds Tk, 31-33, 37, 39, 43, 101-103,
110, 113, 115, 137, 140-41, 143,
145, 175, 178, 181, 183, 189, 197,
204, 206-208, 214, 219, 225, 227,
238, 252-3
2nd Gds Tk, 16, 31-33, 35, 40, 51, 52,
101-103, 110, 113, 140, 143, 146,
169, 171, 174, 197, 199, 206, 214,
225, 227, 230, 238
3rd Gds Tk, 189, 238, 245, 252-3
4th Gds Tk, 189, 238, 243
3rd Shock, 32, 39, 101-103, 110, 115,
138, 140-41, 143-44, 149, 166-68,
170, 193-94, 213, 225, 238
5th Shock, 33, 41, 51, 53-54, 77, 79, 82,
84, 90, 110-111, 113, 115, 138,
140-42, 144, 149, 152, 168-74,
197-99, 214, 216, 238
3rd, 110, 144, 238, 245-6
19th, 102

28th, 245-6
33rd, 33, 37, 40, 58, 60-61, 110, 140,
       149, 153, 184-87, 205, 238
47th, 40, 101-103, 110, 113, 138, 140-42,
       144, 161, 164-66, 192-94, 211, 213,
       238
61st, 39, 40, 101-103, 110, 114, 149, 161-
       62, 191, 227
64th, 14
69th, 31-33, 40, 60, 69-71, 79, 90, 110,
115, 138, 140, 144, 149, 153, 182-83,
204-205, 221-2, 235, 238, 245
70th, 39

Corps:

3rd Cossack Cav, 5
6th Cossack Cav, 5
2nd Gds Cav, 40, 110, 184, 205, 223
3rd Gds Cav, 144, 219
7th Gds Cav, 102, 110, 194, 238
9th Gds Tk, 115
11th Gds Tk, 33, 39, 115, 189, 207-208,
       226
12th Gds Tk, 115, 169, 171, 197, 238
5th Gds Mech, 249
8th Gds Mech, 37, 39, 143, 204, 208,
       219, 234
4th Gds Rifle, 37-38, 55, 84, 86, 144,
       171, 174, 176, 182, 202
9th Gds Rifle, 191
12th Gds Rifle, 167-68, 229
26th Gds Rifle, 35, 169, 173, 214
28th Gds Rifle, 38, 55, 143, 175, 182,
       204
29th Gds Rifle, 174, 176, 182, 204, 226
3rd Tk, 102
9th Tk, 115, 143, 166, 168, 171, 194,
       238
11th Tk, 66, 143, 175, 197, 202
1st Mech, 36, 52, 197, 238
7th Rifle, 167-68, 194
9th Rifle, 51, 77, 169, 171, 174, 197
16th Rifle, 184, 205
21st Rifle, 248
25th Rifle, 60, 182, 204, 222
32nd Rifle, 82-84, 86, 169-70, 173
38th Rifle, 182, 205
61st Rifle, 183, 222

62nd Rifle, 184, 204-205
77th Rifle, 164, 194
79th Rifle, 167-68, 213
80th Rifle, 161, 191
89th Rifle, 161, 191
120th Rifle, 248
125th Rifle, 164, 194
129th Rifle, 164, 194
57th Special, 5
5th Home Air Defense, 146
115th Fortified Region, 184
119th Fortified Region, 184

Divisions:

Combat Trg, 5
1st Moscow Cav, 4
4th Don Cossack Cav, 5
7th Samara Cav, 4
1st Gds Arty, 248
23rd Gds Rifle, 167
35th Gds Rifle, 38, 55, 85, 95
39th Gds Rifle, 219
47th Gds Rifle, 38, 55, 84, 86, 179, 182
52nd Gds Rifle, 167
57th Gds Rifle, 38-39, 55, 84, 182
60th Gds Rifle, 84, 169
77th Gds Rifle, 60
79th Gds Rifle, 38, 55
82nd Gds Rifle, 95, 233
88th Gds Rifle, 182
89th Gds Rifle, 169
94th Gds Rifle, 35, 169
33rd Rifle, 167
39th Rifle, 184
49th Rifle, 184
60th Rifle, 164
64th Rifle, 184
76th Rifle, 164
82nd Rifle, 164
95th Rifle, 184
129th Rifle, 184
132nd Rifle, 164
143rd Rifle, 164
146th Rifle, 167
150th Rifle, 167, 194, 213
171st Rifle, 167, 194, 213
175th Rifle, 164
183rd Rifle, 223

185th Rifle, 165
207th Rifle, 167, 213
222nd Rifle, 184
230th Rifle, 51, 169
248th Rifle, 51-52, 66, 169, 171, 197
260th Rifle, 164
265th Rifle, 167
266th Rifle, 34, 66, 169-70, 197
295th Rifle, 84, 86, 169-70, 197
301st Rifle, 52-53, 169, 171, 197
323rd Rifle, 184
328th Rifle, 164
339th Rifle, 184
362nd Rifle, 184
364th Rifle, 167
383rd Rifle, 184
416th Rifle, 84, 169
16th AA Arty, 37-38, 55
82nd Home Air Defense, 146
Brigades:
2nd Cav, 4
1st Gds Tk, 37
40th Gds Tk, 39
44th Gds Tk, 33
64th Gds Tk, 208
20th Gds Mech, 37, 39
27th Gds Mot Rifle, 39
219th Tk, 36
220th Tk, 173
71st Mech, 253
19th Mot Rifle, 52
29th Railway, 206
Regiments:
10th Dragoons, 4
39th Buzuluk Cav, 4
39th Melekess-Pugachevsk Cav, 4
63rd Gds Rifle, 167
220th Gds Rifle, 55, 57
228th Gds Rifle, 169
242nd Gds Rifle, 233-4
283rd Gds Rifle, 35, 169

286th Gds Rifle, 35, 170
288th Gds Rifle, 197
248th Rifle, 85
266th Rifle, 85
895th Rifle, 52
902nd Rifle, 52
1006th Rifle, 34
1028th Rifle, 197
1038th Rifle, 83, 197
1040th Rifle, 197
1050th Rifle, 171
1052nd Rifle, 172
1054th Rifle, 53
1373rd Rifle, 84
507th ATk Arty, 35
489th Mor, 35
Battalions:
273rd Gds Mot Rifle, 39
20th Pontoon, 39
221st Ind Eng, 194
274th Amphibious Veh, 161
Rear Services: 17, 114, 140, 206

Red Fleet:
Baltic Fleet, 7
Baltic Fleet Air Arm, 144
Dnieper Flotilla, 111, 142, 149

Red Air Force: 14-15, 39-40, 47, 96,
        154, 164, 178, 187, 208, 209, 224,
        250
2nd Air Army, 245
4th Air Army, 144, 158
16th Air Army, 84, 144-46, 149, 160,
        208, 245
18th Air Army, 144-45, 160, 245
9th Ground-Attack Air Corps, 187
29th Air Sigs Bn, 147

Political Dept: 10, 29-30, 137, 146-47

NKVD: 17, 255, 257

Stackpole Military History Series

Real battles. Real soldiers. Real stories.

Stackpole Military History Series

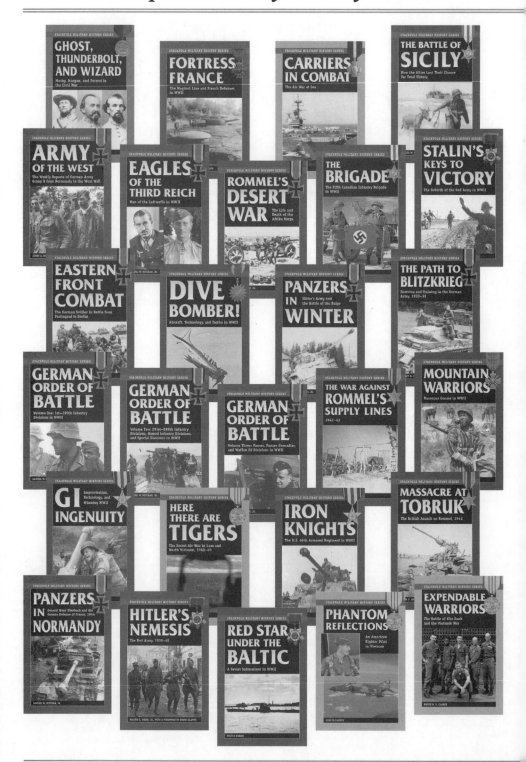

Real battles. Real soldiers. Real stories.

Stackpole Military History Series

STACKPOLE MILITARY HISTORY SERIES

LUFTWAFFE FIGHTER ACE
From the Eastern Front to the Defense of the Homeland

NORBERT HANNING

STACKPOLE MILITARY HISTORY SERIES

PANZER GUNNER
A Canadian in the German 7th Panzer Division, 1944–45

STACKPOLE MILITARY HISTORY SERIES

TWILIGHT OF THE GODS
A Swedish Volunteer in the 11th SS Panzergrenadier Division "Nordland" on the Eastern Front

STACKPOLE MILITARY HISTORY SERIES

THE SIEGFRIED LINE
The German Defense of the West Wall, September–December 1944

STACKPOLE MILITARY HISTORY SERIES

BEYOND STALINGRAD
Manstein and the Operations of Army Group Don

DANA V. SAD...

NEW for Fall 2009

STACKPOLE MILITARY HISTORY SERIES

NO HOLDING BACK
Operation Totalize, Normandy, August 1944

BRIAN A. REID

STACKPOLE MILITARY HISTORY SERIES

THE CANADIAN ARMY AND THE NORMANDY CAMPAIGN

JOHN A. ENGLISH

STACKPOLE MILITARY HISTORY SERIES

BATTLE OF THE BULGE
Volume One: The Losheim Gap / Holding the Line

HANS WIJERS

Real battles. Real soldiers. Real stories.

STACKPOLE MILITARY HISTORY SERIES

THE KEY TO THE BULGE
The Battle for Losheimergraben

STEPHEN M.

STACKPOLE MILITARY HISTORY SERIES

ZHUKOV AT THE ODER
The Decisive Battle for Berlin

STACKPOLE MILITARY HISTORY SERIES

RANGER DAWN
The American Ranger from the Colonial Era to the Mexican War

COL. ROBERT W. BLACK

STACKPOLE MILITARY HISTORY SERIES

SIEGES
From the Siege of Jerusalem to the Gulf War

BRUCE ALLEN WATSON

STACKPOLE MILITARY HISTORY SERIES

CAVALRY FROM HOOF TO TRACK

ROMAN JARYMOWYCZ

NEW for Fall 2009

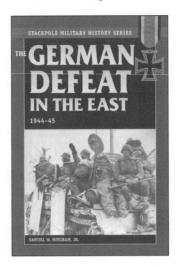

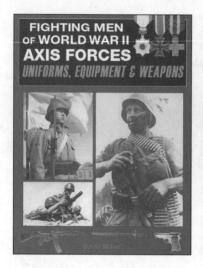